T0247756

THE TRUTH ABOUT BAKED BEANS

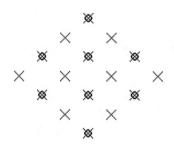

The Truth about Baked Beans

AN EDIBLE HISTORY OF NEW ENGLAND

Meg Muckenhoupt

WASHINGTON MEWS BOOKS

An Imprint of

NEW YORK UNIVERSITY PRESS

New York

Washington Mews Books
An Imprint of New York University Press
New York
www.nyupress.org

References to Internet websites (URLs) were accurate at the time of writing.
Neither the author nor New York University Press is responsible for URLs
that may have expired or changed since the manuscript was prepared.

Library of Congress Cataloging-in-Publication Data
Names: Muckenhoupt, Margaret, author.
Title: The truth about baked beans :
an edible history of New England / Meg Muckenhoupt.
Description: New York : New York University Press, 2020. |
Series: Washington mews | Includes bibliographical references and index.
Identifiers: LCCN 2019041961 | ISBN 9781479882762 (cloth) |
ISBN 9781479812455 (ebook) | ISBN 9781479870646 (ebook)
Subjects: LCSH: Cooking, American—New England style. |
Cooking, American—New England style—History.
Classification: LCC TX715.2.N48 M83 2020 | DDC 641.5974—dc23

LC record available at https://lccn.loc.gov/2019041961New York University Press
books are printed on acid-free paper, and their binding materials are chosen for
strength and durability. We strive to use environmentally responsible suppliers
and materials to the greatest extent possible in publishing our books.

Manufactured in the United States of America

10 9 8 7 6 5 4 3 2 1

Also available as an ebook

CONTENTS

Introduction: What Is New England Food?. 1

1. Who Is a Yankee? 5

2. The Truth about Baked Beans 48

3. The Limits of New England Food. 63

4. Corn and Prejudice 99

RECIPES. 121

5. From River and Sea 165

6. Sweets, Sours, and Spirits 219

7. Cheese and Taste. 254

Conclusion: Giving Thanks for New England Food 267

Acknowledgments 279

Notes 281

Index 329

About the Author 345

Introduction

WHAT IS NEW ENGLAND FOOD?

A fish stick is not fish, nor is it a stick. It is a fungus.
—Matt Groening[1]

THIS BOOK began with a simple question: when did Bostonians start making Boston baked beans? New England isn't known for sweet main dishes like honey-glazed ham or sweet potatoes with marshmallows or Jell-O-based "salads," yet one of the region's iconic foods marries pork and beans with puddles of molasses. Why?

As I began researching Boston baked beans' beginnings, I rapidly realized that most of the origin stories about sweet bean recipes were clearly false. Many authors stated that the Pilgrims had learned a recipe for beans with maple syrup and bear fat from "Indian" cooks and that colonial chefs had simply swapped out the combo for salt pork and molasses. When I checked baked bean recipes in cookbooks, farmers' journals, and newspapers published before the Civil War, though, molasses was rarely mentioned—and in the few cases when it did appear, the quantities were minuscule by twenty-first-century standards, on the order of one tablespoon of molasses to a quart of dry beans.

What I discovered is that the recipe for Boston baked beans wasn't an ancient gift from forgotten Native Americans but the result of a series of conscious efforts in the late nineteenth century to create "New England" foods that happened to coincide with a drop in sugar prices that supersized New England's sweet tooth. Those "New England" foods were cherry-picked from fanciful just-so stories about what English colonists cooked prior to the American Revolution, not from the foods actually cooked by New England's residents—many of whom were immigrants from Ireland, Quebec, Italy,

Portugal, Poland, and a dozen other countries. Those discoveries compelled me to write this book.

This book explores New England's culinary myths and reality through some of New England's most famous foods: baked beans, brown bread, clams, cod and lobsters, "northern" cornbread, Vermont cheese, apples, cranberries, maple syrup, pies, and New England boiled dinner, also known as Yankee pot roast. Each of these foods is frequently featured in popular articles about the history of New England food accompanied by false and sometimes downright bizarre tales—that apprentices were fed lobster until they revolted, that Wampanoag chefs cooked beans with maple syrup, that Pilgrim women roasted turkeys for the first Thanksgiving, that New England's fishermen are heroes battling the elements for food, and that the soil on individual farms makes a discernible difference in the taste of Vermont cheese.

In a period spanning roughly 1870 to 1920, the idea of New England food was carefully constructed in magazines, newspapers, cookbooks, and cooking schools, largely by white middle- and upper-class women who were uninterested in if not outright hostile to New England's immigrant and working-class cooks. Today's New England residents are still struggling with this mythical legacy that has stunted and stymied culinary innovation in the region for more than a century and obscured New Englanders' real struggles with food, resources, racism, and history.

These foods' history confounds their current-day reputations. New England's fishermen have been depicted in films and novels like *Captains Courageous* as strong, independent souls who battle the elements for sustenance—but New England's colonial fisheries depended on sales to slave plantations in the Caribbean. Far from being a beloved treat, maple syrup was unpopular until sugar became scarce during the Civil War, and cornmeal breads were generally abandoned as soon as the Erie Canal started shipping cheap wheat from upstate New York. Lobster is a symbol of Maine only because it has been extirpated in Connecticut and along most of the Massachusetts coast. No one roasts chestnuts over an open fire because all but a handful of American chestnut trees died of chestnut blight almost a century ago.[2] Boston baked beans and steamed brown bread were invented by molasses-smitten Victorians, not thrifty colonial cooks, and the "Pilgrim" traditions for Thanksgiving were largely invented by a novelist in the 1890s.

Because the category of New England regional food as described in chatty cookbooks and on perky tourist websites relies heavily on the Victorian ideal of New England, New England's supposed foodways are unique in America's regional food lists because they exclude the foods cooked by people who actually live here. New England's traditional foods all have origin stories that show that they have been passed down to the modern day straight from the Pilgrims. Most of New England's most famous foods were supposed to have been gifts of the Wampanoag, especially Thanksgiving edibles—corn, pumpkin pie, cranberry sauce. Even foods that can't be linked to Thanksgiving—baked beans, lobster—are explained as the gift of some kindly Native American. These pretty stories are repeated even when there is no evidence that these foods even existed before the late nineteenth century, as is the case with sweetened baked beans.[3]

Outside of New England, most beloved regional cuisines are poured from the American melting pot. Tex-Mex cuisine is thoroughly American, mixing beef from British cattle with Mexican-bred chilis and oozing yellow "processed cheese food" straight from the laboratory. New Orleans cuisine has been influenced by just about anyone who has set foot in the city over the past 400 years: rich French-speaking snobs, poor French-speaking Cajuns, African slaves, Cajuns, Spanish, Italians, Haitians—everyone. Southern food is a salmagundi of European, African, and American techniques and ingredients, largely perfected by African American cooks.[4] North Carolinians savor barbecued pork, not the venison eaten by the pre-Columbian Cherokee.[5] Minnesota hot dish was conceived out of the union of canned vegetables and canned soup, a duo made possible only by the combined labor of thousands of native-born and immigrant peoples to build factories, lay track for railroads, and drive trucks to factories, cocreating a national industrial supply chain. What could be more American than that?

By contrast, New England's foodstuffs are static, superannuated antiques. When writers talk about New England food, they tend to repeat tales of friendly Native Americans welcoming Europeans with their beloved food, building a new nation on a foundation of generosity, charity, and fortitude. Yet New England's European settlers seem to have adopted as few dishes as possible from their Native American hosts. Pumpkin, corn, and beans made the cut, as did venison and chestnuts. The Pilgrims' descendants had less use for acorns, groundnuts, Jerusalem artichokes, and purslane.[6] Two generations after the landing at Plymouth Rock, the descendants of these friendly folk were decimated in the bloody, desperate King Philip's War, a conflict inflamed by the Pilgrims' descendants' obnoxious habit of letting their loose pigs devour the Wampanoags' subsistence crops.[7]

In reality, past and present New England food has always emerged from a mix of cultures. Although all of the colonies founded in the seventeenth century on the East Coast were first populated by English immigrants, by 1700 their food cultures had started to diverge, partly due to what foods were available and how they were prepared, and partly due to who lived where. For example, New Englanders in Boston ate less wild game than their compatriots in New York and the Chesapeake Bay and ate more baked goods and pies—sensible meals for a climate where hot ovens were a household comfort, not a curse, and where most wild game had already been exterminated from nearby woods.[8]

New England stretches from the borders of Quebec to the New York City suburbs, from the shores of Lake Champlain to the Atlantic Ocean. It encompasses both sea-level cities and lofty Mount Washington. Farmers grow turnips on hillsides, tomatoes in greenhouses, and salmon in aquaculture pools. The region has some of the most densely populated areas in the country, like Somerville, Massachusetts, ranked sixth in the United States in 2016, with approximately 19,738 people per square mile.[9] It also has some of the emptiest: Pisacataquis County, Maine, has just 4.4 people per square mile.[10] New England's residents range from the many Algonkin-speaking peoples whose families have lived in the region for up to 10,000 years to immigrants from Ireland, Poland, Korea, and Africa; roughly 7,000 Somali Americans live in Lewiston, Maine.[11]

There is a complicated, dynamic, exciting story to be told about New England's food and the future of a diverse and growing region. This book dispels the accumulated myths about who collected, concocted, grew, and digested New England's food so that we can see the culinary past, and the future, more clearly.

1

Who Is a Yankee?

P ART OF the reason that New England's lists of traditional foods are so stultifying is that writers and publicists are repeating stories about who lives in New England that haven't been true for more than 150 years. Millions of non-English immigrants arrived in the region from 1850 onward, but their histories and foodways have been largely ignored. Popular histories and tourist pamphlets have always included stoic Pilgrims, passionate Minutemen, and thrifty Yankee farmers, but most of New England's people have lived in cities since the 1870s. By 1890, a Massachusetts resident was more likely to be French Canadian immigrant working in a factory than a yeoman farmer raising corn.

New England's nineteenth-century promoters latched onto the ideal of a New England village as the perfect symbol of the region, and of America, despite the fact that very few New Englanders lived in them. These villages fit the concept of the pastoral, a middle landscape between decadent cities and untamed wilderness.[1] Here, Nature with a capital N was cultivated and controlled by independent, hardworking yeoman farmers living in little towns with white-steepled Protestant churches, uncorrupted by city influences such as immigrants from Southern and Eastern Europe and "modern" ideas. Instead, these happy villagers were supposed to be embodying Yankee piety and thrift in their peaceful idyll, which had miraculously emptied of Algonkin-speaking Native peoples just when Yankees' ancestors happened to need a quiet place to live.[2] Visions of New England's peaceful villages rarely mention the current locations of the people who granted the region their quaint, rustic names, like Massachusetts (and Queechee, Ossipee, Aroostook, and Penobscot, among many, many others). Their descendants are still here.

Travelers to New England in the late nineteenth century were disconcerted by how unpastoral the region seemed. Instead of a paradise of orderly farms, they found urban factories and mills full of immigrants. More than 50 percent of Massachusetts residents lived in cities by 1870, and almost a quarter of Rhode Island and Massachusetts residents in that year were born in another country—rising to 30 percent by 1910.[3] The verdant pastures were crowded by encroaching woods as New England forests regrew on abandoned farmland.[4] The state of Vermont did supply the requisite orderly pastures—not because of ongoing yeoman self-reliance, but because railroads enabled farmers to sell cheese, butter, and later fresh milk to Bostonians.[5] When tourists did manage to visit farms in Vermont, they complained about the working-class food they served to their "summer boarders" from the city—too much salt pork and doughnuts, not enough fresh berries and pure, white cream.[6]

As one writer put it, "Taken as a whole, the image of the New England village is widely assumed to symbolize for many people the best we have known of an intimate, family-centered, Godfearing, morally conscious, industrious, thrifty, democratic community."[7] However, that image had very little to do with how most New England residents lived after the Civil War.

How Can You Keep Them Down on the Farm Now That They've Seen Pittsfield?

Although orderly farm villages may be the epitome of New England civilization, those villagers' offspring have been taking off for the big city for at least 200 years. "Hill towns" along the Connecticut River Valley in western Massachusetts started emptying out by the 1820s. Raising subsistence crops on chilly, windy mountaintops was always difficult, and became even less attractive as lowland farmers started getting money for their crops by selling to city folk. Young farmers moved down to the valleys or even to the cities themselves.[8] Only about 20 percent of the farmers who moved out of Massachusetts's Connecticut River Valley in the 1820s moved to the Midwest.[9]

Even if they didn't move to the cities, the farmers who stayed depended on city markets. Between 1820 and 1840, the farm labor force in New England actually increased by 23 percent.[10] These farms grew because the cities grew. Farms near cities or near easy transportation routes to cities (rivers, canals, and later railroads) grew products that were expensive and perished quickly, like fresh milk and strawberries. Farms farther away had to either figure out a way to preserve food for shipment (making milk into cheese, fresh pork into salt pork) or grow foods that could be shipped in bulk (corn).[11] Connecticut River Valley farmers who had crops to sell could float them to New York City on the Hudson River; farmers who stayed on their land until the 1840s could sell their crops to residents of new manufacturing cities like Pittsfield or Springfield.[12]

In 1800, 90 percent of Connecticut's 251,002 residents made their living as farmers, even if they had another part-time occupation, leaving only 25,000 residents to work at any other job.[13] By 1840, close to 50,000 Connecticut residents were earning their living as workers at more than 2,166 "manufactories" producing shoes, cloth, tools, and dozens of other products.[14]

In the nineteenth century, native-born rural New Englanders also started having fewer children. It was a sign and a symptom of two economic trends: the explosion of opportunities in cities, where large families were more of an expense than an asset, and the lack of profitable lands to cultivate, as farms had been divided and redivided over several generations. Women marrying between 1730 and 1759 had nine children, while those marrying from 1820 to 1839 had just five in rural Sturbridge, Massachusetts. Women also got married later and started waiting until their wedding night to start their families; the percentage of women who were pregnant when they got married amounted to a quarter of all brides in 1730 but just 3 percent by 1820.[15] Fertility was reduced by a variety of means—physical and herbal contraceptives, abortions, later first marriage, and, in some cases, complete abstention from any sex at all (the only option in New England's celibate Shaker religious communities).

New New Englanders

Even as the rural New England population was declining in the nineteenth century, cities were growing—largely due to the arrival of hardworking immigrants. Below is a broad description of some of the largest and oldest groups of immigrants who live in New England, when they got here, and what they ate when they arrived.

These are the people whose food traditions should have been included in New England cookbooks from 1850 onward. Instead, most white authors promoted a vision of New England food as cooked from scratch by mothers' loving hands in little towns and white-clapboard farmhouses or perhaps prepared by old Yankee lobstermen in Maine—the smallest populations in the region. To cook and eat real New England food, one had to not look or live like the vast majority of people who were actually here.

The Locals

New England was a giant popsicle 15,000 years ago. The mile-thick Laurentide Glacier extended from Canada as far south as New Jersey. About 10,000 years ago, the popsicle melted, and Native Americans settled all over the region,[16] which was covered with arctic tundra.[17] Grass-covered Maine was Big Sky country.

The Native Americans stayed and watched the region get warmer and develop hardwood forests. And they ate . . . something. We have some guesses. Corn seems to have arrived around AD 1000,[18] but archaeological evidence and scans of old bones show that the locals didn't eat much of it until after European settlement;[19] venison seems to have been a much larger part of their diet. After the Pilgrims started chopping down the forests where the deer browsed and letting their hogs run higgledy-piggledy through what forest was left,[20] there wasn't much for the Wampanoag to eat apart from crops they raised themselves—when the Pilgrims' pigs didn't gobble up their gardens.[21]

When the Wampanoag and other peoples in the region did grow crops during the seventeenth century, they raised plants that weren't native to New England: corn, kidney beans, squash, Jerusalem artichokes, and tobacco. The corn, beans, squash, and tobacco all came from South and Central America, and Jerusalem artichokes (*Helianthus tuberosus*) probably spread northeast from a prairie,[22] as gardeners know they are wont to do. As Anne Mendelson writes, "To this day, pre-Hispanic crops native to those regions, from tomatoes and cacao to potatoes and chiles, not only thrive there but are grown and enthusiastically eaten in many parts of the Old World. By contrast, not a single food plant uniquely native to northeastern North America is still a significant source of food in the Northeast or anywhere else."[23] There is evidence that prior to the seventeenth century other North American plants with edible seeds were cultivated, but corn dominated Massachusetts coastal agriculture by the time the Pilgrims arrived.[24]

But the Wampanoag and other Eastern Woodlands peoples had plenty of contact with Europeans before the Pilgrims deigned to settle in Plymouth. Basque fishermen had been trading along what is now the Newfoundland coast with anyone who would show up with beaver pelts for centuries,[25] and from 1502 onward they were joined by Norman, Breton, Biscayan, Spanish, Portuguese, English, and French fishermen.[26] In 1578 alone, an observer noted 100 Spanish sails, 20 to 30 Basque whalers, 150 French and Breton fishing ships, and 50 English sails along the coast of Newfoundland.[27]

These fishermen landed in harbors from Massachusetts to Maine and traded axes, cooking kettles, and other goods for animal pelts. Through the mid-seventeenth century, New England's Native Americans used those cooking kettles for raw materials for making earrings, pendants, and other decorations, not for cooking—they had their own ways of cooking food using far less precious materials.[28] Eastern Native Americans commonly prepared food by roasting it in fires, wrapping it in leaves and placing it on hot coals or ashes, boiling it in clay pots with heated rocks, or placing it directly on hot rocks by a fire.[29]

These people gathered, grew, hunted, and stored a wide variety of foods: wild game, fish, shellfish, seeds, fruits, roots, and vegetables. That said, they don't seem to have mixed foods much. As one archaeologist put it, "The diet was rich in diversity but scant in what went into a pot at one time."[30] The Wampanoag dried and smoked many foods for winter use, including fish, lobster, eggs, and blueberries.[31]

While the eastern Native Americans had plenty to eat, they did not have several items that later European settlers would consider essential: milk, sugar, honey, salt, coffee, chocolate, tea, and—perish the thought!—beer and alcohol.[32] Imagine making pumpkin pie with no sugar, no milk, no eggs (wild birds wouldn't be laying eggs in the fall when pumpkins ripen), no wheat, and no butter. Stewed squash, anyone?

After the Europeans arrived, the Wampanoag and Narragansett began growing more and more corn—partly to make up for the loss of venison due to the colonists' forest destruction, partly to sell to the settlers. In 1634 alone, the Narragansett sold the Massachusetts Bay Colony 500 bushels of corn: they had promised 1,000 bushels, but "their store fell out less than they expected."[33]

Our information about New England peoples' diets and food preparation will always be limited partly because so much knowledge died with the great epidemics of 1615 to 1619, when somewhere between 30 and 90 percent of the Native American population within 60 miles of the coast in Massachusetts, New Hampshire, Maine, and Newfoundland died. Scholars still argue about just what disease caused the slaughter, but it involved fevers, headaches, nosebleeds, and jaundice and followed contact with Europeans.[34] Plymouth's Native American residents, a branch of the Patuxets, were obliterated by the disease, leaving a ghost town for Pilgrims to settle. In one scouting expedition 40 miles to the south of Plymouth, governor William Bradford recalled that there was "good soyle, and the people not many, being dead and abundantly wasted in the late great mortalitie which fell in all these parts about three years before the coming of the English, wherin thousands of them dyed; . . . ther sculs and bones were found in many places lying still above the ground, where their houses and dwellings had been, a very sad spectackle to behould."[35] Squanto, also known as Tisquantum, the Patuxet man who showed the Pilgrims how to grow corn, had escaped the 1616 epidemic by having been kidnapped to Europe by an earlier expedition. In 1622 he experienced a fever and nosebleed, then succumbed to "the Indean Disease."[36]

After King Philip's War ended in 1675, many Native Americans were enslaved, particularly in Rhode Island. Some of them ended up cooking corn and English food for the men whose ancestors had separated them from their own foodways.[37]

Despite hardship, several Native tribes, including Wampanoag, Nipmuc, Mohegan, Mashpee, and Pequot peoples, continue to live in the region today.[38]

The English, aka Yankees

As the *Encyclopedia of New England* puts it, "To New Englanders, a Yankee is someone of 'original' New England heritage."[39] In short, the Yankees are the descendants of New England's English settlers. English settlers made up most of New England's population between 1620 and 1840, when other immigrant groups started arriving en masse. (It bears repeating, the white Anglo-Saxon Protestants started to lose their grip on New England culture by *1840*.) Today, 13 percent of New Englanders call themselves English and another 1.2 percent say they're "British."[40]

The English immigrants are the default New Englanders—the people we imagine inhabited Ye Olde Neue England, wearing odd black hats and buckles on their shoes. Roughly 60 percent of seventeenth-century immigrants to Massachusetts came from a broad swath of southern England, stretching from Norfolk on the east coast to Somerset in the southwest.[41] Thousands upon thousands of pages have been written elsewhere about their stalwart faith, perseverance in the face of adversity, and unsteady relationships with the Native Americans already living in New England, who were variously placated, infected, admonished, or slaughtered by their colonizers. What follows is a brief description of their diet.

The English appear to have felt that most fruits and vegetables were a waste of precious ship space. When the *Mayflower* set out, the ship carried "15,000 brown biscuit, 5000 white (crackers); half-cooked bacon, dried salted codfish, smoked herring; cabbages, turnips, onions, parsnips," as well as oatmeal, dried peas, and beer.[42]

The stores planned for one of the first ships bound for the Massachusetts Bay Colony in England ten years later with "100 men and 25 mariners" in 1628 was supposed to carry supplies for the 90-day journey measured in "tuns," or barrels holding about 250 gallons: 45 tuns of beer, 6 tuns of water, 22 hogsheads of beef, 40 bushels of peas, 20 bushels of oatmeal, 4 C (2,728 pounds) of dried salt cod, 2 "terces" (one sixth of a tun) of beer vinegar, 1.5 bushels of mustard seeds, 20 gallons of cooking oil, 20 gallons of Spanish wine, 10 firkins of butter, 10 C (6,820 pounds) of cheese, and 20 gallons of aqua vitae.[43]

Shipboard diets were not good for the health. Scurvy struck New England–bound passengers on many ships, including the Pilgrims aboard the *Mayflower* in 1620 and the *Arbella*, which brought settlers to the Massachusetts Bay Colony in Salem in 1630.[44] Once they landed, the English did the best they could to keep eating their traditional foods, with mixed results. They made "pottage," a sort of thick stew of boiled grains, beans or peas, and whatever else might be around—salt meat most of the year, vegetables if handy. This was the easiest possible food to make with a kettle and a fire and a food that everyone could eat whether or not they had teeth (an important feature in meals in the era before modern dentistry).[45]

New England's seventeenth-century European settlers ate pottage every day, all day long. Breakfast, supper, dinner, snacks . . . mush was there. American corn and beans were as easy to make into pottage as English oats and peas, as the Wampanoag and other Native Americans had discovered centuries beforehand. Curiously, as time went on, pottage seems to have separated into distinct New England dishes. Beans boiled with meat became baked beans—called "baked" only because the pot could be set on the embers of a fire—while meat boiled with vegetables became boiled dinner.

Bread and beer were trickier. Wheat didn't grow as well as corn in eastern New England's humid, intemperate climate. Colonists invented concoctions like "thirded," "ryaninjun," or "brown" bread made with mixtures of wheat, corn, and rye, which at least looked a little like wheat bread, even if it didn't have the same taste or texture.[46] For liquid refreshment, the colonists brewed beer from a variety of unlikely ingredients, including spruce boughs and pumpkins, before settling on hard cider and rum as their everyday beverages.[47]

The earliest English settlers irreversibly changed the entire New England ecosystem simply by importing "sweet grass," clover, and other low-growing herbs to feed their livestock, replacing and overwhelming the native browse. Partly, this transformation was simply a side effect of unloading the seed-filled hay brought over as fodder for the animals' ocean voyages and the seeds passing into the animals' manure. The English immigrants raised cattle, let their pigs run wild through the woods to grow fat on acorns (devouring one of the foods the Native Americans had previously collected for their own sustenance),[48] fished in fresh and salt water, collected clams and lobsters, milked cows and made butter and cheese, picked wild blueberries, strawberries, and cranberries, planted fruit trees, and grew beans, corn, squashes, rye, and "sauce"—vegetables to eat with meat and pottage.

During the seventeenth century, vegetables seem to have been a seasonal treat, eaten as they ripened from June through the late fall. They're barely mentioned in wills, probate inventories, and widows' allowances written between October and July, when most other household possessions are detailed down to individual forks. By 1750, winter stores of turnips, onions, carrots, cabbages, and potatoes (introduced in the 1720s to much acclaim) were lasting until spring. Other little niceties for "sallads"—greens, herbs, radishes, and other more perishable crops—were grown in kitchen gardens. These vegetables were not listed in household inventories, although widows were generally allotted space for kitchen gardens.[49]

When amateur historians, party planners, and fair exhibit organizers tried to reproduce "New England" foods after the Civil War, this is the era they looked to . . . or at least, they looked at parts of it. Pottage was never part of these exhibitions, unlike doughnuts and pie.

The city folk always ate a more highfalutin diet than the farmers up in the hills. By 1800, Boston already had a "Restorator" restaurant serving both land turtle and green turtle soup and a caterer who specialized in ice cream and cheesecakes.[50]

However, New England's borders didn't close after the Revolutionary War. Plenty of other people arrived. The largest group in the nineteenth century was. . . .

The Irish

Irish immigrants first alighted on Massachusetts shores by 1640, as Irish Catholics and Scots-Irish Protestants joined the Puritan Great Migration before the English Civil War. Irish kept trickling in through the seventeenth and eighteenth centuries. In 1698, when crops failed and the English government banned wool exports, destroying the Ulster wool industry, still more Scots-Irish immigrated to New England. They settled in many areas that still bear Irish names: Derry, Antrim, and Londonderry, New Hampshire; Belfast and Limerick, Maine; Colrain, Massachusetts; and Londonderry, Vermont.[51] Irish Catholics arrived as indentured servants—some via Barbados, where 50,000 Irish Catholics had been deported by Oliver Cromwell during the 1749–1753 war on Ireland. Irish filled the ranks of the Continental Army during the Revolutionary War: there were at least 695 men named Kelly who fought the British.[52]

Still, Bostonians were suspicious of the Irish Catholics. For example, in the decades leading to the revolution, one charming tradition was Pope's Day. A variation on Guy Fawkes Day, Pope's Day was "a celebration for the lower orders in Anglo-American society," as one author delicately puts it.[53] In Boston, it involved parades through the city's streets by rival factions (really gangs) from the North and South End, a street fight between the gangs, then burning all the floats with effigies of the pope and the devil in an enormous bonfire. What Boston's Catholics did during the whole event is not recorded: presumably, they stayed very, very quiet.[54]

Pope's Day faded after the revolution, partly because George Washington banned the celebration among his Continental Army troops in the name of unity, partly because the Bostonians who would have celebrated it were preoccupied with the British occupation of the city.[55] Anti-Catholic prejudice never really disappeared, though. An angry mob burned down an Ursuline convent in what is now Somerville, Massachusetts, in 1834, and 13 years later a new crop of bigots gained new energy when more Irish came to Boston than ever before.

In 1847, the first wave of emigrants fleeing the Irish potato famine arrived. Boston's population at the time was a little over 90,000; in the single year of 1847, around 35,000 Irish immigrants flooded into Boston. In 1850, there were 37,000 Irish-descended citizens who claimed Boston homes; by 1855, the number was up to 50,000 in a city of 160,000.[56] Massachusetts residents—including many upper-class "Boston Brahmins"— responded by electing almost the entire state legislature from the anti-immigrant Know Nothing Party, whose motto was "Temperance, Liberty and Protestantism."[57]

The sheer number of Irish immigrants in New England ensured that they would influence New England's food, but they had a secret weapon: their women. Whole families emigrated during the famine from 1847 to 1850. From 1850 to 1921, slightly more than half of Irish immigrants were women.[58]

Many of these women went to work as maids. By 1850, 80 percent of the maids in New York city were Irish immigrants, and more than 2,000 Irish women were working as domestic servants in Boston.[59] When they weren't cooking for their families, these women were cooking for New England's middle and upper classes—much to those classes' distress.

Many of these maids weren't familiar with posh Boston food, or much of any home cooking. In the years leading up to the Irish potato famine, 3 million people in Ireland—roughly 37 percent of the population—lived on a diet of potatoes, milk, and salt herring.[60] In 1840, the Poor Law Commissioners for England and Wales listed typical Irish meals for various locations. Here's an example:

KILMALLOCK

Men
- Breakfast: 4 1/2 lbs potatoes, 1 quart skimmed milk
- Dinner: The same, with herring and dripping when milk is scarce
- Supper: The same, but supper is not always eaten

Women
- Breakfast: 3 1/2 lbs potatoes, from 2 1/2 pints to a quart of milk
- Dinner: The same
- Supper: The same[61]

The more daring, desperate types occasionally substituted oatmeal for potatoes at dinner, or boiled onions for herring. The potatoes were boiled in a pot, then set on a table in a basket. Someone would put a salt herring in a dish and pour water on it, and the family would dip their potatoes into the herring water. The "milk" they were drinking was likely buttermilk.[62]

That said, the Irish were better nourished than many modern Americans on this diet. In the century from 1740 to 1840, Ireland's population quadrupled from roughly 2 million to 8 million. At the time of the famine, potatoes were the main, perhaps the only, staple food for an estimated 3 million Irish people.[63] According to USDA values for "potatoes, boiled, cooked in skin, flesh, without salt," four and a half pounds of potatoes would give a man 1,740 calories, 40 grams of protein, 40 percent of his daily value for calcium, 440 percent of the daily vitamin C, and 40 percent of the required iron. Compared to the diet of meat, (corn)meal, and molasses eaten by slaves and sharecroppers in the American South pre– and post–Civil War, this diet is astonishingly nutritious.[64]

Unlike fussy American preschoolers who prefer to live on diets consisting entirely of French fries, the Irish did not come to this arrangement by choice. Before the potato conquered all resistance, Irish farmers ate "stirabout" (oatmeal) and breads made with wheat, barley, oats, or rye. Coastal dwellers ate fish and shellfish and gathered seaweed—Irish moss to thicken puddings, dulse for flavor—and all over the country Irish enjoyed watercress, wild berries, cabbages, hazelnuts, nettles, leeks, and apples. They ate their bread with butter and cheeses, bacon, and roasted and stewed pork, mutton, goat meat, chicken, oxen, and swine—even wild boar, à la Asterix and Obelix—and flavored their savory foods with onions and sweet food with ginger or caraway seeds.[65] Even William Wilde, the Irish surgeon and historian whose 1854 "Foods of the Irish" opined that being well fed with potatoes stymied Irish cultural progress, recognized, "Corn, peas, beans, and possibly parsnips, with cabbages and onions, formed the vegetable food of the people, prior to the introduction of the potato."[66] The butter was sometimes stored over the winter by sinking a wooden tub of the stuff into a bog. The butter was slowly transformed into an odd, sour substance, like "old Stilton cheese," which Wilde termed "adipocere"—the term for the fats of corpses left in bogs. Still, Wilde asserted that "bog butter" remained edible for twenty years or more as long as you didn't mind the taste.[67]

Then came the potato. Productive and easy to grow in Ireland's boggy, cool ground, potatoes were a boon to the poor. Unfortunately, landlords noticed this too and raised their tenants' rents. Tenant farmers still raised some livestock—typically pigs or a cow for milk—but they didn't eat their meat; they sold their animals to pay their rent. English wags joked about the Irish living on "potato and point"—a dish that involves holding up a potato, pointing it at a bit of bacon or salt herring hung up in the chimney for storage, then eating the potato.[68] "Point" was actually a catchall term for any kind of condiment, sauce, or even salty water that a person could dip a cooked potato in to provide a bit of flavor.[69]

Why potatoes? They were easy to grow and produced far more calories per acre than grain, allowing more people to survive on less land. They didn't need to be ground into flour before eating, and they didn't require kneading or a lengthy rising time or a hot oven. All you need to cook potatoes is a pot, water, and fire—and in a pinch, you can simply cook the potato directly on hot embers. There were always enough potatoes to feed the family . . . until 1845.

In 1845, a potato blight, *Phytophthora infestans*, destroyed one-third of the Irish potato crop; in 1846 and 1847, three-quarters of the crop was destroyed, and two-thirds of the crop succumbed in 1848.[70] The blight destroyed the only source of food for more than one-third of the population—people who largely grew their own potatoes on small plots of land. In 1694, one writer had reported that "in hard times, [the Irish] lived on water-cresses, roots, mushrooms, shamrocks, oatmeal, milk, and such other slender diet."[71] But by the 1840s, Ireland's cotters—the poorest—had no money to buy oatmeal and no hope of finding enough mushrooms and roots to feed 8 million people, even if they could remember how to locate them. A few famine survivors dug charlock, a sort of wild mustard.[72]

Between 1847 and 1854, more than 1.25 million Irish arrived in the United States.[73] In 1847 alone, 37,000 Irish arrived in Boston,[74] and people born in Ireland made up more than 25 percent of Boston's population.[75]

By 1860, 20 percent of the Irish-born residents of the United States lived in New England.[76] One-third of Boston's population was Irish,[77] as was 15 percent of the population of Massachusetts, and Irish immigrants made up 12 percent of Connecticut's population and 14 percent of Rhode Island's residents.[78] Today, descendants of Irish immigrants make up 20 percent of New England's population.[79]

Given the sheer number of Irish and Irish Americans in New England, it's strange that tourism boards and local restaurants don't promote local Irish American food traditions apart from Irish pubs. Part of the problem is that twentieth-century Irish culture promoters didn't start talking about Ireland's food traditions until the 1990s. The great Irish traditions that the Celtic revival celebrated at the end of the nineteenth century were unique to Ireland—the Irish language, tales and myths, Irish music, and Irish names. Irish food, by contrast, looks a lot like food found all over Great Britain, apart from a superabundance of potatoes. Talking about, say, the importance of oats in the traditional Irish foodways would have made the Irish seem more like the Scots—or, even worse, the English.[80]

Another explanation may be that the poor, starved Irish who arrived in New England simply didn't have the energy or access to foodstuffs to create new traditions in New England. Coming from poor farming communities where traditional diets had been deracinated for generations, most first-generation Irish immigrants worked as servants or in factories in the United States, not on farms where they would have easy access to fresh, tempting ingredients. Irish women, who did most of the cooking, worked at exhausting jobs, in contrast to Italian American immigrant women, who tended not to work outside the home.[81] Once home, would-be Irish American gourmands often had little access to cooking equipment—a single stove served several families in many tenements—and many of the women servants would have already eaten at their employers' homes.[82] Others either ran or lived in boarding houses that served meals,[83] once again diluting the link between food and family tradition.

However, the Irish aren't the only people who arrived in New England in the nineteenth century.

The French Canadians

About 900,000 French Canadians left Canada to immigrate to the United States between 1840 and 1930. French Canadians from the Eastern Townships immigrated to mill towns in New Hampshire, Vermont, Massachusetts, Rhode Island, and southern Maine. Acadians—residents of New Brunswick's Saint John Valley and descendants of the French speakers who were expelled from Nova Scotia in 1755—settled in many Maine communities.[84]

Thus began a culinary conundrum. Another group of French-speaking residents expelled from Nova Scotia managed to end up in southern Louisiana. The name "Acadian" gradually became Americanized into "Cajun," and French Canadian immigrant cooking spurred one of America's greatest cooking traditions. Combining French techniques with African, Spanish, Caribbean, and Native American traditions and ingredients, from okra to sassafras, the Acadians' descendants showed that they were capable of culinary genius.

Somehow, these same people, sharing the same European culinary heritage, made food in Maine that no one ever noticed. They shared many techniques—starting soups by frying chopped carrots, onions, and celery in fat and making sauces by frying fat with flour to make a roux—and yet no one in New England came up with blackened cod, lobster étouffée, or corned beef jambalaya. Something about living in New England failed to spur these gifted cooks to gastronomic greatness.

That failure may have had a lot to do with where the Acadians ended up: factory towns. Cajun families had to learn to use a variety of ingredients to survive and learned from the people who already lived there—the Houma and Chitimacha tribes, African slaves, and Spanish settlers, among others.[85] Cajuns also lived in communities in the countryside, where they could raise a variety of vegetables and fruits during the long growing season, hunt wild game, collect wild herbs and sassafras leaves, and fish and gather crayfish. The Acadians who went to Maine and Massachusetts lived in towns, their food choices dependent on the mercy of the local grocery store.

Cajuns also had the advantage of having new, tasty ingredients introduced into their region during the twentieth century. Cajuns adopted rice and sweet potatoes as they began to be farmed commercially in the region in the late nineteenth century to early twentieth century, abandoning corn as their favored starch, and they rapidly developed a taste for red snapper, shrimp, and crabs when incomes rose with the post–World War II Louisiana oil boom.[86] By contrast, New England's entrepreneurs focused on factories, not farming, after 1850, and New England's major postwar seafood innovation was fish sticks (see chapter 5).

The early nineteenth-century French Canadian immigrants left after a series of terrible harvests. Later immigrants left their farms due to poverty, overpopulation, debt, and infertile soils.[87] The 1900 US census lists 570,000 New England residents of "French Canadian stock."[88] Some moved to rural areas, but most moved to the burgeoning mill towns. These new Americans were not received warmly. The Massachusetts Department of Labor and Industries commented in 1881, "With some exceptions the Canadian French are the Chinese of the Eastern States. They care nothing for our institutions civil political or educational. They do not come to make a home among us to dwell with us as citizens and so become a part of us, but their purpose is merely to sojourn a few years as aliens touching us only at a single point that of work. . . . They are a horde of industrial invaders, not a stream of stable settlers."[89]

Railroads established routes connecting Montreal, Quebec's Eastern Townships, Rutland, Vermont, and Boston in the 1840s.[90] Rail transportation didn't make life easier for the poor farmers there though. A series of bad wheat harvests in the 1830s due to infestation of ravenous midges made many farmers in southern Quebec turn to raising buckwheat and potatoes for sustenance, and livestock and horses to sell for cash. Unfortunately, in the 1840s, potato blights—much like the Irish potato blight—cut potato yields by 50 to 70 percent, and poor farmers didn't have the resources to feed or house their cows, sheep, and pigs. US railroads and river shipping made it simple and cheap for city folk in Montreal to import flour, meat, cheese, and other foods from Vermont and Ohio, where farmers could easily raise their corn and wheat to feed fat hogs. Most Quebec farms with reported yields of grains, meat, poultry, and dairy products barely produced enough calories to support the families living on them from 1850 to 1900, much less sell any extra food. From the 1840s onward, impoverished French Canadian farmers had to look beyond their failing farms for sustenance.[91]

By 1850, there were French Canadian settlements around Burlington, Vermont, Woonsocket, Rhode Island, and Madawaska, Maine. Later settlers sought out mill towns like Fall River, Springfield, and Lowell, Massachusetts, Manchester, New Hampshire, and Lewiston and Biddeford-Saco, Maine.[92] The most visible French Canadian communities in New England today are in northern Maine and western Vermont, but Canadians of all stripes make up the largest foreign-born population in Maine, New Hampshire, and Vermont.[93]

French Canadians could ride the railroad to Boston or Portland, Maine, in a day, and French Canadian families rapidly filled mill towns. As two Canadian professors wrote, French Canadians "established themselves in 'petits Canadas' that resembled very closely the geographical and social patterns of Quebec . . . in a sense, all they were doing was to slightly enlarge the borders of French Canada. In this sense, there was little difference between settling into New England or into the Saguenay region."[94] In 1900, Fall River, Massachusetts, with 33,000 French Canadian residents, was the third largest community of Francophones in North America after Montreal and Quebec City.[95] French Canadians made up 30 percent of textile workers in Massachusetts and more than 60 percent in New Hampshire and Maine.[96]

About one-third of Quebec's French-speaking residents immigrated to New England between 1870 and 1930.[97] Since New England seemed like an extension of southern Quebec, many viewed their new homes as temporary housing. It's estimated that half of the 900,000 French Canadian immigrants who came to the United States between 1850 and 1930 returned to Quebec sooner or later, and some immigrants shuttled back and forth several times.[98]

These immigrants came to work in the mills, which supplied a better income than Quebec's frigid farms. For several generations, the new French Canadian immigrants showed no interest in assimilating into English-speaking American culture. The French Canadian immigrants were served by Francophone priests and nuns, sent their children to Francophone schools (until they were 14, and old enough to work),[99] and patronized Francophone lawyers, doctors, dentists, and pharmacists.[100] If they married in the United States, they wed other French Canadians. In Fall River in 1880, 86 percent of French Canadian immigrants married within the community.[101] As late as 1926, 50 percent of third-generation French Canadian American children in Woonsocket, Rhode Island, spoke only French at home.[102]

French Canadian American cuisine, like Irish American cuisine, is not celebrated much in New England, apart from occasional articles on *tourtiere* (meat pies) at Christmas.[103] Starting with the same limited northern food palette as anyone else in northern Vermont, New Hampshire, or Maine, French Canadians in New England allegedly ate more pork than beef, using ham or smoked shoulder in their "boiled dinners."[104] They baked beans with salt pork, just as Bostonians allegedly did, but may have used maple syrup with their *féves au lard*. The difference between beans and féves was the basis for some cross-cultural confusion. From an 1897 book by an American traveler in Quebec,

> At our fishing camp we used many baked beans. Now the French for beans is féves, but baked beans are called simply beans. Our cook will frequently ask me if he is to "mettre tremper des féves pour faire de beans," that is, put some beans in soak to make some beans.

So baked beans will be "beans" in French while the unbaked article will continue to be féves.[105]

The same traveler writes about baked beans, "The men are always fond of them but I have rarely known a Canadian family to cook them."[106]

Contrast this to the comment by Philip Marchand, a third-generation French Canadian American raised in Pittsfield, Massachusetts: "I must confess that *tourtiéres* and my family were strangers. In my father's time, the main French-Canadian food concept was baked beans. Pots of navy beans or yellow-eyed beans or pea beans, flavored with salt pork, would be boiling all day Saturday in French-Canadian households across New England, in preparation for the Saturday night baked bean dinner."[107] In the United States, Catholic French Canadians observed meatless Fridays, eating fish in dishes like salmon pie (canned salmon and mashed potatoes baked in a crust) or, in the twentieth century, spaghetti.[108]

Other popular French Canadian dishes include *ployes* (buckwheat pancakes), split pea soup, *tarte au sucre* "sugar pie" made from brown sugar or maple syrup, and *pate Chinoise*, literally "Chinese pie," a casserole made of ground beef, corn, and mashed potatoes. There are many explanations for the "Chinoise." It could have been named for food served at boarding houses near China, Maine (unlikely—then it would be China pie, not Chinese pie) or for a dish served to Chinese railroad workers building the Canadian Pacific Railway in British Columbia (unlikely—why bother making a casserole instead of just serving the meat from pots? And where were these casseroles supposed to have been baked?), or it may be just a garbling of "chez nous," that is, "our house pie."[109] Acadians, French speakers from eastern Canada who settled in Maine, also favor chicken stew with dumplings; *pot-en-pot*, a large, layered meat pie baked in a roasting pan; yellow split pea soup; and two foods that aren't quite their New Orleans equivalents—boudin, a blood sausage made of pork (also eaten on Quebec farms), and Acadia beignets, also called "Grandperes" (grandfathers!). The grandfathers aren't cannibalized old men but floury dumplings that are boiled in water and maple syrup, not fried and doused in powdered sugar like the New Orleans delicacies.[110]

Once they arrived in the United States, poor French Canadians ate dull diets—but they ate more than they did in Quebec, according to an 1886 Massachusetts Department of Labor study. French Canadian men in Massachusetts ate five pounds of food daily, about a pound and a half more than they did in Quebec.[111] The investigators recorded the food consumed in a month by French Canadian families and at boarding houses in Holyoke, Lawrence, Lowell, East Cambridge, and Worcester, Massachusetts. Laborers in Quebec ate one pound of animal products per day, including meat, milk, eggs, cheese, and butter. French Canadians in Massachusetts ate one and a half pounds of those foods each day, while workers from other nationalities ate a little over two pounds.[112] The French Canadians did eat significantly more fat than other ethnic groups, which the writers attribute to eating more salt pork than beef. Curiously, the only vegetables mentioned are cabbage, onions, turnips, and carrots. Apparently, the immigrants had yet to develop a taste for New England's pumpkin, beets, or parsnips. The only fruits mentioned are apples and raisins, which can be stored for long periods of time. This absence may be an artifact of the time of year the study was done, or it could just be that most of the produce available cheaply in cities was the sort that could sit in boxes. By contrast, the diet lists for other "miscellaneous" boarding houses and families in the study include items like broad beans, fresh "green" corn, squash, tomatoes, beets, pole beans, and green peas.[113]

A November 1909 study recorded one week's meals for French Canadian family with 11 members in Lowell, Massachusetts. They survived on $14 a week, and their diet included no fruit or vegetables apart from potatoes. Instead, the family solved "the problem of calories" with bread, butter, milk, potatoes, beans, pork, and lard.[114] A slightly better off family of 13 with 5 members earning a combined $29 a week supplemented their diets with a few cans of vegetables and $0.50 worth of "fresh fruit"—probably apples, given that it was November in New England.[115] By contrast, Irish families who had a little disposable income to spend on food are specifically mentioned as buying cabbage.[116]

These French Canadian families weren't choosing to economize because they didn't care for food. Here are two descriptions of what similar families' lives were like overall from the same study.[117]

SHOEMAKER, FRENCH

Earnings of Father, $396.00

Condition—Family numbers six, parents and four children from one to nine years of age; two go to school. Live in a crowded tenement of three rooms, situated in a very unhealthy locality, in the midst of filth and pollution. On outside of building is a sink-conductor, badly out of repair, and the sink-water, almost black, runs down the clapboards, causing an offensive stench, which can be smelled at a great distance. The inside of the house is on a par with the surroundings; it is poorly furnished, and seems the abode of poverty. Children pale looking, sickly, and wretchedly kept. Father earns from $12 to $15 per week when he has work; but, on account of sickness and dullness of trade, finds it impossible to keep out of debt and live; sees no hope for betterment of condition, till children are old enough to work. Family dresses miserably.

Food:

Breakfast, bread, butter, sometimes salt fish or pork, coffee.
Dinner, bread, meat three days per week, salt fish or pork the remainder, potatoes, sometimes pie, water.
Supper, bread, sometimes brown or oatmeal bread, butter, tea, occasionally gingerbread. Cannot afford luxuries.

LABORER IN MILL FRENCH-CANADIAN (UNSKILLED)

Earnings of Father $420.00
Earnings of Daughter, sixteen. $334.00

[Total] $754.00

Condition—Family numbers five, parents and three children from six to sixteen years of age; two go to school. Have a tenement of four rooms, in a good locality, but the surroundings poor and unhealthy. The house is clean, but poorly furnished. The family is in good health, and dresses moderately well.

Food:

Breakfast, bread, butter, cold meat, gingerbread and coffee.
Dinner, bread, butter, meat, potatoes, vegetables and pie.
Supper, bread, butter, sauce, cake, tea. Soup once a week.

✲ ✲ ✲

French Canadians who ran boarding houses served standard New England foods to their guests. At Polivine Croteau's Lowell, Massachusetts, boarding house in the early twentieth century, breakfast was bacon and eggs and dinner was corned beef and cabbage, with a packed dinner pail with meat, potatoes, and vegetables available for boarders who couldn't leave their jobs at the mills midday. Friday night was for salmon bread pudding and fried rice. Many French Canadian families who didn't run boarding houses began every dinner with soup: pea soup, clam chowder, or vegetable soup thickened with barley. The main meal would contain potatoes, bread, meat, and a vegetable—either turnips, cabbage, or carrots, but never all at the same time. Perhaps multiple simultaneous vegetables were too extravagant?[118]

On weekends, French Canadian mothers in Lowell would cook a *ragout*, a stew with meatballs and vegetables, or beans with a ham shoulder. Holidays meant *tourtiére* and chicken and turkey stuffed with a combination of potatoes and meats—leftover pork or beef roast or other portions of the poultry—seasoned with onions and cinnamon, cloves, or allspice.[119] It's not surprising that people whose grandparents had little access to wheat would find a different carbohydrate for stuffing turkeys.

The "Little Canadas" of Lowell, Woonsocket, and Manchester have generally diffused into general New England whiteness, with few French Canadian descendants speaking French or continuing the old ways.

The African Americans

Historic African American foodways in New England haven't received much attention compared to the traditions of southern African American cooks and chefs. As with the Acadians, New England's African Americans shared ancestors with people who created great culinary traditions in other areas of the country, but either didn't manage to perform the same feat in New England or haven't been recognized for their accomplishments.

African Americans have lived in New England since 1638, when the slave ship *Desire* brought several Africans to Salem, Massachusetts, via the West Indies.[120] Rhode Island actually banned slavery in 1652. That ban was largely ignored, unfortunately, and Rhode Island reaffirmed slavery by law in 1703—shortly before Massachusetts banned intermarriage between African Americans and whites.[121] Rhode Island firms controlled between 60 and 90 percent of the American trade in African slaves until the state legislature forbade the business in 1787,[122] and slaves made up 10 percent of the Rhode Island population in 1750—higher than any other New England state,[123] and far higher than the average 3 percent of the New England population. By contrast, 34 percent of the South's population consisted of slaves in the years leading up to the Civil War.[124] On the eve of the American Revolution in 1775, there were 5,000 slaves living in Connecticut, 4,373 in Rhode Island, 3,500 in Massachusetts, and 629 in New Hampshire. Slavery was banned in Vermont in 1777.[125]

In colonial times, both slaves and free African Americans in New England tended to live in cities along the coast and major rivers, and most slave owners owned fewer than five slaves. In 1755, African Americans made up 2 percent of the population of Massachusetts but 8 percent of Boston, totaling about 900 slaves over the age of 16.[126] In 1790, roughly 2 percent of New England's population was African American—mostly free, at least in name—totaling about 17,000, with 3,763 listed as slaves.

By 1797, all New England states had abolished slavery (although Rhode Island's piecemeal, gradual emancipation didn't release all slaves in the state until 1842), but they did not abolish racism.[127] Bostonian African American leader Prince Hall denounced attacks by mobs of "shameless, low-lived envious spiteful persons" on African Americans who walked on the Boston Common in the 1790s.[128] In 1800, a Boston Selectman tried to have 239 free blacks removed from the city because they didn't have papers stating they were American citizens.[129] Connecticut barred African American men from voting in 1818, and Rhode Island followed suit in 1822.[130]

Very few accounts of slave and free African Americans' diets in New England have come to light. Most New England slaves lived with their owners and did not have the space or kitchen to grow or make their own food, however much they may have yearned to eat food from a different place. In Portsmouth, New Hampshire, one author observed, slaves "usually lived in the same house as their masters, worked beside them, ate the same or similar food at the same or adjacent tables, and were taken to their owner's church."[131] However, that "similar" food might have been leftovers or scraps that could also be fed to hogs, and the "adjacent" tables were often in the kitchen, not the parlor. First-person accounts of slave diets in New York and Philadelphia and archaeological evidence from New York's African burial ground show that slaves in the Mid-Atlantic were frequently malnourished, and enslaved children suffered anemia and rickets.[132] There is some evidence that this mistreatment occurred in Rhode Island, where households kept more slaves and where slaves made up more of the population than in other parts of New England.[133] There, the slaveholders were not always generous with their food. William J. Brown, the son of slaves, recounted his father's diet when he was slave on Moses Brown's Rhode Island farm.

> My father during his youth worked on the farm belonging to Moses Brown, and at one time had occasion to find fault with his food, which displeased Mrs. Brown very much. She was accustomed to save all their turkey carcasses until they were musty, and then make soup for the men. So every morning they were treated to some musty soup for breakfast. Week after week this was continued, and no one dared say anything for fear offending some one. . . . Mr. Brown sent for his wife to come into the kitchen, and said to her in the presence of the men, "Is not my house able to give my help good vituals? Here you have been feeding them week after week on musty soup. I have tasted it; it is fit for nothing but for hogs. I don't wish you to give them any more such stuff; they work hard and should have good victuals, and I am able to give it to them."[134]

Moses Brown went on to become a prominent abolitionist and freed his slaves—after he calculated that they had earned their purchase price.[135]

At the same time, New England slaves lived in such close quarters with their enslavers that they likely had far less freedom to supplement their diets with wild game, herbs, and berries than slaves in more rural areas. As an archaeologist wrote about an excavation at the Royall Estate in Medford, Massachusetts,

> The plant and animal remains from this site suggest that the Royalls' slaves were doing little or nothing to supplement their basic provisions, either through the exploitation of wild resources or the cultivation of domesticated

ones. There was no evidence of a preference for stews or gumbos; no presence of small forest game, aside from a single rabbit; no evidence of fishing; only equivocal evidence of shellfish gathering; and few plant remains—a few hundred wild berry seeds. . . . Since African-American folk culture in other areas is known to have sprung up and flourished in physically marginal areas such as fields and forest clearings and depended largely on enslaved people's ability to get away from the plantation, the possibility that the Royalls' slaves were curtailed in that kind of movement has serious implications for their ability to create and maintain social, cultural, and economic ties outside the bounds of the Royall estate.[136]

To give an example of just how desperate academics can get to find some trace of African identity in postcolonial New England foodways, consider the case of the Plymouth mystery jars. These oddly shaped jars, with a narrow mouth, wide top, and tapering base, were found in archaeological excavations of the cellars of free African Americans' homes at Parting Ways, Plymouth, Massachusetts, and trash pits near homes where African Americans lived in Portsmouth, New Jersey, and Salem, Massachusetts, all occupied ca. 1790–1840. An early researcher opined that these types of jars had been used to ship preserved tamarind fruit from the West Indies to faraway places and suggested that their owners had been preserving African American foodways. A later researcher observed that jars made out of the same materials in the same shape were used to drain sugar cones as they dripped on West Indies sugar plantations. The homes where these jars were found had African American residents, but they were also near major shipping ports where thousands of pounds of Caribbean sugar were unloaded every year. Were the residents enjoying sour tamarind in their food or medicine, savoring the taste of West Africa in their frigid northern homes? Or were they storing sugar or water or maybe old bits of string in attractive red containers, in a postcolonial version of the eternal Danish butter cookie tin? The explanations have not come down to academia.[137]

An excavation of a privy behind Boston's African Meeting House, dating to 1811–1838, turned up a few signs that local African American foodways resembled foodways farther south. The excavation revealed bones from beef, pork, and mutton meals, but also pigs' feet and a butchered snapping turtle—much more common foods in the Mid-Atlantic and Virginia than among white Bostonians.[138] Were the Bostonians eating these foods themselves or feeding guests from southern areas? No one knows. Sea turtle remains, but not pigs' feet, were also found outside a Nantucket house owned by a free African American weaver named Seneca Boston and his descendants, with remains dated ca. 1800–1840.[139] There wasn't much local fish in the privy. Plant remains included local foods like blueberries, apples, and cranberries, but also figs—likely imported dried—and plenty of tomatoes, which weren't mentioned much in cookbooks and menus published by whites in the Federalist era.[140] The privy also contained many specimens of insects that typically infested spoiled grain, implying that the African Meeting House cooks were buying cheap, low-quality flour.[141]

One of the reasons that historians haven't found much evidence of African American foodways in New England is that in the early twentieth century, the African American population in most of New England dropped—even as a million African Americans moved to the North from 1915 to 1930 at the beginning of the Great Migration. Vermont had no all-white counties until 1930. New Hampshire had no all-white counties in 1890 but two in 1930. There's evidence that some New England communities became "sundown towns," legally or socially barring African Americans from staying overnight, much less living there.[142] Other factors may involve the decline of New England industry; why stay in a mill town in Maine when the jobs have moved to steam-powered plants?

While we don't have much information on what New England's slave and free African Americans ate themselves, we do have records of what they served other people. African Americans have worked as cooks and chefs in New England for centuries.[143] White writers remembered slaves and African American servants as excellent chefs. One white historian remarked in 1901, "In many families negroes had an important position, especially as cooks. As compared with the Indians or the Irish, they were epicures. They generally took care to know what they carried upon the table, being their own tasters."[144] New England's African American slaves and their free descendants made pastries, cakes, gingerbread, candy, cheese, and chocolate and, in the case of the improbably named "Cuffee Cockroach," catered "turtle frolic" parties with sea turtle stew.[145] Some of these culinary professionals in Rhode Island earned enough money through overtime work or freelancing to earn their freedom.

Emmanuel "Manna" Bernoon was emancipated by his owner, Gabriel Bernon, in 1736 in Providence, Rhode Island. He added an O to his possibly French Huguenot owner's name and opened his own restaurant, raising local culinary standards, according to a 1910 historian: "Manna now or soon established the first oyster house on Town Street near the location of the subsequent custom house. The rude English-descended efforts in cookery were far surpassed by Huguenot skill and refinement."[146] After she was freed, Duchess Quamino, the "Pastry Queen of Newport," earned enough from her iced plum cakes to buy herself a house in the 1790s.[147]

African Americans also ran restaurants and catering companies in New England from the Federal period onward. Othello Pollard, an African American caterer and restauranteur in Boston from 1796 to 1806 who was a master of cheesecakes, pastries, and creams, had his cakes celebrated in verse by grateful Harvard students:

> When Science has consum'd her classic hour,
> Othello courts the Muses to his bower;
> Each of the Nine his rich libation gives,
> Hence Harvard flourishes, and Pollard lives.[148]

John Remond, an immigrant from Curaçao, lived in Salem, Massachusetts, and catered events including Salem's 200th anniversary dinner in 1826 and a dinner for President Andrew Jackson in 1833.[149] Joshua B. Smith, Boston's premier caterer from 1842 to 1879 (37 years!), created buffets and banquets for up to 2,000 people including roast meats, pâté de foie gras, lobster salad, and Charlotte Russe and blancmange. He also petitioned the Massachusetts legislature to create a memorial to Crispus Attucks, the African American man killed in the Boston Massacre, and led the drive to create the Captain Robert Gould Shaw monument, dedicated to the man who led Massachusetts 54th Volunteer Infantry, the first documented African American regiment formed in the North to fight in the Civil War. Smith had worked for Shaw's father when Robert was a boy.[150]

The culinary history of African Americans in New England became more complex in the nineteenth century as immigrants arrived from Cape

Verde, an archipelago 500 miles off the coast of Senegal. The first Cape Verdeans to arrive were sailors who hired themselves out on whaling ships that stopped by Cape Verde in the late nineteenth century and decided to stay once the ship reached the United States. They considered themselves Portuguese and were often counted as such in contemporary censuses, but Americans treated them as Africans and local Portuguese Americans excluded them from social and religious groups. Still, as historian Marilyn Halter observed, "One of the things that is so remarkable about this migration is that they represent the first group of Americans from Africa to have made the transatlantic voyage *voluntarily*."[151]

These same immigrants built and sailed packet boats back to Cape Verde, exporting trade goods and importing immigrants on the return journey.[152] As the whaling industry crumbled, the Cape Verdeans worked as longshoremen, as dockworkers, and on the cranberry bogs—seasonal jobs that allowed some of them to return to Cape Verde for the winter when work was scarce.[153]

Cape Verdeans largely settled near the ports of New Bedford and Providence and on Cape Cod.[154] By 1880, the entire New Bedford fishing fleet came from the Azores or Cape Verde, and Cape Verdeans continued to immigrate through the 1920s until restrictive immigration laws barred new immigrants from entering the country.[155] Immigration rose again in the 1940s after a series of droughts in Cape Verde produced famines that killed a quarter of the population.[156] Today, one in five Cape Verdeans born abroad who are living in the United States lives in Boston, totaling almost 8,000 people, and close to 90 percent of the total US Cape Verdean population lives in Massachusetts or Rhode Island—about 180,000 people.[157]

"Traditional" dishes, which may or may not reflect what Cape Verdean immigrants ate from day to day when they arrived in the United States, feature cornmeal, beans, and rice. The most debated entrée is a dish named *cachupa* or *manchupa*, which is a reincarnation of colonial "pottage fare"—or another version of the Brunswick stew that was served in the Mid-South, and was also likely created by African slaves.[158] The stew's exact ingredients are the topic of extended arguments, but seem to involve hominy, lima or fava beans, greens, and meat.[159] Leftovers are sometimes fried and served with an egg on top, much like New England's red flannel hash. *Canja*, chicken soup with onion and rice, is also common, as is *jagacita*, rice with onions, kidney beans, and paprika. *Cuscuz*, spelled in a variety of ways, is a type of steamed corn pone and is a traditional breakfast in Cape Verde, while *gufong*, a sweet fried dough with banana, flour, and cornmeal, is a holiday treat.[160] Contemporary versions of gufong are sometimes made with Bisquick.[161]

In the twentieth century, migrants from the southern United States and immigrants from other African countries, the Caribbean, and even Canada joined the mix with a flurry of foods and cultures from Connecticut to Bangor, Maine.[162] As of 2017, 155,000 Caribbean immigrants were living in greater Boston and New Hampshire, making up 3 percent of the population; about half were from the Dominican Republic.[163] More than 100,000 African immigrants were living in the region, mostly in Boston, Providence, and Worcester.[164] Jamaican workers are the majority of seasonal workers in New England apple orchards and have been for decades—but you wouldn't know it from volumes like *The New England Orchard Cookbook*, which features Moroccan peach roasted chicken, not foods prepared by or for the people who pick the fruit.[165]

The Italians

Thanks to earthquakes, crop failures, the eruptions of Mount Etna and Mount Vesuvius, epidemics, and unending taxes, more than four million Italians immigrated to the United States between approximately 1880 and 1924. Of these immigrants, 80 percent were from southern Italy or Sicily,[166] and more than 80 percent of these immigrants settled in urban areas.[167] They settled all around the United States—in New York and Philadelphia, Chicago, St. Louis, Buffalo, and Trenton—but thousands arrived in New England as well. Crowded "Little Italy" neighborhoods full of shoddy tenement housing for the poor, emerged in Boston, Providence, Worcester, Springfield, Bridgeport, and New Haven.[168] Boston's North End shifted from being about one-third Irish, one-third Jewish, and one-third Italian in 1895 to 90 percent Italian in 1910.[169] By 1920, the North End's population had swelled from 28,000 to 37,000 people and was still overwhelmingly Italian.[170] Now, Italian Americans make up the largest ethnic group in Connecticut and the second largest in Rhode Island.[171] More than 10 percent of the residents of Massachusetts and New Hampshire claim Italian American ancestry, and the figures for Rhode Island and Connecticut are close to 19 percent.[172]

It's hard to pinpoint exactly how many Italians settled in New England and when. At least a third of New England's Italian immigrants were "birds of passage"—mostly men, but also some women, who intended to return to Italy as soon as they had earned some money, much like the Cape Verdeans on Cape Cod.[173] Some Italians returned to Italy every winter, then came back to Boston to work once the weather warmed up—much as New England's "snowbirds" decamp to Florida every November today.[174] Many immigrants dreamed this dream, which is one reason that 600,000 Italian Americans were not US citizens when World War II began. In New England, Italian American "enemy aliens" had to keep logs of their whereabouts, and at least 200 Italian American fishermen in Gloucester and Boston lost their ships when the US government requisitioned them for minesweeping or patrol duty (although they were compensated).[175]

Over time, Italian immigrants realized that the southern Italian economy was not getting better and sent for their wives, children, brothers, and cousins in classic chain migration style. North End Italians settled in and started opening businesses instead of working in seasonal employment. Pietro Pastene began what became the Pastene food corporation in 1874 on Hanover Street, in Boston's North End. The Prince spaghetti company opened on Prince Street.

Several authors have noted that Italian Americans bought and ate more fruit and vegetables than other immigrant groups and consumed far less meat and milk than Anglos, much to economically minded Yankee benefactors' dismay.[176] (In Boston, the Italian North End neighborhood was conveniently located next to the city's largest produce markets.)[177] Here's a description of a typical Italian immigrant diet in Boston in 1903, as written by a concerned non-Italian:

> The Italians like their food greasy, highly spiced and flavored with garlic or onions. A dish so dressed will have for a body nothing more substantial than macaroni. With this they will have French bread, beer and some partly spoiled fruit or dried olives.
>
> Such a diet is inexpensive so far as first cost is concerned, but a sturdy growth cannot be made upon it. The frequency of rickets among Italian

children, and the general high average of sickness among adults, is owing very largely to their choice of food. Their liking for this strong-tasting but innutritious food is so deep seated that if they go to a hospital they consider themselves wronged when they are placed upon a diet of milk and beefsteak.[178]

Many Italians in New England went into the produce business. As one 1912 report on Boston put it, "There is a special and permanent fitness in the Italians' choice of abode just next to the great fruit and vegetable markets. The citizens of Boston owe a great debt to the Italians for organizing and developing the retail fruit trade throughout the city. . . . Even the newest immigrant, with his push cart, makes his wares attractive, and unwittingly acts as the dietetic missionary of the back streets throughout the city."[179]

Italian Americans also became produce entrepreneurs—moving from pushcarts and corner stores to truck farms in the country. As early as 1905, a US census study titled *The Italian in America* reported that Italian Americans had established market gardens in the outskirts of cities in Massachusetts, Rhode Island, and Connecticut:

> Six years ago I was invited by one of the leading hotel and restaurant keepers in New Haven to drive out with him to look over a market garden which had been planted by a poor Italian and his family only a few years before near the suburbs of the city. I have never seen anywhere in this country a more thriving garden nor one in which every possible means of advancing the crops that were available to a poor man had been more keenly noticed and grasped. . . . This same gardener has now widely extended [his] most thrifty plantation giving employment in the season to 200 of his poorer countrymen women and children and holding up an object lesson by which many thousands of immigrants to this country should profit.[180]

In the 1920s, Italian immigrants began buying farms in Boston's suburbs. Names like Castella, Rando, Farese, Torola, Tomao, Chicco, Palumbo, Arrigo, and Luongo started cropping up all over greater Boston. Some Italian American families still run farms—often with an eye to tourism, with features like seasonal corn mazes.[181]

Although many immigrant groups kept a tradition of gathering for a family Sunday dinner, in the early twentieth century Italian Americans expanded their culinary ambitions and began creating elaborate multicourse meals every weekend. These dinners often featured separate antipasto, soup, pasta, and meat courses and were cooked not only by the hostess but also by other men and women from the family, creating pan-Italian melting pot meals as family members married spouses from different regions of Italy.[182]

Why? Why did they go to all this effort? Authors like Hasia Diner say that these meals were derived from Italian feast days that landowners would sponsor for local workers, now translated into American meat-laden meals.[183] In America, even poor Italians living in tenements could eat like the rich, relishing meat every day and feasting every Sunday—but so could the Irish, French Canadians, and Portuguese, and the Irish women who worked as maids were certainly exposed to lavish upper-class feasts in the United States. Perhaps the repeated trips the "birds of passage" made to Italy cemented a connection to, and focus on, Italian food; perhaps not.[184]

Italian American food has permeated New England. It's hard to find a town small enough to not have a pizzeria or at least a general store selling Italian sandwiches, called "spuckies" in Boston and grinders in the northern hinterlands. (Although most of those pizzerias are owned by Greeks—more on that below.) The tricky part is that these foods aren't unique to New England, thanks to the rest of the four million Italians who immigrated to the Mid-Atlantic states, Louisiana, and beyond. Pizza is everywhere in the United States, and grinders are sold across the country under the names hoagie, hero, sub, and submarine. Paninis, espresso, and Italian ices are sold at Costco locations everywhere from Miami to Wichita to Seattle.[185] Spaghetti is so omnipresent that flavor-averse young children will eat it along with their recycled-meat chicken tenders and apple juice.

Sadly, New England isn't even one of the top destinations for Italian food in the eastern United States. Food aficionados—aka snobs—will also tell you that Italian Americans make far better pizza in New York and New Jersey than anything found north of Connecticut's Merritt Parkway and that New England's grinder shops simply don't understand how to make a Philly cheese steak. The Italian sandwiches with ham, pickles, and American cheese beloved in Portland, Maine, aren't appreciated farther south, and neither is New England pizza, which is often actually Greek

American pizza and not Italian at all.[186] New England Italian Americans can lay claim to New Haven white clam pizza, but New England cookbook authors generally ignore it in favor of tiresome recipes for chowder and apple pandowdy. Italian recipes still aren't featured in New England cookbooks without some kind of sobriquet like "North End," or they're shunted off into their own cookbooks altogether.[187]

The Poles

Like so many other ethnic groups, Polish immigrants largely arrived in New England between approximately 1880 and 1914 to find work and escape poverty (although a few political exiles came over as well). Another wave of Polish immigrants arrived after World War II, and yet another in the 1990s. Most Polish immigrants in the first wave settled in Massachusetts and Connecticut and, like the Irish and French Canadians before them, went to work in the factories in Lowell and Fall River and up and down the Connecticut River Valley in Hatfield, Springfield, Chicopee, and Holyoke, Massachusetts, Manchester, Vermont, and New Britain, Connecticut. By 1900, Connecticut had the highest ratio of Polish immigrants to native-born residents in the United States. By 1930, 362,285 Polish Americans—more than 10 percent of the total Polish population in the United States—lived in New England, mostly in Massachusetts and Connecticut.[188] In Lawrence, Massachusetts, Polish women sparked the renowned 1912 Bread and Roses Strike when workers at Lawrence's Everett textile mill walked out to protest a cut in their wages, instigating a three-month strike that involved 25,000 workers.[189]

At the end of the nineteenth century, Polish immigrants began to move to western Connecticut and the Pioneer Valley in western Massachusetts; about 70,000 Polish Americans eventually moved to the area.[190] Many of the earlier Polish arrivals were actively recruited by agents to fill labor shortages in the area.[191] The Polish Americans worked on and bought farms from English Americans whose children had been killed in the Civil War or had been wooed away by city life and prairie state soils.[192] Their habits seemed strange to older Yankees. The twentieth-century Polish American farmers raised onions and tobacco—a shift from earlier Yankee farmers who raised beef, fruit, and grain in one place. This was mostly due to railroads' influence on markets rather than some Polish antipathy toward vegetables.[193] Polish women worked alongside men in the fields to make a better life. The strategy paid off: Polish Americans rapidly expanded their land holdings. In 1930, Polish American farmers made up 7 percent of the population of Northampton, Massachusetts, but held 89 percent of the farmland.[194]

The native-born Americans were not always grateful for the Polish Americans' enterprising spirit. Here is a typical contemporary dyspeptic description of Polish diets and farm life—with reference to the habit of boarding house residents cooking many families' meals in a single pot:

> Unmarried men live on a dollar a week. They hang about butchers' shops like hungry dogs, and eagerly snap at some dusty or tainted neck or flank offered for two or three cents a pound. Properly tagged for identification, this acquisition is thrown with pieces belonging to other boarders into the common pot on the boarding-house stove. On such meat, with milk, coffee, rye bread, and a bowl of grease for butter, the Pole thrives, and his round cheeks contrast with the hatchet face of the Yankee who bought the best cuts of beef.
>
> The history of Wawrzeniec Gwozdz is typical. . . . The two little hoards bought a run-down farm that no American would cultivate. Wawrzeniec toils from starlight to starlight, and is now planning to get a barn for a hundred dollars by hewing out the timbers by hand. As domestic, his wife's slashing industry rapidly transferred china from the dining-room to the dump-heap; but since marriage her physical exuberance has found vent in wielding the hoe. . . . In a decade, Mr. and Mrs. Gwozdz will be as prosperous as their Yankee neighbors. Either as farm hand or land owner, the Pole displays industry that adds greatly to the production of the valley. Help is very scarce, and but for him the farms could hardly be tilled.[195]

Polish immigrants in New England maintained their food traditions as best they could. Studies of poor unemployed Polish Americans in early twentieth-century Lowell mostly remark on the rye bread they ate.[196] Polish immigrants in Lowell recall their families gathering to make vast batches of sauerkraut—perhaps to be used to make *kapusta* soup and *bigos* stew with pork and eaten with sausage.[197] Polish American bakeries making *babka*, *strucla*, and *paczki* have been slowly closing, although the

Vermont Country Store will sell you several look-alikes under names like "European Nut Roll Pastries" via its website.[198] *Golubki* cabbage rolls filled with meat and rice aren't exactly New England's most famous food, for no very good reason. Like Italian Americans, Polish Americans settled in many areas, so their food is not unique to New England, which also means that lots of people like to eat it.

Country fairs and food trucks in the Pioneer Valley still serve kielbasa sausage.[199] And in one of the finest examples of New England fusion food, a Fall River pierogi (Polish dumpling) outpost offers them stuffed with French Canadian tourtiere filling, Portuguese *chouriço* sausage, Italian sausage and peppers, or Greek feta cheese and spinach.[200]

The Portuguese

Portuguese Sephardic Jews first arrived in Newport, Rhode Island, in the mid-seventeenth century and established the oldest synagogue in America there in 1759. Catholic Portuguese immigrants started arriving in large numbers in the mid-nineteenth century, when sailors stepped off whaling ships coming from the Azores and Madeira. They settled in southeastern Massachusetts and Rhode Island, particularly New Bedford and Edgartown, Massachusetts, and in the 1880s their families started following them to work at textile mills. By 1910, Portuguese immigrants made up 40 percent of the labor force in New Bedford and Fall River.[201] About 320,000 people of Portuguese descent lived in Massachusetts as of 2010.[202] Today, more than 90,000 Portuguese Americans reside in Fall River alone. Another 100,000 live in Rhode Island, chiefly in East Providence and Bristol. Portuguese Americans are also clustered in Somerville and Cambridge, Massachusetts.

Portuguese Americans arriving in New England up through the 1970s had an easier time finding butter and cow's milk than their traditional olive oil and goat's milk, and they adjusted their cooking accordingly. Everyday Portuguese American food in the United States typically includes *caldo verde* soup with potatoes, chouriço sausage, and kale (in place of hard-to-find Portuguese tronchada cabbage). Fava beans, red beans, and chickpeas appear frequently, along with *bacalhau* salt cod, fresh seafood (typically cod, clams, mussels, and shrimp), potatoes, and pork in all forms. Desserts include eggy custards and tarts. Massachusetts supermarkets frequently carry

Portuguese sweet bread—a slightly sweet, eggy bun.[203] Azoreans brought their own food traditions, such as *malassada* fried doughnuts with cinnamon sugar, that have frequently melded with or been adopted by other Portuguese Americans.[204]

One place where Portuguese American food is actually recognized and even celebrated is Cape Cod. Portuguese Americans have been part of Cape Cod culture for more than 150 years. In the 1870s, a quarter of Provincetown, Massachusetts, schoolchildren were Portuguese; by the 1940s, 90 percent were Portuguese Americans.[205] With the collapse of local fishing and a ravenous vacation home market devouring real estate, the Portuguese American population in Provincetown has shrunk, but they still make up close to 20 percent of the population.[206]

Despite the enormous population of chouriço- and kale-eating Portuguese, Azorean, and Cape Verdean residents in southeastern Massachusetts and Cape Cod, blurbs for cookbooks still read like this one in a Boston cookbook gift guide from 2018—for a book that actually includes recipes like clams with Portuguese *linguiça* sausage and Portuguese sweet bread: "Bring the flavors of the Cape—from New England clam chowder to apple crisp—to the table with this adorable cookbook."[207]

And there you have it—a Cape Cod with all Portuguese speakers removed, eternally spawning generic "New England" food straight out of a convention center grab-and-go lunch counter.

The Greeks

Like migrants from many other nations, Greek Americans primarily emigrated to the United States between 1880 and 1924 and settled in mill towns where the jobs were. Today there are about 100,000 people who claim Greek ancestry living in Massachusetts, Rhode Island, and New Hampshire.[208]

Greek immigrants earned respect, in a way, from a researcher investigating Lowell, Massachusetts, in 1912—for both their hard work and their economical eating habits.

> The men, unmarried or without family ties, live in the home of some brother or relative; or, like an army on the march, eat and sleep together in squads.

A dozen men crowd into three or four small rooms, have one kitchen, one larder, and, like the early Christians, hold "all things in common," which has its disadvantages, as well as advantages, in this case. The breakfast is simple and hasty, and the noon-day lunch consists of the cold remnants of the previous night's meal. Dinner is prepared at night when the men return from the mills, unless, perchance, one of the group is out of work and becomes the cook and quartermaster. The piece de resistance of the evening meal is the leg of mutton, purchased for about fourteen cents a pound. In these narrow quarters, the Greek young men eat, drink, smoke cigarettes, and sleep. They can live on $1.00 a week, some of them depending largely, especially in the summer, on bread and onions.[209]

Greek immigrants to New England weren't as numerous as the Irish or French Canadians, but they have had a major impact on New England's diet through pizzerias and grocery stores. New England has Greek diners too, of course, but they aren't nearly as prevalent or divergent from their Mid-Atlantic counterparts as the pizzerias.

All over New England, "House of Pizza" establishments are run by Greek immigrants and their heirs.[210] The *Boston Globe* counted 200 in 1976.[211] In 2018, New Hampshire had 276 businesses with the words "House of Pizza" in the name for just 221 towns.[212] In the 1970s, an astonishing 76 percent of Greek families in Connecticut worked in the pizza business.[213]

Greek pizza—sometimes also called bar pizza on Massachusetts's South Shore[214]—is a bread and cheese construction that has very little in common with Italian pizza from, well, pretty much anywhere else. It is supposedly the brainchild of a Greek Albanian who set up a pizza shop in New London in 1953 and wanted a more efficient way to prep his pizzas than stretching and forming the dough for each pie.[215] About 10 inches around, these pizzas are made by placing a thick dough in oiled metal tins, not directly on a hot oven floor, producing a puffy crust with a crunchy fried bottom. Some pizzerias add milk, eggs, or sugar to the dough.[216] The sweet, thick tomato sauce is topped with a mixture of cheeses—often mozzarella and cheddar.[217] The combination strikes a note somewhere between Chicago deep-dish pizza and a grilled cheese sandwich. Even New Englanders who grew up on the stuff and should love it with a native's adoration of all foods of their youth call it "The Best Mediocre Food You've Never Eaten."[218]

Greek immigrants have run groceries in New England since they arrived. The most famous Greek supermarket chain is Demoulas Market Basket, with 79 stores in Massachusetts, New Hampshire, and Maine.[219] A series of entertaining lawsuits spanning 1990 to 2014 gave New England residents a glimpse into the dysfunctional relationships of the Demoulas family, culminating in one Arthur T. Demoulas buying the entire chain.

As with its Italian counterpart, Greek food has become American food, thanks to Greek immigrants settling in communities across the country—New York, Chicago, Los Angeles, Washington, Philadelphia, Tampa. Greek salad is sold at national sandwich chains. Spanakopita, gyros, baklava, avgolemono soup, even pita bread are omnipresent in America, but not in New England cookbooks and food blogs. Why New Englanders claim Greek pizza among all Greek American comestibles is a mystery.

The Chinese

In 1870, a man named C.T. Sampson had the brilliant idea to replace his striking workers at his North Adams, Massachusetts, shoe factory with 75 Chinese immigrants brought in from California. Met at the train station by a crowd throwing rocks, the Chinese immigrants knew that their only hope was to work, and work hard; within three months, they were producing boots and shoes faster than the original workers, and Sampson brought in 50 more. Within a decade, Sampson had retired, and all but one of his workers had left[220]—most for Boston, where they founded Boston's Chinatown.[221] Chinese railroad workers coming east joined them.[222]

By 1900, more than 1,000 Chinese Americans were living in Boston, the majority from the Toishan region of Guangdong. The Chinese Exclusion Act of 1882 kept the Chinese from immigrating in large numbers until after 1965, when restrictions were relaxed. In the meantime, white Americans used Chinese Americans as a comparator for other ethnic groups. An 1885 report by the Massachusetts Department of Labor declared, "The Canadian French are the Chinese of the Eastern States. They do not come here to make a home among us, to dwell with us as citizens, and so become a part of us." In 1902, Woodrow Wilson wrote how southern Italians were the "lowest class of Italy. They have neither skill nor energy nor initiative, nor quick intelligence. The Chinese were more to be desired."[223]

Thanks to Chinese government restrictions, most of those immigrants were from the Republic of China (Taiwan) and the British colony of Hong Kong until the 1980s, when increasing numbers of students and immigrants from the People's Republic of China arrived.[224] As of 2010, 120,000 Chinese Americans lived in Massachusetts,[225] 35,000 in Connecticut, and 20,000 in Rhode Island, New Hampshire, Vermont, and Maine.[226]

Most of the information recorded about Chinese immigrants' diets in the nineteenth century comes from the West Coast, where there were more Asian immigrants from all regions. An 1899 study of Chinese American diets in San Francisco showed that they ate more cabbage and greens and far more rice than other immigrants, getting only about 30 percent of their calories from meat. Unsurprisingly, the Chinese Americans ate very little milk and bread—items that were rare in China.[227]

Chinese Americans in New England opened restaurants, much as they did in the rest of the country, and adapted to local tastes.[228] Boston Chinese food is supposedly even sweeter than the usual sugar-infested American Chinese food due to the availability of cheap molasses—or perhaps due to the tastes of the poor Italian and Irish workers who first patronized Boston's Chinese restaurants.[229] This flexibility has led to at least two curious phenomena that have not spread beyond their natal New England cities: a tradition of serving white bread rolls with Chinese dinners and the chow mein sandwich.

The chow mein sandwich—most commonly found in Fall River, New Bedford, Providence, and environs—is a white bread bun topped with fried crispy chow mein noodles, cooked mung bean sprouts, and "brown gravy" made of pork, celery, and onions.[230] It is typically eaten with French fries and an orange soda.[231] Chinese restaurants have historically offered the sauce "strained" so that Catholics could observe meatless Fridays.[232] It is working-class fill-your-gut food.

As one commenter put it, "The chow mein sandwich is a food that's reflective of a part of old Massachusetts culture that's often overlooked—and completely unknown to outsiders—since it doesn't fit perfectly into the state's Boston-centric identity and kitschy Cape Cod stereotypes of clam chowder and Kennedys."[233] Also overlooked is the chop suey sandwich, an even more obscure comestible apparently sold only in the vicinity of the Salem Willows Park in Salem, Massachusetts.

In the 1960s Joyce Chen and other restauranteurs began opening upscale Chinese restaurants with food from northern China in several New England suburbs. Chen even filmed a television show at WGBH, the same public television station that brought the nation Julia Child's *The French Chef*.[234]

Puerto Ricans

Anyone born in Puerto Rico since 1917 is legally a citizen of the United States, not an immigrant, but Puerto Ricans are a distinct ethnic group in New England.[235] They have lived in New England since the early nineteenth century, and they started arriving in Providence in significant numbers in the 1920s, but most arrived in New England in the decades following World War II.[236] Some moved from Puerto Rico, and some came from New York City, a common entry point for Puerto Ricans moving to the continental United States. They generally worked as agricultural laborers, moving north from New York City along the Connecticut River Valley's farming corridor to Connecticut and Massachusetts.[237] Puerto Ricans began settling in New England cities slightly later, moving to Hartford in the 1950s and Boston in the 1960s.[238] More recently, thousands of Puerto Rican migrants settled in Massachusetts and Connecticut following the devastation of Hurricane Maria.

Most Puerto Rican migrants in New England live in Connecticut or Massachusetts. There are more than 300,000 Puerto Rican migrants and their descendants in Connecticut and more than 320,000 in Massachusetts.[239] About 40,000 Puerto Ricans live in Rhode Island, and fewer than 25,000 live in Maine, Vermont, and New Hampshire combined.[240]

Puerto Rican foodways in the continental United States are complicated by the fact that Puerto Ricans have been traveling back and forth between the mainland and the island for more than a century, much like French Canadian and Italian migrants. In recent decades, continental American and Puerto Rican foodways have been converging as more and more fast-food chains like Burger King and Kentucky Fried Chicken, pizzerias, and other branded eateries have arrived on the island.[241] Puerto Rico also imports 80 percent of its food, and farming on the island has declined since the 1950s, making the definition of "authentic" Puerto Rican food even more complex.[242]

The basic flavorings in Puerto Rican cuisine are *sofrito, adobo*, and *achiote*. Sofrito is a combination of onions, garlic, sweet peppers (*ajíes dulces*), an herb named *recao*, and other herbs and flavorings at a cook's discretion. Sofrito serves as a base for beans, rice, stews, soups, and many other savory dishes. Adobo is a combination of garlic, oregano, black pepper, and salt, used as a rub for meats and fish, and achiote, otherwise known as annatto seed, lends a golden color and distinctive flavor to many dishes.[243]

White rice and pink beans—or rice and pigeon peas at Christmas time—are the linchpin of Puerto Rican food on the island and in the continental United States.[244] Puerto Rican cooks in the mainland also value *viandas*, tropical starchy vegetables such as plantains, yuca, yautia, and ñame yams. A two-decade study of Puerto Rican markets in Hartford showed that of all the produce on sale, the many different viandas were the most important to customers. Demand for viandas stayed consistently high over the decades; shoppers bought a variety of different viandas and were willing to pay a higher price for them than for other starchy foods like pasta and rice. For Puerto Ricans living in New England, viandas seem to be a "keystone food group"—foodstuffs that define Puerto Rican cuisine and Puerto Ricans themselves.[245]

Viandas are often boiled and served with olive oil as a side dish or mashed or grated and combined with meat. Common viandas recipes include *tostones*, or twice-fried plantain slices; *mofongo*, mashed fried plantains mixed with pork skins and other flavorings; *pasteles*, the "Puerto Rican tamale," made of grated viandas stuffed with meat, wrapped in plantain leaves, and boiled; and *alcapurrias*, grated viandas stuffed with meat and fried.[246]

A typical Puerto Rican meal in New England includes rice and beans, perhaps some form of viandas, and chicken or pork.[247] Puerto Ricans living in New England eat less fruit, vegetables, and beans than those who stay in Puerto Rico—probably due to the expense of fresh food, lack of access to backyard gardens, and challenges of fitting in cooking around work schedules.[248] Between rice and viandas, Puerto Ricans tend to eat more carbohydrates than other immigrant groups.[249]

Latinos are a large and growing population in New England. There are more than 1.4 million living in New England, making up about 10 percent of the population. There are more than 850,00 Latinos living in Massachusetts, with the remainder residing primarily in Connecticut and Rhode Island.[250] The Latino population accounted for 92 percent of Boston's population growth since 1980. About 42 percent of Latinos in Massachusetts identify as Puerto Rican, with the rest comprising Dominicans, Cubans, Brazilians, and other Central and South American immigrants.[251] More than half the residents of the Massachusetts cities Lawrence, Chelsea, and Holyoke identify as Latino, and Springfield, Massachusetts, and communities around Bridgeport, Hartford, and New Haven, Connecticut, and Providence, Rhode Island, have large Latino populations.

A Snapshot of New England in 1910

By 1910, southern New England was a land of immigrants. Rhode Island's population was 33 percent foreign-born—the highest percentage in the nation—while Massachusetts ranked second at 31.2 percent.[252] The foreign-born populations for New England's eight largest cities ranged from 32 percent (New Haven) to 42.6 percent (Fall River).[253] Were any of them eating baked beans and clam chowder?

If they were, it wasn't for a lack of women from the old country to cook. In 1910, the population of foreign-born residents of the United States overall had a ratio of 129 men to 100 women; in New England, the ratio was just 105 to 100.[254] That lower ratio is partly the result of New England's immigrants being largely Irish, English, and Canadian—three immigrant groups that historically included more women.

A study of poverty in Lowell, Massachusetts, in 1910 noted the ethnicity of people who turned up at the City Dispensary, which provided medical care for poor residents: "The French-Canadians and Irish represent probably four-fifths of the applicants for aid at the office, yet the names of men and women of English, Scotch, Welsh, French, Italian, Spanish, Portuguese, Swedish, Danish, Norwegian, Russian, Polish, Greek, Turkish, Armenian, Syrian, Austrian, German, Hungarian, Belgian, Serbian, Swiss, Lithuanian, Herzegovinian, Jews, West Indians, Brazilians, Nova Scotians, Native Americans, and 'others,' can be found on the books. It is noteworthy that in the last ten years only one Chinaman has applied for and received medical aid from the City Dispensary."[255] These are the people who were eating, buying, and cooking food in New England at the turn of the twentieth century—while white Yankee writers were busy pursuing the Colonial Revival and writing tomes like the 1912 *New England Cook Book*, which instructed readers to boil macaroni for 45 minutes and garnish it by grating "old cheese" over the top.[256]

The Great Pause

The US Congress stopped most immigration dead cold after the First World War. Congress first passed the Immigration Act of 1917, restricting immigration to people who could read and write, then enacted the National Origins Act of 1924, placing quotas on immigration from Southern and Eastern Europe. Immigration to New England—and the rest of the United States—slowed dramatically until immigration laws were liberalized in 1965 and 1980.[257] Puerto Ricans continued to arrive in New England, having been granted American citizenship in 1917.[258] They worked in various factories during World War II, creating communities in Bridgeport and Hartford, Connecticut, Springfield, Massachusetts, and Boston.[259] Before World War II, West Indians arrived in the Connecticut River Valley to work on farms.[260] But overall, immigration was slow. From 1924 to 1960, 98 percent of immigrants to New England were non-Hispanic whites. By 2000, less than 50 percent of immigrants were white. Today, new immigrants are arriving from places like the Dominican Republic, China, Brazil, and Jamaica.[261]

As of 2010, northern New England was clearly showing a different immigration pattern from Massachusetts, Connecticut, and Rhode Island. That year's census showed the foreign-born residents of Maine, New Hampshire, and Vermont made up less than 6 percent of those states' population, while Massachusetts, Rhode Island, and Connecticut had foreign-born populations of 12 to 15 percent.[262]

Some cities in New England have a much higher ratio of foreign-born residents: in 2007, Boston's population was 28 percent foreign-born. The top ten countries of origin for these residents were China (8.6 percent), Haiti (8.5 percent), Dominican Republic (7.9 percent), Vietnam (5.5 percent), El Salvador (4.6 percent), Cape Verde (4.5 percent), Colombia (4.3 percent), Jamaica (4.1 percent), Brazil (4.0 percent), and Mexico (2.4 percent).[263]

The foreign-born population in New England is growing rapidly. From 1990 to 2010, the immigrant population grew 60 percent overall, ranging from 25 percent (Maine) to 74 percent (Connecticut).[264]

Still, as of 2000, the old ethnic groups were still the most populous. Descendants of French Canadians and English immigrants prevail in northern New England, while Irish predominate in southern Vermont, southern New Hampshire, and most of Massachusetts, and Italians are the most populous group in western Connecticut (which is heavily influenced by New York City).[265]

The Truth about Baked Beans

BOSTON BAKED BEANS are beans that are cooked slowly with salt pork and molasses. They endlessly appear on lists of the Top Ten New England Foods, along with unlikely stories about how and when New Englanders came to sweeten their beans. Their true history illustrates how the origins of many New England foods have been distorted in popular media. Like many other New England dishes, Boston baked beans have been attributed to unspecified Native Americans, even though there is ample evidence that the dish was concocted after the Civil War, while the possible influence of immigrants (in this case French Canadians) and industrial food processing (canneries) has been downplayed or ignored.

❦ ❦ ❦

Look up "baked beans" on the internet and you will probably find a history like this one:

> ### BAKED BEANS
> Native Americans flavored their baked beans with maple syrup and bear fat, and baked them in earthenware pots placed in a pit and covered with hot rocks. The Pilgrims most likely learned how to make baked beans from the Native Americans, substituting molasses and pork fat for the maple syrup and bear fat.[1]

These stories never mention a specific tribe of Native Americans or a time or place that these nameless, forgotten people taught the Pilgrims about their food. All we are left with is the notion that European settlers adopted and improved an indigenous recipe—the same way they improved everything else—and created a thoroughly American dish.

Notions aren't a substitute for facts, though, and what we know about New England in the seventeenth century makes the popular story of baked beans extremely unlikely, if not an outright lie. The people who were here before Europeans arrived had names, and the Pilgrims, Puritans, and French knew some of those names, like Wampanoag, Narragansett, Pequot, Abenaki. Wampanoag is an umbrella name for several groups who lived (and still do live) in eastern Massachusetts—the folks who celebrated the "first Thanksgiving" with the surviving Pilgrims.

There aren't any contemporary accounts of Wampanoag baking beans in a pit per se. They may have been "baking" clams in big pits with hot rocks by steaming them in seaweed, although contemporary accounts mention only clams being brought to a "boile."[2] To get rocks hot enough to bake beans in a hole for several hours would require a lot more heat—and a lot more firewood—than the Wampanoag used for clams. During the first decades after the Pilgrims' 1620 arrival, the Wampanoag are not recorded as baking anything, apart from putting small bannock-type cakes in ashes.[3] The few written descriptions we have of Native cooking around the time of the Pilgrim settlement come from Virginia, where Natives placed clay pots in a small depression in the ground and built up fires around the bottom of the pot, or hung metal kettles over fires.[4] Why would anyone bother with such a labor-intensive method of preparing beans in a community that didn't bake anything else? The first people recorded as indulging in this kind of "bean hole cookery," as early twentieth-century outdoors magazines were wont to call it, were cooks at Maine logging camps who had plenty of wood lying around.[5]

It is also unlikely that coastal Massachusetts Native Americans had maple syrup, much less that they squandered it in cooking beans. In 1635, Roger Williams wrote to John Winthrop, Massachusetts Bay Colony governor, concerning Canonicus, the Narragansett chief, "Sir, if any thing be sent to the princes, I find that Canounicus [sic] would gladly accept of a box of eight or ten pounds of sugar, and in-deed he told me he would thank Mr. Governor for a box full."[6] If maple syrup was so plentiful, why would a tribal chieftain petition the governor of the Massachusetts Bay Colony to send a few pounds of the stuff? (For a longer exploration of when and where maple syrup was made in New England, see chapter 7.) Would they have taken this precious elixir and poured it into a pot of beans?

New England in 1620: A Sour Land

In 1620, sweeteners were a scarce commodity in Plymouth. There wasn't any sugarcane growing in Massachusetts any more than there was cotton, tobacco, or pineapples. Sugar beets could have grown in Plymouth, but no one knew how to get rid of the beet parts: sugar was first extracted from beets in the 1740s, and the first beet sugar factory didn't open until 1788.[7] There wasn't any honey oozing around Plymouth in 1620 either. North American honeybees are native to Europe and were first imported to Virginia in 1622; New England didn't get any until sometime in the 1630s.[8] (Pause for a moment and think what it must have been like to spend weeks at a time on a small wooden ship, pitching and rolling on the open, endless sea, knowing that somewhere down in the hold there was a hive of angry, seasick bees.)

Sugar was expensive, and the Plymouth colonists started their New World lives with about a pound apiece to last the year.[9] By the time of the first Thanksgiving, in 1621, the colonists had run out.[10] Sugar was being made in the New World—in Brazil—but it wasn't being shipped off to a few dozen shivering souls in Plymouth; it was being sent to Europe, where people could pay for it. The Pilgrims, with little to trade, were subject to the whims of London merchants for their supplies of sugar, butter, and other culinary comforts. Unfortunately, greed often won out, and some ships arrived stuffed with so much fishing equipment that there wasn't any room for sugar or anything else—much to the Pilgrims' consternation.[11]

By 1620, most Brazilian sugar was being shipped to Amsterdam to be refined.[12] That fact might explain why Dutch colonists had spare sugar on hand while the Pilgrims were deprived. In 1627, Peter Minuit, governor of the New Netherland colony in what is now Manhattan, sent an unsettling letter to the Pilgrims' governor William Bradford cheerfully asserting that, contrary to Bradford's opinions about England's dominion, the Dutch could settle anywhere and trade with whomever they wished in New England, and if the English didn't like it, they could move back home. That letter was accompanied by "a rundlet of sugar and two Holland cheeses."[13] A rundlet is a small barrel for wine, a measure of about 18 gallons (68 liters) in Bradford's day. Presumably that generous quantity of sweets was supposed to help calm Bradford down after he received Minuit's letter.

Between 1624 and 1637, the price of sugar in Europe more than doubled, thanks to Dutch-Portuguese wars that halted sugar imports from Brazil.[14] The price did not decline much until after the English increased the supply of sugar plantations in Barbados in the 1640s. By the time any form of sweetener became cheap enough to use in everyday meals, the Pilgrims were getting on in years. Between 1650 and the early 1660s, the price of sugar declined by more than 80 percent,[15] and consumption increased accordingly.[16]

Still, Barbados exported a negligible amount of molasses to Massachusetts in the early years of production. Molasses and rum together made up only 7 percent of Barbados exports in the 1660s.[17] Molasses became important to American colonists only when plantations started to grow— big enough for a wealthy owner to invest in refining sugar on site instead of sending murky-looking sugar lumps off to Europe for a nice bleaching. The more refining was done on site, the more molasses was extracted and made locally available for making rum, feeding to animals, or shipping to nearby colonies like Massachusetts. By 1688, Massachusetts alone was importing 156,000 gallons of molasses a year from the British West Indies.[18]

Of course, the sons and daughters of the Puritans were not spending all that money to lick treacle off their pancakes. They were making small beer, a very mildly alcoholic sort of colonial soda generally brewed at home.[19] Massachusetts became a major producer of rum after 1700, but didn't have much in the way of distilleries during the seventeenth century.[20] William Penn commented in 1685 that molasses beer "with sassafras or pine infused into it, makes a very tolerable drink."[21] That was in contrast to plain water, which was an intolerable if not outright hazardous drink in an era predating municipal sewers.

But Yankees were not content with small beer. The first rum distillery in New England opened in Boston in 1700; by 1712, the Massachusetts sugar-addled citizenry was importing 325,000 gallons of molasses every year, along with the same amount of rum—at a time when the entire population of Massachusetts at that point was about 62,000.[22]

Wampanoag Bean Recipes

The Wampanoag probably didn't have any maple syrup, and the Pilgrims certainly didn't have much sweet stuff until the 1650s or later, depending on just how generous those boat-addled bees could be. What were the Wampanoag putting in their beans? What did the Pilgrims put in their beans?

Beans were certainly popular. The Wampanoag planted them as one of the "three sisters" of corn, beans, and squash—when they bothered to plant them. The coastal Wampanoag lived next to a bay chock-full of clams, crabs, fish, even an occasional beached whale.[23] There's strong evidence that pre-Pilgrim Wampanoag life centered on estuaries, not villages or fields. The Wampanoag engaged in "conditional sedentism," traveling back and forth between a few nearby sites each year. Anthropologist Kathleen Bragdon writes, "Such regionally based sedentism had not a single bounded village or series of individual 'homesteads' as its focus, but the estuary itself, its human community seeming (to our partially obscured vision at least) joining and splitting like quicksilver in a fluid pattern within its bounds."[24]

Exactly what all those "human communities" ate varied depending on which estuary they chose. Offshore, archaeologists have performed radio isotope studies on the bone collagen of the Wampanoag who lived in Nantucket in the late Woodland period (ca. 1000–1600 CE) and found no evidence that they ate corn at all.[25] It appears their diet consisted almost entirely of shellfish, land animals, fish, turtles, and crabs.[26] Although corn has been discovered in inland riverside sites along the Connecticut River Valley dating back to at least 1000, as of 1991 archaeologists had found a grand total of 12 corn kernels in all of coastal southern New England.[27] Analyses of pollen show that there wasn't much large-scale clearing for growing corn or anything else on Cape Cod until the early 1600s[28]—100 years after first contact with European fisherman and explorers along the East Coast.

It makes sense that the Wampanoag wouldn't depend on subsistence agriculture when there was so much around them to eat. Nobody goes to a clam bake for the corn on the cob. The answer seems to be that the Wampanoag of Cape Cod overharvested their shellfish beds and were compelled to start supplementing their diets with corn around 1300 CE.[29] The Pilgrims were taught to sow corn by Squanto, that cross-cultural Patuxet-Wampanoag phenomenon who was called Tisquantum before English slavers kidnapped him in 1614—but there is evidence that he acquired his corn-growing expertise during his five-year European ordeal.[30]

The Pilgrims had much more on their minds than recording the eating habits of their Wampanoag neighbors. They did manage to record their storage habits, though. According to Pilgrim William Bradford and Edward Winslow's journal, a few days after the *Mayflower* arrived on Cape Cod, one of the Pilgrims' scouting parties found what appeared to be graves, then stumbled onto a recently vacated native settlement. They found a metal pot "which had been some ship's kettle," and what appeared to be a house site, then dug into "a heap of sand . . . newly done," and found many things:

> We digged up and in it we found a little old casket full of faire Indian corn and digged further & found a fine great new basket full of very fair corn of this year with some 36 goodly ears of corn, some yellow and some red and others mixed with blue which was a very goodly sight. The basket was round and narrow at the top. It held about three or four bushels. . . . At length after much consultation we concluded to take the kettle and as much of the corn as we could carry away with us, and when our shallop came if we could find any of the people and come to parley with them we would give them the kettle again and satisfy them for their corn. So we took all the ears and put a good deal the loose corn in the kettle for two men to bring away on a staff. Besides they that could put any into their pockets filled the same. The rest we buried again for we were so laden with armor that we could carry no more.[31]

A few days after this corn rustling, the Pilgrims discovered another cache of corn, beans, and a bottle of oil. So yes, the local Native Americans had beans. But what did they do with them?

The closest we get to a description of Wampanoag bean cookery is from William Wood's 1635 *New England's Prospect*, where Wood describes New England natives' approach to corn: "They seldom or never make bread of their Indian corn but seethe it whole like beans eating three or four corns with a mouthful of fish or flesh, sometimes eating meat first and corns after filling up the chinks with their broth."[32]

"Seethe" meant "to boil." The Pilgrims and other English settlers were very familiar with boiled grains and beans. Various beans and peas had been eaten for centuries in Europe, and the most common food in seventeenth-century New England was something called "pottage," a sort of stew made of some sort of grain boiled with meat, vegetables, and herbs. For many families, it was the only food. According to historian Sarah

McMahon, "When seventeenth-century New Englanders 'dressed their victuals,' they were readying the food for consumption rather than enhancing its flavor. The result was a daily 'pottage' fare, and many families ate 'one continued round' of meat and legume or vegetable stews morning, noon, and night."[33]

Pottage is also the key to one of the most complete accounts we have of the Wampanoag diet as recorded by Daniel Gookin in 1674, on the eve of King Philip's War, more than 50 years after the Pilgrims arrived in Plymouth. By that time, the Wampanoag existence had been completely transformed by European settlement. Settlers had cleared fields and wood-lots, reducing the population of deer the Wampanoag relied upon for food. Wayward hogs and cattle drove the remaining deer out of the forest and devoured Wampanoag corn fields and storage pits; by the 1660s, many Wampanoag were raising hogs themselves.[34] Gookin wrote,

> Their food is generally boiled maize, or Indian corn, mixed with kidney-beans, or sometimes without. Also they frequently boil in this pottage fish and flesh of all sorts, either new taken or dried, as shads, eels, alewives or a kind of herring, or any other sort of fish . . . venison, beaver, bears flesh, moose, otters, rackoons, or any kind they take in hunting. . . . Also they mix with the said pottage several sorts of roots; as Jerusalem artichokes, and ground nuts, and other roots, and pompions, and squashes, and also several sorts of nuts or masts, as oak-acorns, chestnuts, walnuts; these husked and dried, and powdered, they thicken their pottage therewith.[35]

That's a pretty long list, and it doesn't include "syrup" or "sugar" or any fruit besides pumpkins. A journal written by Captain Edward Johnson, an ensign during the Pequot War in southern New England from 1634 to 1638, states that the Narragansett ate blackberries and chestnuts, which "are very sweet, as if they were mixt with sugar"—but these sweets were all prepared for a banquet, not an after-hunt snack.[36] None of these ingredients were wasted on plain old boiled corn pottage. In his 1642 *Plain Dealing*, lawyer Thomas Lechford went so far as to claim that the local tribes of coastal Massachusetts and Rhode Island "will not taste sweet things."[37]

The Wampanoag had beans, and they ate them enough for even the colonists to notice. They don't seem to have had any sweeteners apart from fruit and chestnuts, and there isn't any evidence that they even cooked these foods with their beans.

At the same time that the Wampanoag were boiling up vats of pottage, the Pilgrims were eating peas—or, rather, "pease." Looking at estate inventories from Middlesex County, Massachusetts, from 1620 to 1840, McMahon found few mentions of beans before 1674; colonists preferred to raise the "pease" they knew from Ye Olde Englande. Sometime around the end of the seventeenth century practicality won out, and the colonists started eating local beans instead.[38]

So where did this impulse to sugar baked beans come from? Keith Stavely and Kathleen Fitzgerald argue that the beans are descendants of a Staffordshire dish of dried beans baked with honey-and-mustard-cured ham overnight.[39] That would be quite reasonable if there were any evidence that the colonists from Staffordshire ever put any sweeteners in their beans, or that they baked them, or that the tradition crossed the ocean before the nineteenth century. Other authors argue that the Pilgrims learned to bake beans with meat overnight from the Jews of Amsterdam, who would prepare their pots of *cholent* the night before Sabbath, the day when work is forbidden.[40] Or perhaps they were introduced to the Pilgrims' children by New England sea captains who traded with Sephardic Jews on the North African coast who cooked something like cholent, or maybe they learned how to make *cassoulet* in Quebec from French settlers, as Ken Albala suggests.[41] The possible explanations go on and on.

The fact of the matter is there aren't any records of the colonists baking beans in America, much less adding anything sweet to them, before 1800. None. No cookbooks, no diaries, no letters, no official reckoning of banquet dishes, no residue in a privy. But that absence might just mean that beans were below notice, too common to even be mentioned in a book or a journal. After all, very few cookbooks feature recipes for peanut butter and jelly sandwiches.

Baked Beans in Print

Fortunately, cookbooks aren't the only publications that feature food. The first printed source that mentions baked beans in New England is an 1803 essay from *Boston Weekly Magazine*, and it isn't terribly complimentary. A dashing young financier who has just wheedled a loan of $1,000 from a miserly old man confides in a friend, "Egad! Old skinflint, rich as a Jew[!] knows nothing of life, got a house like a palace, lives like a hermit, eats baked beans twice a week."[42] Baked beans sound like the nineteenth-century tightwad equivalent of a cold cheese sandwich.

In 1817, baked beans were mentioned in a footnote to a heroic ode, *Blue Lights, or the Convention: A Poem in Four Cantos*,[43] which describes some of the grislier alleged atrocities performed by the English during the War of 1812. The author praises the "steady habits" of Connecticut's people and illustrates his point with an anecdote about a "southern gentleman" traveling through the state. This "gentleman" is supposed to have remarked, "At Saturday the never-failing repast of baked beans was as administered as the hog and hominy of Carolina and the warm toddy was as much expected as the mint sling in Virginia."

That is all very interesting, but begs the question, why, if this ritual is so universal, is the author remarking on it? Did everyone know that all Connecticutians served baked beans every Saturday? If so, why does he need the testimony of a "southern gentleman" to confirm it? Modern folklorists who study urban legends and rumors call this sort of person a FOAF: a friend of a friend—the person who actually saw the ghost or the four-foot-long rat. No one can ever locate the FOAF for questioning.

By 1827 beans are definitely part of the "local color" reporting about America. An 11-page rant by the author of the novel *The Buccaneers: A Romance of Our Own Country, in Its Ancient Day* includes this tidbit about poor folk who rise above their station:

And lastly the pedlar, whose whole employment had been to take in the fellers and gals with trumpery baubles, whose best meals were the charity of the farmers where he stopped: Indian pudding, baked beans, "sarse and innards,"[44] whose happiness had been to rest in a barn upon straw or among the corn stalks, and whose highest ideas had been to mount the horse which he stole from his customers or to sit on the ducking stool, this creature is changed in a short period by the prosperous trade of deception and knavery he has pursued to the lofty nosed merchant who would fain carry his head as high as the mast of one of his own ships.[45]

Baked beans were eaten by farmers—not sophisticated city folk who could afford meat for their dinners. And they were old-fashioned. By 1840, beans were being served at occasions like the centenary celebration of Farmington, Connecticut:

> At the close of the exercises within the house the assembly were invited to repair to the green in the rear where the ladies of Farmington had pre-pared a range of tables bountifully and tastefully spread. Apart from the others were two round tables, which have been in Farmington for a num-ber of generations and which were spread with some of the dainties which graced boards of our ancestors such as a huge Indian pudding, a large dish of baked beans, pumpkin pies and some other imitations of the cookery of our fathers.[46]

What would they do to imitate the cookery of their mothers? Note that the baked beans and other dainties were set apart from the tables "bountifully and tastefully spread" with the 1840 equivalent of hot dogs and hamburgers.

The Connecticut Historical Society's 1840 notes accompanying E. S. Thomas's *Reminiscences of the Last Sixty-Five Years: Commencing with the Battle of Lexington* also reveal a peculiar attitude toward baked beans. At the belated 1840 celebration of the 200th anniversary of the adoption of the first Constitution of Connecticut, one Dr. Palfrey of the Massachusetts Historical Society gave a toast:

> Dr Palfrey responded . . . to urge the necessity of keeping alive the New England feeling of doing all that we can to keep the sons and daughters of New England at home and if they must and will pour themselves out into the broad avenues of wealth and enterprise in the West, so to imbue them with love to the old homestead, the old church, the old school house, the old pastimes, customs, and peculiarities of New England, that these shall all be introduced into Wisconsin, Iowa, or a still more western region. He con-cluded with an anecdote told him by a gentleman from Norwich respecting the old Connecticut fashion of ringing the eight o'clock bell on Saturday night and the orthodox dish of baked beans and pork still observed by the emigrants from this State in some parts Ohio. The remotest town of the far

west where the dish of baked beans and pork is regularly served on Saturdays and salt codfish on Wednesdays.[47]

Once again, we have a report of a fine New England tradition—in a Midwestern state, as reported by Dr. Palfrey via a man from Norwich who knew about baked beans in Ohio because . . . we'll never know. But the story has a feeling to it. The beans represent what is good about New England—Scott's "steady habits," the old homestead, the fathers and mothers watching their children ride off to the West.

But still—these beans are clearly famous, but they are clearly beans and pork, not beans, pork, and molasses. At some point, Boston baked beans went from being a fairly obvious foodstuff to a sticky sugarfest.

The Molasses Revolution: How Americans Became Sweet Fiends

The baked beans the Ohioans yearned for in 1840 were probably very different from today's beans; they were most likely not very sweet. The earliest printed reference to putting any sort of sugar into bean dishes in the United States that I could locate comes from 1825 and calls for a "spoonful" of molasses for two quarts of dry beans.[48] Assuming that a "spoonful" is roughly a modern tablespoon, that comes out to sugar-to-bean ratio of about 1:100, or 1 percent. By contrast, modern recipes commonly have a sugar-to-bean ratio of 1:3, or 33 percent.

Sweet foods aren't a new part of the American diet; what's new is how much of our diet is made up of various sugars—table sugar, corn syrup, beet sugar, maple syrup, and, yes, molasses. Colonists on the *Mayflower* brought a pound or two of sugar along with them as medicine. Molasses and sugar weren't generally available to New England's earliest settlers. Britain restricted the colonies' trade partners to other British ports. Most New World sugarcane in the earliest years came from Dutch-occupied Brazil, and Britain was more concerned with squelching Dutch trade than with ensuring the colonists could sweeten their tea. By the 1650s, though, British-owned Barbados began producing sugar, and North American colonists discovered that molasses-pressing French and Spanish colonists were happy to trade their sugars for northern goods like salt fish and barrel staves.[49]

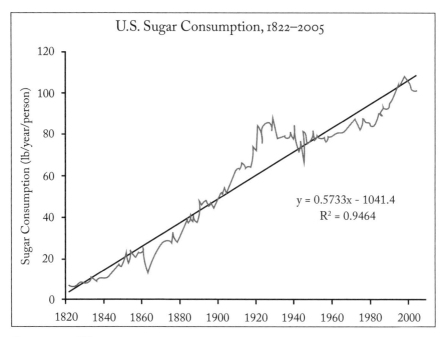

FIGURE 2.1. US sugar consumption, 1822–2005.

Britain's Parliament passed the Molasses Act in 1733, creating tariffs to inflate the price of detestable foreign sugar, but American colonists simply ignored it. As one author wrote, even though the tariff was reduced by half in 1763, "in 1763, out of 15,000 hogsheads of molasses that were imported into Massachusetts, 14,500 were smuggled in."[50] (At 100 gallons per hogshead, that's 1.45 million gallons of molasses.) "Smuggled" is a strong term for what was happening. Although 14,500 hogsheads came from French and Spanish colonies,[51] I doubt that Massachusetts's practical sea captains bothered hiding what they were doing. They were too busy attacking British customs agents. As one author put it, "In 1772, a British schooner attempting to prevent smuggling ran aground on the New England shore while chasing a sloop. The sloop escaped and reported the location of the grounded British ship. An armed force was recruited which attacked the British vessel and destroyed it by fire."[52]

Once the revolution was won, the new US government promptly installed its own tariffs on molasses and sugar—at first simply to fund the government, then to protect the nascent New Orleans sugar industry after the 1803 Louisiana Purchase. Apparently, Massachusetts's native brigands weren't quite so eager to burn American ships, as there isn't any record of smugglers burning US Customs sloops. They really didn't need to; over the course of the nineteenth century, sugar became extremely cheap thanks to expanded production and advances in refining. In 1850, loaf sugar was relatively expensive—20 cents a pound, and still 14 cents a pound by 1870; but by 1902 the stuff was only 2 cents a pound[53]—the equivalent of declining from $5 a pound to $0.50 a pound in 2010.

As sugar grew cheaper, Americans ate more of it, white, brown, and molasses: 9.5 pounds per person per year in 1822, 32.6 pounds per person in 1860, and 80 pounds in 1900.[54] World War I interrupted the trend toward ever sweeter diets, but sugar started creeping back in by the 1930s, when people also started eating a lot more beans due to high meat prices and perhaps longed for some small luxury in their meals.

Molasses also got a boost from desperate efforts to assert Yankee pride during the Colonial Revival and post-centennial era following the celebrations of 1876. In the last quarter of the nineteenth century, Yankee New Englanders were engaging in soul searching about how their region had devolved from the center of the American Revolution to an also-ran with a smaller population than New York, Philadelphia, and Chicago.[55] They also squandered gallons of ink on printed laments bewailing the growing population of Irish immigrants in their precious ancestral Puritan cities. Boston's old Yankee Brahmins made mournful statements about how the region's noble past was rapidly disappearing, such as Harvard professor Barrett Wendell's 1893 maudlin declaration, "We Yankees are as much things of the past as any race can be. I feel a certain regret that I had not the fortune to be born fifty years earlier."[56]

One side effect of this New England identity crisis was a push to preserve "historic" landscapes around the region that seemed to be imperiled by development such as the Boston-area Middlesex Fells and Blue Hills.[57] Another manifestation was a sudden emphasis on homely New England ingredients—especially molasses—in cookbooks. In the 1880s, as Keith Stavely and Kathleen Fitzgerald observed, gingerbread recipes that had previously been concocted solely with white sugar (and spices grown 8,000 miles away) were abruptly reengineered to feature molasses, and often only molasses, as their sweetener. This molasses obsession was prominent in the popular 1881 *Aunt Mary's New England Cook Book*, written by "A New England mother"—not a mother, or a Vermont mother, but a New England mother—which has three recipes for gingerbread, all made with molasses.[58]

After 1900, Americans discovered another reason to buy more molasses—brands.[59] Molasses manufacturers started selling pints and quarts in individually packaged jars and cans, instead of sending out barrels for grocers to pour into customers' jugs. A writer in a printing press trade magazine complained in 1905, "So far as I am able to learn no one has attempted to make popular by advertising in general mediums a single brand of this article of food."[60] That changed quickly. Brer Rabbit Molasses, founded 1915, stormed the market with an advertising campaign aimed at shoppers frustrated with World War I shortages, running newspaper ads with the headline "Don't Worry about Sugar—Your Grocer Has Brer Rabbit Molasses."[61]

Why did people start adding so much molasses to beans? It got cheaper, and it seemed like a New England sort of thing to do at a time when Yankee cooks despaired of losing New England to the Irish. As molasses got cheaper, people added more of it to beans.

There may also have been more people in New England who were accustomed to pouring sweet syrup on savory dishes. More than 500,000 French Canadian immigrants settled in New England between 1880 and 1930, all from areas with active maple syrup farms. Current-day Quebec maple boiling "sugar shacks," or *cabanes à sucre*, put pitchers of syrup out on the table for customers to pour on beans, pork, and everything else served at the cabane. Perhaps French Canadians adopted sweetened beans because of their prior experience with syrup extravagance, easing Boston baked beans' infiltration of broader New England communities.

I gathered baked bean recipes from 274 cookbooks published between 1880 and 1950 and calculated the average ratio of sugar to beans in recipes by decade, then sampled the Boston baked beans recipes from ten contemporary cookbooks and websites—the Food Network, Martha Stewart, the *Boston Globe*. The result appears in Figure 2.2.

American cookbook writers' expectations for how sweet beans should be plummeted during World War I, but they eventually rose anew. Since 1880 the amount of sugars in the American diet has roughly tripled, but the amount of sugar in Boston baked beans increased by a factor of ten.

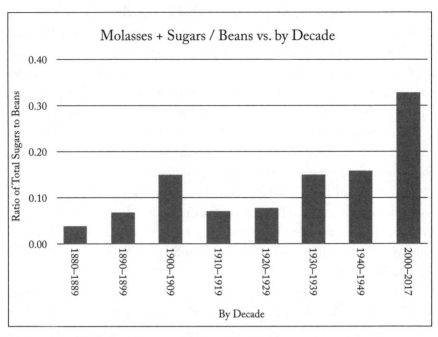

FIGURE 2.2. Molasses and sugar to beans ratio by decade.

As of 2005, Americans were eating a little more than 130 pounds of sweeteners, including sugar, molasses, and corn-based sweeteners like high-fructose corn syrup, a year, or about five and a half ounces a day.[62] One author wrote the headline "By 2606, the American Diet Will Be 100% Sugar." Will Boston baked beans, a foodstuff that would be completely unrecognizable to the colonial forebears, contain more molasses and sugar than beans? Will we continue to "revive" a past that did not exist?

The Limits of New England Food

BETWEEN 1876 and 1900, a particular version of New England food was carved into cultural granite. This was the era when the public ideal of the region's food was created and promoted by nostalgic theme park planners, earnest home economists, bewildered housewives, and anxious preservationists—an ideal that reflected Victorian fantasies of what colonial New Englanders were supposed to have eaten (roast turkey and carefully plated corned beef and parsnips), as opposed to what they actually did eat (boiled bean pottage).

It didn't have to be this way. Thousands of immigrants with vital, flavorful foodways were arriving in New England every year during these decades. In other regions, cooks mixed and recombined the traditions from multiple cultures to create new American foods. Unfortunately, several forces stunted New England's regional foodways just as life was getting interesting.

Although every US region had its identity change and shift after the Civil War, New England was unique because so many tastemakers, so to speak, focused on the distant past of the colonial era, neglecting the current-day urban, largely immigrant population. In 1900, a quarter of the region's residents were foreign-born.[1] Yet instead of celebrating the tourtiere, kielbasa, pasta fagioli, and soda bread cooked in common kitchens, magazine writers lauded the New England boiled dinner—a completely undistinguished assemblage of corned beef and boiled vegetables. Boiled dinner's sole virtue is that it was allegedly served in country farmhouses on pewter platters, colonial-era tableware that nineteenth-century urban housekeepers had long abandoned in favor of fragile, upscale china. Writers declared New England the "Pie Belt," even though urban homemakers preferred to buy cakes at bakeries.[2] Sweeteners like molasses and maple syrup started cropping up in middle-class cookbooks chiefly to make the recipes seem more authentic and historic, and some writers aggressively poured molasses into "traditional" recipes that were previously made with plain white sugar.[3]

All over the region, commentators bemoaned the thinning of the Yankee blood of the region—in fisheries, in Berkshire hill farms, in Boston—even as the immigrants revitalized fields that Anglo-Saxon Protestants had abandoned.[4] In other parts of the country, immigration led to endless culinary innovations. Immigrants created Creole and Tex-Mex dishes, cinnamon-raisin bagels, and American Chinese dishes. In Boston, new foods were suspect because they were deemed unnutritious or destructive to the digestion, unfashionable, or simply new.

The dinner table wasn't the only place where immigrants were dis-invited. In the 1890s, Boston's Metropolitan Parks Commission didn't name hills in the new Middlesex Fells Reservation after the Irish, Southern European, and Eastern European immigrants who had regularly visited the park over previous decades to enjoy a dance hall, music, and a merry-go-round on privately owned land. Instead, they named the reservation's hills after Native Americans who had been dead for 200 years, with no obvious link to the site: Nanapeshemet Hill, Squaw Sachem Rock, Wenepyokin Hill. As Michael Rawson writes, the practice of renaming sites with "Indian" names "was particularly popular in New England, where Indians were fewer and sentimentalism about their removal was stronger than in other regions."[5] Even the name Middlesex Fells was invented in 1879 to evoke an imaginary Old Saxon past that was more compelling than its existing name, Five Mile Wood.[6]

Overall, five factors combined to stunt New England foodways between 1875 and 1900—just when immigration, railroads, and innovations like baking powder were enabling other regions to develop vibrant cuisines: urbanization and industrialization, "New England Kitchen" exhibits, social reformers who sought to feed the poor cheaply, the Colonial Revival, and the New England elites' relationship with their cooks.

Urbanization and Industrialization

By 1900, almost 70 percent of New Englanders were living in urban areas,[7] according to the US Census Bureau, and much of New England's grain, meat, and produce was brought in from the Midwest via railroads. Fruits and vegetables frequently arrived in a can from a factory. New Englanders were city people, living at increasing spatial and temporal distance from fresh food.

The erasure of immigrant food is especially tragic. From the 1880s onward, Americans who wrote cookbooks frequently included Americanized versions of foods from abroad—"eggs a l'indienne" and so on—and recipes learned in foreign lands from French pastry chefs, Mexican caterers, and their ilk. They almost never included recipes cooked by immigrants who had brought their recipes to the United States.[10]

In 1900, thousands of industrious immigrants were living in New England's vital cities and farming communities and cooking delicious food from dozens of traditions. Their descendants still live in the region today, yet the words "New England" and "Yankee" cookery evoke apple crisp and clam chowder, not spumoni and caldo verde.

The New England Kitchens

The New England Kitchen movement may have done more to destroy New England cooking than all the graham-cracker-munching, immigrant-loathing, science-quoting Yankee snobs put together. New England Kitchens were fantasy displays for fairs, cousins of Sleeping Beauty's Castle and Chuck E. Cheese. These "kitchens"—really stage sets—featured various artifacts that were supposed to evoke "New England farm house life of the last century."[11] The Brooklyn and Long Island Fair of February 22, 1864, managed to round up "interesting trophies. . . . Among these was a rifle that belonged to Patrick Henry; several Bibles of the days of the Puritans; a canteen carried in the Revolutionary War; a file of the Yankee newspaper published in Stonington Ct in 1826; an exact copy of the famous *Newport Mercury*, dated 1760; the *New England Chronicle* 1775 to 1778, containing an affidavit recounting the particulars of the Battle of Lexington; a piece of a bride's dress of a hundred years ago, and many other very interesting relics of olden tyme."[12]

Here is an example of the sort of gushing descriptions of Grandma's drafty old house, from 1864: "The idea is to present a faithful picture of New England farm house life of the last century. The grand old fire place shall glow again, the spinning wheel shall whirl as of old; the walls shall be garnished with the products of the forest and the field, the quilting the donation and the wedding party shall assemble once more while; the apple paring shall not be forgotten; and the dinner table, always set, shall be loaded with substantial New England cheer."[13] (Heaven knows you wouldn't want to forget the apple paring.)

This New England kitchen was planned entirely by women from Brooklyn for the 1864 Brooklyn and Long Island Sanitary Fair—distinguished not by its cleanliness compared to the Staten Island Filthy Fair or the Queens Fair of Untidiness, but by the fact that it supported the US Sanitary Commission, the organization that worked to improve sanitary conditions for Union soldiers during the Civil War.

Of course the kitchens served refreshments as well, with as broad a range of New England dishes as a typical hot dog stand. The Brooklyn fair featured these delicacies:

> . . . a gigantic pot in which from time to time were cooked great messes of unctuous chowder or steaming quantums of "mush." From the ovens at the side emerged at stated periods spicy Indian puddings, smoking loaves of Boston brown bread, and famous dishes of pork and beans crisped to delicious perfection. . . .
>
> On the tables were bountiful supplies of toothsome viands—pork and beans, cider apple sauce, Boston brown bread, pitchers of cider, pumpkin, mince, and apple pies, doughnuts and all the savory and delicate wealth of the New England larder.[14]

No fresh fruit or vegetables, no blueberries, cranberries, cabbages, beets, or parsnips for these fine folks—not even potatoes were on the menu (perhaps because they'd seem too Irish?).

These fantasy "kitchens" stayed popular after the war, with roughly the same bill of fare. The menu for the Log Cabin Restaurant at Philadelphia's Permanent Exhibition (1877) read as follows:

Ye Baked Beans, prepared as in ye
fashion of ye Olden Tyme in ye
Ancient City of Boston, Brown
Bread, Coffee or Tea
Cold Ham, Bread and butter,
Coffee or Tea
Cold tongue
Roast Beef
Corned Beef
Potatoes, boiled
Boiled Eggs (2)
Fried Eggs

Sandwiches
Oat-Meal and Milk
Bread and Milk
Pie
Doughnuts
Molasses Gingerbread
Sponge and other Cakes
Iced Tea or Coffee
Bread and Butter
Ice Cream
Soups[15]

This menu is also a recipe for beriberi, rickets, and scurvy, but perhaps nutritional deficiencies made the New England experience more authentic by imitating the conditions in the first years of the Plymouth Colony.

Who Doesn't Like Mush? The Reformers

The root of all culinary misery in New England is Victorian food science. Here's a sample from 1869:

> The articles containing most of the three articles needed generally in the body are as follows: for fat and heat-making—butter, lard, sugar, and molasses: for muscle-making—lean meat, cheese, peas, beans, and lean fishes; for brain and nerves—shell fish, lean meats, peas, beans, and very active birds and fishes who live chiefly on food in which phosphorus abounds. In a meat diet, the fat supplies carbon for the capillaries and the lean furnishes nutriment for muscle brain and nerves. Green vegetables, fruits, and berries furnish the acid and water needed.[16]

Green vegetables provide water and "acid," but nothing else—certainly not heat or muscle. Vitamin C wasn't isolated until 1928.[17] Investigators looking into problems like scurvy outbreaks in prisons knew that something in citrus fruit, vegetables, and potatoes could cure the disease, but they didn't know what it was, and some researchers claimed that it was due to some kind of "vegetable albumen" protein.[18] In the mid-nineteenth century, German scientists were busily "separating foods out into water, carbohydrates, fat, protein, and minerals, and concluding that each nutrient performed specific physiological functions. These chemists recommended that foods be selected on the basis of their components, rather than taste, appearance, or other considerations."[19]

What's more, bad diets made for bad people. In the 1880s, Connecticut-based food chemist W. O. Atwater became concerned that Americans were wasting money on the food they wanted rather than buying cheaper food with the same nutrition—that is, lots of cheap grains instead of more expensive meat. Atwater wrote in 1888,

> The poorer communities and classes of people almost universally select those foods which chemical analysis shows to supply the actual nutrients at the lowest cost. But unfortunately, the proper proportions of the nutrients in their dietaries are often very defective. Thus, in portions of India and China rice, in northern Italy maize-meal, in certain districts of Germany and in some regions and seasons in Ireland potatoes, and among the poor whites of the southern United States maize-meal and bacon make a large part of the sustenance of the people. These foods supply the nutrients in the cheapest forms but they are all deficient in protein. The people who live upon them are ill nourished and suffer physically intellectually and morally thereby.
>
> On the other hand, the Scotchman, as shrewd in his diet as in his dealings, finds a most economical supply of protein in oatmeal, haddock. and herring; and the thrifty inhabitants of New England supplement the fat of their pork with the protein of beans and the carbohydrates of potatoes, and supplement maize and wheat flour with the protein of codfish and mackerel; and while subsisting largely upon such frugal but rational diets are well nourished, physically strong, and distinguished for their intellectual and moral force.[20]

Although Atwater's assertions about the superior protein of Scottish and New England nutrition sound bizarre and frankly racist to modern readers, Atwater had a point. In the 1880s, more than 90 percent of the population of Massachusetts spent over 50 percent of their income on food.[21] A Boston-based businessman named Edward Atkinson was intrigued by the idea of reducing food spending. If you could get the working classes to spend less on food, you could improve their sorry lot "without resort to labor unions, unnatural increases in wages, or other measures which went against the immutable laws of supply and demand," as food historian Harvey Levenstein coolly notes.[22] Atkinson and his cohort found it much more beneficial to harangue and instruct the poor rather than rolling up their sleeves to help them. Thus, the New England Kitchen was born.

The brainchild of an innovative chemist and Boston Brahmin philanthropists, the New England Kitchen may have done more to destroy the reputation of New England food than any other single institution. The New England Kitchens, established in the 1890s in downtown Boston, Boston's North End, and Providence, Rhode Island, served foods intended for the poor made with "the most nutritious, inexpensive, and efficient recipe possible," as Laura Shapiro put it.[23] Note that "tastiest" doesn't make the list, or even "edible."

The brain behind the New England Kitchens belonged to Ellen Swallow Richards, the first woman to be admitted to the Massachusetts Institute of Technology, who earned a bachelor of science in chemistry in 1873. Although she began her career analyzing iron ores and sulfite compounds, by the late 1870s she turned her attention to sanitation, water quality, and sewage and what she called "Household Chemistry"—helping women understand the chemistry behind common tasks like cooking, cleaning fabrics and surfaces, and detecting adulterated food (a pressing problem in the years before the USDA existed).[24]

In the late 1880s, Richards decided to establish a Boston demonstration kitchen modeled on the German *Volksküchen*, soup kitchens for the poor operating in Berlin. This kitchen would be a place where working people could purchase clean, inexpensive food made in open kitchens on site. The recipes would be prepared in exactly the same way each time to create standard results. The working people of Boston could learn how to create economical, nutritious foodstuffs for their own families, improving health and saving money.[25]

Richards's project was financed by Pauline Agassiz Shaw, who gave her money to study "food and nutrition of workingmen and its possible relation to the question of the use of intoxicating liquors,"[26] and Edward Atkinson, a businessman and activist who later became notorious for his work with the American Anti-Imperialist League opposing the Spanish-American War. In the 1880s, though, Atkinson was concerned about what American work men were eating: "My immediate incentive in trying to solve the practical problem was my happening to be present, on a cold day, when a number of workmen in a mill which they were building were about to take their dinner. When they opened their dinner pails a mess of cold victuals was disclosed, which seemed to me must require the digestive power of an ostrich to dispose of."[27] Atkinson set about trying to create a kind of automatic lunch warmer—obviously a superior solution to, say, installing an oven where workers could warm up their lunches or setting up a cafeteria. That sort of thing would cost the owners money.

Instead, Atkinson tinkered. Although he did not invent a microwave or even a good way of warming lunches, he did come up with a new way of heating meals: the Aladdin Oven. Alas, no genie tempted users with sweetmeats and delicacies. Instead, the Aladdin Oven was a sort of Victorian crock pot, an insulated barrel plunked on top of a kerosene lamp. The fuel was cheap compared to firing up an iron cook stove with coal, and the oven didn't need much attention once it was set up. You could cook anything you wanted in it, as long as you didn't mind it being simmered for a very long time. Cakes, hash browns, and pies were doomed, but stews made from cheap cuts of meat, pea soup, and various sorts of mush came out—well, about as tasty as they ever did.

Atkinson wrote a book titled *The Science of Nutrition* about what people with less money than he had should eat, and how to use his Aladdin Oven. Here's one of his recommended economy food budgets for 30 days:[28]

22 lbs Flour	2 lbs Butter
3 lbs Oatmeal	2 lbs Suet
3 lbs Cornmeal	10 lbs Potatoes
6 lbs Hominy	2 lbs Sugar

2 lbs Cabbage	4 lbs Bacon
2 lbs Carrots	2 lbs Beef liver
2 lbs Onions	1 lb Veal
12 lbs Beef neck or shin	1 lb Pork
5 lbs Mutton neck	

It's not clear why he bothered including any cabbage, carrots, and onions in the mix, given that vegetables were "less digestible; and higher in cost because animal food is cheaper in cost than vegetables when consumed at a given standard of nutrition."[29]

Richards also worked with Mary Hinman Abel, a domestic scientist from Michigan who also believed in economical menus of hideous food. Here are a few daily bills of fare Abel recommends in her 1889 *Practical Sanitary and Economic Cooking Adapted to Persons of Moderate and Small Means*,[30] which includes recipes for feeding a family of six for $0.13 a day— the equivalent of $3.41 in 2016. It involves a lot of bread.

MONDAY MAY

Breakfast
Oatmeal Mush with Milk and Sugar
Bread
Coffee

Dinner
Pea Soup
Mutton Stew
Boiled Potatoes
Bread

Supper
Bread Pancakes
Fried Bacon
Tea

For Abel, vegetables were mere extravagance. She wrote, "Except in the height of their season have nothing to do with green vegetables at least not under the impression that they are cheap. If you buy them, know that you are paying for flavors and variety rather than for food."[31]

Here's one of Abel's sample menus for September, the height of the New England harvest season, when tomatoes, sweet corn, zucchini, broccoli, butternut squash, kale, beets, turnips, lettuce, brussels sprouts, green beans, and dozens of varieties of apples are all fresh, tasty, and cheap:

SATURDAY SEPTEMBER

Breakfast
  Soda Biscuit
  Baked Potatoes with Drawn Butter Sauce
  Cocoa
Dinner
  Pea Soup
  Irish Stew
  Bread
Supper
  Corn Mush and Molasses
  Bread and Grated Cheese
  Tea

Modern readers might suspect that Abel was actually a galley cook on a ship bound for an Australian penal colony. Remember, *vitamins hadn't been isolated*—at least not by scientists—although plenty of ship's doctors and physicians knew that scurvy could be cured with fruit and vegetables. (Actually, a galley cook would have included lemons or limes on the menu to prevent scurvy.) Only starch, protein, and fat were supposed to provide nourishment. As Levenstein put it, "In short, had America turned *en masse* to follow their advice, rickets, beri-beri, scurvy, and other vitamin-deficiency diseases may well have reached epidemic proportions."[32]

Richards and Abel went about producing food under strict guidelines. "The requirements of each dish were: the cost of materials must not go beyond a certain limit; the labor of preparation must not be too great; it must be nutritious and healthful; it must be in a form in which it can be easily served and kept without loss of flavor; and it must suit the popular taste in order to be salable," Richards wrote.[33] Inspired by

Richards's example, philanthropists and social reformers set up New England Kitchen–style establishments in New York, Philadelphia, and Chicago.

There was a problem, though. If you're starting with corn mush, there isn't much flavor to lose. The basic elements of the menus at the New England Kitchen were beef broth, pea soup, fish, clam, and corn chowders, succotash, creamed codfish, corn mush, boiled hominy, oatmeal mush, cracked wheat, baked beans, and Indian pudding—all prepared with as little salt, pork, fat, and sugar as possible.[34]

Apparently, Richards and company were not as good at diagnosing "popular taste" as calculating grams of carbohydrates. There are inklings of discontent in Richards and Abel's writings. Abel wrote of a Kitchen branch in Providence, "One good-natured, affectionate Irish mother, when pressed to take an Indian pudding home to her children, replied, 'My boy says, "Oh! you can't make a Yankee of me that way!"'"[35]

Richards wrote, "The peculiar tastes of the people had to be followed. It was disheartening when our favorite dishes, wholesome, nutritious, and cheap, stayed unsold on the counter though freshly prepared day after day, and when our most scientific receipts produced food that was uneatable; but we consoled ourselves with the thought that the student learned most by defeat."[36] In the end, Richards concluded, "What the poor most need is ability to economize their resources, and what all classes need is knowledge of how to live more in accordance with the laws of health as well as of economy." No one needed more money, or more joy in life, or good-tasting food.

All branches of the New England Kitchen closed by 1893. An 1874 survey of Massachusetts working-class families found that more than half ate meat two or three times a day, and 42 percent said that sweets like cakes and pies were eaten at every meal.[37] Were they really going to be happy with creamed codfish and corn mush?

Apart from chiding immigrants for buying foods they liked, domestic science informed social workers also scolded them for cooking "meat, cheese, beans, and macaroni together" (apparently, minestrone soup wasn't respectable in 1900), combining tomatoes and peppers, eating dill pickles, even feeding their children "Grade A eggs"—the good eggs, taken as a sign of parental overindulgence.[38] There were quasi-scientific justifications for these nags, of course. Mixed foods would hinder digestion, according to theory, and sour foods could damage the urinary tract or cause "irritation" that would make "assimilation more difficult."[39] What sort of assimilation was difficult went unsaid.

By the 1930s, taste had won out over social reform. A scribe for the Federal Writers' Project wrote in 1939 that traditional New England foods had been overrun by "the products of the fast freight and the canning factory and to some extent by the influence of immigrants," and observed at the supermarket "near the cans of Boston baked beans and codfish cakes" were "cans of spaghetti and chop suey . . . or is it chow mein?"[40]

Mush for America

Despite the collapse of the New England Kitchens, Richards and Abel's starchy predilections reached a national audience in 1893 when Richards put together four thrilling menus for the Rumford Kitchen at the 1893 Columbian Exposition in Chicago:

> Baked beans, brown bread, roll, butter, applesauce
> Pea soup, roll, butter, apple cake
> Beef broth, roll, butter, gingerbread
> Escalloped fish, roll, butter, baked apples[41]

Richards also made up a chart of the foods that ought to be available to families of varying means.[42] Keep in mind that most New England workers were spending more than 50 percent of their income on food— and as of 1900, the average family income was $750 per year, about $21,000 today.[43]

FOOD MATERIALS IN RELATION TO COST
For 5 to 15 cents per person, daily [roughly $1.50–4.50 today], the food may
    be chosen from:
        Potatoes
        Rye meal
        Corn meal
        Wheat flour

Barley

Oats

Peas

Beans

Salt codfish

Halibut nape

Any meat with little bone, at 5 cents per pound

Oleomargarine

Skimmed milk

For 15 to 30 cents per person, daily [roughly $4.50–9.00 today], the food may be chosen from

Beef and mutton or any meat not over 25 cents per pound

Wheat bread (purchased at the baker's)

Suet

Butter

Whole Milk

Cheese

Dried fruits

Cabbage and other vegetables in their season

Sugar

Fish

Bacon

Some fruits in season

For 30 to 100 cents per person, daily [roughly $9.00–29.00 today], the food may be chosen from

Choice cuts of beef, mutton, or other meats

Chickens

Green vegetables, garden stuff, and vegetables out of season

Preserves

Confections

Cakes

Tea

Coffee

Poor New Englanders were apparently supposed to live without tea, coffee, and sugar and spend their precious few hours away from work baking their own bread. It is unlikely that poor New Englanders ever paid attention to Richards's advice.

Richards and her team of energetic reformers started to "promote the regional foods of New England as a national cuisine for newcomers," even while New England's newcomers rejected these foods.[44] After the New England Kitchens collapsed, Richards and Abel took a different approach to training the nation to eat cheap, bland food. Instead of setting up communal kitchens run on scientific principles, they decided to teach women to run their own kitchens and homes scientifically.

In 1899, Richards organized the first of a series of conferences in Lake Placid, New York, ultimately establishing the American Home Economics Association in 1908. Richards was the association's first president, and Abel served as editor of the association's *Journal of Home Economics*—enabling them to promote their versions of nutrition and sanitation in schools and colleges around the country.[45] By 1914, 250 colleges and universities offered home economics courses, with 28 offering bachelor's degrees and 20 offering with master's programs, and a PhD in household administration at the University of Chicago.[46]

The idea of using science to improve domestic life was immensely popular. Women who had trained in Boston, attended a Lake Placid conference, or read Richards's work about science in the home went on to found new school programs, university departments, and community lectures to train women in the new discipline combining chemistry, nutrition, and sanitation—with the same types of insipid recipes that Richards and Abel had promoted in the New England Kitchens.

Apart from Richards's New England Kitchen work, dull foods were also promoted by civic-minded Bostonians headed by philanthropist Mary Hemenway, who created a cooking curriculum for the public schools in 1885. The Boston Cooking School's Mary Lincoln published the similarly themed *Boston School Kitchen Text-Book* in 1890. This book was copied and used throughout the country, enabling generations of schoolgirls to learn to make steamed rhubarb, scalloped mutton, and fried corn mush.[47]

Richards's and Lincoln's menus spread very far, dooming generations of schoolchildren to eat the dullest New England foods instead of local specialties. Thirty-four years later, in 1920, home economics students in Saint Paul, Minnesota, were taught that vegetables were supposed to be served with butter or white sauce and that good breakfasts always included oat-meal or corn mush. For lunches the class prepared at school, students had an option of cream of pea soup, veal croquettes, creamed potatoes, or cottage cheese balls. Home economics students in New Mexico—land of chili peppers, beans, and corn tortillas—were given quizzes where the options for a multiple-choice question on "an inexpensive substitute for meat" included baked potatoes, suet pudding, rice, or baked beans, and were served salmon croquettes with white sauce and Waldorf salad for lunch.[48]

The New Englandization of American cuisine met some resistance in colleges. An instructor at Atlanta University supervising African American women in 1896 lamented that "to introduce . . . baked beans, Boston brown bread, codfish balls, creamed codfish, Johnny cake, Graham gems and hash was not by any means an easy task"[49]—not surprising for students from a region blessed with a wealth of produce and inventive African American cooks. But these students couldn't escape white sauce, and neither could the nation.

By 1907, other sorts of "science" were claiming the benefits of home economics, including eugenics. J. H. Kellogg, of the Kellogg Sanitarium and Kellogg's Corn Flakes, remarked at the 1907 Lake Placid conference:

> A great tidal wave of degeneracy is sweeping most civilized nations rapidly down the hill of physical decadence. Public hygiene alone cannot stay the tide. It may even accelerate it by keeping alive thru quarantine and other like measures the weak and feeble, thereby weakening the average stamina of the race. The great hope for the future physical development of the race lies in bettering home conditions, especially in relation to nutrition; so from my standpoint, the salvation of the race really rests in the hands of women who, having become experts in all that pertains to scientific nutrition, shall thru the instruction of other women in cooking schools and schools of domestic economy, bring the principles of food reform and scientific nutrition into every home.[50]

Given that the "salvation of the race" rested on home cooking, it isn't surprising that nonwhite races' foods were systematically excluded from home economics textbooks and from New England–themed cookbooks—and continue to be excluded today.

The Colonial Revival: Bringing Zombie Food Back from the Dead

The idea of New England—separate and distinct from the place—has been important to white Americans for a long time. New Yorkers founded the New England Society in 1805 to provide "friendship, charity and mutual assistance"[51] for New England expats. The New England Society also provided propaganda about the destructive influence of immigrants on the "just principles, high sentiments, intelligence" of New England's Anglo-American forebears, as Horace Bushnell put it in 1837.[52] In 1853, Mark Hopkins, president of Massachusetts's Williams College, decried "a populace . . . giving up the care of their government to the king, and of their salvation to the priest" (i.e., Irish Catholic immigrants) in contrast to "a people . . . reflective, self-governed, feeling their individual and immediate responsibility to God."[53]

The 1876 centennial made New Englanders painfully aware of just how prominent the region had been in 1776 and how much of a national backwater New England had become. The West called youth with endless possibilities, and cities from New York to St. Louis to Denver to San Francisco were growing, dynamic, and flush with new money from oil, coal, railroads, mining, factories, and farms—but New England had history. The centennial sparked the Colonial Revival Movement, when New Englanders clawed back their revolutionary past to prove that the region wasn't just a bunch of has-beens.

All manner of Anglo-Saxon Americans suddenly discovered a new fascination with a time when Boston was important, Americans were throwing off tyranny, and Catholic immigrants lived somewhere else. The Colonial Revival caught New England's architects, writers, artists, and even park planners in its backward snare.

Cookbook writers and home economists became entangled in a gluey nostalgia for times their grandparents never witnessed. A small subset of New England foods—baked beans, pies, brown bread, boiled dinner—were charged with Yankee virtue. They became symbols of New England thrift, hard work, and contentment with simple living rather than just another bunch of cheap things to eat. These foods were also homemade, showing that the cook (always a woman) wasn't wasting the family's money at commercial bakeries and restaurants and that she was wealthy enough to spend her time at home cooking instead of working. Women who worked twelve hours a day in the mills didn't care to steam brown bread for three hours after work.

The Servant Problem . . .

Some of the people who were in charge of preparing the most food in New England were people who were never taught how to make it. From 1850 onward, Irish immigrant women prepared most of the meals for upper- and middle-class families in Boston and beyond as maids, and they cooked for a broad swath of boarding house residents as well. Native-born women preferred to work in mills over servitude, and immigrant women who did not speak English weren't hired to work in homes. That left Irish women as the only group left for hiring as servants. Unfortunately, most Irish women had no idea how to cook American dainties when they arrived—and neither did their employers.

Thousands of Irish immigrant women took on jobs as cooks and maids in Boston in the mid- to late nineteenth century with no experience cooking anything like American foods in American kitchens. Many of the Irish famine refugees had subsisted almost entirely on potatoes (see "The Irish" section of chapter 1). Irish immigrants also had little experience with American cooking equipment. In rural Ireland, some women cooked over open fires with kettles through the 1930s.[54] By the mid-nineteenth century, most Bostonians and a sizable percentage of rural households used stoves.[55]

Unlike other immigrant groups, the Irish had a high ratio of unmarried adult women who arrived alone, without their families. Throughout the nineteenth century a little over half of Irish immigrants were women, and 5 percent were children. By contrast, only 41 percent of the Germans who arrived during the same period were women, and in the late nineteenth century only 21 percent of southern Italian immigrants were women.[56] The Irish had a tradition of late marriage, and men and women lived in largely separate spheres. With no children to take care of and no household to support in America, these women flocked to domestic service—positions as maids and cooks in private homes. The Irish maids, or "Bridgets" as they were called in the press, generally received room and board and higher pay than their peers who worked in factories or sewed at home.

Bostonians hired Irish women to work as cooks in enormous numbers. In 1850, 72 percent of the servants in Boston were Irish,[57] and Bostonians hired more servants than did residents of other cities. By 1850, more than 2,000 Irish women were working as domestic servants in Boston. By 1865, that number was over 11,000[58]—in a city with a total population of just over 192,000.[59] Eight-three percent of Irish domestic servants lived and worked in private homes of their employers in 1860, according to the census; the rest lived in boarding houses.[60] Assuming that the average household had five members,[61] up to 46,000 Bostonians were eating meals cooked by Irish women every day—not including the residents served by Irish women in boarding houses, public institutions, and restaurants.

This pattern of employment persisted across time; in 1900, 34 percent of Boston's servants and waitresses were born in Ireland,[62] and 54 percent of Irish-born women in the United States worked as domestic servants.[63] Second-generation Irish tended to find other occupations, working as teachers, stenographers, and other higher status jobs; by 1908, close to 50 percent of the schoolteachers in Worcester, Massachusetts, were second-generation Irish immigrants.[64]

Women servants per 1,000 families,[65] by year	1880	1900	1920
New York	188	141	60
Boston	219[66]	202[67]	73[68]

Although white upper-class Yankees relied on Irish servants for food, they mocked their meals and insulted their cooks. Magazines published jokes and cartoons about the awful Irish maids who couldn't soft-boil an egg, served "undressed tomatoes" in their underwear, and burnt and ruined anything they touched.[69] Grumpy writers complained about the Irish Bridgets' meals "of burnt steaks, of hard boiled potatoes, of smoked milk."[70] Yet these women ate what they cooked. In New England households with few servants, the help generally ate "the remains of the family meals,"[71] and servants would complain and quit if the household food was not up to their standards.

Irish women knew full well that their Yankee employers didn't have many alternatives for hiring servants if they wanted the filthy work of cooking done—and they weren't necessarily eager to get instruction from the boss on how to do their work. One labor researcher wrote in 1904, "There is a . . . class of girls, chiefly American and Irish, which is aggressively opposed to training. They say: . . . 'Shure, now, why should I be l'arnin' when I kin shove my ear in anywhere and get a good job?'" A respondent to a survey in the same book wrote, "I can't see that there is any such big [servant] problem as you suggest. I have solved it by living on nuts and fruit and having my work done out."[72]

Bostonians kept hiring Irish maids to cook anyway, and by the turn of the century they were paying them more than Irish women could make in any other legal profession besides being a schoolteacher.[73] Irish women immigrants continued to choose domestic service over working in mills and factories throughout the nineteenth century. Several authors claim either that the Irish had no effect on New England's food or that food "exercised little power and occupied no special place" in Irish American culture; that spot was reserved for whiskey.[74] Yet Irish American women spent the nineteenth century feeding an astonishing proportion of New England's residents, for good and for ill.

. . . and the Employer Problem

Having all these servants around meant that middle-class women could avoid preparing food, a task that involved "eviscerating birds and scrubbing dirt from carrots."[75] The brownstones built in American cities in the mid-nineteenth century—including Boston's Back Bay neighborhood—were constructed with kitchens in "dark, airless basements," making cooking on a coal stove unpleasant on frigid winter mornings and hot summer days alike. Bloody meats and grimy vegetables were delivered to the ground floor, where the maid whisked them inside. Later, mysteriously, miraculously, food was sent upstairs via a dumbwaiter, with no sign that it was once something dirty and alive.[76] Kitchen conditions weren't any better in working-class neighborhoods, where tenement apartments were cramped, several families often used the same stove, and every ounce of water had to be hauled up—and down—stairs.[77]

Even if the mistress of the house did trouble herself to walk down into the dim, cramped kitchen, she wasn't actually supposed to *touch* anything. Upper-class ladies were meant to tell their servants what to do, not actually cook. Housekeeping advice books for the lady of the house featured recipes like Catharine Beecher's 1850 instructions for bread: "She [the mistress] must, if needful, stand by and see that the bread is wet right, that the yeast is good, that the bread is put where it is warm enough, that it does not rise too long, so as to lose its sweetness (which is often the case before it begins to sour), that it is moulded aright, that the oven is at the right heat, and that it is taken out at the right time."[78] For most upper-class families, though, Beecher's bread advice was irrelevant—something people might aspire to but would never actually do, like the intricate instructions offered up nowadays by Martha Stewart or Gwyneth Paltrow. Very few women were making their own bread in 1850 if they could help it. Sylvester Graham, the notorious, pure-living health reformer whose legacy has been largely reduced to a name for children's crackers, lamented in 1837,

> In cities and large towns, most people depend on public bakers for their bread. . . . The public bakers have been led to try various experiments with chemical agents, and there is reason to believe that in numerous instances, they have been too successful in their practices, for the well-being of those who have been the consumers of their bread. . . . Alum, sulphate of zinc, sub-carbonate of magnesia, sub-carbonate of ammonia, sulphate of copper, and several other substances, have been used by public bakers in making bread.[79]

Graham's efforts to revive New England's pure, virtuous, subcarbonate-free bread-making traditions were futile. In 1840, 27 percent of Massachusetts residents lived in "cities and large towns": by 1900, 86 percent did.[80] From roughly 1820 to 1900, native New Englanders moved to cities old and new to work in mills and factories—joined by hundreds of thousands of immigrants from Ireland, Canada, Southern Europe, and elsewhere. In 1800, roughly 8 percent of New Englanders lived in cities and towns.[81] By 1900, almost 70 percent of New Englanders were city dwellers; 88 percent of Rhode Island, 86 percent of Massachusetts, and 60 percent of Connecticut residents lived in urban areas.[82]

The poorer urbanites generally lived in rented apartments that had only small stoves,[83] not the luxurious ovens available to Catharine Beecher.

Most of the cooking that was done was "as it had been in the eighteenth century—one pot cooking: either gruels, soups, or stews which could be boiled on top of the stove or bacon, fish, or occasionally chops, which could be fried."[84]

Even if they did have access to adequate cooking equipment, ventilation, and food, nineteenth-century New England urban dwellers didn't necessarily even know *how* to cook. Living apart from the grandmothers, aunts, mothers, and other older members of a culture meant that many young people didn't get instructed in all the intricacies of their natal cuisine, as political economist Charles Stanton Devas noted in 1901 (with a strong prejudice against Polynesians):

> The art of cooking, like other arts, must be learnt and transmitted from one generation to another; a disorganization of family life and irrational education may in a few years reduce a civilized population to the culinary level of Polynesians.
>
> Thus many Americans in spite of large earnings have no choice but to feed in great part on tinned provisions and rancid bacon; and amid the urban population of England, the high wages of the workpeople sometimes fail to secure them a decent meal at home, because their wives have not been given the capacity or the wish to be good cooks; and the downward progression in depraved consumption is fostered by the ease of buying close at hand the materials of makeshift meals, salted meats, sausages, pickles, or bad cakes and pastry; and a new source of mischief is the practice of preserving meat, fish, milk, and other perishable foods by means of chemicals such as boric acid, thereby rendering them indigestible.[85]

The Boston Cooking School: Kitchens Paved with Good Intentions

One of the major sources of bland, well-intentioned, stereotypical New England recipes was the Boston Cooking School. Founded in 1879 by the Women's Education Association (WEA), the Boston Cooking School sought to bring science and purpose to the kitchen, with the motto "better ways, lighter burdens, more wholesome results."[86]

The WEA was an ambitious group, spurring Harvard to establish Radcliffe College and MIT to permit Ellen Swallow Richards to set up a women's chemistry laboratory, and was supported by prominent philanthropists. Their approach to teaching women how to cook was also ambitious, scientific, and divorced from human pleasure. For example, as the cooking school was being organized, the WEA committee spent time at many meetings arguing about what the students should do with the food once it was prepared in class. The obvious answer, "Eat it!," doesn't seem to have occurred to them.[87] In the end, the committee allowed students to taste their food, but sold most of it to the poor at cost.[88]

Classes began with public lectures by celebrity cookbook writer Maria Parloa and private lessons by a local cooking instructor named Joanna Sweeney. Sweeney's first lesson, voted on by the WEA's Industrial Education Committee, included tomato soup, Irish stew with mutton and potatoes, steamed apple pudding, and bread dough: solid, nutritious, unexciting food. A few days later, Parloa gave a public cooking demonstration on Saturday. It was a great success, so great that the Industrial Education Committee began planning the menus for both Sweeney's classes and Parloa's demonstrations. Parloa's second demonstration included larded grouse with bread sauce, lobster croquettes, potato souffle, cream meringues, and orange sherbet—the sorts of foods that the Parker House Hotel, not a scientific nutrition laboratory, might serve.

The WEA decided that celebrity sells and quickly fired Sweeney and hired Mrs. Mary J. Lincoln to teach instead. Lincoln, a founder and editor of New England Kitchen Magazine, emphasized "plain food," such as brown bread, fish balls, doughnuts, and Indian pudding.[89]

The WEA also quickly discovered that although they aspired to educate cooks, upper-class women were loath to give their cooks time off to attend the school. Instead, the ladies themselves came to learn—and to admire Maria Parloa and Mrs. Lincoln. After Parloa left for New York and Lincoln quit to write and lecture, the school quickly ran up debts.

Instead of mixed, flavorful meals, the polite ladies of Boston and beyond aspired to make what modern middle-class Americans would call "toddler food." As one eager student of Fanny Farmer at the Boston Cooking School gushed, "Miss F. Says if a cook can make a good cream cake, baking-powder biscuit, & creamed codfish, she can cook almost anything!"[90] These pale, bland, vegetable-free white flour delights were the building blocks of all cuisine. I'm sure some respectable households served nothing but cream cakes, biscuits, and creamed codfish (until the residents died of scurvy or pellagra).

Fanny Farmer's 1896 *Boston Cooking-School Cook Book* helped women cook, but it made them worse at cooking. She emphasized exact measurements over sensory learning—cooking without tasting, touching, or understanding, as cooks have for generations. Women become instruments of the author's cooking, not creators. Yes, the recipes were consistent, but the person cooking them was not empowered to make anything her own. By making every recipe a scientific exercise, Farmer reduced women's expertise and creativity. She also helped spread her sweet tooth all over the country; a third of her cookbook is devoted to candies and desserts.

The same employers who never touched bread or allowed foods to mix in a pot were pressured to create ridiculously elaborate meals whenever guests arrived. The New England tastemakers who prescribed fancy menus for aspiring hostesses created meals that a single woman could not possibly hope to serve without one or several servants. Maria Parloa, head of the Boston Cooking School, presented a dinner party plan in her 1880 *New Cook Book* for the following courses in order:

- Two quarts of oysters on a block of ice
- Consommé à la Royale
- Baked fish with Hollandaise sauce
- Cheese soufflé
- Roast chicken with mashed potatoes, green peas, celery, and cranberry jelly
- Oyster patties
- Lettuce salad with French dressing
- Crackers and Neufchatel cheese, orange sherbet, frozen cabinet pudding with apricot sauce, Glacé Meringue [*sic*], sponge cake, fruit and coffee[91]

This crazed hostess needed iced oysters, warm soup, fish that wasn't overcooked, a soufflé that hadn't fallen, oysters that hadn't spoiled, a meringue that hadn't gotten damp, and a frozen pudding—all at the right time, and all before modern refrigeration, freezers, and stoves with thermostats. How many women were willing to pay their cooks enough to deal with all that?

Becoming a New England Food: The Curious Case of the Boiled Dinner

Some foods were consciously claimed by the Yankee literati as New England for no obvious reason. One of these questionable comestibles is New England boiled dinner.

References to New England boiled dinner started popping up in cookbooks in the 1880s.[92] *Aunt Mary's New England Cook Book*, published in 1881, calls New England boiled dinner "an old fashioned but favorite dish,"[93] while the 1896 *Boston Cooking-School Cook Book* simply calls it "Boiled Dinner."[94]

New England boiled dinner is, according to the tastemakers at *Yankee Magazine* (now sporting the hip moniker *New England Today*), corned beef boiled with cabbage, potatoes, and rutabagas. More adventurous eaters and aspiring vampires include beets, which are cooked separately so as not to turn the entire concoction bloody red.[95] Variants include dinners made with smoked or fresh pork instead of corned beef.[96] Although recipes collected in the 1930s by the Federal Writers' Project include onions, some latter-day local informants insist that onions have never, ever belonged in boiled dinner.[97]

Boiled dinner leftovers are supposed to be chopped and fried the next morning into red flannel hash, where the beets are finally allowed to let loose their dye on weakly tinted vegetables.[98] This hash has provoked mixed reactions over the years. As a writer in the *Knickerbocker*, a monthly magazine published in New York, put it in 1848 (and credited to a writer in Angola, Iowa, in 1838, "If every dish has its times and seasons no less truly hath every person their likings and their antipathie. . . . How mincingly will a child pick at its plate of boiled dinner—'pot luck,' the grandmothers call it. How many like the 'old maid's hash up,' where that same boiled dinner appears the second time, salt beef, pork, potatoes, turnips, and cabbage all finely minced, and warmed with the melted butter, a little salt, pepper, and vinegar?"[99]

But What *Is* *Boiled Dinner?*

The questions of what constitutes boiled dinner and how it should be cooked have never been entirely resolved. The 1999 *New England Cookbook* claims that New England boiled dinner contains beets and parsnips, which are "strictly required."[100] Beets and parsnips were omitted entirely from the New England boiled dinner according to the menu served at the Michigan State Prison in Jackson in 1908,[101] which specified corned beef, cabbage, potatoes, and carrots. (Why was a Michigan prison serving a New England boiled dinner? Was the prison populated with Vermont renegades? The record is lost.) An 1891 New York journal even claimed, "If you wish real New-England 'boiled dinner,' you also have carrots, parsnips, and cauliflower."[102]

In the late 1880s, popular cookbook author Jessup Whitehead pondered the ineffable essence of boiled dinner (from the safety of Alabama):

> What preservative principle the New England Boiled Dinner to keep itself together through all the changes encountered while spreading over this great country? Why did it not lose one thing here and there and get mixed up and obliterated? How did it get over the difficulties in the rich valleys of the West when it found the vegetables growing to enormous sizes and the corn fed and pork all fat? How often must there have been spoonfuls of succotash or of beans or a section of squash or pumpkin or peas or corn surreptitiously crowded into the dish? Why did they not remain? How did the New England Boiled Dinner get rid of them and come clean as we see it today? And having passed through so much, how much more could it endure and come out intact? . . . How many of its parts if any could be lopped off before it would cease to be?[103]

Bostonians and "Vermont housewives" had different opinions about how a boiled dinner ought to be cooked. In her 1884 *Appledore Cook Book*, Maria Parloa, doyenne of the Boston Cooking School, declared, "Some boil all kinds of vegetables in the same pot, but there is this objection to this method; you lose the distinctive flavor of each vegetable, and the beef is flavored with the vegetables, which is very unpleasant when it is cold."[104] Some writers dispensed with cooking altogether. The

1888 edition of *Good Housekeeping* (published in New York) made helpful suggestions:

AN OLD CONNECTICUT BOILED DINNER At this season of the year a New England boiled dinner consists of a brisket piece of corned beef, boiled or rather simmered twelve minutes to the pound and served with spring greens instead of cabbage. The meat and the greens are cooked separately; so are carrots, turnips, and potatoes. . . . The quickest way to prepare a boiled dinner is to buy a can of corned beef, heat it fifteen minutes, open the can and turn it out in a dish surround it with the greens alternated with little mounds of boiled carrots, turnips, potatoes, and baked beets.[105]

Fifty years later, a Federal Writers' Project author wrote, "Controversy over the matter of cooking the vegetables separately, or with the meat, leaves Vermont housewives just as certain as ever that they should be cooked together, and they go right on doing so, just as their grandmothers and great grandmothers did before them."[106] A 1933 *Boston Globe* columnist admitted that boiled dinner mystified him: "I haven't the faintest idea when or how a boiled dinner came to be called a 'New England' boiled dinner. Possibly it was at that stage of affairs when a chunk of boiled fat pork was added to the mélange. For this piece of fat pork is the only New England touch that a boiled dinner can possess, and it seldom does possess it today outside of a home-cooked country meal."[107]

Very few of the published descriptions of New England boiled dinner under that title include salt pork—which doesn't mean that people didn't put it in. What it means is that the sort of people who would bother to put the name New England on a dish and publish it in a cookbook didn't want to include salt pork in their recipes. Perhaps the salt pork was old-fashioned, or considered lower class and not worthy of respectable middle-class recipes. Salt pork was cheaper than beef in the 1880s, the sort of food eaten by poor farmers and mill workers.[108] Wealthier New Englanders preferred beef over pork beginning in colonial times.[109]

Who Owns Boiled Dinner?

To an outsider, it's not clear why boiled dinner even has a name. The ingredients look like a statistical average of the food New England households had sitting around the house in the winter in 1850, cooked in the easiest way possible. It's a little like renaming a food "Prairie State Grilled Cheese Sandwiches" or "Rocky Mountain Campsite S'mores."

This concoction wasn't new, and it wasn't unique to New England. A similar dish was described by Henri Misson in his 1698 *Memoirs* describing his travels in England:[110] "The English . . . will have a piece of boiled beef, and then they salt it some days before hand, and besiege it with five or six heaps of cabbage, carrots, turnips, or some other herbs or roots, well peppered and salted and swimming in butter."[111]

Here's a typical New England boiled dinner, from Quebec in November 1775:

> In the evening before bedtime the females of the house prepare the dinner of the following day. It may be particularly described as it was done in our view for a number of days together and during the time was never varied. This was the manner:
>
> A piece of pork or beef or a portion of each kind, together with a sufficiency of cabbage, potatoes, and turnips, seasoned with salt, and an adequate quantity of water, were put into a neat tin kettle with a close lid. The kettle, thus replenished, was placed on stove in the room where we all slept and there it 'till the time of rising, when it was taken to a small fire in kitchen where a stewing continued till near noon, when they dined. The contents were turned into a large basin. . . . The meat required no cutting as it was reduced a mucilage or at least to shreds.[112]

What New England cookbooks call a New England boiled dinner is the same as the dish called boiled dinner in Cape Breton and Jigg's dinner in Newfoundland and Labrador.[113]

Still, boiled dinner's reputation as a symbol of New England was firmly established before the turn of the century. An 1882 church operations manual from Mansfield, Ohio, described the "New England kitchen" at a bazaar fund-raiser held in 1870: "Refreshments were served here every day and evening of the bazar in the most attractive forms. One feature of the fair was the New England kitchen. . . . There were doughnuts, and pumpkin pies, baked apples, and baked beans on the old-fashioned table, while in the centre steamed a good hearty boiled dinner in a pewter platter of most ample dimensions."[114]

Boiled Dinner Dissent

Boiled dinner was not universally admired. Even while Ohioans were serving extremely authentic boiled dinner reproductions on polished platters, Bostonians were sneering at such homely food. From the 1891 *Boston Cooking-School Cook Book* by Mrs. Lincoln, "An old-fashioned Boiled Dinner (Mrs Poor): Notwithstanding that this dish has fallen into ill repute with many people it may be prepared so as to be both palatable and nutritious for those who exercise freely. It is more suitable for cold seasons. The most healthful and economical way, though perhaps not the old-fashioned way, is to boil the beef the day before."[115]

Fannie Farmer deplored boiled dinners in her 1896 edition of the *Boston Cooking-School Cook Book*: "Corned beef has but little nutritive value. It is used to give variety to our diet in summer when fresh meats prove too stimulating. It is eaten by the workingman to give bulk to his food."[116] Farmer includes cabbage, beets, turnips, carrots, and potatoes in her boiled dinner, though she believes firmly in vegetable segregation. In Farmer's recipe, cabbage and beets are served on separate platters from the rest of the dinner. Perhaps she was afraid they would tarnish the pewter?[117] Or perhaps she didn't want her proper Boston food to look too much like Irish corned beef and cabbage?

Boiled dinner was certainly out of fashion beyond Boston by the early twentieth century according to an account of life in Hampton Falls, New Hampshire, in the 1840s (published in 1918): "A boiled dinner consisting of salt beef and pork, with vegetables and sometimes a pudding, were boiled together in a large pot. The older members of the family were fond of this kind of dinner while the younger members were not. This was generally spoken of as biled pot."[118] A journalist's memoir of his life in Boston in 1919 echoes the theme: "Meals at the boarding house up the street were $7 a week. Thursdays it was always boiled dinner and those who could afford it went out."[119]

There were also doubts as to whether it was even healthy to eat boiled dinner. A 1903 Boston city investigation of the alms house and hospital on Long Island, Boston, showed that the Joint Standing Committee on Institutions was highly suspicious of boiled dinner—a very different set of comestibles from the soft, boiled, flavorless pap most "experts" served the sick.

Q. Do the hospital patients in the tuberculosis ward get boiled dinner?
A. They do sir. . . .
Alderman NOLAN It is not what they like, but what is best for them in the judgment of the doctor. I saw one man eating corned beef and cabbage on the bed.
Mrs LINCOLN. He would feel badly if he didn't get it. . . .
Q. By Councilman BRAZZELL: I would like to ask Mr McDermott if he knows of any person who received a boiled dinner when dying?
A. I do, sir; but I could not call them by name. . . .
Q. By Councilman BRAZZELL: I should like to ask Mr McDermott if he knows of a young man who died a few weeks ago who had a boiled dinner before he died.
A. I could not say. I am not out there eating sir. . . .
Q. Some question was raised by one member of the committee as to whether it was proper to give a patient who was in a feeble condition a boiled dinner. What is your judgment as a medical man in regard to that?

. . .

WITNESS. I consider it proper food. I consider it just as nourishing for a patient suffering from the advanced stages of consumption as it is to any other person. In treating patients in the advanced stage of consumption it is not always the desire to give them nourishing food, but the principal desire, or at least one of the aims you are trying to accomplish, is to suit the patient. . . .
Q. I will put it in another way. Do you think it proper food to give to a patient if he wanted it?
A. I do.
Q. Do you think it would do him any harm?
A. I do not.
Q. Do the patients like boiled dinners?
A. They are very fond of them.

Q. Some question has been raised regarding the desirability of serving boiled dinner to any of the patients in the consumptives hospital. Do you consider it proper to have such a dinner served there?

A. I consider it proper that any kind of food the consumptive patient can digest should be served, and if he can take care of boiled dinner, it is perfectly proper to give it to him.[120]

Cabbage Tastes Best on a Big Shiny Plate

So, what's New Englandy about New England boiled dinner? Victorian recipe writers and sentimentalists said the dinner required several types of vegetables and that true New Englanders insisted that the vegetables had to be artfully arranged by type on a big shiny platter.

The *New England Farmer* printed instructions on arranging a New England boiled dinner in 1864: "Put your beef and pork upon a large platter in the centre of the table near the foot where the husband can carve it to advantage. . . . [Do] not pile two thirds of the mass of meat and vegetables helter skelter upon a big platter and the rest upon a smaller one and think it just as well. It is not. A boiled dinner relishes better when neatly dressed up."[121]

Strangely, there's little evidence that people really thought about boiled dinners' geometry before 1860. The *New England Farmer* magazine advised in 1867, "The garden that satisfied our forefathers will but illy satisfy the more cultivated or dainty appetite of the present age. Few at the present day rest satisfied with the salt meat and potatoes of former days which constituted the farmer's boiled dinner. A greater variety is craved and as a general thing we find it conducive to health to gratify the appetite in this particular."[122]

Despite evidence that grandpa was happy with meat and potatoes, many late nineteenth-century writers insisted that after hours of hard manual labor, New England's farmers could not eat unless they were served precisely aligned vegetables on a shiny plate. Was this habit supposed to demonstrate Yankee restraint? The strange compulsions that arose out of New England's rocky soil?

All the descriptions of polished pewter platters I have been able to locate were written at least 30 years after these boiled dinners were allegedly served, usually with a reference to "old New England" to boot. In "old New England," pewter platters and plates of all sizes were certainly used. Farmers didn't buy breakable ceramic plates in the early years of the republic and didn't invest in superfluous serving plates—or flatware. As author Jane Nylander puts it, "The New England custom of eating with a knife and presenting an entire meal on a single serving platter were scorned by prosperous city dwellers and commented upon by European travelers."[123] Nylander also observed that these platters became "bright" by being repeatedly scoured with sand, not any kind of careful, painstaking polishing.[124]

In the nineteenth century, farmers gradually acquired regular ceramic plates, spoons, and forks. The continued emphasis on the "bright silver platters" by Victorian-era food writers reminded their affluent readers just how superior their up-to-date homes were, with pretty tableware and separate serving dishes for every possible food.

The platters seem to have emerged as an important food accessory mid-century. An 1853 memoir by an evangelist pegs those "bright pewter platters" as being used in Herkimer County, New York, in 1820, though he fails to comment on the vegetables' symmetry:

The . . . pudding was snugly tied at both ends. It was soused into a large dinner pot and then boiled with pork, potatoes, and other vegetables, until all was thoroughly cooked; and when the hungry labourers were summoned from the field by the welcome blast of the loud sounding-conch, they were seated down to the above mentioned luxuries, neatly arranged on two large bright pewter platters which had passed down through many generations.[125]

An 1892 *New England Magazine* article titled "Sixty Years Ago: Recollections of New England Country Life" contains a lengthy description of boiled dinner, with special attention to food arrangement. "At dinner time, the beef and pork were put in the centre of a large pewter dish, and the vegetables symmetrically arranged around, all forming the noon meal once or twice a week."[126] This sounds far more like instructions from a Boston Cooking School class for ladies than a description of a rustic farmer's meal.

The same issue claims that in years past New Englanders who had moved to "old Milwaukee" ate boiled dinner every Monday—but those days were long gone of course.[127]

Here's a typical example from a 1900 article in *House Furnishing Review*.

> . . . an accounting of the pieces in the old Summer house in Shrewsbury which has been preserved intact since the Puritan days. In that time all the platters as well as the plates were round. The oval shape was unknown. There are many alive today who remember the New England farmer who clung stubbornly to the usage of having a boiled dinner on a pewter platter. He said that it did not taste quite right unless it was heaped up on a great shining platter.[128]

Who is this fussy farmer? Where did he live? Did he actually do any work? After a long day of haying, milking cows, repairing fences, and hauling rocks out of the fields, most people would have been happy just to have food on the table that wouldn't break their teeth.

You can find the same shiny platter in an 1898 biography of Susan B. Anthony, depicting her childhood in Adams, Massachusetts: "To go to school the children had to pass Grandmother Read's. . . . In the evening they would stop again for some of the left over cold boiled dinner which was served on a great pewter platter, a big piece of pork or beef in the center and piled all round potatoes, cabbage, turnips, beets, carrots, etc."[129]

Likewise, consider an 1894 history of the colonial period in Chataqua, New York: "On shelves against the wall or in the tall cupboard, are displayed rows of bright pewter plates standing edgewise, headed by the great pewter platter always in use at 'boiled dinners' piled with cabbage, turnips, beets, potatoes, and other vegetables, and near its side lies the bag of pudding stuffed with some kind of wild berries, a tempting slice of which is given to each one at the table covered with sweetened cream."[130]

A pewter platter also appears in the 1867 *Me-won-i-toc: A Tale of Frontier Life and Indian Character*, when a character recounts his New England childhood "on the east side of the Connecticut River" in some unnamed state: "Six days in the week, the dinner which was always ready at noon was composed of a dish known by the simple name of 'boiled victuals,' usually composed of salt pork and beef, potatoes, turnips, and frequently beets, carrots, parsnips, and cabbage, all cooked in one great dinner pot and brought to the table upon a large pewter platter."[131]

Curiously, pewter platters were also apparently popular in Cornwall, England, in 1830, judging by this tale of "A St. Just Feast 50 Years Ago" in the 1880 *Stories and Folk-Lore of West Cornwall.*

> In the large vessel were boiled a rump of beef, a couple of fowls, and a nice piece of streaky pork to eat with them as well as turnips carrots and other vegetables all in kipps net bags to keep them separate and for convenience in taking up. The vegetables were placed to drain on bars called kipp sticks placed across the crock, the beef was dished up on a round pewter platter, the fowls had melted butter and parsley some of the butter poured on them the rest served in a boat.[132]

Madame Whitney's Cabbage-Scented Confection

Over and over again, boiled dinner was evoked as the essence of New England times gone by. It makes one wonder if there was a secret Boiled Dinner Quickie Mart where all the farm wives were buying takeout after an exhausting day of chores. Here's a typical 1883 description from the children's magazine *Wide Awake* about the boiled dinner prepared by a Vermont-based Madame Whitney of "the very new New England of 100 years ago": ". . . A piece of pork and a quantity of garden 'sauce'—beets, cabbage, turnips, carrots, and potatoes—followed the beef at the appropriate time, and, best of all, a *pudding.*"[133]

A word about that pudding: the author specifies that this particular pudding was boiled in the same pot as the boiled dinner and served as dessert with maple syrup and cream. I cannot say for certain that Vermonters of past ages did not relish desserts that were seasoned with corned beef and cabbage broth, but it seems unlikely.

There are many ex post facto boiled dinner descriptions that insist that housewives boiled hasty pudding or Indian pudding for dessert in the pot.[134] Earlier American cooks, Jigg's dinner aficionados in Nova Scotia, and English cookbook writers specify a *pease* pudding boiled in the pot to serve with boiled beef or pork—a savory side dish, not a dessert.[135] This dessert "tradition" may have been invented by latter-day cooks with multi-burner stoves and more than one pot.

As an 1890 pamphlet on all things corn observes, if you boil a corn pudding with a boiled dinner, "When done it will be a rich red"—presumably due to the beets.[136] None of the fond recollections of great-grandma's boiled dinner mention that their dessert was dyed this striking hue.

A bad boiled dinner could sink even a woman's marriage plans—perhaps intentionally. From yet another probably spurious publication titled "Our Grandmother's Dishes" (1896),

> In country houses, the home-cured beef and pork on the great pewter platter, occupying the middle of the table was garnished by a picturesque array of vegetables on the edge of the same platter. "A girl was fit to be married," so the old saying went, "when she could cook a boiled dinner." And really it required much care and judgment to put in the same pot meat, cabbage, beet, turnip, carrot, parsnip, squash, and potato, each according to its own need of time for cooking, so that all should be ready to be taken up at the same time and all perfectly done. So this qualification meant more in a girl's character than simply cooking a good dinner. The work must have been more difficult where the only time keeper was a noon mark on the threshold of the kitchen door or a sun dial in the garden.[137]

The Decline of Boiled Dinner

Apparently, the tastiest sorts of boiled dinner were long gone by 1915. This paean to a boiled dinner appeared in a 1915 syndicated newspaper column by Canadian American writer Walt Mason:

THE BOILED DINNER
How dear to my heart is the luscious boiled dinner,
which fond recollection brings back now and then,
that balm to the stomach that forty-time winner—
oh, give me an old-time boiled dinner again!
So often I've sat at the restaurant table,
and down through the menu I've hopefully looked
for something to comfort my northeastern gable

for such a boiled dinner as grandmother cooked!
The steaming boiled dinner, the noble boiled dinner,
the grand old boiled dinner my grandmother cooked.
I'm tired of the fodder you're constantly shovin',
the things out of box and the things out of can,
the dofunnies baked in a gasoline oven,
the chafing dish horrors which frighten a man;
your cooking school triumphs are weird and uncanny,
That sort of refreshment too long I have brooked;
I long for the skill of my dear sainted granny,
I long for the dinner that grandmother cooked!
The fragrant boiled dinner, the juicy boiled dinner,
the cultured boiled dinner my grandmother cooked![138]

Since grandmother's time—whenever that was—the published recipes for boiled dinner have become less amenable for polished platter presentation as well. Recipes from the 1860s to 1900 call for five or six different timings for when to add the beef, potatoes, cabbage, parsnips, turnips, beets, and squash into boiling water for noon dinner.[139] A 1947 recipe says just to add cut-up vegetables "during the last hour of cooking."[140] In an introduction to the chapter, though, the authors repeat the old canard of how colonial housewives lined all their vegetables up on a pewter platter to serve the great boiled mess: "sliced carrots at one end, sliced turnips at the other, beets on one side, cabbage opposite. Only the potatoes had a dish of their own."[141]

In 1930, under the heading "How to Prepare a Real New England Boiled Dinner," the *Boston Globe* recommended that since so many visitors from other regions of the country were going to be arriving to attend Bay State tercentenary events, local housewives should serve them dishes "which are distinctive of New England."

All those visitors might have asked, if these dishes are so common in New England, why would a newspaper need to print a recipe for them? Why would a proud New England housewife need a recipe out of a Saturday newspaper to show her guests what people in her state like to eat? Because New England boiled dinner is what Massachusetts residents are supposed to be eating, not what they actually ate. The *Globe* went on to list three different recipes for boiled dinner: New England boiled dinner with corned beef, a boiled ham dinner, and "Vermont boiled dinner," which included both fresh and salt pork.[142]

Apart from all these different ideas of what boiled dinner is, who serves it, and what tableware is necessary, boiled dinner conceals a lingering mystery: when did pottage lose its grains? Food historians generally agree that seventeenth-century European Americans in New England made most of their meals from pottage (stew with grain) consisting of corn, beans, or corn and beans with some salt meat mixed in, with vegetables tossed in depending on the season.[143]

By the mid-nineteenth century, the corn had evaporated and pottage split into two dishes. The salt meat and vegetables stayed in the boiled dinner pot, while beans and salt meat migrated to the baked beans pots. The corn was largely left to feed the animals. Why didn't New Englanders still boil up beans, salt meat, and vegetables in the same pot? Only Madame Whitney knows.

Boiled Dinner Today

Boiled dinner has not completely vanished from New England life. A 2017 headline on the satirical *New Maine News* site read, "Classic Boiled Dinner in Decline as More Maine Youth Discover Flavor."

> Statewide—Once a staple of Maine households, boiled dinners have suffered a tremendous falling out as more of the meal's biggest fans die of old age. Boiled dinners, in which a ham, potatoes, cabbage and other greens are boiled to remove toughness and flavor, aren't exciting Maine's young people, who are used to tasting things other than salt.
>
> "We used to eat it at my great-grandmother's house," Cherryfield native Travis Smith said.
>
> "I remember when we'd walk in, the house smelled like feet. But the food tasted like nothing," Smith said.[144]

4

Corn and Prejudice

ALL OF New England's most notorious foods harken back to ye olde colonial times, but some genuinely old-fashioned comestibles have been quietly removed from that list. They aren't "acquired tastes" that have to be learned, like, say, anchovies, or black pudding. They're foodstuffs that are appreciated, even enjoyed, today by millions of Americans from a wide range of backgrounds, but have slid silently out of the canon of New England foods. One of these foods is cornbread—the most important food to New England's first settlers, yet it is almost never mentioned in the same breath as "New England" at all.

Corn Mattered

Indian pudding. Hasty pudding. Ryaninjun bread. Anadama bread. Boston brown bread. Hoe cakes, Johnny cake, Jonny cakes, and journey cakes (all very different, really), pone and porridge and plain old mush: corn was everywhere in colonial New England, and the colonists weren't happy about it.

When Squanto taught the Pilgrims how to farm the sandy soil of Cape Cod, he planted corn. The surviving Pilgrims probably ate corn at the first Thanksgiving,[1] and they were grateful for it. William Bradford reported, "They had about a peck a meal [two gallons!] a week to a person, or now since harvest, Indian corn to that proportion, which made many afterwards write so largely of their plenty here to their friends in England, which were not feigned but true reports."[2]

It's not clear why corn and not some other plant became the North American staple of choice. It took time for northern flint corn to become New England's all-American food plant. Maize didn't become wildly popular among Native American agriculturalists in the Northeast until sometime after 1000 CE,[3] when maize, and northern flint in particular, took over farming. Before Europeans arrived, American peoples grew plenty of different grains, including by not limited to little barley (*Hordeum pusillum*), maygrass (*Phalaris caroliniana*), panic grass (*Panicum* spp.), and wild rice (*Zizania* spp.),[4] as well as other seed plants including goosefoot (*Chenopodium berlandieri*) and erect knotweed (*Polygonum erectum*), squashes, and sunflowers (*Helianthus annus*).[5] Several of these species are also native to modern lawns, where they grow vigorously despite firm opposition.

The northern flint corn the Pilgrims encountered isn't the same as Mesoamerican maize. It's genetically different enough from other types of corn that some authors consider it a different species. It is the product of human work, of repeated selection and cross-fertilization by Northeast Woodland tribes over hundreds of years.[6]

A latter-day observer (1674) commented about the Native Americans' diet, "Their food is generally boiled maize, or Indian corn, mixed with kidney beans, or sometimes without."[7] Although there were many Native American words for boiled beans and corn in different languages, English immigrants eventually started calling the stuff "succotash."[8]

Despite the fact that corn was the most popular food crop in eastern North America, the earliest English settlers strongly preferred using wheat for their daily bread when they could get it. Corn had all manner of unfortunate associations. Wheat bread was the food of the gentry back home, the stuff that lords would eat when the common folks would get by with coarser grains—rye and oats—and corn was more similar to those grains than wheat. Corn was also a strange new plant eaten by Indians, the unfamiliar people the colonists were displacing, killing, and infecting with smallpox. Corn was a grain "tainted by savagery"[9] and by deep ambivalence.

Some of the earliest settlers blamed their stomach ailments on corn—although in the absence of any medical care, it's hard to tell if they simply got sick from corn or something else. Edward Johnson wrote of the Plymouth settlers in his 1653 history *Wonder-Working Providence*, "The want of English graine Wheate Barly and Rie proved a sore affliction to some stomacks who could not live upon Indian Bread and water yet were they compelled to it till Cattell increased and the Plowes could but goe."[10]

Corn's other problem was that it's hard to make real bread out of it. As millions of dieters and fad followers know, wheat contains gluten, the magical mystery protein that gives bread its soft, resilient structure. Knead bread, and the gluten's proteins stretch and fold and catch and connect to make a springy matrix that holds together when it's puffed up by yeast making little air bubbles, and retains its soft, chewy texture for days.

Corn, alas, has no gluten. You can knead cornbread dough all day long, and you'll still end up with a crumbly, rapidly-drying lump after it's baked. If you keep cornbread for more than a few hours, it will start to get stale.

Unfortunately, New England, like the American South, is a terrible place to grow wheat. In the 1640s and 1650s, Massachusetts plots planted with corn yielded twice as many bushels of grain per acre as did wheat plots.[11] From 1660 on, southern New England's wheat was repeatedly attacked by a fungus known as "the blast" (black stem rust), Hessian flies, wheat midges, and plagues of other insects, and wheat yields fell as the local soil lost its fertility.[12]

Corn was hardy. It was the perfect crop for colonists who were expending most of their labor trying to make fields out of forests and didn't have much energy left for plowing. The "hill" method of growing corn, which Squanto demonstrated to the Pilgrims, worked well in fields full of dying trees and stumps where plowing wasn't possible anyway. Corn also didn't require emergency all-hands-on-deck harvesting in the late summer between rains. Families could leave the drying cobs on the stalks through the early winter until they had the time and hands available to bring them in (assuming that a cow didn't get loose in the field in the meantime). A single farmer with six to eight acres of land could harvest enough corn to support five to seven people for a year.[13] Even better, local corn varieties had been selected by Native Americans for more than 500 years and flourish in New England's damp, changeable, short growing season—unlike wheat, which never did like it here.

Corn, or maize, was declared a legal currency in Massachusetts in 1631, and in 1635 the Massachusetts General Court declared that taxes could be paid in corn.[14] Boston's population reached 1,200 by 1640, far more than the meager, hilly, swampy farmland on the Shawmut Peninsula could support, and the city began importing food; by 1708, the south side of the Boston town dock was called "Corne Market"[15]—which meant that all manner of grains were shipped there, as "corne" could refer to any grain. "Indian corn" was the preferred title for the ear-borne variety.

When the Minutemen threw off their homespun breeches for Continental Army uniforms, the Massachusetts Provincial Congress begged towns for "flour, wheat, rye, and Indian corn to nourish the troops."[16] The Continental Congress assigned each soldier one pint of cornmeal per man per week (or a half pint of rice) to supplement their seven pounds of flour.[17]

There were even efforts to make rum out of "molasses"—a sort of corn syrup made from crushed cornstalks—in eighteenth-century Connecticut. Although at least 1,000 gallons of rum were distilled from this curious material, it appears to have been more economical for New Englanders to obtain liquor by trading for slave labor, and the industry seems to have vanished by the 1780s.[18]

Corn, the Breakfast of Losers

So what was the problem? Why hasn't cornbread made the Most Beloved New England Foods list? Part of the problem had to do with where it was cooked; part of it had to do with how it was cooked; and part of it had to do with when it was cooked.

Cornbread was cooked in the country. Corn was the staple grain of New England homesteads, the righteous farmers who built a republic—or, as their city-bred grandchildren sneered, those backwoods yokels. Wheat was always available in New England, but it cost more than corn and was generally imported from other parts of the country. Flour arrived via ocean ports through the late eighteenth century and via the Erie Canal and railroads from the 1820s onward. In eighteenth-century Boston, the bread available in bakeries was made of wheat flour, and wheat bread was generally available only at bakeries.

Most urban families relied on bakery bread because baking wheat bread required

- an oven, which in colonial times meant either an outdoor beehive oven—a misery to fire and use in the winter—or an indoor oven attached to a fireplace, which was a misery to use in the summer
- the time to fire a hot oven up to 500°F or more, which could take several hours

- the money to buy enough firewood to bring the oven up to 500°F or to pay bakers for space in their oven
- the space to have a wood-fired oven in or near your house
- enough space in that oven to contain as many loaves of bread in a day as days you'd like to wait before embarking on another 10-hour bread-baking ordeal

Much like the twentieth-century New England home builders who neglected to include air conditioning in basic house designs, colonial urbanites also liked to pretend that summer doesn't exist, and did not include outdoor "summer kitchens" in their homes. Producing wheat bread during summer months would have made houses astonishingly overheated. Humble cornbread or corn-and-rye bread could be baked in an iron "spider" skillet with a cover right on top of a few coals,[19] minimizing the heat inside the house.

Bostonians seem to have ignored their cornmeal options even when wheat was scarce. During a series of 37 Boston food riots in Boston up to and during the Revolutionary War (1775–1778), "the people" reportedly seized bread, flour, tea, sugar, and coffee—but never cornmeal.[20]

By the 1850s, most New England homes switched from cooking on tree glutton fireplaces to iron stoves fired with wood or coal.[21] They were far more fuel-efficient, but they changed how women cooked. In general, their ovens were smaller, so home bread bakers had to bake it more frequently if they wanted to keep their families carbo-loaded. And unlike fireplaces, which sent most of their heat up the chimney, stoves projected much more of their heat straight into the room, making summer high-temperature bread baking almost unbearable.[22]

Cornbread, gentle, forgiving cornbread, could be cooked on the family hearth. All of the most common colonial corn foods—cornbread, hominy, samp (another name for hominy), Indian pudding, and so on—were boiled or baked at home, and most were far from delicate morsels. They were heavy and dense because they weren't leavened.

Does Your Cornbread Have Chemistry?

Today's commercial cornbread mixes produce a pale, light, sweet cornbread thanks to that miracle of nineteenth-century industrial chemistry, baking powder. Before baking powder, baker's options for making a cornbread fluffy were pretty much limited to either using yeast and waiting—and waiting—or beating a bunch of eggs until they foamed, folding them into the dough, and hoping that the whole thing wouldn't collapse in the oven like a date-night disaster souffle.

The first widely available leavening that didn't require beating eggs with iron biceps or waiting for yeast to deign to reproduce was pearl ash or potassium carbonate, a chemical leavening which came into American culinary use in the 1790s. Pearl ash enjoyed the honor of being a subject of the first ever US patent, granted on July 1, 1790, for "the making Pot ash and Pearl ash by a new Apparatus and Process."[23] Before then, colonial chefs had three options for leavening their foods: yeast, potash, or hartshorn.

Hartshorn, or baker's ammonia, was available in colonial Boston and was used by apothecaries for smelling salts to revive people from fainting spells.[24] As you might imagine from its name, when it is used in baking, hartshorn releases ammonia, stinking up the kitchen.[25] The gas rapidly dissipates, but in the era before electric kitchen fans, the stench was discouraging.

If the colonial baker brewed beer or hard cider at home or lived near a brewery or distillery, she would have had a ready source of yeast in "emptins"—the yeasty substance left at the bottom of barrels of beer or cider after they're emptied.[26] Amelia Simmons's *American Cookery*, reputed to be the first American cookbook, gives a recipe for propagating emptins by combining them with water boiled with hops, but some emptins are needed to start the process.[27] And once you have emptins, of course, you have to deal with wild yeasts that might or might not raise your corn bread depending on how warm and moist your drafty New England kitchen was in the middle of January.

Pearl ash is a refined version of potash, and adds a bitter aftertaste to baked goods. As historical gastronomy author Sarah Lohman observes, "The earliest recipes to use pearlash were gingerbread recipes. Of the four recipes in [Amelia] Simmons' [1796] cookbook, half of them were for gingerbread. A highly spiced gingerbread probably did a lot to hide the taste of the bitter base chemical."[28]

All in all, making leavened home-baked goods was a challenge during the colonial era—and even more so for city dwellers who might not have a ready supply of wood ashes and emptins or a brick oven. Any boiled corn dish was liable to become mush. Any baked corn dish was liable to be thick, dense, and leaden. So there was dogged, reliable corn: dependable, reliable, dull, and heavy, the sort of thing people eat at home. How could it compete with fine, fluffy wheat bread, bought in big-city bakeries?

It couldn't. Opting for wheat bread wasn't cheap, although it was likely more economical than renovating a wooden house to include a brick oven. During the colonial period, wheat flour cost anywhere from 35 percent to 100 percent more than cornmeal—but people bought it anyway, whenever they could.[29]

"Bostonians were faced with the paradox of short supply at the same time quantities of grain passed through the city, bound for foreign ports."[30] There were grain riots in Boston in 1713 because of a shortage of wheat; the price had increased from 7 to 9 shillings per bushel.[31] On May 20, 1713, Bostonians attempted to loot a warehouse where they thought wheat was being stored. The warehouse was empty, but Boston's Selectmen were sufficiently spooked by the violence that they voted for funds to supply a public granary to store wheat and sell it when the price climbed too high.[32] This granary was never actually used; after the 1713 riot, Bostonians began substituting cheaper corn and rye for wheat. When the price of wheat increased again in 1719, the Selectmen talked about buying wheat in Connecticut to feed Boston—an odd parallel to the West Indies approach of buying food instead of raising it on land devoted to sugarcane.

Ashes to Ashes

In the 1790s, pearl ash was a relatively new, refined form of potash. Potash is the residue left behind when wood ashes are soaked in water to make lye, then heated to evaporate the water. Using ashes in cooking corn wasn't new. The Abenaki had boiled whole corn with ashes to make hominy and soups for hundreds of years,[33] as had the Navajo, Hopi, and every other Native American group who ate corn.[34] Cooking or soaking corn kernels with an alkaline substance—wood ash lye is alkaline—and then cooking them is also called nixtamalization. This process makes corn's vitamin B3 (niacin) and protein much more accessible to human digestion.

People who get a majority of their calories from corn and don't nixtamalize it end up with a miserable vitamin deficiency disease called pellagra, which causes peeling, scaly skin, hair loss, chronic diarrhea, dementia, and death.[35] Europeans and their slaves didn't adopt Native American corn traditions, and when Americans in the Southeast began to rely on corn, the results were grim. From 1900 through the 1940s, more than three million cases of pellagra were recorded in the American Southeast, causing 100,000 deaths.[36]

But pearl ash was what modern-day activists would call an industrial chemical, used to manufacture pottery, china, and soap.[37] Who thought of putting it in cookies?

Pearl ash wasn't used by European Americans to make baked goods until at least the mid-eighteenth century, although the historical record about the stuff is muddy. The first published recipe using potash was a 1753 Dutch recipe for pretzels,[38] and some authors think that American home cooks learned to use pearl ash from Dutch immigrant professional bakers in New York's Hudson River Valley.[39]

Pearl ash was a finicky leavening. It worked only if the dough was acidic, and baked goods made with pearl ash had to be baked immediately after mixing so they wouldn't deflate. Traces of undissolved pearl ash could leave a bitter aftertaste, and pearl ash concentrations weren't standardized, so baked goods sometimes failed to rise even when baked goods were catapulted straight into a waiting oven.[40]

A commercial baking soda called saleratus became available around the 1830s, and baking powder was introduced about two decades later.[41] Saleratus was just pearl ash with carbonic acid added to make it rise more reliably. Saleratus's reign was short, though, as it still had a bitter aftertaste. Saleratus was also viewed suspiciously compared to wholesome (unreliable, unstandardized) yeast.

An 1855 *Scientific American* column warned of the dangers of chemical leavenings:

> There must be great danger indeed, in such a free and ignorant use of saleratus, without an acid, as a pound per month in any family. It is a common

thing, however, in the country, to use sour milk with the saleratus, and there is not so much danger in its use when so combined, but, we must say, that saleratus, and those combinations of chemicals which merely produce effervessence, and not vinous fermentation, should not be used in cooking.

Experience is the only way to tell what is good and what is evil to use as food or drink, and so far as our experience goes, and we have paid close attention to it for the past three years, we must conclude that yeast alone should be used for raisings in domestic cookery.[42]

Baking soda, or sodium bicarbonate, came on the market in 1846. It wasn't as bitter as saleratus, but still needed an acid to make its lovely bubbles. The 1860s saw Eben Horsford's commercial introduction of what we now know as baking powder—a combined acid and sodium bicarbonate in a can, ready to raise whatever comes near.[43]

Baking powder came to New England too late to save its cornbread, though. By the 1860s, New England was using corn—the Pilgrims' sustenance, the carb that nourished the Puritan forefathers—as animal feed and an occasional amusement, not as a dietary staple.

Some Americans doubted that animals could be raised without corn at all. In a 1911 congressional hearing about trade with Canada, one Mr. Crumpacker of Indiana declared, "Talk about raising cattle and hogs in Canada! They have no corn to feed them. They feed all the oats they raise to their horses and sheep. Oats, hay, and barley are all the feed they have."[44] Somehow, the fact that the entirety of Europe had raised cattle without recourse to corn for several millennia escaped the gentleman's attention.

The Collapse of Corn Bread

Port cities like Boston, Providence, and Portland always had an easy supply of wheat flour grown in the fecund, fertile Mid-Atlantic states of New York, Pennsylvania, and Virginia. After almost two centuries of relying on corn for sustenance, if not pleasure, New Englanders in inland areas began to abandon all their cornmeal concoctions as soon as the Erie Canal was finished in 1825 and wheat flour from upstate New York could be bought cheaply.[45] Wheat flour also got substantially less expensive around 1790 to

1840 as technology made it easier to harvest wheat and mill the flour[46]—
and to mill fluffy white flour without pesky wheat germ or bran instead of
dour old brown whole wheat.[47] Yet New Englanders have historically had
an ambivalent attitude toward wheat bread, as the yeast used to make the
bread was taken from the yeast used to brew beer.

With railroads linking New England to New York State from the 1840s
onward, wheat was everywhere—especially in the new "mill towns,"[48] the
explosively expanding manufacturing cities from Connecticut to Maine
that attracted thousands of immigrants. Most of these immigrants from
French-speaking Quebec and Ireland came from communities that never
used cornmeal in the first place.

It wasn't just rich city folk who decided to stop eating corn. Between
1795 and 1830, New England farmers transformed themselves from hale
and hearty yeomen of yore into capitalists. As New England farmers made
more money, they spent less time growing—and eating—subsistence crops
like corn. The percentage of New England farming households that kept
corn and rye on hand fell from 83 to 70 percent, judging by probate records
for rural residents of Middlesex County, Massachusetts.[49] The actual percentage of people using corn was probably even lower than that in 1830
because probate records tend to be lagging indicators of social change. The
people whose belongings are recorded in probate courts were generally old
enough to be dead, so they tended to be a little behind the times. However,
New Englanders weren't adopting a low-carb diet. In the same period, the
percentage of households left with potatoes at the time of death swelled
from 37 percent to 59 percent.[50]

New England's urban population also began expanding rapidly even
before the textile mills were built in Maine, and smart farmers who lived
near waterways, roads, and later railroads quickly realized that although
they could make a decent living by growing most of their own food, they
could make cold, hard cash by selling milk, butter, cheese, and fresh fruit
and vegetables to city markets.[51]

New England farmers also abandoned growing grain because they couldn't
predict from one year to the next whether they could actually grow a crop.
Between 1750 and 1850, New England's climate became much warmer, which
normally would have been a good thing. But as today's weather watchers
know, change can be terrifying when it's *your* weather that's changing.

In New England, the shifting winds and weather patterns meant that the growing season wobbled and lurched, making it impossible to figure out when to plant and harvest corn. The growing season—the time between the last spring frost and the first killing frost of fall—was roughly 240 days in Massachusetts in 1815 but just *80 days* in 1816—the famous "year without a summer"—according to contemporary temperature records from Cambridge, Massachusetts. There were at least 13 years in that interval when there weren't enough growing days for corn to mature at all. Under those circumstances, growing food for your family was a losing proposition.[52] Better to ship off beef and timber to the West Indies and buy your corn from some luckier farmer in Pennsylvania.

By the 1840s, corn also had an unsavory association: slavery. Cornmeal was generally the only grain given to southern slaves.[53] An 1842 health book reported, "The house slaves partake of the fare of their superiors with the exception of a more restricted use of wheat bread; but this cannot be called a privation among a people with whom as in the case of those of the south and west, maize is the bread corn and the preferred one of the country. . . . Indian corn is in many States the chief bread corn, and to the slave population almost entirely so."[54]

Corn for the Poor

Some New Englanders had nauseating experiences with corn before they even arrived in the United States. The Irish introduction to corn was appalling. In 1846, to help alleviate the famine caused by the 1845 potato blight, English authorities imported "Indian meal" (cornmeal) from America as a cheap food source. Asenath Nicholson, a Vermont-bred Protestant who had the moxie to become a missionary to Catholic Ireland, wrote in 1851 about the Irish experience with the rice and Indian meal that had been imported from America:

> The rice and Indian meal, both of which are excellent articles of food, were cooked in such a manner that in most cases they were actually unhealthy and in all cases unpalatable. So unused were they [the Irish] to the use of that common article rice that they steeped it the night before, then poured the water off without rubbing, and for three and four

hours they boiled stirred and simmered this till it became a watery jelly, disgusting to the eye and unsavory to the taste, for they never salted it; besides unwholesome for the stomachs of those who had always used a dry potato for food. The poor complained that it made them sick; they were accused of being ungrateful, and sometimes told they should not have any more; and the difficulty, if possible, was increased by giving it out uncooked—for the starving ones in the towns had no fuel and they could not keep up a fire to stew it for hours, and many of them ate it raw which was certainly better when they had good teeth than cooked in this unsavory way.

But the Indian meal! Who shall attempt a description of this frightful formidable! When it first landed the rich, who had no occasion for using it, hailed it with joy, and some actually condescended to say They believed they could eat it themselves. . . . The Indian meal by some was stirred in cold water with a stick, then put quite dry upon a griddle, it consequently crumbled apart, there was no turning it. . . . Others made what they call "stirabout"; this was done too by first steeping in cold water, then pouring it into a pot, and immediately after swelling it became so thick that it could not be stirred, neither would it cook in the least. The "stirabout" then became a "standabout," and the effect of eating this was all but favorable to those who had seldom taken farinaceous food. They were actually afraid to take it in many cases, the *government* meal in particular, fearing that the "Inglish intinded to kill them with the tarin and scrapin," but when hunger had progressed a little, these fears subsided, and they cared neither what they ate or who sent it to them.[55]

The Irish weren't entirely to blame. The corn that the English sent wasn't hulled, and its hard shell made it difficult to grind the flour into edible meal[56]—no one thought of boiling it with ashes to make hominy—and much of the imported corn was water damaged and spoiled.[57]

Meanwhile, Back in New England . . .

By 1840, cornmeal and rye were already going extinct in New England. As the Massachusetts Agricultural Commissioner complained that year,

Public manners in this matter have undergone considerable change within the last quarter of a century. Bread made of rye and Indian meal, was then always to be found upon the tables in the country; and, in parts of the state, was almost exclusively used. Wheat flour was then comparatively a luxury. Now brown bread, as it is termed, is almost banished from use. No farmer gets along without his superfine flour, his bolted wheat; and the poorest family is not satisfied, without their wheat or flour bread.[58]

Although it might sound like the commissioner was about to launch a paean to the virtues of humble corn, he didn't. Instead, he went on in a lengthy harangue about how Massachusetts sends too much money off to Upstate New York for wheat flour, and that Massachusetts farmers ought to grow more wheat. Clearly, Massachusetts farmers weren't interested.

Around the time that various authorities claimed that no one in the North ever ate corn bread, northerners started claiming there were differences between northern and southern cornbread. The author of the 1854 *Hall's Journal of Health*, published in New York, stated

Corn Bread, the "Indian" of the North, when properly made and of suitable materials, is a sweet healthful and delightful article of food. We seldom see southern corn bread on a northern table because the meal is ground entirely too fine and becomes soggy in the baking: to obviate this sogginess and its effects on the system, northerners put physic in their meal and make it *sometimes* apparently as good as the southern bread, whose only constituents are meal itself, a little milk, and some salt.[59]

The author goes on to give a corn bread recipe with "physic"—cream of tartar and baking soda—and a physic-free version with flour.

In the 1850s, eating cornmeal was humiliating, according to an 1858 *American Farmers' Magazine* article: "There are thousands of poor families in New England who do not know one week where the next week's supplies are to come from, who would feel a sort of degradation in living on corn bread and if they resort to it occasionally eat slyly and by stealth that it may not be known that they are so poor as to live on Indian meal."[60] Or as a New Hampshire writer put it in 1851, "There is a stupid prejudice throughout Free States against the use of corn as an article of human food, which seems to be on a presumption that it is a coarse and homely grain, designed for hogs and cattle. In the South this prejudice is unknown and bread of various kinds and other of this grain are constantly provided and used in every household from highest to lowest."[61]

Still, consumption of corn, physic-free or not, continued to decline in New England. Even cows stopped eating New England corn after the Civil War. From the 1870s onward, farmers began making silage—livestock fodder out of green plants that are fermented in a silo. Green corn stalks and half-ripened ears were perfect for feeding dairy cows and reduced the amount of pasture land farmers needed.[62]

A 1926 Connecticut agricultural report also talked about human corn-meal consumption in the past tense:

> We have seen that maize was the staple crop and staple cereal food of the settlers in the seventeenth century. Gradually, wheat displaced it, at first only among the more prosperous in the centers. But baked in thin cakes, forerunner of the "hoe cake" of the South, cooked as "hasty pudding," with molasses as a sauce, later made into bread with rye ("rye and Injin"), corn meal was widely used in the country in the eighteenth and early nineteenth centuries, and now, while it has almost passed as a family food, it has not passed from some of us as a not unpleasant boyhood memory. . . .
>
> The fact that corn is the only food crop which has not declined but actually increased since 1880, is explained by its extensive use in dairy feeding.[63]

Corn for the Ungrateful Poor

One New Englander who was enthusiastic about corn was Ellen Swallow Richards. Her 1890s New England Kitchens, the outlets for training young women in economical cookery and selling cheap food to the poor, were practically corn sales outlets. Out of 32 items sold at the New England Kitchen to poor immigrants living in Boston slums, eight were forms of corn and five were variations on boiled corn: corn soup, corn mush, boiled white hominy, boiled yellow hominy, corn cakes, Indian pudding, brown bread, and "Aladdin Hash" (hominy with meat.)[64]

Richards, the industrious, brilliant, and misguided scientist and social reformer, complained that the poor were spending too much money on wheat flour: "The $200 which a Lowell factory operative spends on food out of his $360 total income is largely spent on costly meat, sugar, butter, and fine flour instead of on well-chosen cuts of meat, peas, beans, and cornmeal. He could have secured better nutrition for $100 and have $100 to put into better shelter and a dress for his wife who had had none since her marriage seven years before."[65] In 2017 dollars, the $200 of food spending that Richards is discussing comes to about $6,000 per year, or $16 per day. In 2018, the average American household spent roughly $7,000 per year on food,[66] or $19 per day—but many Lowell factory "operatives" were supporting a wife and children.

Of course, Richards didn't ask the wife if she would prefer to save a few pennies by spending hours simmering a batch of split pea mush or just fry up a juicy steak at the end of a long day of tending children, re-darning socks, and washing coal soot out of her family's clothing by hand. Immigrants who arrived in Boston and mill towns around the region in the nineteenth century had few pleasures. Factory work was hard, hours were long, and gray, damp winters were miserable in cramped, underheated (or unheated) apartments, especially as the cheerlessness extended into months when Sicilian lemon trees would be unfurling their blossoms and old neighbors in Quebec would be laughing together and boiling down maple sap to make taffy on new-fallen snow. One of the few pleasures poor and working-class immigrants had was the ability to buy and eat foods that were rare and expensive in their home countries—especially large pieces of meat.[67]

In America, even poor work men could buy fresh steaks and chops cut to savor in great gaping mouthfuls, not just tough salted meats to provide faint flavorings in cauldrons of gruel. Americans ate an average of a half a pound of meat per person per day in the nineteenth century, and even more if they were affluent.[68] As Richards wrote, "'Where in the old country do you find a workman that can have meat on his table three times a day?' said one of our German neighbors. For this man American freedom and prosperity had a very limited meaning." And yet it did have a meaning, a very strong, concrete, positive meaning for people who had faced starvation and had watched stunted children wither from malnourishment. Why *shouldn't* American prosperity mean that a work man could eat three meat meals a day?

Or, to put it differently, why were American work men being paid so poorly that they could not afford middle-class food, decent shelter, and a new dress every few years? As Harvey Levenstein wrote about Edward Atkinson, the main financial backer of Ellen Richards's New England Kitchen, "A lifelong Democrat and laissez-faire man, he sought ways to break through the Malthusian knot and improve the lot of the working classes without resort to labor unions, unnatural increases in wages, or other measures which went against the immutable laws of supply and demand."[69]

Even some of Richards's supporters were leery of corn. An 1895 edition of *New England Kitchen* features an essay by Dr. Mary E. Green titled "The New Era in Food Supplies," which blames industrial processing for corn's demise.

> The corn of the long ago was carefully dried and cured in the home. It was then crushed into meal or coarsely ground into samp. The whole grain was soaked in a lye then cooked making an excellent food. Again, it was crushed and made into a cake similar to the polenta of the Mexicans. How sweet and nourishing it was we know for the merits of hasty pudding have long been sung by our poets.
>
> Today our corn is so hastily stored and cured that its flavor is lost. By huge steel knives it is cut into hominy grits and meal, but the sweetness of the corn as it developed braided and hung in long rows along kitchen walls outside in the sun or in dry warm attics is no longer known. The corn bread of today has lost its flavor; thus the new era has come into being with the shattering of another ideal. Effort is being made to utilize corn more extensively. This should in a measure succeed, but corn flour cannot replace wheat flour, as it is lower in the strength-giving elements.[70]

Ironically, one of the few places New England flint corn was appreciated was Italy, where so many immigrants to New England had been born in the late nineteenth century. New England Eight Row Flint corn became Italy's Otto File, prized for its flavorful polenta.[71] The fact that a food has been abandoned by a region or a culture doesn't mean it isn't tasty. What it means in this case is that New Englanders simply could not appreciate cornmeal mush, no matter how delicious it might have been.

Suspicious Wheat

Wheat wasn't always pure and beneficent, though. Sylvester Graham railed against commercial bakers in his 1837 *A Treatise on Bread, and Bread-Making*, published in Boston, which stated that bakers "sometimes purchase large quantities of old spoiled flour from New Orleans and elsewhere, which has heated and soured in the barrel, and perhaps become almost as solid as a mass of chalk so that they are obliged to break it up, and grind it over, and spread it out and expose it to the air, in order to purify it in a measure from its acid and other bad properties; and then they mix it with a portion of much better flour and from this mixture they can make as they say the very largest and finest looking loaf."[72] Of course, Graham also believed that white flour would make Americans sick and "soft"—physically weak and weak-willed. He promoted coarse, brown bread made with "Graham flour," which we now call whole wheat, as the cure for all ills.[73]

Sarah Josepha Buell Hale warned in her 1839 *The Good Housekeeper*,

> In Europe, flour is often adulterated that is mixed with other substances to swell its bulk and weight. Whiting, ground stones, and bones and plaster of Paris are the ingredients chiefly used. . . .
>
> The rich will find several advantages in having a portion at least of their bread baked at home even though the saving of money should not be an object. They can be certain that their bread is made of good flour. This is not always sure when eating baker's bread. Much damaged flour, sour, musty, or grown is often used by the public bakers particularly in scarce or bad seasons. The skill of the baker and the use of certain ingredients (alum, ammonia, sulphate of zinc, and even sulphate of copper it is said has been used!) will make this flour into light white bread. But it is nearly tasteless and cannot be as healthy or nutritious as bread made from the flour of good sound wheat baked at home without any mixture of drugs and correctives.[74]

Hale's attitudes toward bakers are a little puzzling because by the time she wrote *The Good Housekeeper*, bakers had been supplying Bostonians' daily bread for more than 200 years.[75] You'd think someone would have noticed that Sam Adams and Paul Revere were eating copper sulfate, or that Hale would see that home baking in urban homes was a losing proposition. Poor women didn't have the time or ovens available for baking; and rich women could afford to buy their bread from bakers with more wholesome reputations. But, like many health enthusiasts across the centuries, Hale believed that the option that consumed the most possible time and energy from women was the best way to promote health—as though draining an urban wife's energy would magically transfuse her invested labor into her family's bloodstream.

Even breads that were only partly made of cornmeal became unrecognizable. In colonial days, brown bread was simply thirded bread—the economical bread made with one-third corn, one-third rye, and one-third wheat flour. This solid if dull bread had a makeover sometime after wheat bread became the norm. By 1850, the rye-corn-wheat bread had been doused with a couple good slugs of milk and molasses and emerged as a kind of gigantic breakfast muffin called brown bread.[76] When your bread is 20 percent molasses by weight, it's hard to taste that there's any grain in the stuff at all, much less that it's made of more than one type of grain. You don't have to worry about how Boston brown bread had "become utterly worthless by the introduction of Western corn meal made often of damaged corn and tasteless Western rye to match," as Thomas Hazard complained in 1915.[77]

Corn Bread: New England Symbol of . . . What?

By 1902, the main way New England residents were enjoying corn, the grain of the forefathers,[78] was at breakfast.

As James O'Connell puts it in his history of Boston restaurants, "Corn bread, which many think of as a Southern dish, was a traditional food item that evolved into a regional specialty. It is still served in local landmark restaurants such as Durgin-Park and Jacob Wirth."[79] In January 2019, Durgin-Park closed after 191 years of serving dull food,[80] and the only place corn appeared on the Jacob Wirth menu in 2018 was in the form of "Jake's Nacho Platter"[81]—and later that year, Jacob Wirth closed as well after a fire. And yet this "regional specialty" was reportedly nearly extinct in Massachusetts in 1840.

What happened? Why did a few "landmark restaurants"—that is, self-consciously Yankee restaurants—decide to adopt cornbread as a sort of culinary pet? A 1925 menu from Durgin-Park doesn't mention cornbread at all.[82] Still, there are glimmers that sweet, wheatey cornbread was identified with the Northeast. A 1912 edition of *The New England Cook Book*—published in New York—features a tourist-restaurant-style "Boston corn cake" cornbread with flour and sugar in the biscuit section of the book.[83]

The transition from historic all-corn breads to corn-and-wheat breads seems to have happened very early among cookbook-reading northerners. An 1886 cookbook published by the New York–based Royal Baking Powder Company lists 21 different recipes for cornbread submitted by women living in states from Rhode Island to Michigan to Nevada. Every single recipe contains wheat flour, a sweetener (sugar or molasses), or both—except for an "Alabama Johnny Cake" submitted by a woman from Preston, Ohio, which contains cooked rice.[84]

At some point in the twentieth century, someone decided that corn bread was a Yankee tradition and that it should be made with sugar, flour, milk, eggs, and baking powder. Was it because of Colonial Revival fervor? A desire to make a cornbread that wasn't southern (as made by southern whites, at least)? Muffin envy? The doctoral dissertation on this subject has yet to be written. What is clear is that this "traditional food item" didn't exist before chemical leavening became available in New England—which was long after most New Englanders had stopped eating cornmeal.

By 2010 cornbread had become a New England tradition because it had been served in restaurants like Durgin-Park since the 1930s. But it wasn't a tradition before then, and it isn't any more traditional or unique to New England than an Italian grinder (sub) sandwich.

Even in 1848, northern writers were prattling about how the only American dishes were made with corn, while ignoring the entire southern United States. For example, a writer in New York–based *The Knickerbocker* magazine—a writer supposedly from "Angola" Iowa—asserted in "A Chapter on Eating," "Americans have few national dishes saving and excepting those made of the Indian corn. What better dish than a good Johnny cake?"[85]

By the end of the nineteenth century, most cornmeal in the United States was grown in the Midwest, not the South. Instead of cooking with the traditional white cornmeal grown on southern farms, most southerners bought their cornmeal at the store—and that cheap Midwestern meal was yellow, not white. Yellow corn was far better adapted to industrial milling than was white meal, which meant that it was also the cornmeal that most northerners used—and Midwesterners, and Seattleites, and pretty much everyone else in the country.[86]

The yellow cornmeal wasn't as sweet as the white cornmeal, so African American cooks started adding sugar to their cornbread—and white tastemakers began declaring that the only proper cornmeal for making cornbread was white (what a coincidence!), with no sugar—that is, the cornbread that wasn't made by African Americans.[87] A 1948 excerpt from the *Los Angeles Times* makes the reasoning explicit: "Northerners, however, prefer the yellow meal. These preferences have their roots in the Civil War. Northern soldiers on the drives into the South learned to make cornbread from the field negroes, who often were cooks for the Union forces. They used the yellow meal and when the boys in blue went back home, they showed their women folks how to do it."[88]

Curiously, African American recipes for cornbread—as recorded in early twentieth-century cookbooks—started adding more and more sugar to cornbread at about the same time that Yankee cooks were submerging beans with molasses. The amount of sugar in these recipes rose from one tablespoon at the turn of the century to half a cup in the 1936 *The Eliza Cookbook* published by the Negro Culinary Arts Club.[89]

Yet southern cooks weren't always cornbread purists. An 1866 cookbook titled *A Domestic Cook Book: Containing a Careful Selection of Useful Receipts for the Kitchen* is the oldest known published cookbook by an African American. The author, Malinda Russell, was a former slave who worked as a cook in Virginia and Tennessee after she was freed. Russell fled northern troops in 1864 and published her cookbook in Michigan in 1866, including a recipe for "Indian Meal Batter Bread" that combines a quart of cornmeal with a half pint of flour—and no leavening.[90]

The idea that "northern" cornbread, made with wheat flour and sugar, is different from "southern" cornbread became a point of pride sometime in the early twentieth century. A writer in a 1925 edition of *Boy's Life* declared, "In North among the Yankees they spoil cornbread by mixing it with wheaten flour and sugar—that is, spoil it for the Southern taste."[91] The 1847 *Carolina Housewife* contains recipes for "Chicora Corn Bread," which has both sugar and wheat flour, and "Virginia Egg Bread," which has wheat flour.[92] A 1901 cookbook published by the *New Orleans Times-*

Picayune features a "Nonpareil Corn Bread" made with both flour and sugar, and a "Steamed Corn Bread," with molasses and flour that looks exceedingly familiar to Boston brown bread devotees.[93]

Still, cornbread fell out of favor in the North—and the Midwest and the West. Europeans in every frontier area of the United States relied on cornmeal and cornbread for calories during pioneer times, but only the South continued to use cornmeal as a primary food source for humans. Even in the Southwest, where corn is the basis for tortillas and essential to Mexican American culture, corn was never as large a part of European American diets as it was in the South—partly because people just ate less grain. A 1941 diet study by the USDA showed that southeasterners ate more than twice as much grain as New Englanders, Midwesterners, and Plains States farmers, about seven pounds of grains per person per week;[94] northerners made up the difference with potatoes. As culinary writer Mark Essig puts it, in the South "cornmeal is food, not feed."[95]

There are several reasons that could explain why cornmeal persisted in the South and not in New England. The South was more rural, which meant that fewer residents could buy bread from bakeries or stores, and there were far fewer immigrants, so a higher proportion of cooks were familiar with cornmeal and its culinary properties. It was also harder to store baked goods in the long, hot, humid southern summers when mold spread quickly over nutritious baked goods. In an era before industrial preservatives, even though kneaded wheat bread's gluten kept it soft, it couldn't keep it from spoiling. There wasn't much point in spending hours kneading and baking loaves of bread at home when you'd just have to make a new batch the next day anyway—and keeping a stove at more than 400°F for more than an hour to bake bread wasn't a very attractive proposition either.

Southerners were also poorer. In 1900, residents of the 11 southern states had about half the per capita wealth of the rest of the country, and a 1919 survey found that the South's per capita income was 40 percent lower than the North's.[96] In 1909—the year of the first southern pellagra epidemic—25 cents would buy 7 pounds of wheat flour but 10 pounds of cornmeal.[97]

Perhaps it was because baking powder became available in the 1870s, making it possible to make everyday cornbread something other than a dense, flat lump, while white flour from Midwestern mills became truly economical only in the 1880s.[98] Whatever the cause, cornbread became identified with the South in a way it never did for the erstwhile corn eaters of the rest of the United States.

Today in New England, "cornbread" is served at "southern" and barbecue restaurants, and cornmeal mush isn't mentioned in polite company. But thousands of New England's home cooks are preparing meals from cornmeal every day—in the form of tortillas, tamales, pupusas, arepas, and atole. The Latino population of New England grew 60 percent from 1990 to 2000 to more than 871,000: today, one in sixteen Massachusetts residents is Latino.[99] Cities from Springfield, Massachusetts, to Manchester, New Hampshire, to Providence, Rhode Island host growing numbers of Mexican, Salvadoran, Guatemalan, and Ecuadorian immigrants. These new Americans are opening markets, running all kinds of restaurants, and baking up a storm at *panaderias*. If "New England" cookbooks and food writers become more open to the foods actually eaten by today's New England residents, perhaps cornmeal will become a northern food once again.

RECIPES

Chapter 1: Who Is a Yankee?

NASAUMP AND SAMP

Adapted from Plimoth Plantation,[1] http://plimoth.org

A traditional Wampanoag dish, nasaump is a sweet variation on "pottage fair"—the dishes of boiled grains, vegetables, and meat that formed the basis of both Native American and English immigrant food in New England in the early seventeenth century.

Samp, by contrast, is the English settlers' variation made with milk. It is supposedly easier to digest than regular boiled hominy, even though it is made of exactly the same corn.

....

NASAUMP

1 1/2 cups cornmeal
1 cup berries strawberries, raspberries, blueberries, or a combination of all three
1/2 cup nuts or seeds such as walnuts, hazelnuts, and/or sunflower seeds, very coarsely ground
1 quart water
Optional: maple syrup or sugar

1. Combine cornmeal, berries, and crushed nuts in a saucepan.
2. Stir in water and cook over medium heat, stirring frequently, until the mixture boils.
3. Turn down the heat to medium-low and simmer, stirring frequently, for 15 minutes, or until the mixture thickens.
4. Taste and add optional maple syrup or sugar if desired. Serve immediately.

Note: Leftover cooled nasaump will thicken. It can be cut into slices and fried.

SAMP

1 cup coarse corn grits—often available in the Latin American food
    section
2 cups water
1/2 cup milk
Sugar to taste

Bring water to a boil in large saucepan with a heavy bottom. Add the corn
grits and stir. Simmer until they are soft, about 10 minutes, and the water
has been absorbed. Serve with milk and sugar.

....

SARAH JOSEPHA BUELL HALE's RYE AND INDIAN BREAD
From *The Good Housekeeper* (1839).[2]

There are many different proportions for the mixture—some put one-third
Indian meal with two-thirds rye; others like one-third rye and two-thirds
Indian; others prefer it half and half.

If you use the largest proportion of rye meal, make your dough stiff so that
it will mold into loaves; when it is two-thirds Indian, it should be softer and
baked in deep earthen or tin pans after the following rules.

Take four quarts of sifted Indian meal; put it into a glazed earthen pan;
sprinkle over it a tablespoon of fine salt; pour over it about two quarts of
boiling water, stir, and work it until every part of the meal is thoroughly
wet; Indian absorbs a greater quantity of water. When it is about milk warm,
work in two quarts of rye meal, half a pint of lively yeast, mixed with a pint
of warm water; add more warm water, if needed. Work the mixture well
with your hands; it should be stiff, but not firm as flour dough. Have ready
a large, deep, well-buttered pan; put in the dough, and smooth the top by
putting your hand in warm water, and then patting down the loaf. Set this
to rise in a warm place in the winter; in the summer it should not be put by
the fire. When it begins to crack on the top, which will usually be in about
an hour or an hour and a half, put it into a well-heated oven, and bake it
three or four hours. It is better to let it stand in the oven all night, unless the
weather is warm. Indian meal requires to be well cooked. The loaf will weigh
between seven and eight pounds. Pan bread keeps best in large loaves.
Many use milk in mixing bread; in the country where milk is plentiful, it is
a good practice, as bread is certainly richer wet with sweet milk than with
water; but it will not keep so long in warm weather.

RYE AND CORNMEAL BREAD, ADAPTED FOR MODERN KITCHENS

4 cups cornmeal
1 teaspoon salt
2 cups rye flour
1 package (2 1/4 teaspoons) dry yeast
2 cups milk, scalded, or 2 cups boiling water

Directions
1. Butter or oil two 9-inch loaf pans.
2. Mix cornmeal and salt in large heat-proof bowl. Pour in 2 cups boiling water or hot scalded milk and stir until well combined. Let rest until lukewarm, 10–15 minutes.
3. Mix yeast into 1/2 cup lukewarm water. Let rest for 10 minutes to proof. Yeast should become foamy; if it does not, discard and get new yeast.
4. Add yeast mixture and rye flour to cornmeal dough. Knead in the bowl until well mixed. Dough should be thick, but not stiff.
5. Divide dough between loaf pans. Smooth the tops with wetted hands, cover with a damp dish towel, and leave in a warm place to rise for an hour, or until the top begins to crack.
6. Preheat oven to 350°F.
7. Bake bread at 350°F for 30 minutes, then reduce oven temperature to 325°F and bake for an additional 30 minutes, or until browned and internal temperature is over 200°F.
8. Serve hot or at room temperature.

ICED PLUM CAKE

Duchess Quamino (1754–1804), a Rhode Island caterer and entrepreneur who used her skill at baking to buy her freedom from slavery, was celebrated for her iced plum cakes. A plum cake is what modern-day cooks would call a fruit cake, and icing at the time would have been a hard, sugary coating cooked onto the cake in a cooling wood oven.

Quamino's recipe is lost to time (if she even shared it). Below are copies and modern adaptations of two contemporary recipes: a plumb cake from Amelia Simmons's 1796 *American Cookery* and "Icing for Cakes" from Maria Eliza Rundell's *A New System of Domestic Cookery*, first published in the United States in 1807.[3]

The plumb cake is not very sweet; the only sugar in the recipe comes from the candied and dried fruits. Modern diners will observe that the cake tastes more like raisin bread or Irish soda bread than today's sugar-laden fruitcakes. This cake is very good eaten warm with butter, or toasted and served with stewed fruit and ice cream.

....

SIMMONS'S PLUMB CAKE

Mix one pound currants, one drachm nutmeg, mace, and cinnamon each, a little salt, one pound of citron, orange peel candied, and almonds bleached, 6 pounds of flour (well dried), beat 21 eggs, and add with 1 quart new ale yeast, half a pint of wine, 3 half pints of cream, and raisins.

....

ADAPTED PLUM CAKE

1 1/2 packages active dry yeast (ca. 1 tablespoon)
1/2 teaspoon sugar
3/4 cup raisins
1/2 cup currents
1/4 cup candied citron, chopped
1/4 cup candied orange peel, chopped
1/4 cup blanched almonds
1/4 teaspoon apiece of ground nutmeg, mace, cinnamon, and salt
6 cups all-purpose flour
6 eggs
2/3 cup heavy cream
1/3 cup sherry or other sweet wine

Directions
1. Preheat oven to 350°F.
2. Place 1/4 cup lukewarm (90–100°F) water in small bowl. Stir in sugar, and sprinkle yeast onto water. Leave yeast to proof while assembling other ingredients, 10 to 15 minutes. Yeast should become foamy; if it does not, discard and get new yeast.
3. Butter two 9-inch loaf pans or a Bundt pan.
4. Mix candied fruit with one tablespoon flour. Set aside.
5. Mix remaining flour, spices, and salt in a large bowl. Set aside.
6. Whisk eggs to combine.
7. Stir in cream, eggs, wine, and proofed yeast into flour mixture. Stir in dried fruit.

8. Pour or spoon batter into prepared pan. Let it rest for 10 minutes to allow yeast to begin rising.

9. Bake cake at 350°F for 30 minutes. Turn oven temperature down to 325°F, and bake for an additional 30 minutes.

10. Insert knife into the center of the cake to test for doneness. If the knife gains gooey or wet crumbs, return the cake to the oven for an additional 10–15 minutes.

11. Follow instructions for plum cake icing, if using.

12. Allow cake to cool completely in the pan before removing.

. . . .

RUNDELL'S "ICING FOR CAKES"

For a large one, beat and sift eight ounces of fine sugar, put into a mortar with four spoonfuls of rose water, and the whites of two eggs beaten and strained, whisk it well, and when the cake is almost cold, dip a feather in the icing, and cover the cake well; set it in the oven to harden, but do not let it stay to discolor. Put the cake in a dry place.

. . . .

PLUM CAKE ICING

8 oz. (1 cup) superfine sugar
4 tablespoons rose water or 1 teaspoon vanilla extract
2 egg whites, beaten and forced through a strainer

Directions

1. Pasteurize egg whites by combining them with the sugar. Place the mixture in a small saucepan, and heat, stirring constantly, over low heat until the mixture reaches 160°F. Remove the pan immediately and strain the mixture into a mixing bowl.

2. Beat egg whites with sugar until frothy. Add rose water or vanilla extract.

3. Spread egg white mixture over surface of cake and return to cool oven (200°F) until frosting is dry, about 20 minutes.

AGNES MCCLOSKEY HEFFERNAN'S BRAN BISCUITS

Born Agnes McCloskey in 1864 in County Londonderry, Ireland, Heffernan immigrated to the United States in 1881 and lived in Thomaston and Bristol, Connecticut. She worked as a servant and in a clock factory before marrying Daniel Heffernan in 1894. In 1909, the Heffernans bought a house, and Agnes began cooking meals for guests—essentially running a restaurant out of her home.

Heffernan's life has been extensively documented by Mary F. Wack—including her recipe notebooks. Many of Heffernan's recipes are clearly copied from popular published sources such as Maria Parloa's cookbooks and include fashionable recipes for "classy" foods like wine jellies, but some seem to reflect what Wack calls the Ulster "leanness principle"—employing far less butter and far more molasses than contemporary American recipes, which relied on sugar. Below is Heffernan's recipe for bran biscuits, a type of cookie. The instructions are adapted for modern kitchens.

....

AGNES MCCLOSKEY HEFFERNAN'S BRAN BISCUITS

Adapted for modern readers from Mary F. Wack's "Recipe-Collecting, Embodied Imagination, and Transatlantic Connections in an Irish Emigrant's Cooking."[4]

2 cups wheat bran
1 cup all-purpose flour
1/2 teaspoon baking soda
1/2 teaspoon salt
1 cup milk
1/4 cup of molasses

Directions
1. Preheat oven to 350°F. Oil a baking sheet, or cover it with parchment paper.
2. Mix bran, flour, baking soda, and salt in a large bowl. Gradually mix milk into molasses in a small bowl, stirring thoroughly to combine.
3. Mix milk mixture into bran mixture. Dough will be stiff.
4. Pat dough or roll dough on lightly floured surface to 1/4-inch thick. Cut into squares or rounds and place on prepared sheet. To make "farls," pat dough into a circle directly on the prepared baking sheet, then cut into eighths.
5. Bake biscuits for 15 minutes or until lightly browned.

FRENCH CANADIAN YELLOW SPLIT PEA SOUP

Adapted from Denise Pare-Watson and Marc Miron.[5]

Some Quebec chefs claim that yellow split pea soup can be traced back to the explorer Samuel de Champlain. Whatever its origin, it has been a popular dish among French Canadians living in New England for at least 150 years. From 1938 to 1983, the Habitant soup company—named for the French Canadian farmers who settled along the Saint Lawrence river from the seventeenth century onward—operated a soup factory outside heavily Franco-American Manchester, New Hampshire, that produced upward of 50,000 cans of yellow split pea soup per day to feed regional demand.

This recipe is a composite of two chefs' French Canadian yellow split pea soup derived from two current-day Canadians, stripped of contemporary imported additions such as bay leaves and lemon juice.

2 tablespoons lard or oil
1 onion, large, diced
2 carrots, diced
2 stalks celery, including leaves, chopped
1 teaspoon dried thyme
10 cups water or broth
1 cup diced ham or 1/2 cup diced salt pork
2 cups dried yellow split peas, rinsed
Salt and pepper to taste

Directions
1. Heat the lard or oil over medium heat in a large stock pot. Add the onion, carrots, and celery. Stir and cook until the vegetables are softened, about 5 minutes.
2. Stir in the water or broth, the ham or salt pork, and the yellow split peas.
3. Bring to a boil, then reduce the heat to a simmer and cover. Simmer, stirring from time to time, until the split peas are soft, about one hour. Add water if soup becomes too thick.
4. Season with salt and pepper and serve.

AUNTIE LAURA'S GUFONG/FUNGINE (CAPE VERDEAN SWEET FRIED DOUGH)

Adapted from Nuala, http://thecoolcook.wordpress.com.[6] There are many, many variants of gufong recipes; this particular one employs an American ingredient (Bisquick) as well as bananas for flavor.

  1 1/2 cups sugar
  1 cup boiling water with a pinch of salt (1/8 teaspoon) added
  1 cup cornmeal
  3 ripe, mashed bananas
  2 cups Bisquick mix
  2 cups all-purpose flour, plus flour for mixing
  Vegetable oil for frying

Directions
1. Mix sugar and salted water in a large saucepan. Bring to a boil over medium heat, then remove from stove.
2. Mix in cornmeal, then add bananas, Bisquick, and flour. Stir until smooth: do not overmix. Mixture should be consistency of bread dough. Let sit until cool enough to handle, 10–20 minutes.
3. Roll dough into 24 logs or 48 small balls. Fry in 350°F oil until golden brown. Drain on paper towels and serve warm.

STUFFED PEPPERS (*PEPERONI RIPIENI*) TWO WAYS

Adapted from *Specialita Culinarie Italiane: 137 Tested Recipes of Famous Italian Foods*, published by the North Bennet Street Industrial School, a nonprofit serving immigrants in Boston's North End in 1936.[7]

These two recipes illustrate North End Italian immigrants' diverse, inventive ways of serving vegetables at a time when Yankee cuisine focused on meat and potatoes, and not much else.

....

STUFFED PEPPERS I

  8 small green bell peppers
  2 cups white bread crumbs
  1/2 cup tomato pulp
  2 anchovy filets
  1/2 cup pitted black olives, finely chopped

1 teaspoon tarragon vinegar, or 1 teaspoon vinegar plus 1/2 teaspoon
    tarragon
6 tablespoons olive oil or vegetable for frying
Salt and pepper to taste

Directions
1. Slice off tops of peppers and remove seeds and veins.
2. Mix remaining ingredients except for oil, tasting before adding salt and pepper—the anchovy filets and olives may add enough salt. Stuff peppers.
3. Heat oil in a frying pan over medium heat. Sauté peppers on each side until browned, 3–5 minutes per side. Serve immediately.

....

STUFFED PEPPERS 2

6 medium green peppers
1 cup bread crumbs
1 glove garlic, minced or crushed
1 teaspoon vinegar
6 sprigs parsley, minced
1 tablespoon raisins
3 tablespoons olive oil plus oil for frying
Salt and pepper

Directions
1. Slice off tops of peppers and remove seeds and veins.
2. Mix bread crumbs, garlic, parsley, and raisins. Add oil and vinegar, and mix until the stuffing is a consistence of a soft paste. Add salt and pepper to taste. Stuff peppers half full.
3. Pour 1/2 inch oil in a frying pan and set pan over medium heat. Sauté peppers on each side until browned, 3–5 minutes per side. Serve immediately.

PIEROGI (POLISH DUMPLINGS)

Adapted from Polish Plate, http://polishplate.com, and the *Polish American Journal*,
http://polamjournal.com.[8]

Pierogi are one of the most common Polish American dishes. Although classic fillings include potatoes, cheese, sauerkraut, mushrooms, and pork, American pierogi makers have used everything from blueberries to Buffalo chicken.

PIEROGI DOUGH

2 1/2 cups flour
1/2 teaspoon salt
1 large egg
2 tablespoons oil
1/4 to 1/2 cup hot water (130°F)
Flour for rolling dough

Directions

1. Heat a large pot of lightly salted water. Beat egg with oil until combined.
2. Mix flour and salt in a large bowl. Pour egg mixture into center of flour and mix. Slowly add hot water to dough, only adding as much as needed to make a smooth, soft dough. Knead briefly in bowl until dough is soft and no longer sticky. Cover bowl with a damp towel and let dough rest 10 minutes, or up to an hour.
3. Roll out 1/3 of the dough at a time on a lightly floured surface to 1/8 inch thick. Cut out dough rounds with a large glass, biscuit cutter, or cookie cutter. Rounds should be 3–4 inches in diameter.
4. To fill and cook: Place 1 tablespoon filling on pierogi rounds. Fold and crimp edges closed with a fork. Drop in boiling salted water, and adjust heat so that water boils gently. Cook pierogi for 7–10 minutes, or until dough is tender.
5. Drain and serve, or fry drained pierogi in 2 tablespoons lard, butter, or oil until lightly browned on both sides. Serve with sour cream, caramelized diced onions, bacon bits, or applesauce.

....

POTATO PIEROGI FILLING

Adapted from the *Polish American Journal*.

There are many, many variations on this filling. You may add farmer's cheese, cheddar cheese, or some fried bacon, or dispense with the potatoes altogether and use sauerkraut, mushrooms, cabbage, leftover meat, blueberries . . . dumplings are a forgiving medium.

3 large potatoes (3 cups), cooked and peeled
2 medium onions, chopped
3 tablespoons butter or oil
Optional: 1 egg, 2 tablespoons bread crumbs, 1 tablespoon diced bacon or
  salt pork

Directions

1. Fry onions in butter or oil over medium heat, stirring, until lightly browned, 8–10 minutes.
2. Mash potatoes with onions. Add water if potatoes are too stiff.
3. Add optional ingredients, if using. Mix.

NEW ENGLAND GREEK PIZZA

Adapted from J. Kenji López-Alt, http://seriouseats.com, and Terrence Doyle, http://vice.com.[9]

The most authentic way to eat New England Greek pizza is to order takeout from your local House of Pizza. A slightly less authentic version can be made by baking pizza at home in a cast-iron skillet, topping it with a combination of cheddar and mozzarella cheese.

Homemade or store-bought refrigerated pizza dough to make a 10-inch pizza
2 tablespoons olive oil

Sauce
2 tablespoons olive oil
1 medium clove garlic, pressed or minced
1/2 teaspoon dried oregano
1/4 teaspoon red pepper flakes
1.5 ounces tomato paste
1 15-ounce can crushed tomatoes
Salt and pepper

Cheese
1/4 pound shredded mozzarella cheese
1/4 pound shredded mild cheddar cheese
Toppings of your choice

Special equipment: 10-inch ovenproof cast iron skillet or other large, oven-safe, rimmed pan.

Directions
1. To make sauce: Heat oil in a saucepan over medium-high heat until the oil simmers. Add garlic, oregano, and pepper flacks and stir for 30 seconds, then add tomato paste. Stir and cook for a minute, then add crushed tomatoes, stir, and reduce heat to a simmer. Cook for an hour, then remove from heat. Add salt and pepper to taste.
2. To assemble and bake pizza: Preheat oven to 500°F and place oven rack in bottom position. Coat cast iron skillet with olive oil. Stretch pizza dough to a 10-inch circle, then place in skillet.
3. Spread 1 cup sauce on dough in skillet. Sprinkle evenly with grated cheese, allowing cheese to reach the pizza edge. Then add toppings.
4. Bake pizza 20 minutes, or until cheese has begun to blister and char. Slide a knife around the pizza edge, then extract pizza carefully with 1 or more long, thin spatulas. Consider waiting for it to cool, then serve.

TILLIE'S PORTUGUESE AMERICAN SAUSAGE, KALE, AND POTATO SOUP

Adapted from Clotilda Medeiros Steele, *Provincetown Portuguese Cookbook*, http://iamprovincetown.com.[10]

The *Provincetown Portuguese Cookbook* features several different variants on kale soup, with various combinations of chouriço and linguiça sausage, commercial soup bases, and flavorings such Campbell's soup, Kitchen Bouquet, and Worcestershire sauce, fresh pork, beans, and vegetables. This recipe is adapted from a soup recipe created by Clotilda "Tillie" Medeiros Steele, a Portuguese American resident of Provincetown.

1 2-inch piece of salt pork (2 ounces)
1 bunch fresh kale, chopped (1 pound / 7 cups chopped)
1 pound linguiça sausage, sliced
1 pound chouriço sausage, sliced
5 large waxy potatoes, diced
2 large onions, sliced
1 15-ounce can (2 cups) of beans such as navy beans, cannellini, or kidney beans

Directions

1. Heat stockpot on medium heat and add salt pork. Cook to render fat, about 5 minutes. Add onions and sauté until soft, about 5 minutes.
2. Add sausages, potatoes, and kale to pot. Pour in enough water to cover (6 cups or more), then bring to a boil. Reduce heat to low and cook until the kale and potatoes are tender, 15–20 minutes. Add the beans and heat through.

....

FALL RIVER CHOW MEIN SANDWICH

Celebrity chef Emeril Lagasse, who grew up in Fall River, Massachusetts, before he moved to New Orleans, created a recipe for making chow mein sandwich gravy from scratch, available at http://splendidtable.com. Most local restaurants and Fall River natives use the Hoo-Mee mix.

Hamburger bun
1 box Hoo-Mee Chow Mein Mix, including gravy and fried chow mein noodles, available at www.famousfoods.com
1 cup cooked chicken, diced
White vinegar to taste

Directions

1. Prepare gravy according to box instructions.
2. Place fried chow mein noodles on bottom bun. Top with chicken and pour on gravy. Place top bun and serve.

Chapter 2: The Truth about Baked Beans

1832 BAKED BEANS

This version of baked beans comes from Lydia Maria Francis Child's 1832 household manual *The American Frugal Housewife*.[11]

Baked beans are a very simple dish, yet few cook them well. They should be put in cold water, and hung over the fire, the night before they are baked. In the morning, they should be put in a colander, and rinsed two or three times; then again placed in a kettle, with the pork you intend to bake, covered with water, and kept scalding hot, an hour or more. A pound of pork is quite enough for a quart of beans, and that is a large dinner for a common family. The rind of the pork should be slashed. Pieces of pork alternately fat and lean are the most suitable; the cheeks are the best. A little pepper sprinkled among the beans, when they are placed in the bean pot, will render them less unhealthy. They should be just covered with water, when put into the oven; and the pork should be sunk a little below the surface of the beans. Bake three or four hours.

....

1832 BAKED BEANS FOR 2019

Adapted from Lydia Maria Francis Child's 1832 household manual *The American Frugal Housewife*.

    2 cups dry small white beans, such as navy beans
    8 ounces salt pork, cut into thin slices
    Pepper

Directions

1. Soak beans overnight in 8 cups water. Drain.
2. Preheat oven to 300°F.
3. Place 1/4 of beans in ovenproof pot with a lid. Cover with 1/4 of salt pork strips and a few grinds of pepper. Continue alternating layers of beans and pork, ending with pork.
4. Pour in enough water to just cover the beans and place in the oven, covered. Cook for three hours, checking occasionally to make sure that beans are still moist. Add water as needed to keep beans just under water.
5. Remove lid and bake for an additional hour, or until beans are tender.

PAUL MAYOTTE'S FRENCH CANADIAN AMERICAN BAKED BEANS

Adapted from Le Comite Franco-Américain de Lowell, Massachusetts.[12]

1 pound small pea beans
1 medium onion, coarsely chopped
1/2 pound salt pork
1/2 teaspoon dried
1 teaspoon black pepper
1 cup maple syrup
Salt

Directions
1. Soak beans in 8 cups water overnight. Drain.
2. Preheat oven to 250°F.
3. Place beans in ovenproof pot with lid with all ingredients except salt and salt pork. Stir. Cut salt pork into 1-inch pieces and place on top of beans. Add enough water to cover beans and pork. Bake in slow oven (250°F) for 8 hours.
4. If you will not be checking beans frequently, cover. Otherwise, bake uncovered and check each hour to see if top of beans is dry. Add water to cover beans to prevent beans from drying. Pork may be left uncovered to brown.

....

LOWELL'S FAMOUS ROCHETTE'S BAKED BEANS

Adapted from Marguerite Lyons, *Lowell Sun*.[13] Rochette's was a longtime French Canadian grocer and deli in Lowell, Massachusetts.

2 pounds dried small white beans, such as pea beans
1 1/2 teaspoons salt
1 pound salt pork cut in 2-inch squares
1/4 cup ketchup

Directions
1. Preheat oven to 350°F.
2. Wash beans thoroughly. Drain beans and pour into 4 1/2-quart bean pot or other tall oven-safe covered baking dish. Add pork, ketchup, salt, and a little water. Stir to mix thoroughly.
3. Add enough water to cover beans and come to 2 inches from the top of the pot. Cover pot and bake for 5 hours at 350°F.
4. Remove lid and cover beans with 1/2 inch of water. Continue baking beans uncovered for 2 hours more, or until the salt pork is cooked to taste. Some people prefer crispy, browned pork on top of their beans; watch to make sure the beans underneath are not dry.

BOSTON BAKED BEANS

Adapted from the Pot Shop of Boston, one of the few remaining purveyors of Boston bean pots.[14]

1 pound (2 cups) dry navy beans
1 1/2 quarts cold water
1 teaspoon salt
1/3 cup brown sugar
1 teaspoon dry mustard
1/4 cup molasses
1/4 pound salt pork
1 medium onion, thinly sliced

Directions
1. Soak beans overnight in 6 cups water in a large saucepan.
2. Add salt to beans and soaking water. Cover and simmer until tender, about an hour.
3. Drain beans, reserving liquid.
4. Preheat oven to 300°F.
5. Measure 1 3/4 cups bean liquid, adding water if needed. Combine with brown sugar, mustard, and molasses.
6. Cut salt pork in half, score one-half, and set aside. Slice the remaining salt pork thinly.
7. Fill an oven-safe pot with a lid with the beans. Place a layer of beans in the pot, then add layers of onion, salt pork slices, and sugar mixture in the pot. Repeat the sequence of layers, then top with the piece of scored pork.
8. Cover pot with lid and bake at 300°F for 5–7 hours, or until beans are tender. Add more liquid if beans become uncovered.

Chapter 3: The Limits of New England Food

SOFT GINGERBREAD

This gingerbread recipe, which appeared in the 1878 *Massachusetts Woman's Christian Temperance Union Cuisine,* may have been similar to the "Molasses Gingerbread" served in the New England Kitchen at the New England–themed Log Cabin Restaurant at the 1877 Philadelphia Permanent Exhibition.[15] Contemporary recipes vary widely in the proportion of ginger to flour, type of leavening—soda, cream of tartar, saleratus, whipped egg whites, or sometimes nothing at all—and methods of mixing—when the methods of mixing are mentioned at all.

> One cup of molasses; one cup of sugar; one half cup of butter; one cup of milk; four cups of flour; two eggs; two teaspoonfuls of cream of tartar; one and one fourth teaspoonfuls of soda; one teaspoonful of ginger; and one half teaspoonful each of cloves and cinnamon.

....

SOFT GINGERBREAD FOR MODERN COOKS

Adapted from the 1878 *Massachusetts Woman's Christian Temperance Union Cuisine* and Maria Parloa's 1880 *Miss Parloa's New Cook Book and Marketing Guide.*

1 cup sugar
1/2 cup unsalted butter (one stick), softened
1 cup molasses
2 eggs
4 cups all-purpose flour
2 teaspoons cream of tartar
1 1/4 teaspoons baking soda
1 teaspoon ginger
1/2 teaspoon cloves
1/2 teaspoon cinnamon

Directions
1. Preheat oven to 350°F. Grease or line a 9-inch square baking dish.
2. Sift flour with dry ingredients in a medium bowl and set aside.
3. Cream softened butter with sugar in a large bowl until light and fluffy. Add molasses and eggs and beat well.
4. Add flour mixture and stir until combined.
5. Bake until lightly browned and a knife inserted in the center comes out clean, about 40 minutes. Cool before slicing and serving.

NEW ENGLAND KITCHEN BEEF BROTH—ALADDIN OVEN RECIPE

This recipe by Mary Hinman Abel and Maria Daniell was featured in *The Science of Nutrition*, an 1895 treatise on the Aladdin Oven they coauthored with Edward Atkinson.[16] The Aladdin Oven was something akin to a kerosene-powered nineteenth century slow cooker that could cook only on low.

The method adopted in the New England Kitchen for making beef broth, for the sick or for the well, is as follows: (Samples may be found at 142 Pleasant street, where many useful ideas may be gathered.)

A large tin vessel has been pre- pared which fills the inside of the oven. Into this twenty pounds of coarse beef bones broken up and twenty pounds of neck or shin cut in moderate-sized pieces are placed; to this material is added fifteen quarts of water, sufficient to cover well.

This is placed in the oven at four o'clock p.m., and the lamp is then lighted.

At seven o'clock p.m., the lamp is refilled, lighted, and left to burn itself out during the night, or in about eight hours.

At six a.m., the broth will be found still nearly at the boiling point, about 204°F. The soup is then strained and cooled, and is ready to be put into jars for sale or seasoned for use.

This broth is a nutritious and easily-digested food, differing from the ordinary beef tea which is mainly a stimulant rather than a food. The meat in very tender condition still contains much nourishment; it is chopped and seasoned so as to be eaten after or with the soup.

MARY HINMAN ABEL'S BREAD PANCAKES

This economical recipe appeared in Abel's 1890 *Practical Sanitary and Economic Cooking Adapted to Persons of Moderate and Small Means.*[17]

FOUNDATION OF EGG BREADS

1 quart milk, 3 eggs, 1 tablespoon butter, and 1 teaspoon salt

To mix: First beat the eggs very light, whites and yolks separately, then the yolks smoothly with the flour and milk, stir the whites in at last very lightly and bake immediately. The eggs must be beaten *very* light, and the batter just of good pouring consistency, thinner than if no eggs were used.
Bread pancakes: Add to the foundation mixture 1 cup flour and 2 cups bread crumbs that have been soaked soft in milk or water and mashed smooth. The batter should be rather thick.
Bake in small cakes, adding more flour if they stick.

SCALLOPED FISH

Ellen Swallow Richards's menu for the economical, terribly nutritious Rumford Kitchen at the 1893 Columbian Exposition in Chicago included "Escalloped Fish." This moniker appears to have been a slightly pretentious title for what other recipe writers called "scalloped fish," or leftover cooked fish baked with white sauce. Various contemporary cookbooks call for making scalloped fish with a stuffing, or oysters, or a variety of other frivolous editions.

Below is a recipe for scalloped fish that appeared in an 1875 edition of *Godey's Lady's Book and Magazine*, a popular women's magazine akin to today's *Good Housekeeping*.[18] In the interest of economical, unsurprising, uninspiring food, Richards would have undoubtedly eliminated the mace and the anchovy sauce—and perhaps the pepper as well.

> *Scalloped Fish*—Any cold fish, one egg, milk, one large blade of pounded mace, one tablespoonful of flour, one teaspoonful of anchovy sauce, pepper and salt to taste, bread crumbs, butter. Pick the fish carefully from the bones and moisten with milk and the egg; add the other ingredients, and place in a deep dish or scallop shells; over with bread-crumbs, butter, the top, and brown before the fire; when quite hot, serve.

....

FISH BALLS

Reformatted from an 1890 edition of the *Boston School Kitchen Text-Book*, this recipe is similar to codfish ball recipes later foisted on home economics students around the nation.[19] Strangely, this recipe does not call for presoaking the salt cod for hours before using—only for a brief wash. It is not clear how or why cooking students were supposed to divide an egg in half.

1 cup potatoes
1/2 cup salt fish
1 teaspoon butter
1/2 egg
Sprinkle of pepper
Fat for frying

Directions
Wash the fish and shred it into half-inch pieces. Pare the potatoes, and if large cut into quarters. Put the potatoes and fish in a stew pan and cover with boiling water. Cook 25 minutes, or until potatoes are soft. Drain very dry, mash fine, add butter, seasoning, and beaten egg. Beat well, shape on a spoon, drop into smoking hot fat, fry till brown, and drain on paper. The same mixture may be cooked as hash.

CATHARINE BEECHER'S WHEAT BREAD OF DISTILLERY, OR BREWER'S YEAST

Author and social reformer Catharine Beecher insisted that homemade bread was essential for family health, but making Beecher-approved bread was a lengthy, tedious process. Below is a bread recipe from her 1846 *Domestic Receipt Book* that calls for yeast acquired at a local distillery. Most of Beecher's recipes call for yeast cultures made at home, another time-consuming step that convinced many American women to patronize their local bakery.

Beecher's instructions for how long to allow the bread to rise, when to put it in the oven, how to prepare a bread oven for baking, and how to tell if the oven is hot enough run to several pages. When a baker is using stone-age cooking technology with no thermostat, she needs to pay close attention to many, many things.

....

WHEAT BREAD OF DISTILLERY, OR BREWER'S YEAST

Reformatted from Catharine Beecher's 1846 *Miss Beecher's Domestic Receipt Book*.[20]

> Take eight quarts of flour, and two of milk, a tablespoonful of salt, a gill and a half of distillery yeast, and sometimes rather more, if not first rate. Take double the quantity of home-brewed yeast.
>
> Sift the flour, then make an opening in the middle pour in a part of the wetting, and put in the salt. Then mix in a good part of the flour. Then pour in the yeast, and mix it well, then add the rest of the wetting, using up the flour so as to make a stiff dough. Knead it half an hour, till it cleaves clean from the hand.
>
> This cannot be wet over night, as, if the yeast is good, it will rise in one or two hours.
>
> Some persons like bread best wet with water, but most very much prefer bread wet with milk. If you have skimmed milk, warm it with a small bit of butter, and it is nearly as good as new milk.
>
> You need about a quart of wetting to four quarts of flour. Each quart of flour makes a common-sized loaf.

MARIA PARLOA'S CREAM MERINGUES

This recipe, which appeared in Parloa's 1880 *Miss Parloa's New Cook Book and Marketing Guide*, was probably similar to the recipe featured in her second demonstration lecture for the new Boston Cooking School in 1879.[21]

....

KISSES

Beat the whites of six eggs to a stiff froth. They should beaten until so light and dry that they begin to fly off of beater.

Stir in a cupful of powdered sugar gently and quickly.

Spread paraffine paper over three boards which about nine by twelve inches.

Drop the mixture by on the boards having perhaps a dozen on each.

Dry in a warm oven for about three-quarters of an hour; then brown them slightly.

Lift from the paper and [group] them together at the base by twos.

A dozen and a [half] can be made from the quantities given.

....

CREAM MERINGUES

These are made similar to kisses but are put on the paper oblong shape and dried two hours.

Take from the board with a spoon remove all the soft part.

Season half a of rich cream with a tablespoonful of sugar and one of or a speck of vanilla and whip it to a stiff froth.

Fill shells with this and join them. Or they may be filled [with] ice cream.

If the meringues are exposed to much heat [they will be] spoiled.

ANCHOVY TOAST WITH EGGS

This recipe, which is essentially scrambled eggs on toast, appeared in the first edition of the *New England Kitchen Magazine* in April 1894, where it was listed under "CHAFING DISH RECIPES, Recently used in Demonstrations by MISS FANNIE FARMER, Principal of the Boston Cooking School."[22] The use of a fashionable table-side cooking appliance—the chafing dish—the emphasis on presentation, with instructions on how to trim the toast squares, and the author's assumption that readers didn't know what anchovies are show the editor's assumptions about the audience's aspirations and lack of culinary sophistication.

ANCHOVY TOAST WITH EGGS

Beat five eggs slightly, add half a teaspoonful of salt, half a spoonful of pepper, and half a cupful of milk or cream.

Put a heaping tablespoonful of butter in the chafing dish, and when melted, add the egg mixture. Stir until the egg is creamy.

Spread slices of toast thinly with anchovy paste, arrange on a platter and pour over them the scrambled eggs. If the crust is cut from the slices of bread before toasting, and the slice cut in squares, it gives a daintier appearance.

The anchovy paste can be had in bottles at thirty-five cents a bottle, and gives a good relish. The anchovy is a fish belonging to the herring family, and has something of the same taste, yet different.

MARIA PARLOA'S FROZEN CABINET PUDDING WITH APRICOT SAUCE

This pudding, which appeared in Parloa's 1880 *Miss Parloa's New Cook Book and Marketing Guide,* was the dessert course in a dinner party that also included roast chicken, baked fish, fried oyster parties, and a cheese souf-flé.[23] All these dishes required different cooking techniques at different temperatures, most likely by different servants.

FROZEN CABINET PUDDING

Two dozen stale lady fingers
One cupful of English currants
One pint of cream
One pint of milk
One small tea cupful of sugar
Three eggs
Three tablespoonfuls of wine

Put the milk in the double boiler. Beat the eggs and sugar together and gradually pour the hot milk on them. Return to the boiler and cook two minutes, stirring all the while.

Pour the hot custard on the lady fingers, add the currants, and set away to cool. When cold, add the wine and the cream whipped to a froth. Freeze the same as ice cream.

When frozen, wet a melon mould in cold water, sprinkle a few currants on the sides and bottom, and pack with the frozen mixture. Pack the mould in salt and ice for one hour.

At serving time, wipe it and dip in warm water for a moment. Turn out the pudding on a dish, pour apricot sauce around it, and serve.

APRICOT SAUCE

One cupful of canned apricot
One of sugar
One of milk
One tablespoonful of corn starch
Half a cupful of water

Put the milk in the double boiler. Mix the corn starch with a few spoonfuls of cold milk and stir into the boiling milk. Cook ten minutes.

Boil the sugar and water together for twenty minutes. Rub the apricot through a sieve and stir it into the syrup. Beat well, and then beat in the boiled milk and corn starch.

Place the sauce pan in a dish of cold water and stir for about eight minutes. Set away to cool.

If you have cream, use it instead of the milk. All kinds of fruit can be used in pudding sauces by following this rule. If the fruit is preserved, use less sugar, and if very acid use more.

BOILED DINNER: FROM THE *New England Farmer*, 1864

This "recipe" is really just general advice about technique and timing.[24] Note that this dinner includes pork and squash.

To get dinner ready at twelve o'clock, the general hour for dinner at the farm-house, corned beef should be put on by eight, or half-past eight, in hot water; beets washed clean, but not cut, by nine, cabbage by half past; pork about ten; pease, parsnips, and turnips by half past; squash by eleven and potatoes by half past.

By making this your rule, your dinner will be nicely done so that you can take out your squash and butter it, adding pepper and salt and a spoonful of sugar if it is not nice and sweet; mash your turnips smooth, adding pepper and salt—don't forget the pepper; peel the parsnips and beets, cutting the beets into quarters if large, having peeled by dropping them hot into a pan of cold water, and slipping the outside off with the hand, using now fork or knife, and have you dinner nicely dished, without confusion, at the proper time.

SIMPLE MODERN BOILED DINNER

This contemporary version of boiled dinner, adapted from Woodman's restaurant in Essex, Massachusetts, is a "staff meal"—the food served to restaurant workers during their breaks. It's filling and cheaper than serving all the staff fried clams and lobsters.[25] The smoked pork shoulder has been a favorite of French Canadian and Portuguese American families for decades, while Irish American New Englanders more often use corned beef.

NEW ENGLAND BOILED DINNER

6 pound smoked pork shoulder or corned beef brisket
1 large turnip, peeled and cut into 1/2-inch chunks
3 pounds potatoes, peeled and quartered
1 medium head of cabbage, core removed, cut into fourths or eighths
1 pound carrots, peeled and cut into 1/2-inch chunks.

Directions
1. Place meat in a tall stockpot and pour in enough cold water to cover meat. Bring water to a boil. Reduce heat to low and simmer meant until almost cooked through, 60–90 minutes.
2. Add turnip chunks and cook for 20 minutes. Add cabbage and potatoes and cook for another 15 minutes. Add carrots and cook until all vegetables are tender.
3. Drain and serve with cider vinegar and yellow mustard.

PORK SHOULDER BOILED DINNER (COZIDO)

This recipe is adapted from the Portuguese American Mom blog, written by a second-generation Portuguese American living in New England.[26]

1 10-pound smoked pork shoulder
6–8 potatoes, peeled
3 large onions, peeled
1/2 medium cabbage
1/2 pound hot Portuguese chouriço sausage

Directions
1. Place pork shoulder and potatoes in a tall stock pot and cover with water. Add onions, cabbage, and chouriço.
2. Cover the pot and bring to a boil over high heat. Reduce heat to low and simmer for 90 minutes to 2 hours, or until meat is tender and vegetables are cooked.

Chapter 4: Corn and Prejudice

JOHNNY CAKE, OR HOE CAKE

Adapted from Amelia Simmons's *American Cookery* (1796).

> Scald 1 pint of milk and put to 3 pints of Indian meal, and half pint of
> flower—bake before the fire. Or scald with milk two-thirds of the Indian
> meal, or wet two-thirds with boiling water, add salt, molasses and shorten-
> ing, work up with cold water pretty stiff, and bake as above.

....

MODERN ADAPTATION

1/2 cup milk
1 1/2 cups cornmeal
1/4 cup all-purpose flour
Oil for frying
Optional: 1 teaspoon salt and/or 1 teaspoon sugar

Directions
1. Combine cornmeal, flour, and optional salt or sugar if desired.
2. Bring milk to a boil. Stir milk into cornmeal mixture, mix well, and let sit
for 10 minutes to thicken.
3. Heat 2 tablespoons oil in a 9-inch frying pan or griddle. When oil is
hot, spoon thickened cornmeal mixture onto hot pan. Flatten Johnny cakes
with oiled spatula to 1/2 inch thick. Cook 2–3 minutes, or until underside is
lightly browned.
4. Before flipping Johnny cakes, drip a few drops of oil on top of the cake
from a spoon to prevent sticking. Flip cakes and cook until bottom is lightly
browned, 1–2 minutes.
5. Serve immediately with butter, maple syrup, or other pancake toppings.

HASTY PUDDING (CORNMEAL MUSH)

This recipe from an 1832 edition of Lydia Maria Francis Child's *The Frugal Housewife* instructs readers to pour in cornmeal gradually, reducing
the chances of lumpy or too-thin mush—while increasing the attention
needed to produce the meal.[27]

HASTY PUDDING

Boil water, a quart, three pints, or two quarts, according to the size of your family; sift your meal, stir five or six spoonfuls of it thoroughly into a bowl of water; when the water in the kettle boils, pour into it the contents of the bowl; stir it well, and let it boil up thick; put in salt to suit your own taste, then stand over the kettle, and sprinkle in meal, handful after handful, stirring it very thoroughly all the time, and letting it boil between whiles. When it is so thick that you stir it with great difficulty, it is about right. It takes about half an hour's cooking.

Eat it with milk or molasses. Either Indian meal or rye meal may be used. If the system is in a restricted state, nothing can be better than rye hasty pudding and West India molasses. This diet would save many a one the horrors of dyspepsia.

CORN CAKE

This recipe from Mrs. Lincoln's 1890 *Boston School Kitchen Text-Book* has more flour than cornmeal.[28]

1 cup flour
1/2 cup fine yellow corn meal
1/4 cup sugar
1/2 teaspoon salt
1 teaspoon cream of tartar
1/2 teaspoon soda (mashed fine)
1 cup sweet milk; if sour milk is used, omit the cream of tartar
1 egg
1 tablespoon butter or dripping

Directions
Mix the dry ingredients thoroughly in the order given. Add the milk with the egg (well beaten), and the melted butter last. Beat well and bake in muffin pans, or a shallow pan in a hot oven about 20 minutes.

This cake is very good without the egg, and when it is to be eaten with meat the egg is unnecessary; but when this is the most substantial part of the meal, the egg should be used.

DURGIN-PARK CORNBREAD

Adapted from the *Durgin-Park Cookbook*.[29]

This recipe is an approximation of the cornbread that arrived at every table in lieu of bread rolls at Durgin-Park, the storied, stuffy Boston restaurant that closed in 2019 after 192 years of serving fairly pedestrian and bland food.

The published recipe calls for 3 teaspoons of salt, which may seem excessive to current-day palates. I have given a range of salt here; the lower number approximates the salt in flour-sugar-sweet-milk cornbread recipes from other northern sites such as King Arthur Flour and *New England Today*.

> 3 cups all-purpose flour
> 2 cups yellow cornmeal
> 1 to 3 teaspoons salt, depending on taste
> 3/4 cup sugar
> 2 tablespoons + 2 teaspoons baking powder
> 2 large eggs, lightly beaten
> 2 1/2 cups milk

Directions

1. Preheat oven to 375°F. Butter an 11- × 13-inch baking dish.
2. Mix dry ingredients in a large mixing bowl.
3. Add 1/2 of beaten eggs, to dry ingredients, stir briefly, then add half of milk and stir briefly. Repeat. Stir only until just mixed.
4. Pour mixture into prepared pan. Bake 35–40 minutes, or until knife inserted in center of cornbread comes out without wet crumbs attached. Serve hot.

TWO SOUTHERN CORNBREAD RECIPES
BY MRS. ABBY FISHER

Mrs. Abby Fisher was an African American cook and author who was likely born a slave and lived in South Carolina, Alabama, and California. Her 1881 volume *What Mrs. Fisher Knows about Old Southern Cooking, Soups, Pickles, Preserves Etc.* was likely the second cookbook published by an African American in the United States, after Malinda Russell's 1866 *A Domestic Cook Book: Containing a Careful Selection of Useful Receipts for the Kitchen.* These two recipes are for hoe cake and versions of sugar- and wheat-free "southern" cornbread from her cookbook.[30]

PLANTATION CORN BREAD OR HOE CAKE

Half tablespoonful of lard to a pint of meal, one teacup of boiling water: stir well and bake on a hot griddle. Sift in meal one teaspoonful of soda.

....

CORN EGG BREAD

Two eggs, one pint of meal, half pint of sour milk, one teaspoonful of soda—beat eggs very light—one tablespoonful of melted lard or butter, mix all together, well stirred or beaten. Bake in an ordinary pan.

....

CHEESE AND LOROCO PUPUSAS

The University of Massachusetts Extension Nutrition Education Program has created a variety of recipes for dishes "featuring ethnic crops grown in the Northeastern United States and available in Massachusetts." This adapted recipe is for pupusas, a cornmeal-based stuffed grilled flatbread commonly eaten in El Salvador. About 60,000 native- and foreign-born El Salvadoran Americans live in Massachusetts, making up the third largest Latinx immigrant group in the state.[31]

1/3 cup loroco (canned or frozen)
1/3 cup mozzarella, part skim cheese (3 ounces)
1/3 cup farmer's cheese or white semisoft cheese
1 tablespoon light cream
2 cups of Maseca (whole-grain white corn flour)
1 cup warm water

Directions
1. In a medium bowl, mix the loroco with both cheeses and light cream.
2. In a large bowl, mix the Maseca and water and mix well. Cover and set aside to rest 5–10 minutes.
3. Divide dough into four parts, making a ball with each one.
4. Press a hole in each ball with your thumb. Put about 1–2 tablespoons of cheese filling in each hole and fold the dough over to cover the filling. Flatten each filled ball between the palms of your hands to form a flat circle about 1/2 inch thick.
5. Heat an ungreased skillet over high heat. Cook each pupusa for about 1–2 minutes on each side until lightly browned.

Chapter 5: From River and Sea

CODFISH

From Amelia Simmons's 1796 *American Cookery: The Art of Dressing Viands, Fish, Poultry, and Vegetables.*

....

FOR DRESSING CODFISH

Put the fish first into cold water and wash it, then hang it over the fire and soak it six hours in scalding water, then shift it into clean warm water, and let it scald for one hour, it will be much better than to boil.

....

MODERN SALT COD

Directions
Soak salt cod in cold water in a large bowl for 24 hours, changing water at least 4 times. Use in any cod recipe, such as cod fish cakes.

....

COD FISH CAKES

Adapted from Maria Janoplis, *Provincetown Portuguese Cookbook*, http://iamprovincetown.com.

1 pound salted cod, soaked overnight or up to 24 hours in cold water, water changed 4 times.
3 large potatoes
4 eggs
1/3 cup fresh parsley, chopped
1/3 cup onions

1/2 teaspoon black pepper
All-purpose flour, optional
Oil for frying

Drain the soaked cod and place in a large stock pot with potatoes. Cover with water and bring to a boil. Cook until the potatoes are tender, about 20 minutes. Drain.

Mash the cod and potatoes with the eggs, parsley, onion, and pepper until well mixed. If the mixture is too wet to hold a shape when you squeeze it in your hand, add flour one tablespoon at a time until mixture just holds together. If it is too dry, add another egg.

Shape into round patties 1/2 inch thick. Pour a thin layer of oil into a skillet and heat on medium-high until oil shimmers. Fry patties until browned on bottom, 3–5 minutes, then slip and continue cooking until browned. Serve immediately.

FISH CHOWDER

Boston Evening Post, September 23, 1751.

First lay some Onions to keep the Pork from burning

Because in Chouder there can be not turning;

Then lay some Pork in slices very thing,

Thus you in Chouder always must begin.

Next lay some Fish cut crossways very nice

Then season well with Pepper, Salt, and Spice;

Parsley, Sweet-Marjoram, Savory, and Thyme,

Then Biscuit next which must be soak'd some Time.

Thus your Foundation laid, you will be able

To raise a Chouder, high as Tower of Babel;

For by repeating o'er the Same again,

You may make a Chouder for a thousand men.

Last a Bottle of Claret, with Water eno; to smother 'em,

You'll have a Mess which some call Omnium gather 'em.

....

FISH CHOWDER FOR MODERN COOKS

Adapted from the G. H. Bent Company.

21/2 pounds firm white fish (haddock, cod, or similar)
1/2 cup diced salt pork or 1/2 cup diced bacon
1 teaspoon dried thyme, savory, parsley, or marjoram, or a mixture
Salt and pepper
Up to 4 cups unsalted crackers such as oyster crackers, saltines, or Bent's
   Pilot Crackers

Directions
1. Fry salt pork or bacon until it begins to brown in a large saucepan. Remove pork from fat.
2. Place half of pork in the bottom of a large saucepan. Layer half of the fish on top, then crumble a layer of crackers on top of the fish. Sprinkle in 1/2 teaspoon of chosen herbs. Repeat layers.
3. Add enough water to cover the fish (about 3 cups). Bring to a simmer, and cook gently for 10 minutes.
4. Add salt and pepper to taste. Serve with more crackers.

TWO LOBSTER SALADS

These lobster salads from the 1896 *Boston Cooking-School Cookbook* show how lobster was served by the up-and-coming classes—with fancy celery curls.[32]

....

LOBSTER SALAD 1

Remove lobster meat from shell, cut in 1/2-inch cubes, and marinate with a French dressing. Mix with a small quantity of mayonnaise dressing and arrange in nests of lettuce leaves. Put a spoonful of mayonnaise on each and sprinkle with lobster coral rubbed through a fine sieve. Garnish with small lobster claws.

....

LOBSTER SALAD 2

Prepare lobster as for Lobster Salad 1. Add an equal quantity of celery cut in small pieces kept one hour in cold or ice water then drained and dried in a towel. Moisten with any cream or oil dressing. Arrange on a salad dish, pile slightly in center, cover with dressing, sprinkle with lobster coral forced through a fine sieve, and garnish with a border of curled celery.

To Curl Celery
Cut thick stalks of celery in two-inch pieces. With a sharp knife beginning at outside of stalks, make five cuts parallel with each other extending one-third the length of pieces. Make six cuts at right angles to cuts already made. Put pieces in cold or ice water and let stand overnight or for several hours when they will curl back and celery will be found very crisp. Both ends of celery may be curled if one cares to take the trouble.

....

PORTUGUESE CLAMS AND RICE

Adapted from Nancy Meads's recipe in the *Provincetown Portuguese Cookbook*.[33]

1 cup long grain rice
1/2 cup olive oil
2 small onions, chopped
1 green pepper, chopped
4 dozen littleneck clams
4 cloves garlic, minced
3 cups whole tomatoes, chopped, juice drained
1 teaspoon saffron
1/2 pound linguiça, with the casing removed

Salt and pepper to taste

Directions
1. Place clams in a large stockpot with a lid or covered skillet, and add 1/2 cup water. Steam clams until they open, about 5 minutes. Discard unopened

clams and set opened clams aside. Reserve the cooking liquid, avoiding any sand from the clams that may remain in the pot.

2. Heat olive oil in a large pot with a lid over medium heat. When hot, sauté the rice in the olive oil until golden brown. Add the onion, green pepper, garlic, and linguiça and cook for 5 minutes, stirring occasionally.

3. Add tomatoes and 1 cup clam cooking liquid to the rice mixture. Bring to a boil, then lower heat, cover, and cook until the rice is soft, 15–20 minutes, checking and stirring every few minutes. Add more of the reserved clam juice if necessary to keep rice moist.

4. Shell the clams; leave 8 clams in their shells for garnish. Add the clams and saffron to rice mixture, stir, and serve garnished with clams.

....

WINNING STUFFED QUAHOGS

This recipe is for "stuffies"—stuffed Quahog clams, as enjoyed in Rhode Island. This recipe is an adaptation of a version that was a finalist in the Wickford, Rhode Island, International Quahog Festival, and appeared in the *Providence Journal* in 1999.[34]

15 quahogs, shucked and then ground or chopped
2 loaves day-old Italian bread, broken into crumbs
2 tablespoons oil
2 medium onions, chopped
1/2 green pepper, chopped
2 to 3 cloves garlic, chopped
2 tablespoons crushed red pepper
2 tablespoons parsley, chopped
Paprika
Margarine or butter
Optional: 1 stick Portuguese chouriço sausage, ground

Directions

1. Preheat oven to 375°F.

2. Shuck quahogs, placing meat and juice in separate bowls. Save shells. Grind quahogs or chop very finely.

3. Place bread crumbs in large bowl and enough clam juice so bread becomes moist but not soggy. Add quahogs.

4. Heat a frying pan on medium heat. When hot, add oil, onion, green pepper, and garlic, and ground chouriço, if using. Sauté vegetables until soft, about 5 minutes. Remove from heat and mix with breadcrumbs, adding crushed red pepper.

5. Wash shells and separate into halves. Mound stuffing into shells. Sprinkle tops with parsley and paprika, and dot with butter or margarine.

6. Place stuffed shells on a rimmed baking sheet or baking dish. Bake until heated through, about 25 minutes.

Chapter 6: Sweets, Sours, and Spirits

SARAH JOSEPHA BUELL HALE'S APPLE PIE

Hale took a dim view of pies and complained that pies were bad for the health and that baking ruined most fruits—except for apples. Here is her apple pie recipe from her 1839 *The Good Housekeeper*.[35]

....

APPLE PIE

Apples of a pleasant sour and fully ripe make the best pies—pare, core, and slice them, line a deep buttered dish with paste, lay in the apples, strewing in moist brown sugar and a little pounded lemon peel or cinnamon; cover and bake about 40 minutes. The oven must not be very hot.

When apples are green, stew them with a very little water before making your pie. Green fruit requires a double quantity of sugar.

THREE PIES FROM HOLYOKE, MASSACHUSETTS

These pies were featured in the 1886 community cookbook *625 Choice Recipes from the Ladies of the Second Cong. Church, of Holyoke, Mass.*—a Protestant church, likely with few (if any) immigrant members.[36] Like all community cookbooks, it presents likely aspirational recipes—those that women made to show off their skills or culinary sophistication, and not necessarily the foods they ate day to day. The recipes below show a slight departure in ingredients or technique from today's pie fare. The choice of crust is left to the reader.

....

DELICATE PIE

Dissolve one tablespoonful of corn starch in a little cold water; add one cup of boiling water; when cool add one beaten egg; one lemon (juice and grated rind); one cup of sugar; a little salt; bake in two crusts. —Mrs. Dr. Tuttle

MOCK MINCE PIE

Four crackers rolled fine; one cup of sugar; one cup of molasses one-half cup of vinegar; one-half cup of cold water; two eggs well beaten; one cap of chopped raisins; one-half teaspoonful of cinnamon; the same of nutmeg and salt; one-quarter of a teaspoonful of cloves; make three pies.
—Mrs. J. E. Bronson

NICE APPLE PIE

Line your dish with paste; then cut your apples into eighths and fill your dish; cover lightly with a top crust; bake; when it is baked, while hot remove the upper crust; put in ginger, nutmeg, and a little butter; stir this together and spread evenly in the pie; then replace the top crust. —Mrs. F. K. Blodgett

FRENCH CANADIAN AMERICAN RAISIN PIE

Adapted from Georgette Bégin and Le Comité Franco-Américain de Lowell, Massachusetts.

2 cups seedless raisins
1 cup water
1 cup brown sugar
1/2 cup orange juice
1/3 cup lemon juice
2 tablespoons grated orange peel
1 tablespoon grated lemon peel
1/4 teaspoon salt
1/4 cup plus 1 teaspoon flour mixed with 1/4 cup water
Uncooked double piecrust of choice

Directions
1. Preheat oven to 450°F.
2. Mix all ingredients except flour and water paste in a medium saucepan. Bring saucepan to a boil, lower heat, and simmer until raisins are plump, about 10 minutes.
3. Add flour and water mixture to hot raisin mixture and stir well. Continue to cook until mixture thickens, 5–10 minutes. Remove from stove and cool for 10 minutes.
4. Pour mixture into piecrust and cover with top crust. Slit or cut top crust to release steam. Bake at 450°F for 10 minutes. Lower heat to 350°F and bake for an additional 30 minutes or until lightly browned. Cool before serving.

MYRLE SYLSBY'S ONE-CRUST BLUEBERRY PIE

Adapted from a 1957 edition of the *Peninsula Gazette*, Winter Harbor, Maine.[37]

> 1 quart blueberries, divided
> 2 tablespoons flour
> 3/4 cup sugar
> Cinnamon to taste
> Pinch of salt
> 1/4 cup water
> Prebaked pie shell

> *Directions*
> 1. Combine 1 cup blueberries and flour, sugar, cinnamon, salt, and water in a medium saucepan. Heat on medium, stirring, until mixture comes to a boil and thickens slightly, 5–10 minutes. Remove from stove and slowly stir in remaining blueberries.
> 2. Pour mixture into baked pie shell and cool thoroughly. Serve with whipped cream.

....

WASHINGTON PIE

This handwritten 1875 recipe collected by the Maine Historical Society is for a "pie" that, like Boston cream pie and whoopie pies, is actually a cake. The "pie" cakes would be stacked with a layer of fruit or jelly in between.[38]

> One cup sugar. One cup flour, 3 eggs, bit of butter the size of a walnut, 1/2 teaspoon full cream of tartar mixed in the flour and sugar, 1/2 teaspoonful saleratus dissolved in three teaspoonfuls cold water. Orange peel or nutmeg for spice.
> The eggs and butter put into the flour without previous beating. This makes two round cakes. Bake 10 or 15 minutes.

> *Filling for Washington Pies*
> From *The Kirmess Cook-Book*, published by the Boston Women's Educational and Industrial Union, 1887[39]

> Grate three or four apples, juice of one lemon, one cup of sugar, two eggs. Let it boil a few minutes, then add the grated rind of a lemon. This will fill two pies. —M. B. Scudder.

DOUGHNUTS

Mrs. Lincoln comments in her 1884 *Mrs. Lincoln's Boston Cook Book* that yeast-raised doughnuts are "more wholesome than those made with soda"—but she offers three soda doughnut recipes and only one yeast recipe. Apparently, convenience won out over wholesomeness.[40] Mrs. Henderson's identity is shrouded in mystery.

....

SOUR MILK DOUGHNUTS—MRS. HENDERSON

Two eggs beaten light
One cup of sugar
Three even tablespoonfuls of melted butter
One cup of sour milk or if sweet milk be used add one teaspoonful of
    cream of tartar
Four cups of flour with half a teaspoonful of soda and one salt spoon-
    ful each of cinnamon and salt. [Use] enough flour to make just soft
    enough to roll out.

Mix the dough rather soft at first. Have the board well floured and the fat heating.
Roll only a large spoonful at first. Cut into rings with an open cutter.
Mix the trimmings with another spoonful. Work it slightly till well floured, and roll again.
Roll and cut all out before frying as that will demand your whole attention. Remember that the fat should be hot enough for the dough to rise to the top instantly.

ACADIAN BEIGNETS, AKA GRAND-PÈRES DANS LE SIROP, AKA MAPLE SYRUP DUMPLINGS

Adapted from "Les Repas de Mon Enfance: Growing Up Franco-American" by Dr. Daniel G. Parenteau.[41]

Maple syrup was used by the Abenaki and other northern Native American tribes. French Canadians adopted the maple syrup and made a variety of sweet dishes with them. This simple dish of dumplings is associated with Acadian immigrants to Maine's mill towns.

2 cups all-purpose flour
1/4 cup sugar
2 teaspoons baking powder
1/4 teaspoon salt
1/4 cup unsalted butter
1 cup milk
1 cup water
2 cups maple syrup
Warm maple syrup for serving

Directions
1. Combine flour, sugar, baking powder, and salt in a food processor work bowl or large mixing bowl. Add butter and pulse or "cut" butter into mixture with a fork until the mixture is the texture of coarse sand. Add milk and stir until dough is smooth.
2. Mix maple syrup and water in a saucepan with a lid and bring to a boil. Shape the dough into about 12 balls. Drop balls into the boiling syrup.
3. Cover, reduce the heat to low, and simmer for 15 minutes. Serve with the hot syrup.

MAPLE MOUSSE

This ice cream recipe from a 1912 Woodbury, Connecticut, community cookbook, *Tried Recipes Collected by the Ladies of the Mission Circle of the First Church*, is one of the more detailed versions of this recipe. It appears to be a slightly adapted version of the "Maple Parfait" recipe that appeared in the third edition of Fannie Farmer's *The Boston Cooking-School Cook Book*, which featured several new maple recipes that did not appear in the 1896 edition.[42]

MAPLE MOUSSE

Yolks of 4 eggs
1 cup Maple Syrup (hot)
1 pt Whipple Cream

Beat eggs, add slowly syrup, and cook to a custard in double boiler. When cold add cream and bear well. Turn into mould tightly covered and stand in equal parts of ice and salt for 4 hours. —Miss Ruth B. Smith.

CRANBERRY SAUCE AND CRANBERRY JELLY

Fanny Farmer included both cranberry sauce and cranberry jelly in her 1896 *Boston Cooking-School Cook Book*.[43] Much like today's Ocean Spray jelly logs, the jelly has a higher ratio of sugar to cranberries than sauce and is cooked longer.

CRANBERRY SAUCE

Pick over and wash three cups cranberries. Put in a stewpan, add one and one-fourth cups sugar and one cup boiling water. Cover, and boil ten minutes. Care must be taken that they do not boil over. Skim and cool.

CRANBERRY JELLY

Pick over and wash four cups cranberries. Put in a stewpan with one cup boiling water, and boil twenty minutes. Rub through a sieve, add two cups sugar, and cook five minutes. Turn into a mould or glasses.

CHAMPAIGN CIDER

This recipe, which originally ran in the magazine *The Cultivator and Country Gentleman* in 1870, was reprinted and collected by a Maine farmer in 1890.[44] Clearly, interest in hard cider continued through the end of the nineteenth century.

Champaign Cider.—I have been looking through the back numbers of the COUNTRY GENTLEMEN for a receipt for making champaign cider, but fail to find one. If you have such a receipt, will you be kind enough to give it to your readers? J. F. L. Xenia, O.

> Our correspondent did not go back far enough. The following appeared in vol. 35, p. 711: "Take one barrel of pure cider made from sound apples, no decayed ones; mix it with forty pounds of light brown sugar, dissolving it with some of the cider in a tub while it is perfectly free from fermentation; place the barrel in a cool cellar and let it work thoroughly from the bung-hole, filling it up as it evaporates, with some that has been saved out for that purpose; when it has worked a week or so, bung it up securely, draw it off in March, and put it in a clean cask, stopped tightly. It can be bottled in May or June, and it is well to coat the corks with melted tallow and rosin, using one ounce of the former to one quarter of a pound of the latter."

TWO GINGERBREADS FROM PORTLAND, MAINE

These recipes from the 1877 community cookbook *Fish, Flesh, and Fowl: A Book of Recipes for Cooking Compiled by Ladies of State Street Parish* illustrate two of the main schools of gingerbread—a soft, molasses-based fruit cake and a hard, sugar-based cookie. Note that "Boston Gingerbread" cake does not contain any actual ginger.[45]

BOSTON GINGERBREAD

One pound of sugar, one pound butter, two pounds of flour, six eggs, one pint molasses, one gill of water, one teaspoon soda, two teaspoons each allspice, cloves, and mace, one quart of fruit, half a pound of citron. Bake in two loaves three hours.

GINGERBREAD 2, SUGAR

Three-quarters pound sugar, same of butter, one and a half pounds flour, four eggs, ginger, small teaspoon of soda. Roll very thin and bake on tin sheets.

Chapter 7: Cheese and Taste

HOW TO STUFF PINEAPPLE CHEESE

Sarah Tyson Rorer gave advice in her 1907 *My Best 250 Recipes*.[46]

....

CHEESE

Shells of Edam or pineapple cheese after being scooped out nearly clean may be saved to use as a baking dish for creamed spaghetti, macaroni, or rice. After the dish is completed, pour it in the shell, stand it on greased paper in a baking pan, and bake for fifteen minutes. Serve in the shell.

....

HERB AND CHEDDAR EASTER TOMATOES

Adapted from Crowley Cheese. Operating in Vermont since 1824, the company built a factory in Winfield in 1882. Although Crowley Cheese is not cheap—several of their cheddars cost more than $18 a pound—the recipes on the Crowley website are less complicated and use more readily available, inexpensive ingredients than Vermont's artisanal goat cheese producers. They seem to be intended for more everyday cooks who splurge on good cheese as a special ingredient, rather than for affluent urban foodies.

6 ripe large tomatoes
2 cups fresh white bread crumbs
1/4 cup scallions, finely minced
1/4 cup fresh basil, finely minced
1/4 cup parsley, finely minced
1/2 t fresh thyme leaves, finely minced
Salt and pepper
1 cup grated medium sharp cheddar cheese
Olive oil

Directions
1. Preheat oven to 400°F.
2. Cut tomatoes into halves, removing core. Remove seeds and juice and place in baking dish. Sprinkle with salt and pepper.
3. Place bread crumbs in a large bowl. Gently mix in scallions, basil, parsley, garlic, thyme, and 1 teaspoon salt.
4. Generously fill tomatoes with bread crumb mixture, creating a mound on top. Drizzle tomatoes with olive oil. Bake tomatoes for 15 minutes or until tender.
5. Sprinkle baked tomatoes with shredded cheese and return to oven for two minutes, or until tops are slightly browned. Serve hot or at room temperature.

SHAVED ASPARAGUS SALAD WITH GOAT CHEESE

This recipe, adapted from the Vermont Creamery website, is representative of the Nouvelle-Vermont cheese world.[47] The recipe, which makes just two servings—not enough for a farm family—involves intricate preparations of expensive asparagus, watercress, and microgreens, olive oil, and terms like "chiffonade."

Dressing
1/4 cup crème fraîche
1 teaspoon honey
1 teaspoon mint leaves sliced into thin strips (chiffonade)
1/2 teaspoon freshly grated lemon zest
Juice of one lemon
2 tablespoons olive oil
Salt and pepper

Salad
3 cups watercress or mesclun
2 cups asparagus, shaved into thin slices with a vegetable peeler
1/2 cup microgreens
1/2 cup fresh peas or thawed frozen peas

Toppings
2 ounces goat cheese, crumbled
1/4 cup toasted pistachios, chopped

Directions
1. Mix all dressing ingredients except olive oil, salt, and pepper in a small bowl. Gradually whisk in olive oil. Season with salt and pepper.
2. Mix salad ingredients in a large bowl. Add dressing and toss to coat leaves.
3. Add toppings and serve.

KIMCHI GRILLED CHEESE

This recipe is adapted from Must Be the Milk, a campaign and website supported by the New England Dairy Promotion Board.[48] Although it specifies two types of cheese, the original recipe says nothing about what type of kimchi to use. I leave the decision up to the reader.

2 slices bread
1 tablespoon of butter
1 slice mozzarella cheese
1 slice Monterey Jack cheese
1 tablespoon kimchi, chopped

Directions
1. Arrange cheese on bread slice. Top with kimchi, then second slice of bread.
2. Melt butter in grill or frying pan over medium heat. Cook sandwich until browned on bottom, flip, and cook until cheese is melted. Serve.

Thanksgiving

....

AMELIA SIMMONS' POMPKIN PIES

These recipes appeared in Simmons's 1796 *American Cookery*.[49] By the turn of the eighteenth century, cooks in New England had ready access to sugar and molasses via the West Indies trade, although these ingredients were more expensive than they are today, and may have been used more sparingly.

No. 1. One quart stewed and strained, 3 pints cream, 9 beaten eggs, sugar, mace, nutmeg and ginger, laid into paste No. 7 or 3, and with a dough spur, cross and chequer it, and baked in dishes three-quarters of an hour.
No. 2. One quart of milk, 1 pint pompkin, 4 eggs, molasses, allspice and ginger in a crust, bake 1 hour.

ESTHER HOWLAND'S CHICKEN PIE

This recipe appeared in Esther Howland's 1845 *The New England Economical Housekeeper, and Family Receipt Book*.[50] She listed it as part of her Thanksgiving menu.

....

CHICKEN PIE

Cut up your chicken, parboil it, season it in the pot, take up the meat, put in a flour thickening, and scald the gravy; make the crust of sour milk made sweet with saleratus, put in a piece of butter or lard the size of an egg; cream is preferable to sour milk, if you have it. Take a large tin pan, line it with the crust, put in your meat, and pour in the gravy from the pot; make it nearly full, cover it over with crust, and leave a vent; bake it in a moderate oven two hours, or two and a half.

FRENCH CANADIAN TURKEY STUFFING

Adapted from *The Providence and Rhode Island Cookbook*, this recipe reflects the French Canadian heritage of Woonsocket, Rhode Island.[51] As the cookbook authors note, it is similar to the meat mixture used in French Canadian American tourtiere, the traditional holiday meat pie.

1 tablespoon butter
1 onion, chopped
2 large potatoes, peeled and quartered

1 pound ground pork
1 pound ground beef
Salt and black pepper to taste
Turkey or chicken broth (optional)

Directions

1. Heat a saucepan with enough water to cover the potatoes. Bring to a boil, add potatoes, and cook until tender, 15–20 minutes.

2. While the potatoes are cooking, melt the butter in a large frying pan over medium heat. When the pan is hot, add onions and cook until softened, 5–7 minutes. Add ground beef and pork to the frying pan and sauté until browned, 8–10 minutes.

3. Drain cooked potatoes. Add potatoes to frying pan and mash them into the meat mixture. Season with salt and pepper.

4. Allow stuffing to cool enough to handle, then use to stuff turkey. If baking in a separate dish, pour 1/2–1 cup turkey or chicken broth over stuffing to keep it moist while heating.

....

PUERTO RICAN THANKSGIVING TURKEY (PAVOCHON)

Adapted from Delish D'Lites and Goya Foods.

1 12- to 16-pound turkey, fresh or defrosted
24 cloves garlic
2 tablespoons + 2 teaspoons Goya Adobo All Purpose Seasoning
6 teaspoons Goya Sazon seasoning
2 teaspoons black pepper
2 teaspoons dried oregano
3 tablespoons olive oil
3 tablespoons vinegar

Directions

1. Remove giblets and neck from turkey. Place in a large nonreactive container or Ziploc plastic bag.

2. Combine remaining ingredients except for 2 teaspoons adobo in a food processor and pulse until combined in a paste. Alternately, pound ingredients together in a mortar and pestle.

3. Separating skin from turkey with your gingers, push mixture underneath skin on breast, thighs, and back. Sprinkle turkey with remaining adobo.

4. Cover turkey or close bag and allow to marinate for at least 4 hours or overnight.

5. Preheat oven to 325°F. Place turkey breast side up in roasting pan. Cook until meat thermometer reads 165°F, 3–4 hours depending on size.

EMMIE GALARZA'S PUERTO RICAN AMERICAN PLANTAIN STUFFING

Adapted from Emmie Galarza, Hartford.

10 green plantains
5 tablespoons olive oil
1 cup pork skin or 1/2 cup bacon
5 cloves garlic
1 teaspoon onion powder
1 teaspoon Goya adobo seasoning

Directions
1. Peel plantains and slice in half. Cook plantains in a pot of boiling water until soft. Mash plantains until very smooth using a mortar and pestle or food processor.
2. Heat olive oil in a frying pan and fry pork skins or bacon until crisp. Mash the pork into a coarse paste with mortar and pestle or food processor. Mash garlic.
3. Mix plantains, mashed garlic and pork, onion powder, and adobo. Use to stuff turkey or serve immediately.

From River and Sea

Salmon, shad, and alewives were formerly abundant here . . . until the dam and afterward the canal at Billerica, and the factories at Lowell, put an end to their migrations hitherward . . . Perchance, after a few thousands of years, if the fishes will be patient, and pass their summers elsewhere meanwhile, nature will have leveled the Billerica dam, and the Lowell factories and the [Concord] River run clear again.

—Henry David Thoreau, "A Week on the Concord and
  Merrimack Rivers" (1849)

People have [an] intimate relationship with birds because you can hang a bird feeder out the window and you can admire birds. But you can't put a fish feeder outside your window and admire fish. You have no relationship with them. You see them only as a slab of meat. It's as though our whole relationship with birds was the experience of being in the poultry section of the supermarket.

—Carl Safina

Nᴇᴡ ᴇɴɢʟᴀɴᴅ's seafood is a conflicted business. Cod, chowder, and lobster are symbols of the region, but most locals never eat fresh fish or boiled lobster, and haven't since the eighteenth century. Salt cod and canned lobster were the most popular seafood up through the twentieth century, and frozen fish sticks are the entrée of choice today. New Englanders trawl in some of the most productive natural habitats for fish in North America, and lobsters are thriving, but many edible species have been nearly exterminated like some kind of ocean pest. According to a 2018 market survey only about 15 percent of seafood in New England grocery stories comes from New England; the rest comes from the West Coast or abroad or isn't labeled as coming from anywhere.[1]

How New Englanders eat seafood is the result of how they have managed, or destroyed, habitats in rivers and the ocean, and those actions are partly due to the stories we have told about fish, fishermen, and the sea. Fish and shellfish are mostly invisible to landlubbers. It's far easier to see and hear the workers in mills that dam rivers or the fishermen who scrape the ocean floor with giant nets than to see that there are fewer cod in fewer places than there were 50 years ago. Popular histories recount specious stories about how there were so many lobsters that people grew disgusted with them, ignoring the fact that they disappeared because so many gourmands lusted after their flesh.

Fish the First: Lobster

How New England Didn't Eat Lobster

When fishermen, regulators, and environmentalists are trying to judge if fishing practices are helping or hurting a species, they often look to historical documents for accounts of how much people were eating or fishing the species in question. The problem is that certain types of stories are more fun than others, and writers tend to repeat them without asking too many questions.

One of these stories is the tale of the lobster revolt. It goes like this: Lobsters were so common that they were fed to prisoners, or indentured servants, or slaves, or schoolchildren, or nuns, or Santa's elves, or some other group of people who didn't have much choice over their food. Those people rebelled, and there was a law passed that forbade the awful authorities from ever serving that food to those poor, poor people ever again. The most curious part of the whole story is that no one can ever say exactly who those people were, or what year the revolt occurred, or where this forced lobster feeding took place.

As food historian Sandra Oliver put it, "Salmon and lobster used to be so abundant that, it is said, pick one—the apprentices, servants, boarders, lumbermen, occupants, prisoners, and slaves of—pick another—Newcastle, England, Boston or Lowell, Massachusetts, Puget Sound, Bristol, Rhode Island, Islesboro, Maine, the Maine State Prison, or the South—refused to eat either lobsters or salmon, more than twice a week."[2] Most of these stories seem to originate in town histories written in the last quarter of the nineteenth century—always at least 50 to 100 years after the revolt took place, Oliver notes.

Similar stories have also been told about:

SHAD (1983)

Shad was so abundant that farm hands insisted their job contract include provisions limiting the number of times they could be given shad as part of their meals.[3]

HEATH HENS (1905)

Heath hen . . . was formerly so common . . . that laboring people or servants stipulated with their employers not to have the Heath Hen brought to table oftener than a few times in the week.[4]

SALMON (1887)

Salmon have allegedly been force-fed to servants in both the US and Great Britain, where a Victorian author credited the rumor to medieval times:

"It has been questioned whether the amount of salmon in our rivers is really much less than was formerly the case. . . . Although many authors have of late years held that the widely spread belief that laws formerly existed prohibiting giving salmon to servants or apprentices more than three times a week was a popular fallacy, it seems more probable that it is the recent authors themselves who are in error. . . .

"That such prohibitions were not unknown in other countries can be demonstrated, thus in Western Pomerania on the river Oder and its affluents, the monastic accounts show that a regulation was in force prohibiting salmon being given as food more than three days in a week."[5]

Those monks had objected to their salmon hundreds of years before this 1887 book was published. Salmon were locally exterminated in the Oder by a combination of overfishing and habitat destruction in the Middle Ages,[6] and by the fifteenth century salmon were being imported salted in barrels to areas of Prussia that had once been salmon fishing ports.[7]

In short, the best evidence for a ban on a particular seafood comes from vague reports about monks living prior to 1500. There aren't any American records of indentured servants, prisoners, or slaves being force-fed lobster.

As Oliver puts it, "Plain fact is that most rationed diets on land and sea in the 1700s and 1800s relied on salt pork, salt beef, bread, potatoes and once a week in some places, salt cod. No lobsters in sight."[8]

The old story about salmon-suffering servants seems to have originated in England, and it wasn't true there either. As historian Newton C. Brainard wrote,

> Let us review the old story of the apprentice agreements which were supposed to have protected the poor by a clause stipulating that he was not to be required to eat salmon more than twice a week. This story was intended to show how plentiful and cheap salmon was here [Connecticut River], and has been generally accepted as true. As a matter of fact, it is an English or Scotch tradition which is not true, even in the land of its origin. As long ago as 1867 the London Field offered a reward of five pounds to anyone who would produce one of these agreements. The reward was withdrawn a year later, unclaimed.[9]

How New England Did Eat Lobster

In colonial times, there was no lobster fishery per se. Anyone who had working legs and arms could simply pick lobsters up out of the shallow water right offshore.[10] Reverend Francis Higginson wrote from Salem, Massachusetts, in 1630, ". . . and aboundance of Lobsters that the least Boy in the Plantation may both catch and eat what he will of them. For my owne part, I was soone cloyed with them; they were so great and fat and lussious I haue seene some my selfe that have weighed 16 pound, but others have had divers time so great Lobsters as have weighed 25 pound as they assured me."[11]

By 1850, New England's lobstermen from Connecticut to Maine were using sea-bottom traps to catch their prey.[12] Lobsters managed to survive in southern New England only as long as it was difficult to ship them to Boston and New York. The effort and outlay involved in transporting lobsters in "smacks"—boats containing wells of seawater for transporting them live—were enormous. Once lobster meat started being canned, lobstermen depleted the populations from Connecticut to Maine in less than 50 years.[13]

William Underwood began canning lobster meat in quart jars in Boston in the 1820s.[14] (If his name sounds familiar, it's because his family's Underwood Deviled Ham still lurks in the canned meat aisle of supermarkets and gas station convenience stores.) In 1842, a Maine entrepreneur opened the first lobster cannery in Harpswell. By 1844, Underwood had bought out that cannery and built another cannery of his own in the same town.[15] Lobster canning was a competitive business from the very start.

Canned lobster was relatively cheap—the Maine workers who picked the meat out of the lobsters didn't get paid much—and far more convenient for fashionable hostesses than acquiring the skills and tools to extract meat from a lobster in a Boston townhouse. Many of the most popular Victorian lobster dishes, like molded lobster salad and Lobster Newburg, were made with canned lobster meat, not whole lobsters.[16]

By the 1860s, posh New York hotels were commonly offering lobster salad as a second course, and "currie of lobster" was served from Boston to Minneapolis to New Orleans.[17] Before you get excited at the idea of curry teasing the tongues of America's most daring palates, here's a fairly representative recipe from Sarah Josepha Buell Hale's 1857 *Mrs. Hale's New Cook Book*.[18]

CURRIED LOBSTERS

Lay the meat in a pan, with two or three of blades of mace, and equal quantities of veal gravy and cream; then rub with butter, two teaspoonsful of currie powder, and half the quantity of flour; which put into the pan, and simmer the whole an hour, adding salt, and the juice of half a lemon.

Canned lobsters were big business. In 1880 alone, 9 million pounds of lobsters were picked in 23 canneries, yielding 2 million pounds of meat.[19] The poor picked-on lobster population soon started shrinking, both in numbers and in actual size. In 1870, lobster canning magnate George Burnham—more famous nowadays as the B in B&M Baked Beans—reported to the US Fish Commission, "In the fall of 1854 I went to South Saint George, not the coast of Maine, to pack lobsters, and sent a smack to Deer Isle, where the fishermen used hand nets, and 1,200 lobsters then caught filled the smack's well. It would take of the lobsters we now catch from 7,000 to 8,000 to fill the same well."

Maine responded slowly, by closing the seasonal lobster fishery from August 1 to October 15, then banning canning altogether from August 1 to April 1. Massachusetts and Maine both passed laws prohibiting taking lobsters bearing eggs—"berried" lobsters—or those shorter than 10.5 inches in length. Mr. Burnham, who was so concerned for lobsters dwindling size, promptly moved 16 of his 21 canneries to Nova Scotia, which did not have these laws. By 1895, there were no lobster canneries left in Maine[20]—but there were 650 in eastern Canada, where the near-shore lobsters had not yet been fished out.[21]

Those canned lobsters were easy to use, but sometimes were less than fresh. Canned lobster was the subject of some of the first research into canned food spoilage. In 1896, William Underwood—grandson of the Underwood who started the cannery—worked with Professor Samuel Prescott at MIT to figure out how canned food spoiled. The pair discovered that clams and lobsters commonly bore four types of bacteria that would survive in underprocessed cans and spoil their contents—a smelly but necessary piece of research for food safety.[22]

Over the next 40 years, Maine lobstermen concentrated on keeping lobsters alive. One difference between lobster and fish is that if the price isn't right, lobstermen can just keep their charming new pets in tanks in "lobster pounds" for days or weeks until they're offered a better deal. If fishermen can't sell right away, their precious seafood quickly dissolves into fertilizer.

The market for fresh lobsters remained ravenous in the early twentieth century, and lax enforcement of a variety of laws about equipment, licensing, trap numbers, and lobster size didn't help the species. The Great Depression did ease lobsters' lives a little. With no market for the grandest, most expensive lobsters, fishermen let them go—inadvertently ensuring that the lobsters capable of bearing the most eggs would survive.[23]

During World War II, lobster was one of the few meats that wasn't rationed. It was considered a luxury food and not necessary for the troops' nourishment. The price of canned lobster went from about 18 cents per pound in 1941 to 40 cents per pound in 1945, thanks to increased demand.[24] (Lobster rolls—essentially lobster salad on a hot dog bun—seem to have cropped up after World War II in midcoast Maine,[25] although lobster sandwiches were available in the 1930s.)[26]

Consumers kept eating lobster after World War II, and lobstermen kept obliging them by pulling up lobster traps, and the lobsters got smaller. Lobstering wasn't significantly more efficient in the 1950s than the 1880s—there was no equivalent of the otter trawl or seine nets to annoy old fishermen—but in 1957, lobstermen needed four times as many traps to catch the same amount of lobster as they had in 1888, snaring 24 million pounds in 565,000 traps.[27] By 1980, there were two million lobster traps in the Gulf of Maine, and biologists estimated that 90 percent of lobsters were being caught within a year of molting—that is, just when they had reached breeding age. Massachusetts and Maine passed new laws about minimum length, and notching the tales of female lobsters bearing eggs, and Massachusetts even started requiring licensing and limiting lobstermen to 800 traps.

Today, lobstermen tend somewhere between 300 and 1,000 traps apiece, checking them every day or two: lobsters left more than 48 hours tend to figure out how to escape. The traps are set at depths from 10 to 250 feet inshore and up to 1,500 feet for offshore lobstermen and are hauled in by winches.[28] Maine lobsters must measure between 3.25 and 5 inches from eye socket to carapace[29]—too small, and they're too young to have reproduced. The smaller lobsters weigh in at about one and a quarter pounds, or a single serving.[30] The lobsters that grow beyond five inches are more valuable as potential parents than as dinner entrées because they produce up to 100,000 eggs at a time—more than ten times as much as the smaller lobsters' 10,000 egg hauls.[31]

What Lobster Means in Maine

Lobster is the biggest seafood fishery in Maine, netting $569 million in 2017—more than 30 times as much as herring (largely used as bait for lobsters) and soft-shell clams.[32] Maine lobstermen collect 80 percent of the lobsters in the United States, and lobster is the state's most valuable export commodity.[33]

The reason that Maine dominates the lobster market and that lobsters dominate the state's tourism isn't because it is the only place that lobsters can live; it's because Maine is the last part of the Northeast where lobsters haven't been driven to near extinction. Lobsters have been nearly or entirely wiped out in all the other places they once lived in the Northeast: coastal Connecticut, Cape Cod, Boston. As early as 1880, lobsters had become scarce on Cape Cod and Long Island Sound thanks to the endless appetites of New Yorkers and Bostonians.[34]

While lobsters were being devoured south of New Hampshire, wealthy northeastern urbanites were building summer homes in Maine, the Hamptons, and Newport, Rhode Island—far from the environments they'd built in their home cities, where poor immigrants lived in slums and worked in the factories that made their owners rich.

The Maine vacation contingent celebrated the year-round Mainers by imitating their accents at cold-season cocktail parties and by talking about how much better lobster is when it's eaten fresh straight out of the shell at the dock—that is, in Maine.[35]

The people who actually lived in Maine were not impressed. Most Mainers either had far too much lobster in their lives, from collecting, picking, or packing it, or none at all, if they didn't live on the coasts—and rich city folks made it far too expensive to eat. As one author wrote, "In the high season, a lobsterman has to think twice, and seriously, about dipping into his catch to put this high-priced food on his own table."[36]

Monetarily, Maine has always trailed the other New England states. In 2018, Maine's median household income was a little over $51,494—almost $10,000 less than the national median income of $61,372,[37] and far less than the princely incomes of nearby Massachusetts ($70,628) and New Hampshire ($70,303).

In the mid-1980s, Maine's state legislature voted to put Maine lobsters on license plates at the behest of newer, wealthier residents in tony towns like Portland and Kennebunkport. Both coastal and inland Mainers objected strenuously, suggesting alternatives like chickadees, blueberries, potatoes, and mosquitoes, and there was a fad for painting over the red lobster—which is the color of cooked lobster, not the living animal. As one resident commented, "We are the only state with a dead creature on the license plate. Think about it."[38] Dorcas Gilpatrick of the Maine Civil Liberties Union suggested, "If we have to have something on our license plates, the only thing that'd work is a black fly. It's everywhere. It gets everybody, inland and on the coast, tourist and native, rich and poor. It's ubiquitous."[39]

Still, lobsters are part of the Maine tourist experience, if not Maine life. With more than 37 million visitors spending more than $6 billion a year,[40] Maine produces plenty of lobster pounds, rolls, keychains, T-shirts, salt shakers, and plushies to collect tourists' money.[41] Putting aside the question of how a creature with a chitinous exoskeleton could ever be plush, this alien bounty raises a question. Tourists outnumber year-round Maine residents by roughly 27 to 1, and devour lobster by the ton. Is a food a New England culinary tradition when the locals barely ever eat it?

Game of Traps

The lobster catch was constant in Maine for roughly 100 years despite an increase in both lobstermen and traps. In 1892, 2,600 Maine lobstermen caught 17,599,502 pounds of lobster; in 1989, 6,300 Maine lobstermen landed 23,369,000 pounds.[42] Since then, Maine lobster catches have more than quintupled, reaching more than 120 million pounds and $300 million in 2012. That astonishing increase may be *because* lobsters are being trapped—or, as one researcher put it, farmed.[43]

Lobster traps are photogenic symbols of seaside Maine, but they're not particularly good at holding lobsters. One experiment with video cameras aimed at undersea lobster traps showed that everyone's favorite ocean arthropod managed to escape after eating the bait 94 percent of the time.[44] That bait is herring, and lobstermen are feeding roughly 60,000 metric tons of herring to the lobster each year via traps; that 132,277,000 pounds of fish weighs slightly more than the total pounds of lobster they're collecting.[45] The result: lobsters in lobster-fishing areas (as opposed to closed areas) grow 16 percent faster than those without those yummy herring supplements, and about half of trapped lobsters' diet is herring.[46]

As you might expect, this wholesale herring slaughter appears to be having an effect on the herring population. Gulf of Maine herring catches have dropped 40 percent in the past decade, and four of the past six years have had the lowest counts of newly hatched herring ever. The price of a pound of herring spiked from 15 cents in 2015 to 60 cents in 2018.[47]

And those fish-fattened lobsters may move on—but not because they're tired of herring. Warm water stresses lobsters' respiratory and immune systems, and there's strong evidence that lobsters have been shifting from southern waters up to the Gulf of Maine for almost two decades. From 1996 to 2014, commercial lobster landings in Connecticut and New York dropped almost 97 percent, and Rhode Island's landings fell more than 70 percent.[48] In 1999 alone, almost the entire lobster fishery in Long Island Sound died off, and most of the lobstermen still operating caught no lobsters at all.

From 1996 to 2014, New York's registered lobster landings dropped almost 98 percent—from 9.4 million pounds in 1996 (the state's most profitable year) to 215,980 pounds in 2014. The story is the same in Connecticut, where landings fell 96.6 percent from the most profitable year, and in Rhode Island, which saw a 70.3 percent drop. The Atlantic States Marine Fisheries Commission noted in 2017 that the local Massachusetts lobster stock was "in need of protection," and that the warming waters have jeopardized lobsters. Industry groups basically argued that the lobsters were doomed already and that lobstermen deserved to exterminate the ones that remain. "It would devastate [the lobstermen] if there were greater conservation efforts," said Beth Casoni, executive director of the Massachusetts Lobstermen's Association. "The waters aren't going to cool."[49]

During roughly the same period—1994 to 2014—Maine's lobster harvest increased by 214 percent, from 60 million to 124 million pounds.[50] The recent Maine lobster boom seems to have been caused by three factors. Cod were overfished, so there were fewer predators around to snack on baby lobsters. Sea urchins were also overfished, so the amount of kelp increased (because the sea urchins weren't snacking on it), providing more spots for little lobsters to hide. And finally, the Gulf of Maine warmed enough to make the lobsters start accelerating their lives. They began molting earlier in the season, and sometimes molted twice in the summer and again in the fall, instead of once per season. They also started breeding repeatedly before they reached legal size—the size that was supposed to be when most lobsters had bred once.[51]

Warming temperatures seem to accelerate lobster lives—up to a point. In 2013, 11 million lobsters died in Long Island Sound off Connecticut when the water got too warm—essentially expiring of heat stroke.[52] Since then, the lobster population has moved north, abandoning Connecticut for Maine's still-frosty waters.[53] The 300 lobster fishermen trapping in Connecticut in 1999 dwindled to just 14 by 2016.[54] Lobsters, which were supposedly so numerous they were once the food of choice in local prisons, are moving away from warming water all over southern New England, and Massachusetts lobstermen may be facing a five-year moratorium on trapping.[55]

Individual lobsters aren't moving to Maine; their little claws can't scuttle that fast. Instead, over the past 50 years fewer and fewer little lobsters in the waters off New York and Connecticut have survived to adulthood, while lobsters in Maine have thrived.[56] That difference in juvenile survival rates has translated into a huge difference in the number of adult lobsters—and may well doom the Maine lobster industry as the ocean gets even warmer.

The Gulf of Maine is projected to warm by up to 4°F by the end of the century. What will the lobsters do then? One researcher commented, "We're keeping our eye on Newfoundland and the north shore of the Gulf of St. Lawrence as a new frontier for lobster."[57]

There is one glimmer of hope. Lobstermen in Maine generally belong to "lobster gangs," groups of 8 to 50 boats of lobstermen who set traps in a particular territory. The gangs keep outsiders away from their territory and have strong motivation to perform basic conservation measures like putting notches in the tails of egg-bearing females. Having more lobsters benefits the group, and every lobsterman will see the rest of his gang at the dock, at the grocery store, at the bar. There's not much escape from your neighbors in coastal Maine's small towns. Social pressure benefits the gang, and the lobsters.[58]

Fish the Second: Ocean Fish
Who Sees Seafood?

Until the late nineteenth century, most New England locals never ate fresh fish at all, even if they lived in seaport towns, because fishermen didn't sell it. Most of the fish available in New England was cod, which was salted at sea and either "pickled" wet in barrels or dried on shore. Even then, most of New England's fish didn't end up in New England, or even in North America. The finer grades of salt cod were exported either to Catholic countries, including Portugal, Spain, and France, where the faithful ate fish on Fridays, or to England and other European countries where meat was expensive. The nastier grades, which were discolored, shredded, or even rotten, were known as "refuse fish" and shipped to the West Indies and the American South to feed slaves.[59] New England's signature fish formed yet another leg of the infamous triangular trade, where human bodies were shipped from Africa to produce sugarcane and New England ships supplied cheap protein to keep those bodies alive.

This fact bears repeating: New England's fish-based fortune was made not because Portland or Providence residents loved baked scrod but because Caribbean slave overseers preferred to buy cheap protein so that every arable inch of the islands and every ounce of their slaves' strength could be used to grow sugarcane instead of food. In 1763 alone, Massachusetts fishermen exported 137,794 quintals (1,544,928 pounds) of dried salt cod to the West Indies.[60]

Are You Really Going to Eat That?

Before the era of ice making and mechanical refrigeration, in New England fish was a poor man's food. An archaeological survey of the privy of Katherine Nanny Naylor, who lived in Boston from 1636 to 1716, shows that a significant number of fish bones appeared only in the period after her 1671 divorce,[61] when Nanny had to support four children on a pittance.

(In case you're wondering what it took to get divorced in Boston in 1671, Katherine Nanny Naylor reported that her husband Edward threw "earthen platters," food, and chairs at family members and servants and "[his daughter Lydia] down the garet stayres," and that after Edward had impregnated their servant, Mary Read, Read may have tried to poison Katherine by putting henbane in her beer. A jury found Edward guilty of adultery and "inhuman carriage and guilty of flogging his wife and children.")[62]

Despite Boston's proximity to a vast ocean supporting more than 200 species of edible sea life, studies of the colonial privies unearthed during excavation of Boston's Central Artery yielded up only seven species of fish—cod, haddock, striped bass, sturgeon, herring, alewives (another type of herring),[63] and, weirdly, shark, which may have been sold under a false name. Halibut, salmon, sole, shad, and dozens of other types of fish just weren't eaten.

Through the eighteenth century, New Englanders never ate fresh cod, herring, or mackerel unless they visited a coastal town.[64] Any ocean fish that made it to inland towns was salted or dried. All fresh fish came from their rivers, and most came from the spring migrating fish runs, although some enterprising farmers began building fish ponds on their land in the 1730s.[65]

One reason for this pescaphobia is that fish, weird creatures resting somewhere between beef and vegetables in a sort of eighteenth-century nutritional Great Chain of Being, were generally suspect in New England.[66] Here's a fairly typical passage from the 1837 *The Parlor Book: Or, Family Encyclopedia of Useful Knowledge and General Literature*.[67]

> Fish has generally been considered holding a middle rank between the flesh of animals and vegetable food. Though not so nourishing as beef or mutton, it is sufficiently so for all the purposes of active life, but a quantity is required to satisfy the appetite, which returns sooner after fish than after meat. It gives less excitement during digestion than most meat or other nourishing food, and is therefore a useful article of diet to persons recovering from acute diseases, but though reputed light and nourishing, it is not so proper for patients laboring under stomach complaints, with whom it very generally disagrees.[68]

Apart from its inability to "satisfy the appetite," preparing fresh fish also involved labor-intensive removal of lots of little bones, and nineteenth-century New England writers complained that it was tasteless, as Sarah Josepha Buell Hale wrote in 1839 in *Godey's Lady's Book*: "Fish cannot be rendered so palatable because it does not admit the variety of cooking and flavors that other animal food does."[69]

As food historian Sandra Oliver notes, fish also falls apart into little bits once you cook it—unlike stalwart, sturdy beef, which stays in chunks!— and unless you live next to a seaport, it won't be terribly fresh (unless it's iced).[70] Who would want this stuff?

Part of the problem is that New Englanders weren't terribly creative about cooking their fish, judging by nineteenth-century cookbooks. Salt cod was cheap and generally soaked and boiled into submission. Small fish were breaded and fried; larger fish were poached and served with white sauce, butter, cream, or fried salt pork scraps. Leftover fish were mixed with potatoes to make fish cakes and fried, or warmed up in cream and poured on toast. Chowder was a kind of combination of all the other cooking methods, simmering fish with salt pork and potatoes and adding milk or cream.

New Englanders were also early adopters of canned fish, innovating by passing off small herring in cans as "sardines" in the 1870s. Maine continued to be a canned sardine powerhouse through the 1950s, when California and Norwegian sardines seeped into the market. The last Maine sardine cannery closed in 2010.[71]

Why didn't New Englanders do better? Why didn't they develop a bouillabaisse, smoked salmon, sole meunière, or even decent fish and chips? Or pickled herring? Apart from chowder, New England's main popular contribution to oceanic gastronomy is one of the most abstract, industrialized forms of seafood: the fish stick.

The issue seems to be the same problem that impoverishes all of New England's food. By the time high-quality ingredients became widely available, most of the people cooking them were busy with their urban, industrialized lives and were so accustomed to canned, preserved, salted, and just plain *old* food that they did not aspire to anything tastier. As a 1910 skeptic wrote, "Indeed, the inventions by which food can be preserved for long and transported from afar may be liable to the drawbacks of fostering a concentrated instead of a scattered population and eliminating better food to make way for worse. Thus it is by no means pure gain that fishmongers by the use of ice can now keep their fish so long."[72]

In the meantime, industrial entrepreneurs in Gloucester were trying to make it as easy as possible for consumers to use their fish—ensuring that increasing numbers of people who bought it would never have to look a cod head in the eye or ever learn how to cook a filet. Gloucester fish processors started to produce "boneless" salt cod in 1869 and turned out 14 million pounds it per year—at a time when workers had to remove every single bone by hand. The process wasn't even partly mechanized until the 1880s. The first boneless fresh fish filets were commercially produced by Boston's Bay State Fishing Company in 1921.

The market for unsalted fish continued to grow with advances in refrigeration, freezing, processing, and transportation. By 1935, New England's fishermen were regularly supplying fresh fish to areas 600 to 700 miles beyond Boston.[73] By 1940, 60 percent of New England's fresh fish was being shipped over 200 miles.[74]

A Fresh Start

In the mid-nineteenth century, an influx of Catholic immigrants from Ireland, Italy, and Quebec created a large local market for New England fish for meatless Fridays. Middle-class consumers were also happy to pay a premium for fresh fish as cheaper salt cod and "pickled" fish became increasingly associated with poverty, immigrants, urban working classes, and southern blacks.[75]

Fishermen had attempted to produce "fresh" fish for New England before then; they were kept in freshwater mill ponds, tidal pools, or wooden "cars" sunk into the ground and filled with salt water—much like today's lobster pounds. From the 1820s through the Civil War, fish were also kept in "well smacks"—ships with a special hold with holes that allowed sea water to flow in and out to keep fish and lobsters alive, mostly. Shallow-water fish did fairly well, but deep-water fish like cod caught in the Banks tended to float to the top and expire unless their swim bladders were punctured.[76]

For the most part, until ice became common, most New Englanders got their "fresh" fish from peddlers going door to door with pushcarts. As fish canner Frank E. Davis wrote in his biased recipe book in 1907, "The fish you see in a dealer's store has probably been dead some time, exposed to the air, to germs, to flies, and other contaminating influences."[77]

Steam engines, railroads, and ice all made it easier to get fresher fish out to people in more places more quickly. As a Provincetown sea captain testified before the Senate Committee on Foreign Relations in 1866, "The demand for salt fish today is not as large in proportion to our population as forty years ago. . . . Our population has increased threefold in the last forty years, yet we do not use much more salt codfish than we did then."[78]

Fresh Fish Folly: Halibut

By 1845, most Gloucester fishing boats had converted to using ice to preserve fish—and halibut became the new "it" fish. It also became one of the first major overfishing disasters of the nineteenth century.

Halibut was once so common that Captain John Smith wrote in 1624, "There is a large sized fish called a Hallibut, or Turbut, so bigg that two men have much a doe to hall them into the boate; but there is such plenty, that the fisher men onely eate the heads & finnes, and throw away the bodies."[79]

Halibut wasn't popular with New England's fishermen until the 1840s, though, because it was a big, thick fish, which made it difficult to salt and preserve. Before the 1840s, fishermen would eat the halibut they caught themselves because it was worthless, unlike the money-making cod.[80] But with ice, halibut could be preserved without salting, and the fish's firm, dense flesh also held up better in freezing conditions than cod, haddock, pollock, and cusk. Halibut was also a big-boned fish, which made it much easier for frustrated wives to prepare and for tired husbands to eat than small-boned, fussy fish like alewife herrings or shad.[81]

By midcentury, the combination of ice and railroads made it easier to ship fish fresh from port. Middle-class consumers were also happy to pay a premium for it. Cheaper salt cod and "pickled" fish became increasingly associated with poverty, immigrants, urban working classes, and southern blacks.[82] Halibut was the perfect fish for icing and shipping, and it became the subject in the first test of unregulated, year-round Georges Bank fishing with bottom-scraping trawl lines.

Halibut fishing was a wasteful business. Fishermen threw away fish that weren't absolutely perfect. Starting in 1848, Gloucester halibut were graded by buyers as white, gray—which was worth half the price of white—and sour—which brought a quarter the price of white. The only difference between the white and gray halibut was the color of the underbelly, which most customers never noticed, but the price difference meant that fishermen threw hundreds of dead gray fish overboard to make room for more whites on each trip. As Glen Grasso wrote, "Throwing fish overboard in port instead of selling them led to more trips, more fishing pressure, and ultimately, more halibut taken out of the ecosystem."[83]

Halibut are also big fish when they're allowed to mature, with females commonly reaching 150 pounds; the record holder in Maine weighed 600 pounds.[84] Like other big, slow-growing fish, they don't reach reproducing age until they're 7 to 12 years old.[85] Altogether, they were perfectly suited for extinction.[86]

Up to the 1830s, most halibut was fished—when it was fished at all—in Massachusetts Bay. By the 1850s, the species had been exterminated there, and fishermen traveled to Georges Bank to pursue their prey. As fishermen killed off most of the mature halibut, they began a "chicken halibut" fishery for smaller juvenile fish—which reduced the number of halibut growing old enough to reproduce.[87]

By 1870, Georges Bank had been fished out as well, which apparently didn't teach anyone anything.[88] Commentators claimed that the fish had gone "farther out to sea" in a sort of miraculous mass migration. In a pathetic reversal of sixteenth-century fishermen's journey to the New World to seek out new fisheries, Gloucester fishermen seeking halibut in the 1880s sailed eastward to Greenland and Iceland—a bit far for a fresh fish—and returned with salted halibut to be smoked for market.[89]

By 1885, Captain Chester Marr reminisced about Georges Bank in the 1840s: "Whole surface of the water as far as you could see was alive with halibut . . . we caught 250 in three hours; the crews of some vessels would go and cut the fins off the fish and let their bodies go. . . . No wonder they were broken up. We thought they were always going to be so. Never made no calculations that we were going to break them up."[90] Soon, the fish served in New England didn't even come from the Atlantic Ocean any more. In 1897, an article in *Harper's Magazine* noted that "car-loads of fresh halibut are sent from Seattle to New York, and even to Gloucester, the headquarters of the New England deep-sea fishery."[91]

Even Rudyard Kipling noticed that the halibut were disappearing. As Kipling had his mouthpiece character Dan say in *Captains Courageous*, "The fish are runnin' smaller an' smaller, an' you've took baout as logy a halibut as we're apt to find this trip. Yesterday's catch—did ye notice it?—was all big fish an no halibut."[92]

By the 1930s, fishermen in Georges Bank who caught 10,000 pounds of halibut in five trips thought they were "doing well," when at the height of the nineteenth century a halibut ship could snag 35,000 pounds of fish in a single outing.[93]

In the twentieth and twenty-first centuries, Atlantic halibut have been struggling. Halibut has been listed as a "species of concern" by the National Oceanic and Atmospheric Administration (NOAA) since 2004.[94] Total Atlantic halibut landings have plunged from a high of 10.8 million pounds in 1896 to record lows of about 40,000 pounds between 1998 and 2000.[95] The stocks have recovered a little since then, but they are far, far below historic levels. The NOAA still lists them as "overfished,"[96] and the fishery is tiny by West Coast standards. In 2015, East Coast fishermen caught 215,000 pounds of Atlantic Halibut, while Alaskan fishermen marketed 20 million pounds of Pacific halibut to a hungry nation.[97]

Fish the Third: Ye Olde New England Fish

Although salt cod was the most commonly produced seafood in New England (if not the most commonly consumed), New Englanders did eat other creatures too. Whales, salmon, and shad happen to illustrate useful principles of New England's tastes and attitudes toward fresh, local food—many of them grim. When there was a conflict between fish and industry, industry always won out.

Whales

One seafood the near-starving Pilgrims did not adopt was whale meat. Whales washed up on Plymouth's shores regularly, according to accounts by Plymouth colony leader William Bradford, who describes *Mayflower* scouts encountering "ten or twelve Indians" on the beach "cutting up a great fish like a grampus"—probably a stranded pilot whale.[98] An early settler in Acadia, Maine, reported that the local M'iqmaks ate whale blubber "as one does bread," from the dead whales that frequently drifted onto local beaches. There isn't much evidence that Native Americans hunted whales in the Northeast before European colonization—enough whales drifted onto the beaches to meet local demand.[99]

The Massachusetts Bay colonists and their ilk valued whales far more for their oil than for their meat. Governor John Winthrop wrote in 1635 that some of the Massachusetts Bay men went to Cape Cod to make whale oil, and by 1652 it was taxed by the Plymouth colony.[100] Massachusetts whalers began fishing for whales near the shore by the 1660s, and by 1720 the *Boston News-Letter* recorded that the Cape Cod whales had disappeared, writing, "We hear from the towns on the Cape that the Whale Fishery them has failed much this Winter, as it has done for several winters past."[101] By the 1760s, whalers from Cape Cod and Nantucket had to sail off to Newfoundland and Labrador to find their prey.

Salmon

One of the most bemoaned lost New England fish is Atlantic salmon—yet another fish that was supposed to be so plentiful that colonists could walk across their backs to cross rivers during the spring, and allegedly was the subject of laws passed to keep servants from eating it more than twice a week.

In Europe, salmon was known as the "king of fresh-water fish," and its luscious flesh was expensive, a luxury good. Early European records of fish in the Americas tended to be written by promoters writing seventeenth-century advertisements for how wonderful life was in frigid, forested New England. Instead of describing a land of milk and honey, they talked about the rivers of salmon—although some of these writers seem to have been confused about what exactly salmon was. At least two seventeenth-century writers say the rivers were full of "white salmon," which isn't a real fish. They probably meant shad.[102] When the writers did take the time to describe fish species, salmon was never at the top of the list of fishy bounty, and they showed up at the middle or end, if they appeared at all, implying that the salmon was not the most exciting fish in the sea or the river. Salmon is a little different from shad, though, because instead of relying on hearsay, archaeologists have attempted to locate physical evidence of salmon via surveys of fish bones in middens along rivers where Native Americans lived and ate before Europeans arrived in Maine.[103]

Consider for a moment the lengths that academic archaeologists will go to make a point. Catherine Carlson sifted through 30,000 fish bones at 21 archaeological sites in Maine at estuaries, on the coast, and along the Sheepscot and Damariscotta rivers. Carlson found almost no salmon bones at all.[104] This is a little odd if the rivers were brimming with tasty, fatty fish. The local Native Americans caught and ate plenty of shad, ale-wives, and other smaller, bonier fish. And in the Pacific Northwest, where there are still salmon runs today, there are plenty of salmon bones in pre-European middens.

Two conditions changed in Maine rivers once Europeans arrived: the temperature and the rivers' flowing, thanks to dams. The Little Ice Age began around 1550, cooling New England rivers and making them more amenable to cold-loving salmon. Salmon eggs and fry can tolerate only a narrow range of temperatures, and today New England's waters lie at the warmest end of that range. It could be that New England's Atlantic salmon were just European salmon that swam over during the Little Ice Age, which coincided with the beginning of European settlement on the Maine coast. Genetic tests indicate that Atlantic salmon in New England and Europe separated into two populations only very recently.[105]

That salmon-friendly Little Ice Age waned around 1800. One writer complained that by 1749 the salmon on the Merrimack and Connecticut rivers was "not of a good quantity, and is not so good quality, and is not so good for a market as the salmon of Great Britain and Ireland."[106] By the time dams and mills began to appear on Maine's rivers, the salmon were already disappearing. Strangely, the salmon disappeared in areas *downstream* from where the dams were being built on the Connecticut River—but persisted in the dammed, polluted Penobscot.[107]

Unfortunately, several unsuccessful salmon-restoration efforts have been attempted based on old fish tales. Since 1970, more than $100 million has been spent attempting to restore salmon to the Connecticut River, with up to 10 million fry released each year. Over the course of the next 30 years, the largest Connecticut River salmon run consisted of just 600 fish, and as of 2004, fewer than 50 fish were returning each year—during a period when the global average temperature increased by 1°F.[108] Ironically, attempts to restore salmon to rivers have resulted in a resurgence of alewives and shad, the "poor man's salmon."[109]

Sturgeon

Sturgeon is a great, boney-plated, bottom-feeding fish, so highly esteemed and overfished in Europe that fourteenth-century French and English cookbooks listed instructions for making "sturgeon" out of veal. Sturgeon was abundant in precolonial America and appears to have been a mainstay of the diets of coastal Native Americans, especially during the spring sturgeon runs.

William Wood wrote in the 1630s, "The sturgeons be all over the country, but the best catching of them is upon the shoals of Cape Cod and in the river of Merrimac, where much is taken, pickled, and brought for England. Some of these be twelve, fourteen, eighteen foot long."[110] Those sturgeon lengths may sound a little exaggerated, but they don't even re-produce until they're at least four feet long. They're armored, slow-moving, bottom-feeding fish who don't have much else to do. Why not grow to the size of a small whale? What else do you have to do when you spend your whole life sucking up algae?

As John Josselyn wrote in his 1674 *An Account of Two Voyages to New England*, "In dark evenings when they are upon the fishing grounds near a Bar of Sand (where the Sturgeon feeds upon small fishes), Indian lights a piece of dry Birch-Bark which breaks out into flame and holds it over the side of his Canow, the Sturgeon seeing this glaring light mounts to the surface of the water where he is slain and is taken with a fish gig."[111]

By 1673, Massachusetts was licensing sturgeon fishers, and export regu-lations soon followed. By 1793, regulations on fishing by the Massachusetts General Court (the legislature) did not even mention sturgeon; there were too few to bother regulating.[112] So much for Paul Revere's caviar.

Shad

Shad was a popular fish but was not a very fashionable food in the sev-enteenth century. As Sylvester Judd wrote in his *History of Hadley*, "The shad, which were very numerous, were neglected by a large portion of the English for near 100 years in the old towns of Connecticut, and for about 75 years in these Hampshire towns above the falls. It was discreditable for those who had a competency to eat shad; and it was disreputable to be des-titute of salt pork, and the eating of shad implied a deficiency of pork."[113]

Like Alewife herring, shad swam up river to spawn at a convenient time in the spring when the fall stores of salt pork and vegetables were gener-ally depleted, but before spring crops could be harvested and spring lambs slaughtered. Fishing helped farmers survive.[114] These late spring fish runs, ranging from April in southern Connecticut to late June in frigid Maine, were an important source of food and cash for pretty much anyone with a net who lived near a river, with fish ranging as far inland as the Green Mountains of Vermont and the White Mountains of New Hampshire.[115] In the eighteenth century, farmers and townsmen would gather in groups at the local falls, using dip nets or large nets called seines to catch hundreds of fish at a time—some for food, some for barter, some to sell in local markets.[116] In 1800, most large rivers hosted spring fish runs. By 1900, these fish were functionally extinct.[117]

Battles over fish runs started early. In 1645, residents of Sandwich, Massachusetts, complained that bass fishermen had set up fishing nets that blocked alewives from migrating to the upstream town weir.[118] Two decades later, North Shore residents of Topsfield and Rowley said that a dam in Ipswich had blocked alewives for several years, "and, as a consequence, the fish might be wholly diverted from the river."[119]

By the beginning of the eighteenth century, New England's population was doubling every twenty years, and increasing numbers of people were tearing up riverbanks for farmland, cutting trees from the banks, and building dams for mills—all of which made it harder for fish to get to their spawning grounds.[120] The dams physically prevented fish from traveling upstream, while clearing the land of trees and vegetation increased the runoff into streams, silting in the rocky bottoms fish needed to spawn.

Local fishermen started seeing declines in the numbers of fish in the streams. Beginning in 1710, colonial assemblies in Massachusetts, Connecticut, and Rhode Island started passing laws to protect their fisheries, forcing mill owners to open their dams during fish runs, banning weirs and seine nets, or limiting fishing in certain areas to particular days of the week.[121] New England legislatures passed 39 laws limiting fisheries and dam openings between 1710 and 1775—and that's not counting all the local laws, hiring of fish wardens, and other fishy debates.

These new rules didn't increase the number of fish, and didn't prevent private interests from more fish-stopping dams. In 1788, the town of Falmouth on Cape Cod listened to freshwater fishermen's complaints, but ultimately accommodated a grist mill owner who dammed the river, only requiring that he open the dam gates during fish migrations in the spring, not demolish the dam altogether. The claims of private industrialists were becoming as strong as those of fishermen. The fishes' claims, if there were any, went unrecorded.[122]

The complaints—and dam building—continued into the nineteenth century, when the dams' effects became clear. When two dams were built on Maine's Penobscot River between 1830 and 1835, the rental value of nearby fishing sites plunged 90 percent, while a Kennebec River dam at Augusta, Maine, in 1838 brought local salmon to "just short of utter extinction."[123]

The latter half of the nineteenth century was full of struggles over fish and dams. Dam owners in Holyoke, Massachusetts, refused to build fish ladders that would sap a single drop of water from their mills' power. When they did build the ladders, the fish, now bred in state hatcheries, wouldn't climb them. River fish populations also declined due to excess organic waste rotting and sucking the oxygen out of the water, as well as polluted runoff from sewers, tanneries, and paper mills.[124] The most successful fish-restocking programs of the 1860s onward served resident, nonmigratory fish that happened to be the favorites of wealthy vacationers. Tourist fishermen angled for trout, and resort owners petitioned legislators to allow fishing year-round—except for late summer when the city folk were around.

By the 1830s, though, New England was more concerned about "progress" than fish eggs. When mills and factories were chartered by the state, their new dams were protected by eminent domain, and they were specifically protected from lawsuits by people who could no longer catch fish. A few rural folks petitioned the government for relief, or tried to tear down the dams, but their efforts were futile. The factories were here to stay; the fish weren't. As historian Daniel Vickers wrote, "During the nineteenth century, an emerging class of capitalist manufacturers seized control of the state and imposed their will upon the rivers." In 1800, most large rivers hosted spring fish runs; by 1900, shad were functionally extinct in New England—just like the passenger pigeon.[125]

It's not clear that the shad would have survived if there hadn't been any dams, but it might have taken a little longer to exterminate them. Short of continuous fish patrols on every New England river, towns didn't have any way to stop a growing population from overfishing the spring fish runs, and individual fishermen and women didn't have any motivation to stop catching the fish until they were completely gone.

Mill owners controlled the inland rivers and dams, destroying the fish runs, refusing to put fish ladders in their dams. Various groups opposed their selfish practices, but in the end the mill owners won out, and the tradition of spring shad runs and seasonal freshwater fishing was no more.

Fish the Fourth: Shellfish
Oysters

Oysters have struggled for decades, and clams are having a hard time nowadays too. Oysters have been popular in New England for more than a millennium, eaten raw or roasted in fires. Mounds of oyster shells from shellfish eaten by Native Americans more than 1,000 years ago still linger along parts of Maine's Damariscotta River.[126]

By the mid-nineteenth century, everybody was eating oysters, and working hard to find even more ways to devour them. Cooks were frying, scalloping, stewing, roasting, broiling, and baking oysters, even boiling them into something called "Oyster Ketchup."[127] Victorian cookbooks have more recipes for oysters than any other seafood.[128] Fanny Farmer's 1896 *The Boston Cooking-School Cook Book* has 26 recipes for oysters, including delicacies neglected by modern cooks such as "Beef Steak with Oyster Blanket" (which is just what it sounds like) and "Chicken and Oysters a la Metropole," or diced chicken cooked with fresh oysters in a white sauce. Truth be told, "Chicken and Oysters a la Metropole" is reheated leftovers with oysters, a dissonant dish to contemplate today when fresh oysters cost more than $1 apiece.[129]

Most oyster eaters preferred to eat oysters away from home. Ordinary working men ate their bivalves in "oyster saloons," cheap fast-food joints with red and white awnings where you could buy a beer with your oysters for breakfast, lunch, dinner, or hangover pick-me-ups. Oyster saloons were often stand-up establishments with counters in lieu of chairs. They offered raw, fried, stewed, or roasted oysters accompanied by typical fast-food condiments: mustard, ketchup, vinegar, salt, and red and black pepper.[130] More elaborate establishments might have special rooms for women and families and a slightly larger range of items on the menu, like oyster pies.[131] Fancy restaurants served oysters on a block of ice or on special oyster plates. When author Charles Dickens visited the United States in 1842, he later recalled in his *American Notes* that at fancy Boston dinner parties he encountered "at every supper at least two mighty bowls of hot stewed oysters, in any one of which a half-grown Duke of Clarence might be smothered easily."[132]

Oysters are filter feeders, extracting nutrition from their surrounding waters along with pollution, bacteria, and anything else that might happen to lurk in the water. Abundant, tasty, and easy to gather from seabeds in shallow water, oysters were collected up and down the coast by Native Americans. Once Europeans colonized New England, they started devouring oysters as well, depleting the supply along the northern coast of Massachusetts and New Hampshire in the eighteenth century.[133]

The declining oyster population was noticed. Connecticut first passed laws to allow towns to restrict shellfish harvesting in 1750. In the early nineteenth century, oystermen in Connecticut figured out how to repopulate oyster beds by transplanting them from one seabed to new "oyster farms" in state by scattering spawning oysters over a layer of old oyster shells.[134]

These farms were enormously successful for more than 60 years. Oysters were shucked and packed in wooden kegs in the 1830s for transport throughout New England, and many were "pickled" in brine for shipping. By the 1880s, New England oysters were being shipped as far as Chicago.[135] In the early 1900s, a third of Rhode Island's Narragansett Bay—30,000 acres—was devoted to oyster farms.[136]

If oysters had persisted, New England culinary life could have been very different. Oysters were popular, low-cost sources of protein and minerals, enjoyed by millions of people from all walks of life throughout the eastern United States. Today, New England oysters are a luxury, a footnote food eaten in cloth-napkin restaurants, like squab or passion fruit mousse.

After 1910, the New England oyster business gradually collapsed. Farmers suffered "set failure" and hurricanes, but the ultimate killer was human pollution. A combination of industrial vileness dumped into rivers, runoff from farms, and fecal contamination from ignorantly located sewage led to shellfish die-offs and occasional typhoid epidemics spread by contaminated oysters.

From the 1830s onward, Connecticut oystermen had farmed oysters by taking young "seed" oysters from natural beds and putting them in privately owned underwater plots to mature. Since World War II, oysters all over Long Island Sound have been threatened by development—or, rather, by covering up the earth. When rain falls on a forest or an open field, the water soaks into the earth and gradually travels underground to rivers, streams, lakes, and ponds. That's why rivers run when it isn't raining—groundwater is still flowing in. As the water flows through the soil, most pollution sticks to the dirt and clay it flows through, so the water that flows into the river is purified.

Unfortunately, water can't flow through rooftops or driveways or interstates (unless they've been designed to let water through—and not many are built that way nowadays). Instead, it's flushed into storm drains, which empty right to the nearest river. Instead of being filtered by flowing through soil, this rainwater picks up all the contaminants lying on the pavement—drops of motor oil and gasoline, dog feces, candy wrappers, whatever's lying around—and carries it straight into waterways and the ocean. The number of homes on the Connecticut coastline rose from 1.7 million to 3 million from 1940 to 1970.[137] At peak production (1890–1910), Connecticut's oystermen harvested 10 million pounds of oysters a year. By the 1960s, only 133,000 pounds were being collected annually.[138]

Today, nearly 50 years after the Clean Water Act was passed in 1972, eastern seaboard states have cleaned up coastal waters and oyster farmers are beginning to try their luck again. There were more than 530 oyster farms in Maine, Massachusetts, and New Hampshire in 2018. In 2016, Rhode Island was hosting 70 farms on 275 acres of seabed—or roughly 1 percent of the area that was farmed in 1910.[139] That same year, Connecticut oysterers harvested more than 200,000 bushels (1.2 million pounds) of oysters worth $17 million from more than 20,000 acres of beds—even more astonishing considering that a series of oyster epizootics nearly wiped out the species in the state in 1998.[140]

New England's oysterers face new competition from growers in balmy Virginia and Maryland. Unlike lobsters, oysters thrive in warm water and are reproducing happily as climate change wrecks the water for cold-loving species.[141] (So does the stomach-wrenching vibrio bacteria, which forced shellfishery shutdowns in Massachusetts in 2013.)[142]

Clams

Clams have a happier history and are still dug out of mucky mud flats—or dredged with nets from the ocean floor—but they have their own problems. The first problem is that the word "clam" refers to several different species of shellfish.

Littleneck or hard clams, *Mercenaria mercenaria*, are also known as qua-hogs; in Rhode Island, they're the most common chowder clam. They're also chopped up and made into fritters called clam cakes or "stuffies," also known as stuffed clams, as well as spaghetti with clam sauce. They live in the sand below the high tide level from Massachusetts on south, and they're the clams you can harvest with a clam rake.[143] Depending on their size, they're called cherrystones, mediums, or—surprise!—chowders.

Mya arenaria are called soft shell clams, long clams, long necks, or steam-ers. They can also be gathered from mud flats between high and low tide with rakes, and the steamers are, yes, commonly steamed.[144] They're also the clams used to make "belly" fried clams, those squishy-centered tidbits that unnerve delicate eaters unaccustomed to eating entire organisms.[145]

Spisula solidissima are known as surf clams, bar clams, hen clams, or sea clams, and they live offshore in depths up to 60 meters as well as in inter-tidal zones.[146] Historically, they were used for bait.

Clams have always been a harder sell than oysters. They're too tough to eat raw and chewy when they're undercooked or overcooked; and if your clam isn't a steamer (*Mya arenaria*), they're chewy no matter how you cook them and impossible to swallow unless cut into small enough pieces. No one offered bowls of steamers to Charles Dickens at a party.

Clams were also once reviled as the food of desperation by Plymouth's prissy Pilgrims, equated with eating acorns and groundnuts by nineteenth-century historians.[147] Native Americans were enthusiastic about clams, and shorelines from Connecticut to Maine harbor middens filled with clam shells. This fact may have contributed to the Pilgrims' reluctance to em-brace their chewy benthic neighbors, although the association doesn't seem to have bothered oyster fans. Victorian cookbooks don't have much to say about clams, especially compared to their fan-girl adulation of oysters.[148] More likely, tidy people eschewed clams because they were most often used for bait. A resident of Newburyport, Massachusetts, recalled that in the early nineteenth century clam peddlers roamed the streets hawking raw (unshucked) and cooked clams, stating that "clams were considered a plebeian dish, from which many persons turned in disgust."[149]

Clams became one of New England's most beloved foods when two traditions were invented. A shipboard stew of fish and hardtack biscuits was transformed into chowder with clams, potatoes, and cream; and the clambake was created as an excuse for a beach party.

Clambakes are a curious undertaking. Clams can be steamed open in a few minutes, but clambakes involve burying them in a pit with hot stones or coals and seaweed for several hours along with a selection of corn, potatoes, Portuguese chorizo sausage (if you're on Cape Cod), or whatever other food cooks wish to forget about for a few hours.

Nineteenth-century writers loved to describe Native American origins for their seaside parties that involved rustic cooking outside in the sand, making assertions that a clambake "perpetuates this practice of the aborigines." However, Victorian-era American authors were notorious for inventing Indian names and origins for everything from recipes to public reservoirs to make them seem more "rustic."[150] There is no record of Wampanoag or anyone else performing or sharing this cooking method with Pilgrims or other colonists. Native Americans may well have discovered this method of cooking clams slowly for a crowd. The tradition of cooking food in pits over coals has emerged independently in many areas of the world, and certainly could have been invented in New England as well. Nowadays, Mashpee and other Native Americans hold clambakes for special occasions, as do white people of all backgrounds. The traditions may be parallel, but they are separate.[151]

Clams started popping up in commemorative dinners celebrating the Pilgrims from 1720 onward. Forefathers' Day, the eighteenth-century approximation of Thanksgiving hosted by the Plymouth Old Colony Club, was celebrated as a "feast of shells," which they also called a "squantum"—presumably because that sounded "authentic." That dinner featured both clams and oysters in the 1790s.[152] Clambakes are an outdoor version of squantums.

As nineteenth-century Americans became wealthier and had more leisure time on their hands, and as railroads made travel easier, Americans began indulging in all manner of outdoor picnics and cooking.[153] Chowder parties and clambakes both began with the jolly fun of digging around in the seaside mud for clams and making a fire outdoors—both fascinating activities for children. People tended to bring along all manner of picnic items to these events: pie, cake, watermelon, drinks that were fizzy or alcoholic or not, even fried chicken(!).[154] As historian Sandra Oliver notes,

"Clams were not serious food, much as hot dogs are not serious food today, and this made them particularly suitable for recreational eating."[155]

Although clambakes may have begun as gatherings of friends and families, businesses quickly started hosting them—sometimes very, very large ones.[156] Clambake "pavilions" serving "shore dinners" appeared anywhere there was a coast.[157] On July 4, 1840, 100,000 supporters of presidential candidate William Henry Harrison assembled for a clambake and chowder festival in Rhode Island.[158] There is no record of just how many acres of sand were dug up for the clambake pit, if there was one at all.

Chowder has a slightly more obvious genesis than clambakes. Soups with chowder's basic ingredients—fish, salt pork, onions, water, and ship's biscuit crackers—seem to have been a tradition among New World fishermen dating to colonial times. The word "chowder" itself may refer back to the French word for cauldron, *chaudière*—or it may not.[159] What we do know is that dairy products would not have been available on most fishing boats, and milk wasn't included in eighteenth-century chowders. Dairy products seem to have first made their way into chowder in the 1840s. Since the 1870s, some kind of milk or cream has been included in most New England fish and clam chowders, except for Rhode Island chowder, which doesn't use milk.[160] (New Englanders will point out that tomato-based Manhattan clam chowder is not chowder at all.)

Between milk and mud-flat shellfish, clam chowder is clearly a landlubber's dish. Chowder parties in the nineteenth century hung a rustic kettle over a fire during a day at the beach. Stale ship's crackers were replaced with potatoes, which also help thicken the soup. In the twentieth century, there were many, many pointless arguments about the proper ingredients of clam chowder, but at heart it seems to be a milky, clam-based soup, suitable for serving in New England–themed airport lounges.[161]

Now New England's intertidal clams are threatened by warming waters, new predators, red tides, and moon snails. The clam harvest from Cobscook Bay, Maine, fell from 800,000 pounds to 100,000 pounds from 2006 to 2009 thanks to ravenous snails,[162] and red tide regularly closes New England clam, mussel, and scallop fisheries.[163]

In 2018, surf clam habitats were closed to dredging off the Rhode Island coast to protect fish spawning habitats, putting 500 families out of work.[164] In Maine, clams are threatened by the dreaded green crabs, invasive crustaceans that can obliterate entire flats and are expanding their range and becoming more energetic as the Maine waters warm. Clammers are reluctantly turning to solutions like fencing in mud flats, "farming" the clams—but the nets don't keep out toxic algae blooms, which are also stimulated by warmer temperatures.[165]

How We Actually Eat: Fish from Cans

Once upon a time in the Victorian era sardines were a luxury food.[166] Cans of tiny fish were a novelty, and fine dining sets came with special plates and forks for enjoying their oily, pungent taste. But as canneries expanded and fishermen grew more ambitious, sardines turned into bar food, then a staple in work men's lunch boxes, then a vaguely unfashionable food found in expired tins at the bottom of grandma's pantry.

The canning industry transformed Maine's herring from fertilizer and lobster bait into a bar snack. Herring became sardines, salted, smoked, and packed into little metal boxes that were sent to gin mills and saloons around the nation to stimulate patrons' thirst. Passamaquoddy Bay alone hosted 19 smokehouses for sardines by 1890.[167] Unfortunately, these salted, smoked fish were never deemed suitable for upstanding, calm, bland family meals, and when Prohibition forced bars to close, most of the canneries closed too.[168]

Sardine canneries were Maine's largest employers in the 1950s, with 6,000 Mainers stuffing herring into cans all over the coast in towns like Belfast, Lubec, and Eastport.[169] The last sardine cannery in Maine—and the United States—was Stinson Seafood in Prospect Harbor. It closed in 2010.[170] A newspaper article displayed typical fishing industry logic when the writer declared, "Once plentiful and unregulated, the supply of herring (unprocessed sardines) has been diminished by federal limitations and overfishing." Outside observers would note that those federal limitations were actually a response to overfishing.

Maine's sardine plants were also doomed by a lack of modernization for environmental and health codes. As the New England Historical Society wrote, "In Stonington, the waters around the factory turned red on days when the sardines were packed in tomato sauce, yellow when they were packed in mustard. The factory burned coal, so soot and dust settled on clothes drying on nearby lines."[171]

Now, miles of Maine's crinkled, crumpled seacoast look "natural" and "unspoiled" because the canneries, shipyards, and mills that served the herring fishermen and blueberry harvesters at Passamaquoddy, Mount Desert Island, Tremont, Southwest Harbor, and dozens of other ports have had time to rot and disappear.[172] Bostonians and New Yorkers can come to relax in an atmosphere where the work of thousands of men and women has been erased from the shores, where they can forget New England's industrial past.

Sardines have given way to tuna, a milder-tasting fish that isn't packed in glops of oil and comes from distant shores—and is also being fished to extinction.

How We Actually Eat: The Perfect Fish

New England's most appreciated contribution to the nation's seafood menu is the fish stick, "the industry's greatest contribution to modern living."[173] Introduced in 1953 after three years of painstaking laboratory development, the fish stick is the perfect exemplar of New England food. The fish itself is unrecognizable—the bland breading-entombed substance could be cod, pollock, haddock, or some unmeasurable combination of fishes—and its only consistent relationship with New England waters is that it may have been produced in a coastal factory. Gorton-Pew—better known as Gorton's of Gloucester, Massachusetts—has been getting its fish stick innards from sources like the Polish Distant Water Fleet for decades.[174]

Simply producing and getting a fish stick to consumers involved developing enormous industrial supply chains for freezing fish at sea in factory ships, finding freezers in grocery stores, and persuading consumers to install freezers in their homes. In 1952, when the US population was 152 million, only 4 million homes even had freezers.[175] But the rewards for fish stick shoppers were enormous. As the label said, "No actual cooking is required."[176]

The fish stick suppliers were devoted to scientific improvement too. In 1956, Paul Jacobs, the president of Gorton's, recapitulated Underwood's journey to MIT for help with food science. This time, Jacobs sought to improve the fish stick's freshness and taste, not to diagnosis the ills of canned lobster. Although the MIT scientists dabbled in irradiating the fish, courtesy of funds from the Atomic Energy Commission, among other sources, in the end it turned out to be less expensive to just improve Gorton's refrigeration and sterile handling procedures.[177]

Within a few months of going on sale, fish sticks made up 10 percent of noncanned fish sales from New England firms.[178] Congress pitched in a few years later, allotting $45 million to promote new fish products in supermarkets—mostly fish sticks.[179]

And yet, despite all this energy and promotion, fish sticks aren't viewed as classic New England food. In most places they're viewed as barely food at all. A staple of school lunches (thanks at least in part to Gorton's energetic promotions to schools in the 1950s), fish sticks are what one author called "the hot dog of the sea"—a foodstuff that is edible and known, but known as something children eat, not a food adults turn to for deep nourishment or pleasure. And hot dogs at least get served with interesting toppings and in exciting places like baseball stadiums and amusement parks. Where do fish sticks get served? Elementary school cafeterias, the antithesis of excitement and joy.

Fish the Fifth: Eels

According to John Goodwin's *The Pilgrim Republic*, on April 4, 1621, "Samoset and Tisquantum were still guests of the Colony. In the afternoon, the latter went to Eel River, apparently, and by treading in the mud caught, with his hands alone, as many fat, sweet eels as he could bring back to his entertainers."[180] As recently as 1989, Massachusetts eel fishermen harvested close to 30,000 pounds of eels from the commonwealth's rivers—a far cry from the 400,000 pounds plucked from local waters in 1880.

Glass eels are the youngest eels, so named because they're virtually transparent. Once they reach 2.25 inches, their skin grows dark and their name changes to "elvers."[181] The only two states where fishing for elvers or glass eels—tiny eels swimming upriver from the ocean spawning grounds where they were hatched—is permitted are Maine and South Carolina, and most elvers are fished in Maine. Florida has so few elvers that commercial fishing is futile. The vast majority of elvers caught in Maine are shipped live to Asia, where they are raised in aquaculture ponds to adult stage and then harvested as seafood.

Global demand for Maine's elvers has been high since 2010, when the European Union outlawed all imports and exports of elvers to protect its collapsing eel stocks.[182] Japanese gourmands enjoy 70 percent of the world's eels, or unagi. Japanese coastal workers have been farming eels since 1891, taking wild-caught young glass eels or elvers and raising them to maturity. Eels won't reproduce in captivity, so the world eel supply depends on hunting and catching the young as they swim upriver.[183] The Japanese eat about 130,000 tons of full-grown eels a year.

Between 1965 and 2000 the Japanese glass eel catch dwindled from 140 to 40 tons, a 71 percent decline over 35 years, and fell further to 15 tons in 2017.[184] The Japanese government even listed mature wild eels as an endangered species in 2013.[185]

Today, most of Japan's glass eels come from China—some from Hong Kong, which has no eel harvest to speak of, but appears to be a convenient layover for eels obtained from questionable sources.[186] A tsunami in Japan destroyed much of that country's cultivated eel stocks in 2011.[187] In just two years, the value of Maine's eel harvest spiked from less than $3 million in 2010 to more than $40 million in 2012, with prices reaching more than $2,000 a pound.[188]

Glass eel prices zoomed from $185 per pound in 2010 to $2,600 per pound by the end of the 2012 eel fishing season (roughly May–June in Maine).[189] The price has varied, but has stayed above $800 a pound, reaching an average of $2,000 a pound again in 2018.[190]

Maine licenses eel fishers, and in 2014 the state started regulating them; it banned cash sales of elvers and instituted a quota on harvests of both glass and mature eels due to concerns about overfishing. Where there's money, though, there are crooks. In 2013, 19 men were arrested in Operation Broken Glass for poaching and selling $5.25 million worth of glass eels caught outside of Maine but sold in that state to Asian sellers. The eels were stolen from New Jersey, Massachusetts, Rhode Island, and several other states.[191] In 2018, Maine shut down the elver season two weeks early because of concerns about illegal cash sales concealing poaching and overfishing—but not before Maine eel hunters had netted more than $20 million.[192]

In 2017, the Atlantic States Marine Fisheries Commission (ASMFC) declared that the Atlantic eel fishery "remains depleted," but did not take any action to limit the fishery.[193] Maine reduced its yearly quota in 2015 from 11,749 to 9,688 pounds,[194] and has kept the quota steady since then.[195]

There is one bright spot in yet another tale of resource depletion. Maine eel fishers can't point to generations of proud eel fishing because harvesting glass eels in Maine began only in the 1970s[196]—and it wasn't the sort of fishing for building a family dynasty. As recently as 2001, elvers brought in only $25 a pound[197]—a nice price, but not an overwhelming return for a business that operates only a maximum 8 weeks a year. And as recently as 1981, fishers landed more than 3 million pounds of adult eels—compared with averages below 1 million pounds per year since 1998.[198] There are reasons why the ASMFC considered the Maine eel population "depleted."

The "eel rush" is the ugly opposite of the supposed virtues of the old-time New England fishermen—the stalwart, hardworking, honest men who braved incredible peril and battled with fierce determination and skill against the titanic forces of the sea itself. Instead, elver fishers stand around on riverbanks catching baby fish with dip nets, much like colonial fishermen scooping up the seemingly endless shad run. Some of them don't even use dip nets but set "fyke nets," which are just giant funnels set up in the river, and empty them at low tide. Sometimes they can set up a little net in a stream and catch 15 pounds in one night.[199] It's slightly harder than getting a goldfish out of a tank at the pet store, but only because riverbanks are slippery. It's hard to make an emotional appeal for people making windfall profits by just living in the right place at the right time, but who are also depleting a species that is already going extinct in East Asia and Europe. Even William Sheldon, who was the Maine Department of Marine Resources employee who worked with Japanese seafood interests in the 1970s to figure out whether Maine had enough glass eels to ship overseas, was convicted of $500,000 in eel trafficking in 2017.[200]

Corruption has never been touted as a New England virtue. Miserliness, hard bargaining, and obstinacy, yes, but not outright theft and cheating. A sample of the postings on the Maine Elver Fisherman's Association Facebook page (August 8, 2018) reads,

> We are sorry to say that the ASMFC American Eel board voted to NOT give us an increase in our quota. All because of the illegal dealers and elver fishermen that decided to get greedy and not follow the laws. For those people that poached and bought illegal elvers you have hurt us from getting an increase on our elver eel quota. I hope you illegal people are proud of yourselves. And if this happens again, you can be proud of closing this fishery down."[201]

Fish the Sixth: Cod

> Along with deforestation, plow agriculture, river fishing, and the construction of milldams on hundreds of river sites, all of which affected estuaries, the relentless ocean harvest led not only to depletion of some marine resources, but to a restructuring of marine environments. It changed the sea.
> —Jeffrey Bolster, "Putting the Ocean in Atlantic History"

> We aren't stupid like they think, we'll learn the loopholes. A good fisherman these days must know when and how to break the law.
> —Gloucester fisherman

New England's cod, clams, and lobster are symbols of the region's rocky coasts—but only the lobster harvest is healthy. The 2018 Maine clam harvest was the lowest since 1930, about half of a typical 1980s haul, thanks to warming ocean temperatures that boost predators and harmful algae blooms.[202] Lobsters are thriving, but the cod catch has collapsed to 5 percent of early twentieth-century levels. Whether New Englanders will enjoy these iconic seafoods 50 years from now may depend more on today's fishermen than on tomorrow's eaters.

Dried cod contains up to 80 percent protein, making it a portable, very nutritious food that can be transported over very long distances.[203] Apart from feeding Caribbean slaves, salt cod was also one of the cheapest ways the Continental Army was fed. At the time of the American Revolution, Massachusetts residents could purchase a pound of "merchantable" salt cod for about a fifth of the cost of a pound of pork, and less than a third of the price of beef.[204]

Connecticut's Continental Army troops could have salt fish substituted for meat three times a week, while the Continental Congress called for fish on Mondays and Wednesdays.[205] The Massachusetts Committee of Supplies decreed in June 1775 that every soldier in the Massachusetts Army should get these daily rations:

> One pound of bread.
> Half a pound of beef and half a pound of pork; and if pork cannot be had, one pound and a quarter of beef;
> and one day in seven they shall have one pound and one quarter of salt fish, instead of one day's allowance of meat.
> One pint of milk, or, if milk cannot be had, one gill of rice.
> One quart of good spruce or malt beer.
> One gill of peas or beans, or other sauce equivalent.
> Six ounces of good butter per week.[206]

New England's fishing industry also helped *start* the Revolutionary War. New England's fishermen squabbled with seasonal English fishermen who frequented the Grand Banks off Newfoundland—and often fished for the same fish and dried cod on the same Newfoundland beaches. New England fishermen and merchants competed with the English fishermen for the West Indian slave market, sold and smuggled their fish to French merchants and the French West Indies, and flaunted British authority and control over the oceans. British attempts to control Atlantic shipping lanes and international commerce were futile and ended in war.[207] New England fishing ships also traded in the Caribbean for supplies for the Continental Army, including muskets and gunpowder.[208] Fishermen even showed up in Revolutionary War art. In the famous painting of Washington crossing the Delaware, the men rowing are all Marblehead, Massachusetts, fishermen.[209]

Fishing the Very, Very, Very Old-Fashioned Way

One reason that cod became such a popular fish to kill is that they live near coasts. Cod eat smaller fish like capelin and herring that feed on phytoplankton, single-celled plants. Phytoplankton need to absorb light near the surface of the ocean, but they also need nutrients from sediments from the seafloor. Some New England cod historically lurked near shore (until they were eaten), but they also lived in places where tides and ocean currents stir the sediments up to the surface—the vast shallow areas known as Georges Bank and the Grand Banks.

These banks were once hills and plateaus in a coastal landscape. They were submerged when the Laurentide glaciers melted more than 10,000 years ago. Imagine a flooded Boston with shimmering schools of fish circling Beacon Hill's summit, and you'll get some idea of how high the banks reach above the neighboring seabed. The Grand Banks and Georges Bank are less than a few hundred feet deep, and in many places the ocean bottom is only a few dozen feet away from the air and light.[210] That's great for fishermen because cod are groundfish—they lurk and linger near the ocean floor.[211] A higher ocean floor means more convenient fishing.

For the first 300 years of the New World cod fishery, working life was fairly predictable apart from the constant threat of violent death at sea. Fishermen would venture out and drop hooked lines over the side. Each man had eight to twelve 500-foot lines weighted with lead. On a good day a man could catch up to 400 cod.

Once the fish were caught, someone would split the fish, remove their heads, coat them with salt, and put them in the hold. If the ship was from a country that had easy access to Mediterranean sea salt—say from the French coast—they might bury the fish in enough salt to take them home "green," stashed in the hold. If they were from England, though, where salt was more expensive, the fishermen would return to shore each day to dry their fish on land. This procedure required much less salt, but far more land and labor.[212]

The first North American fishing ground to attract Europeans was the Grand Banks off the Newfoundland coast. The Grand Banks aren't really in New England, but are close enough that thousands of New Englanders have fished there over the centuries. Explorer John Cabot wrote after his 1497 voyage to the Grand Banks, "The sea is covered with fish which are caught not merely with nets but with baskets, a stone being attached to make the baskets sink with the water."[213] Within two decades of Cabot's journey, there were Portuguese, Breton, and Basque fishermen angling off Newfoundland, and the Spanish and English followed by midcentury, partly because the British had exhausted the cod fishery off Iceland's coast.[214]

Being a fisherman off Newfoundland in the sixteenth century was like working on a submarine. The crews would sail to Newfoundland in the spring, fish, take the fish to shore to salt and dry them on special platforms called flakes, then return to Europe in the fall with their dry cargo. There were no bars or horse races on the Newfoundland shore for sailors' amusement, although they did trade with local Native peoples.[215] Over time, the fishing concerns began leaving caretakers to overwinter in Newfoundland and keep warehouses, bunkhouses, and the flakes in shape for the coming season.[216]

Similarly, New England's first fishermen were transient workers, much like the farm workers who pick strawberries and lettuce in California fields today. In the seventeenth century, fishermen working in Marblehead generally came from English West Country towns such as Plymouth, Dartmouth, Exeter, and Barnstable—which later gave their names to towns in Massachusetts, Connecticut, and New Hampshire.[217] Because there was a local labor shortage, merchants didn't pay wages. Fishermen got a share of the profits in exchange for guaranteeing the merchants exclusive rights to their catch.[218] Presumably, the wages earned this way were more attractive than being a farm laborer back in Barnstable.

Cod also schooled in the Gulf of Maine, and in the seventeenth century fishermen set up operations in what is now the Massachusetts North Shore. In 1624—just four years after the Pilgrims landed in Plymouth—at least 50 vessels from Gloucester "fished with handlines in the offing of Maine and Massachusetts."[219] By 1653, the General Court of Massachusetts Bay had decided that fishing was so important and profitable that fishing vessels and equipment were exempt from taxes.[220]

By 1675, there were reportedly 440 boats and 1,000 men fishing between Boston and Maine's Kennebec River, exporting 6 million pounds of salt cod a year.[221] In eighteenth-century Salem, most young men put in some time at sea and did well for themselves—if they lived. About 30 percent of the young men of Salem who went to sea died before their 30th birthday, but out of those who survived, 70 percent were promoted to mates and 39 percent became captains of their own ships.[222]

The Business of Fishing

The people who actually made money fishing were the ship owners. In the first two decades of the Massachusetts Bay Colony (1630–1650), "grains profited the farmers who produced them, the local merchants who sent them on to Boston, and the Boston merchants who sold them for shipment abroad; fish, on the other hand, profited a scattering of fishermen located primarily along the northern coast, the English houses which . . . controlled the trade in this early period, and those Boston merchants acting as agents for English firms."[223]

As the revolution approached, fish made a few Americans very, very rich. After merchants in Marblehead expanded their dried cod trade to Europe in the mid-eighteenth century, the wealthiest 10 percent of the population held more than 60 percent of the town's wealth, while the poorest 30 percent owned slightly less than 2 percent of the money, land, and housing.[224] Interestingly, as Marblehead's labor force expanded and became cheaper to hire, fish merchants abandoned the traditional profit-sharing system for fishermen and instead paid straight wages to their hired hands.[225]

Bostonians were so proud of their *Gadus spp.* that a wooden cod was hung in the Massachusetts State House chambers. Between 1768 and 1772, fish represented 35 percent of New England's total export revenue.[226] In 1775, about 10,000 New Englanders, or 8 percent of the adult male working population, worked in fishing.[227] By 1787, 30 percent of Massachusetts's $3.5 million in exports was fish; 13 percent was whale oil.[228]

At the time of the revolution, 500 fishing boats and 5,000 fishermen from Massachusetts were taking cod from anywhere from Georges Bank to the Grand Banks to Nova Scotia, and about 10,000 people were working on short processing, drying, and packing the fish for export.[229] Gloucester and Marblehead combined took in 60 percent of the catch, with another 18 ports rounding out the total.

After the American Revolution, the 1783 Treaty of Paris officially gave Americans the right to fish in what are now Canadian waters on the Grand Banks off Newfoundland and in the Gulf of Saint Lawrence. They weren't allowed to dry fish on the Newfoundland shore, though, so American cod fishing trips were relatively short—a month at sea packing wet salted fish into barrels before returning to coastal towns to dry their catch.[230] About 1,230 New England boats sailed off to Canadian waters each year from 1790 to 1810.[231]

Part of the reason hardworking New England fishermen were setting off to sea is because the federal government was giving them a handout. From 1789 to 1803 and from 1813 to 1866, the government gave a bounty to every cod exporter, first as a "drawback," or credit for using imported salt, to ease the burden of tariffs.[232] Fish merchants seized the funds at first, but in 1792 the law was revised to direct the money to ship owners and fishermen. The fishermen quickly became accustomed to this handout. In 1839, one John Williams of Kittery, Maine, wrote,

> The bounty now paid is the sole means which many have to procure their outfits for the voyage; and that, if it be taken away, all such persons will have to abandon the business, which will thereby fall into fewer hands, and will, in fact, be monopolized by capitalists; the inevitable result of which will be a vast reduction in the quantity of fish taken, and a corresponding augmentation in the price, which will thereby drive our fish from foreign markets, when they can now barely sustain a competition with the British exporters of the same.[233]

Williams was right, but not about the order of events. By the time the bounty was repealed in 1866, the fishing industry had consolidated, and most of the capital—ships, equipment, money to buy supplies—was in the hands of fish merchants in Boston, Gloucester, Newburyport, and even Portland, Maine, not the captains or the crew.[234] These merchants didn't care if the bounty was repealed. They weren't especially interested in sharing money with their fishing crews anyway.

Without the bounty, it became slightly harder for individual fishermen and captains to earn enough money to buy their own boats—yet another reason that native-born New Englanders abandoned the fisheries to immigrants. Writers in popular publications lamented the thinning of the Yankee fishing stock, much the same way their college classmates were lamenting the Polish immigrants taking over Berkshire hill farms. This 1896 comment is an example: "The change in blood and personnel in the New England fisheries becomes interesting mainly from . . . the decay of coast villages and the disappearance of a sturdy type of American citizen."[235]

By 1840, cotton mill workers earned $14 a month, while unskilled seamen made less than $9.[236] An eighteenth-century fisherman in Essex, Massachusetts, probably owned land; nineteenth-century Gloucester sea captains probably didn't even own their own boats. Fishing increasingly became a poor man's occupation—a major reason why Massachusetts fisheries became dominated by immigrants. By the end of the nineteenth century, fishing was dominated by Newfoundlanders in Boston, Italians in Gloucester, Portuguese in Provincetown, and Portuguese and Scandinavians in New Bedford.[237]

In 1898, the year after Rudyard Kipling published the classic sea tale *Captains Courageous*, Boston fish dealers founded the New England Fish Exchange to "stabilize" their businesses through vertical integration. Like the fish merchants of colonial Gloucester, they controlled the ships, piers, and marketing—and, by extension, the fishermen, who earned a share of the catch, not a wage. A waterfront worker in the 1970s commented, "Fishing is the rottenest goddam business in the world . . . everybody's out to screw you."[238]

The Great Slaughter Begins

It took a little while, but fishermen eventually came up with more efficient ways to kill fish. In the early nineteenth century, ships began to take along small rowboats called dories and send fishermen out in them to catch more fish farther from the main ship. In the 1850s, fishermen added "bultow" or "trawl" longlines. Instead of tossing a fishing line off a boat, ships using trawl longlines would sink a long fishing line with hundreds of hooks attached to it, anchoring the line near the seafloor.[239] Ships began using dories to set up multiple longlines, and the payoff was enormous, for a little while. In 1880, New England fishermen landed 294 million pounds of cod.[240] A schooner crew of 8 to 12 men with dories could catch between 20,000 and 30,000 pounds of cod in a day.[241]

But even fishing from dories soon became a quaint historic custom. As Caribbean slave colonies withered, New Englanders began to crave fresh fish, and with new refrigeration technology, fishermen were happy to supply them. The last quarter of the nineteenth century saw the introduction of steam- and diesel-powered ships, power equipment like winches, and otter trawling—the practice of dragging enormous nets across the ocean floor to dredge up whatever was down there. New England fishermen started exterminating cod fish at an astounding rate. From roughly 1880 to World War I, New England fishermen killed up to 120 million pounds of cod per year on Georges Bank alone.[242]

Catches generally declined between 1920 and 1960, except for a brief period in the 1940s. During World War II, fisherman avoided Georges Bank out of fear of having their ships blown up by German submarines, and the fishermen who did venture out generally fished for halibut, not cod.[243]

Postwar Fish Frenzy

After World War II, fishery biologists supported their countries' efforts to kill as many fish as quickly as possible in the name of efficiency and progress. Economics, not the environment, was the main concern. The oceans seemed to be infinite resources, and fishermen had a patriotic obligation to exploit every possible resource for protein, progress, and profit. Fishery scientists talked of maximum sustainable yields and embraced a German forestry principle that removing older, larger fish would enable young fish to grow faster.[244] It is unclear why any scientist thought that management principles for dealing with trees on land competing for light would apply to ocean fish species, which had already had their largest specimens systematically slaughtered for more than 300 years. Perhaps something was lost in the translation from German. As a Canadian fisheries historian wrote, "The postwar deep-sea fisheries could . . . be characterized as a frenzied free-for-all. . . . Fisheries biology's focus on efficient resource exploitation made it a handy tool for the U.S. government; since nobody could actually see the resource, geopolitical ambitions were successfully projected onto the fish. . . . Cold War resource policy extirpated formerly sturdy fish populations."[245]

In the 1960s, New England fisheries had their own Red Scare. Research ships from the Soviet Union found a plenitude of herring in Georges Bank in 1961, and for the next six years fleets of trawler "factory ships" with fast-freezing capacity flocked there from the Soviet Union, Poland, East Germany, Spain, and Romania. Between 1960 and 1965, fish landings from Georges Bank increased from 96,000 tons to 578,000 tons—nearly a billion pounds of fish a year.[246] The fleets would search out the most common fish at the time, which led to depleting Georges Bank species by species: haddock, whiting, redfish, red hake, mackerel, and herring all disappeared in turn.[247] The International Commission for Northwest Atlantic Fisheries imposed catch quotas in 1973, and the 1975 Magnuson Fishery Conservation Act excluded all foreign ships without special fishing permits from venturing within 200 miles of the US coast.[248] The fish belonged to the Americans, who quickly proved that they were just as bad at fishery management as the Soviets.

When the United States and Canada established a 200-mile fishing limit in 1977, they effectively excluded all foreign trawlers from the New England cod fishery.[249] Euphoric fishermen bought new boats and new electronic fish detecting rigs. Between 1977 and 1983 the New England fishing fleet increased 42 percent, from 825 to 1,423 boats.[250] The New England Fishery Management Council (NEFMC), the local regulatory body largely staffed by fish processors and fishermen, did away with catch quotas entirely in 1982.[251] For a couple of years New Englanders caught a lot of fish. Then, catches started plummeting.

The story is the same for every fish in Georges Bank, although the timing is a little different between species. Cod landings, after averaging about 500,000 tons from 1895 to 1945, rose after World War II, peaked at 1.9 million tons in 1968, then collapsed. Despite a brief uptick in the 1980s to 700,000 tons, the catch dwindled down to 1,590 tons in 2016—or less than 1 percent of the 1968 catch.[252] Haddock peaked in 1965 at 250,000 tons, then fell to 25 tons by 1992. Redfish fell from a high of 400,000 tons in 1959 to 100,000 tons in the 1980s.[253]

There are many reasons for the decline. Overfishing is clearly one—but the North Atlantic Ocean has also been warming, driving away cold-loving fish like cod. The National Oceanic and Atmospheric Administration (NOAA) and other regulatory agencies overestimated how much fishermen could catch without destroying the stocks, and there have been problems with fishermen underreporting catches, discarding and dumping immature fish, and using technologies that destroy the environment. Foreign fishermen sailing just beyond the Grand Banks have been overfishing as well.[254] As a Canadian fisheries agency analyst wrote, "The fishery crisis cannot be related to a single cause or blamed on a single group: it is the failure of our whole fisheries system."[255]

In 1991, the Conservation Law Foundation sued the NEFMC to force it to manage cod responsibly. New regulations were put in place in 1994 to reduce the number of days fishermen spent at sea by 10 percent a year for five years—but it was already too late. The National Marine Fisheries Service calculated in 1993 that New England fishermen had caught 55 percent of the remaining cod living in Georges Bank that year. The entire bank was closed as an emergency measure.[256] Since then, fishing has resumed on a limited basis, but the NOAA stated that as of 2017 the Georges Bank cod population is "significantly below target population levels" and predicted that it would take until 2027 to recover.[257]

What took them so long? Why didn't the NEFMC regulate the cod catch before the lawsuit? Part of the problem is that fishermen, or at least the idea of fishermen, have enthralled Yankee New Englanders for almost two centuries. The consensus seems to have been that these admirable men (always men) deserved to keep fishing even though they were rapidly destroying the fishery itself.

Fishermen

Hail the stalwart, grizzled, salty New England fisherman! He bows to no man—except maybe the millionaire who owns his boat—and accepts only the purest subsidies from the US government as he relentlessly battles the elements in pursuit of his quarry. His prey? The mighty cod, which still persists in New England's George's Bank fishing grounds, barely. Cod landings in New England sank by 98 percent between 1945 and 2017.[258]

Part of the reason it has taken so long to regulate New England's fisheries to keep the fish from being obliterated from the face of the sea is that fishermen were given a privileged position in New England's culture. Victorian writers adored the idea of the heroic, stalwart, silent fisherman battling the elements and prevailing through sheer tenacity, and the idea continues to warp fishery management today. Fishermen are entitled to drive edible species extinct because they virtuously work hard and expose themselves to danger while they make money. As one scholar wrote about the emotional force of fisheries, "But somehow [the land] does not have the same emotional quality as do the boats. No one ever died digging potatoes; there is no danger planting barley."[259]

This hero worship was an astonishing reversal from Puritan-era attitudes toward sailors, when the men were known for cursing, fighting, and skipping church.[260] One creative Marblehead sailor threatened to have his dog baptized just to spite the Puritan authorities.[261] Most Puritans preferred stable lives on land to the changing fortunes of the sea. Sailors had to be recruited from beyond Puritan communities and were viewed as a shifty lot.[262]

Americans started worrying about fisherman in the 1880s. After more than 50 years of industrialization, the nation's centennial, and surges of immigration from Europe, Francophone Canada, and Asia, New England's white Anglo-Saxon Protestant middle-class Americans started fussing that their values were disappearing along with the honest, hardworking fishermen.[263]

In 1883, the story of Gloucester fisherman Howard Blackburn thrilled landlubbers across the nation. Abandoned in his dory at sea with his shipmate in January, Blackburn survived by allowing his hands to freeze to his oars so he could continue rowing through a storm to reach Newfoundland. Blackburn lost most of his fingers and toes but gained notoriety as the most perfect example of fishermen's virtues: hand work, persistence, and courage in the face of nature's cruelty. The tale made for thrilling reading in Beacon Hill's carpeted, coal-warmed parlors.

Blackburn's story also didn't involve the capitalist, consolidated, near monopoly that actually ran most New England fishing ports. Late nineteenth-century fisheries were largely controlled by fishing firms, not independent captains. By 1885, almost 40 percent of the Gloucester fishing fleet was owned by just 11 firms—143 ships out of a total fleet of 388.[264]

New England's fishermen had also stopped taking many thrilling journeys. The new demand for fresh fish meant that it didn't make economic sense for fishermen to venture to the distant Grand Banks—any fish that wasn't cod would rot before they could get back to harbor. Instead, they mostly dawdled around their home ports. Between 1901 and 1915, fishermen made four times as many trips to "Shore, General"—the inshore fisheries—than they did to the Grand Banks.

The act of fishing had also become more mechanized. No one needed to sail to the Grand Banks when they had otter trawls, giant weighted nets dragged over the seafloor. New England fishermen started to use these trawls in the 1890s. These nets captured all manner of fish that wouldn't take bait, including bottom-dwelling flounder and fish that had just finished spawning and weren't interested in eating. Add in the steam engines introduced in the early 1900s and typical New England fishermen weren't ocean adventurers so much as drivers, a bunch of hired hands guiding sea tractors few miles from home.[265]

And drive them they did. Between 1901 and 1905, fish landings in Gloucester and Boston inflated from 70 to almost 150 million pounds—and then dropped. By 1913, these fishermen were only catching 110 million pounds of fish, and taking twice as many trips to get them. The yield per trip fell from 22,000 to 11,000 pounds by 1913.[266]

In 1897, Rudyard Kipling published the most famous contemporary fishing adventure novel (and there were many, many fishing adventure novels at the time): *Captains Courageous*, a yarn about a Gloucester trawl schooner crewed by Portuguese American fishermen. Kipling later wrote, "I wanted to see if I could catch and hold something that was already beginning to fade."[267]

Mr. Fisherman Goes to Washington

In the late nineteenth century there were bitter fights over who should be allowed to plunder the sea, and why. In 1892, Congress debated the Latham bill, a measure that would have forbidden states from regulating any form of offshore fishing—basically giving over every bit of the coastline to industrial trawls and seine nets.

Stopping fishing regulations was so important to the US Menhaden Oil and Guano Association, a consortium of trawl fishers, that they threatened fishing regulators, bribed newspaper reporters, and paid a stenographer to alter the transcript of the testimony on the bill—all to no avail. The consortium was no match for Maine fish and game commissioner Dr. Edwin W. Gould, who opposed the bill and had the New England Fisherman™ on his side. Gould said the bill "would strike down the strong arm of the State, which is raised, as it were, to defend [the fishermen] against a most merciless and crushing competition by combined capital."[268]

The reason the US government should care about these imperiled fishermen wasn't that they were better at fishing than Menhaden Association members or that they contributed more to the economy, but because they were simply better people than other men (like, say, Menhaden executives). Gould said the fishermen were "hardy, fearless, inured to hardship and accustomed to brave the elements at all seasons, [and as such] are an ideal body of men. . . . But for the care of these men, among her most valued citizens, our State has always shown extreme solicitude, and the force of facts which would crush so splendid a race of men should receive careful scrutiny. . . . The Nation has a manifest interest in the welfare of this class of men."[269] The bill died in committee, and menhaden fishers were restricted for a few more years.

This appeal to fishermen's character didn't always work. In 1913 the Gloucester Board of Trade asked Massachusetts congressman Augustus P. Gardner to ban the landing of fish caught with the giant sea-bottom-dredging nets called otter trawls.[270] One pessimistic fishing boat captain commented, "Well, you could not get a better thing to do away with the fish on Georges Bank. In 10 years from now I do not believe there will be a fish there."[271]

Unfortunately, Gardner decided to invite as his chief witness James B. Connolly, a novelist who wrote about fishermen in books with titles like *The Seiners* and *Out of Gloucester*. When Connolly spoke before the Merchant Marine and Fisheries Committee, he praised fishermen's stalwart character. Then he was demolished by William F. Garcelon, the fishing industry's lawyer, who questioned Connolly about topics like the difference between cod and hake and fisheries statistics. Connolly could not answer—he wrote about fishermen, not fish.

Garcelon won the day by talking about how the new gear made fish cheaper and more sanitary and was safer for fishermen than rowing out in dories with fish hooks.[272] Fishing was an industry now, and the fleet owners weren't going to stand for regulations that would interfere with getting more fish out of the ocean more cheaply—and driving the remaining small-boat hook-and-line operators out of business. The fishes' thoughts on the matter are not recorded.

What's Love Got to Do with It?

Another reason why it has been so hard to create sustainable fishing regulations in New England is that some fishing isn't just a business—it's a *family* business.

Through the 1970s and 1980s, most Gloucester fishing boats were run by and for Italian families, and about half the boats out of New Bedford were owned by Portuguese families. (During World War II, Italian Americans were restricted from fishing off New England's coast due to fears of loyalty to Mussolini, and some Gloucester fishermen had their boats seized and were imprisoned.)[273]

These families used what economists call "kinship" systems of employment. If you weren't born into a fishing family, you did not work on these boats. Crews were sized according to how many family members needed to be employed, not for maximum efficiency, and family members were rotated on and off boats to share the work. The advantage of having families own boats is that the crew is more motivated to work for the good of the family, and family members pool resources so they have access to more money to reinvest in equipment—and to keep from selling off equipment when times are bad.[274] The disadvantage is that when the fish start disappearing, the entire family is threatened.

The other problem with these kinship boats is the "lay" or shares system of payment. Traditionally, in the lay system the captain, boat owner, and crew are given shares of the income from the catch instead of fixed pay. That means that when the fish are biting and prices are high, crew have even more of an incentive to catch as many fish as possible, legally or not.

Boston's fishing fleet had almost no kinship boats, and the entire Boston fishing fleet closed down between the 1950s and 1970s when falling fish stocks and competition from foreign ships made fishing unprofitable.[275] When the prices for fish fluctuated in the 1970s and 1980s, the ships that didn't hire family-based closed and sold their equipment at a much higher rate than the kinship operations.[276] In the 1980s, though, price increases gave fisherman incomes two to three times higher than those of landlubber factory workers.[277]

The shares system isn't unusual. Fisheries all over the world use it to spread the risk around so the ship's owner doesn't have to pay fixed wages when there's a bad catch—but the more expensive it is to set up a fishing boat, the more shares go to the owner, not the crew.[278]

Shares systems make it hard for Gloucester and New Bedford fishermen to change jobs because their entire families are invested in fishing.[279] Outside observers might question why anyone is still fishing for cod given the collapse of fishing stocks. One answer is that the family investments make it very hard for fishermen to leave the industry and get other jobs.[280] Kinship employment systems usually arise in the United States when it's hard for immigrants to find employment due to discrimination—often in businesses like ethnic groceries and restaurants. Gloucester's Sicilian immigrants no doubt encountered discrimination when they arrived in the country. Movies like *The Godfather* that featured Sicilian crime families didn't help.

As of 1990, only 548 men worked as fishermen in Gloucester, but a researcher estimated that 40 percent of Gloucester's economy depended on fishing, including ice companies and seafood dealers and processors.[281] Those companies include Gorton's—the home of the "Gorton's Fisherman"— which grew out of a business started by Slade Gorton in 1833. Today Gorton's is one of the top ten seafood suppliers in the world, with $350 million in revenue in 2000.[282] But Gloucester's seafood plants don't rely on Gloucester fishermen. They import frozen blocks of fish from Canada, Iceland, and Norway, fillet them, bread them, and stuff them into boxes.

The factories aren't staffed by extended Gloucester families. Most Gloucester seafood plants aren't unionized, and many employees work seasonally for minimum wage. The factory surveyed by the MIT Sea Grant program in 2001 brought in most of its workers from urban Chelsea, not Gloucester—and most of the workers were immigrants from El Salvador or Guatemala.[283]

The Sad State of Cod

All evidence gathered by people who do not stand to lose money from bad news points to the same conclusion: New England's cod stocks are on their way to extinction. Centuries of grand cod harvests, salted and shipped around the world, stalled and then stopped altogether when modern, efficient ships eviscerated the sea.

The 2016 cod catch was "the lowest in recorded history," 80 percent less than the catch of just five years earlier, down from close to 8,000 metric tons to 1,400 metric tons. Twenty-six years earlier, in 1990, the catch was 30 times larger.[284]

The cod population in the Gulf of Maine isn't a single giant cod, suspended in the ocean, staring at fishermen with one vast empty eye. There are ongoing debates about whether there is just one population of cod with members who shift locations or several different schools that don't interact much. What does seem to be clear is that the fishery "has been inexplicably devoid of cod for nearly two decades."[285]

When confronted with dismal statistics, New England's fishermen generally answer that NOAA scientists don't understand fish, and there are plenty of cod in the ocean where the fishermen know to go presumably because fishermen don't bother to linger in the empty, dead spaces where the cod have been exterminated. In 2016, Massachusetts governor Charlie Baker, ever sympathetic to the stalwart, energetic, and very well-organized fishermen of Massachusetts's historic fishery, decided that the state would conduct its own survey, just to show the NOAA what was really happening in the Gulf of Maine.[286]

The Massachusetts Division of Marine Fisheries (MDMF), under the direction of scientist Micah Dean, committed to correcting every possible flaw in the NOAA's surveys. The MDMF spent more than $500,000 and sent out a cod industry trawler—not one of those namby-pamby science ships!—to sample ten times as many locations as the NOAA ships, put out nets every month for ten months straight, instead of a mere two times

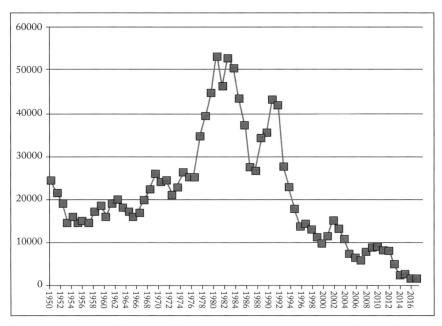

FIGURE 5.1. Annual New England cod catch, 1950–2016, in metric tons. Source: National Oceanic and Atmospheric Administration, National Marine Fisheries Service, "Commercial Landings," www.st.nmfs.noaa.gov.

a year, and kept the nets in the water 50 percent longer than the NOAA. And they found . . . nothing. As Dean commented in the *Boston Globe*, "It was an exhaustive survey meant to provide an answer to the questions that the fishermen were posing," Dean said. "But the fish weren't there."[287] The cod population was down 80 percent from the early 2000s, and, more ominously, very few of the cod the MDMF found were juveniles—the future market fish.

The scientists also had an explanation for why the fishermen are still seeing so many fish. Cod tend to cluster together when there are fewer of them in the ocean, and they seem to be gathering in water near Gloucester, where many of the most vocal, organized Massachusetts fishermen make their homes. No one sails out to the empty eastern Gulf of Maine, and since modern fishing nets are designed to release small juvenile cod, no one notices they're missing.[288]

From 2005 to 2015, the New England cod catch declined by 75 percent,[289] and from 2004 to 2014, the number of people claiming to work in fishing, hunting, and trapping in New England decayed by 42 percent.[290] As one writer put it, "Freedom to work when and how they want is one of the things that draw people to fishing; many believe they have a right to fish. What the cod crisis demonstrates is that the world has become too small, and our own numbers too large, for such a right to be acknowledged anymore. It is a privilege that has been abused. That is hard to accept."[291]

Even herring—the bait fish used to catch tastier things like cod and lobster—have been all but eliminated from New England waters. The herring population in the Gulf of Maine has declined by 90 percent since 1967.[292] In 2018, the NEFMC approved a ban on herring fishing within 12 miles of shore from the Canadian border to Connecticut, and slashed catch limits for the next three years.[293]

Codfather

In 2017, New Bedford fishing mogul Carlos Rafael, known as the Codfather, was convicted of flouting federal fishing quotas and smuggling money out of the country to the Azores.[294] Rafael owned one of the largest fishing companies in the country, with 32 ships and 44 permits. He admitted that he falsified records, lied to the NOAA, underreported how much fish he caught, and mislabeled fish as cheaper species that didn't have a quota—then turned around and sold them under their true identity to a New York wholesaler for hundreds of thousands of dollars.[295] In response, the NOAA banned 60 permit holders from fishing, representing a quota of 20 million pounds, or 10 percent of the region's quota of cod, flounder, and other ground fish.[296]

In the midst of a sea of complaints from captains, crew, net menders and other fishery boosters, New Bedford's mayor made the interesting observation that fish—actual fish—make up only a small fraction of New Bedford's fishing economy. Most of the money in New Bedford is in scallops.[297] In 2016, Portuguese fishermen landed $327 million in seafood, and three-fourths of that money was from scallops—which are really dredged from the ocean bottom, not fished at all.[298]

One of Rafael's former captains was convicted of using illegal fishing equipment in 2018. When Coast Guard inspectors boarded his vessel for a routine inspection, instead of letting them examine his net, he severed the line and let it sink to the ocean floor. Unsurprisingly, the Coast Guard knows something about ocean rescue, and when they retrieved the net, they found it was actually three nets, stacked so as to shrink the mesh size so the ship could catch smaller fish than the regulations allow.[299]

Fishermen in Gloucester's Northeast Seafood Coalition have claimed that in recent years the cod quotas have been so low that they couldn't intentionally fish for cod. Tom Testaverde Jr., Gloucester captain of the *Midnight Sun*, said that in 2017 he caught three times his 850-pound cod quota accidentally while fishing for haddock, and that he had to buy another fisherman's quota to make up for the cod.[300] Gloucester fisherman Al Cottone said that the cod had been getting in the way of catching flounder. "There's way too many fish out there," Cottone said. "It's a vicious cycle we're stuck in right now."[301]

Cod with the Wind

There are also signs that as the Atlantic Ocean warms, fish are moving farther north.[302] Scientists predict that 90 percent of current cod habitat in US waters will be too warm for the species to survive by the end of the century.[303] By 2100, the habitat for cod is predicted to be north of Newfoundland.[304]

Part of the reason that New England cod populations collapsed between 2004 and 2014 is that the Gulf of Maine warmed faster than any other oceanic region on earth. The water became too warm for young cod to survive to adulthood, perhaps because their food sources disappeared, or because they moved to deeper, cooler waters where more predators can devour them.[305]

As fish move north, New England's remaining fishermen have a new problem. Plenty of tasty southern species like black sea bass are schooling in northern waters, but the fishing quotas are still allotted to southern fishermen. In 2018, half of the fishing quota for black sea bass was allotted to fishermen south of Delaware, when surveys showed that 99 percent of the bass were swimming somewhere between New Jersey and Rhode Island.[306]

Aquaculture, or fish farming, doesn't really help. Most of the most marketable fish, like salmon, are carnivorous. On average, it takes five pounds of fish meal—made from fish like anchovies or menhaden—to grow one pound of salmon. How long can stocks of smaller fish hold up to the demand for salmon?

New England's smaller coastal towns lost most of their economy in the latter half of the nineteenth century. Petroleum was discovered in Pennsylvania in 1859, dooming the whalers of Nantucket and New Bedford (although the whales' near extinction would have ended whaling sooner or later). Salt producers in Onandaga, New York, drove Cape Cod's salt industry out of business soon after the Erie Canal opened in the 1830s, and New England shipbuilders found the market for wooden schooners evaporated once steamships began to dominate the seas in the 1860s. New England's seaside granite and lime went out of favor as new construction methods and new quarries sprang up in the West, where most of the building was taking place. Even New England's ice industry melted with the appearance of refrigerators.

In the twentieth century, larger seaports overwhelmed smaller harbors. Places like Gloucester built refrigerator plants and rail depots, while smaller ports "assumed a look that tourist promoters optimistically described as rustic or quaint, with old vessels lying on their beams at the tideline, wharfs sagging over rotted pilings, upland pastures growing back to bramble, and barns and fish-houses tilting precariously."[307]

Culturally, New England's maritime economy just isn't that important anymore. Although Boston was the second most active US port in 1900—bested only by New York—a century later it was ranked 35th, beaten out by dynamic cities such as Paulsboro, New Jersey, and Valdez, Alaska. Portland, Maine, New England's second largest port, was ranked 44th as of 2013.[308] As one author notes, "Tractor-trailer trucks using the federal highway system and the port of New York turned Boston into a backwater."[309]

In 2017, the United States imported 6 billion pounds of seafood—more than ever before—and 90 percent of the seafood Americans eat is imported.[310] How much longer will people eat any seafood from America, much less from New England?

Sweets, Sours, and Spirits

Maple syrup, cranberries, and apples are all made into pies and are all symbols of New England's fall and winter harvest bounty, but they were homely, unpopular foods until the 1850s. Maple syrup was a poor man's sugar, a country bumpkin's food that was gradually disappearing until Civil War sugar shortages and Colonial Revival rural chauvinism finally made it fashionable. Latter-day stories about maple syrup being a gift from "American Indians" are belied by a lack of evidence that anyone was making maple syrup in New England before sugar-craving Europeans arrived. Apples were mostly used for making hard cider, not pies, until Americans moved to the cities and discovered that industrial-scale factories made beer that was cheaper and easier to ship than Grandpa's favorite tipple back on the farm. New England writers promoted the idea that Massachusetts-born Johnny Appleseed planted sweet fruit to tame the American frontier, not to promote alcoholism.

Cranberries weren't associated with poverty or backcountry farmers, but they also weren't widely cultivated or eaten until the mid-nineteenth century, when a series of maritime industries failed and left many Cape Cod residents out of work and searching for new opportunities. Today, far more cranberries are farmed in Wisconsin than in New England, and climate change and poor yield management are making it even harder for cranberry farmers to survive.

Pies themselves have been exalted as the epitome of quaint New England domestic economy. Alas, New England cooks aren't any more interested in lengthy sessions of rolling out dough, peeling fruit, and waiting for pastry to bake and cool than residents of other parts of the country. New England residents are far more likely to eat whoopie pies from a minimart than to bake an apple pie from scratch.

Sweets

Maple syrup is one of the few foods that is actually produced in New England, identified with New England, and eaten and genuinely enjoyed throughout the United States. Although 80 percent of the world's maple syrup is actually produced in Canada, Vermont's trees supply about half of the United States' sweet stuff.[1]

Maple syrup doesn't exactly grow on trees; it grows *in* trees. As New England schoolchildren learn on sticky midwinter field trips, maple syrup is concocted by draining sap from sugar maple trees in the late winter. Warm days coax trees into sending stored sugars from their roots to their branches by day, then collecting their sugary sap back in their roots at night. The children's-book picture of maple syrup collecting is of a covered bucket hung on a maple tree over a spile, a short length of pipe stuck into the tree trunk. Modern-day tree tappers use plastic tubing linking multiple trees to polyethylene storage tanks that can hold hundreds of gallons of sap.[2] Some producers install underground pipelines to extract their trees' value without worrying about branches falling onto tubing or hungry squirrels gnawing into profits.[3]

In Maine, the average yield per maple tap is 5 to 15 gallons of sap per tree—but that's sap, not syrup. To make maple syrup, you need to boil down the pale, watery sap that's roughly 3 percent sugar until it's about 60 percent sugar. Ten gallons of sap produces just one quart of syrup—a ratio of 40 to 1 sap to syrup. Sap collected earlier in the season makes pale, lightly colored syrup. As the weather grows warmer, maple sap fills with more dark-colored, strong-tasting elements.

That collecting and boiling takes a lot of time, a lot of space, and a lot of fuel. This intense use of resources has led to bitter battles over how maple syrup came to be. Was collective syrup making a centuries-old community tradition passed down by Native Americans? Or was it a late-winter novelty, more like licking ice chips, that became a community project once European technology and consumers arrived? Although the typical pancake-soaker may not care if maple syrup is the product of Abenaki know-how or an innovation by immigrants from Barbados, anthropologists care deeply about who first started to make maple syrup, and they have gone to extreme measures to prove that they are right.

What We Know about Maple Syrup

The Micmac and Abenaki probably did have something like maple syrup. There are several references from 1557 onward to drinking maple syrup with Micmac and Abenaki peoples in what is now Canada.[4] It's referred to as "a sweet and very pleasant liquor" or "a beverage . . . of the color of Spanish wine."[5]

As close observers of their environment, the Micmac and Abenaki people also may have noticed that red squirrels will bite into sugar maple trunks in late winter and drink up the sap that drips out—a behavior that has been recorded in western Maine and elsewhere. The squirrels could also have been observant themselves and may have developed the habit as a result of encountering human taps.[6]

But most European American New Englanders, including the Pilgrims, didn't live in the Canadian woods. Sugar maple trees weren't nearly as common in coastal New England as in northern New England hill country and Canada.[7] It's possible to make syrup from the sap of other maple trees, such as red and silver maples, but it's harder. In most maple species, the sap has a lower sugar content or the sugaring season is much shorter due to early bud break, which renders the sap inedible.[8]

What We Don't Know about Maple Syrup

French explorers roaming Canada reported drinking a tree sap that had a taste "resembling that of the good wines of Orleans or Beaune" as early as 1543, but there are no written records of any of the Native peoples living in New England tapping trees for maple syrup before 1664.[9] Given how rare sugar and honey were at the time, this is a little odd. Southern New England Native Americans were certainly interested in sweet foods. Around 1635, Roger Williams of Providence wrote to Governor Winthrop at Boston about Canonicus, a chief of the Narragansett peoples, "Sir, if anything be sent to the princes, I find that Canonicus would gladly accept of a box of eight or ten pounds of sugar, and indeed he told me he would thank Mr. Governor for a box full."[10]

One piece of evidence that people near the Massachusetts Bay colonists weren't making maple syrup is that they were systematically making the coastal environment less hospitable for sugar maple trees, which didn't generally grow in coastal New England anyway. On Cape Cod, the Wampanoag regularly burned the woods.[11] Sometimes they used the fires to clear land to grow beans and corn; they may have used fire to keep hunting grounds open and "fresh and sweet" by killing off the woody brush.[12] Unfortunately, the fires also would have killed off sugar maple trees, which are far more sensitive to fire damage than are oak or pine.[13]

Red maples vigorously resprout after their main trunks are singed by fire, but red maple saplings aren't much use for food unless you're a beaver and haven't traditionally been used to make syrup.[14] Sugar maple trees generally prefer cooler upland areas to the damp New England shores where the first European colonists lived. As a nineteenth-century author put it, "The shores of the sea and the tidal streams were not the common home of the Sugar Maple."[15]

Still, suppose that New England's Native Americans did find some maple trees and tapped them. Next, they would have had to take on the laborious task of boiling down the sap to syrup, reducing 40 gallons of sap to a quart of syrup with a high enough concentration of sugar that the syrup wouldn't ferment (approx. 65 percent sugar).[16] It's possible to do this with the technology available in eastern North America before European metal kettles arrived. Sap can be boiled down by placing heated rocks in birch bark pans or wooden troughs. (Native Americans had ceramic vessels too, but they don't work as well.)[17] Freezing the sap repeatedly and then removing the low-sugar ice from the top works too.[18]

It would have made sense for New England's Native Americans to make maple syrup. It tastes good, it's a source of calories that's available in late winter when other food is scarce, and the effort involved in hauling and boiling maple sap would have provided an excuse for families and friends to gather and enjoy syrup together.[19] The problem is that there isn't any documentary or physical evidence any Native Americans gathered to make maple syrup in New England before 1674. No one wrote a description of Native Americans boiling down sap, and no one has found an abandoned sugar bush with syrup residue in broken pots or preserved wood (and archaeologists have tried, repeatedly).[20]

Maple sugar—the hardened, crystallized form of syrup—is even more likely to have arrived in New England after European colonization. Maple sugar is a lot easier to store than maple syrup, but it's virtually impossible to make it without a metal kettle. Put hot rocks in thick syrup, and the syrup sticks to the rock and scorches.[21] The words for sweet maple products in Native American languages ranging from Siouan to Algonkin all have to do with liquid coming from a tree, not sugar—"wood water," "tree juice," "sap."[22]

Sugar was precious in the early colonial period. There weren't any honey bees in New England until sometime in the 1630s.[23] Sugar was in short supply before the infamous Caribbean sugar trade began in Barbados in the 1640s—and Barbadians produced only small amounts of low-quality molasses-soaked sugar at first. These first sugar farmers ran small, self-sufficient farms. Sugar production didn't increase significantly until wealthy owners drove thousands of small landholders out of business, bought up all the land, and switched to producing sugar as a massive slave-grown monoculture crop around 1650 to 1665. Between 1645 and 1655, Barbados landlords also imported 12,000 political prisoners—English, Scotsmen, and Irish Catholics who had been involved in various rebellions. These light-skinned men could pass for free and escaped to North America and New England as quickly as they could, bringing their sugar-making experience with them.[24]

Even with all this coerced labor, business was slow; molasses and rum together made up only 7 percent of Barbados exports in the 1660s.[25] Then, Massachusetts farmers began getting large supplies of cheap molasses. Barbados's landlords traded that molasses for lumber, salt cod, beef, grain, and other basic foodstuffs to keep their slaves alive; not an acre of the island could be spared to grow food.[26]

Plain old sugar was expensive in the Pilgrims' time. Before the Barbados plantations began producing large quantities, England's sugar was being shipped in from Brazil's cane fields via Lisbon.[27] In 1650, the price of sugar in England was roughly 25 pence per pound, or bit less than 0.25 percent of a typical family income.[28] By comparison, 0.25 percent of an American family income of $50,000 today would be $125. By the 1670s, when prices had fallen by half, the average English citizen was still consuming only two pounds of sugar per year.[29]

By 1664, the Wampanoag and other New England peoples had been living in contact with Europeans for over 40 years, a population that from the

1650s onward included hundreds of refugee farmers from sugar plantations in Barbados.[30] These people had plenty of experience boiling down sweet liquids into hard, sweet crystals—a process that works for both sugarcane juice and maple sap.

Molasses and sugar became important to American colonists only when plantations started to grow big—big enough for a wealthy owner to invest in refining sugar on site, instead of sending brownish sugar off to Europe for a nice bleaching. The more refining was done on site, the more molasses was available for making rum, feeding to animals, or shipping to the other colonies like Massachusetts. By 1688, Massachusetts alone was importing 156,000 gallons of molasses a year from the British West Indies.[31] Sugar prices collapsed over the next 50 years as the supply increased, and by the 1720s Bostonians were eating about ten pounds of sugar and a gallon of molasses per year.[32]

Through the eighteenth century, though, sugar was still expensive for New England folks living outside the big city, and many whites and Native Americans boiled and sold maple sugar.[33] But maple sugar was considered inferior because it wasn't as white and pure (that is, bland) as cane sugar, and it was cheaper. Colonial farmers in New Hampshire and Vermont made plenty of sugar, and sold it to inland towns, but didn't have much success selling it to the coastal cities where Caribbean molasses and refined sugar were omnipresent.[34]

Maple syrup and sugar might have disappeared altogether, turning into a quaint regional memory, if not for the Civil War. Before the war, maple sugar was one of the sweeteners favored by abolitionists who deplored the use of slavery in producing cane sugar. An antislavery society even tried to mass-produce maple syrup in New York in 1792 to compete with slave sugar, but the effort collapsed due to mismanagement.[35] Once the shooting began, the North was cut off from cane sugar supplies by the hostilities. The maple tappers enthusiastically increased their production to feed the sweet-craving North, and northerners developed a taste for the stuff. By 1890, Vermont alone was producing 14 million pounds of maple sugar a year, about a quarter of the nation's supply.[36]

New England's cookbooks, always trailing indicators of popular food fashions, featured more and more maple recipes after the Civil War. Lydia Maria Francis Child's 1833 *The American Frugal Housewife* has no recipes involving maple syrup or sugar at all, and Maria Parloa's 1872 *Appledore Cook Book* (republished in 1880) simply suggests pouring maple syrup over a single apple pudding.[37] By 1896, Fannie Farmer's *The Boston Cooking-School Cook Book* suggested pouring maple syrup on cornmeal mush, waffles, and buckwheat pancakes, and making candy, fondant, frostings, and pralines.[38] A volume titled *The New England Cookbook*, published in 1999, mentions maple syrup 108 times and includes recipes for maple-braised turnips, barbecue sauce, and "Maple-lacquered Game Hens."[39]

Even after the Civil War ended and New Englanders were annually downing thousands of tons of maple sugar, maple sugar producers tried to compete with refined white sugar by producing the least maple-tasting and -looking sugar possible. It's an impossible task. The palest maple sugar is still beige, and even syrup made from the freshest spring tapping has a pale gold cast and a faint caramel flavor, like a buttery chardonnay.

Rising Sap

In autumn, the wild hills of Vermont, New Hampshire, and the Berkshires blaze with brilliant orange, red, and yellow sugar maple leaves, courtesy of more than 300 years of intensive crop management. When the Pilgrims landed in Plymouth, New England's northern forests were only about 10 percent maples. About 40 percent of northern hillsides were covered with beech trees whose leaves turn a pleasant (if monotonous) golden bronze. Evergreens like spruce and fir made up most of the rest. Today, beeches represent just 15 percent of the total, and sugar maples and red maples have soared to make up almost 30 percent of northern forests.[40]

Between 1620 and 1860, most of New England's forests were logged, cleared, or burned. During the "sheep craze" of 1810 to 1840, Vermont alone reduced its forested land from 70 percent to just 20 percent of the state, mostly for sheep pasture.[41] The stone walls running through all the "wild" parks and forests in the northeast are relics of an age when almost every acre that wasn't a cliff or under water was occupied by sheep, cows, pigs, or crops.[42]

Today's maple sugar industry extracts sweetness from an incredible regional rebirth, an unparalleled reforesting. As the price of wool collapsed in the 1840s, New Englanders began abandoning their farms, leaving them to grow wild. The woods returned. Today, Vermont is 78 percent forest, New Hampshire 84 percent.[43] As those hill-town homesteads grew back into forests, they were reseeded by the "sugar bushes" colonial farmers had planted, groves of sugar maple trees persisting on old farms.[44]

The maple syrup industry also benefits from its renaissance as a distinctive, regional, "locavore" food. In earlier times, maple sugar competed with white sugar for market share—a losing battle as sugar became cheaper and maple syrup more expensive. From the early twentieth century onward, local state and then USDA maple syrup grades reflected this hierarchy of blandness. The palest, least flavorful maple syrup was "Fancy" or "Vermont Fancy," with darker, tastier grades earning monikers like Grade A Dark Amber, Grade B, and Grade C, or just No. 1 and No. 2.[45]

In 2015, after petitions from syrup producers, the USDA changed the maple syrup classification system. Now, like children in a pretentious yet mediocre school, no maple syrup gets a B—at least not if it's edible. Fancy is now US Grade A Golden Delicate, Grade A Medium Amber is now US Grade A Amber Rich, Grade B is now US Grade A Dark Robust, and Grade C—imagine such a thing!—is now US Grade A Very Dark Strong.[46] Maple syrup's flavor, its onetime flaw, has become a source of strength.

Alas, maple syrup's future in New England may not be Grade A Golden Delicate. Quebec's maple industry dwarfs New England's. Worse still, New England's warming climate has already made it harder for sugar maples to survive in southern New England, and fluctuating spring temperatures are making it harder for syrup makers to time their taps.[47]

Maple syrup is one New England's foods——well, Canada's foods—that's easy to love. New England chefs make all manner of cured meats, barbecue sauce, breads, cookies, pies, ice cream, root beer, and even cocktails with the stuff. But love doesn't pay the rent. Everyday shoppers can see that maple syrup costs roughly 400 percent more than corn-syrup-based "table syrup," costing upward of $15 per quart, and many opt for more economical pancake toppings. Maple syrup is a genuinely historic New England regional food, but how long can a food represent a region, or a culture, when it isn't produced there, and most of the people there can't afford to buy it?

To Pie or Not to Pie

To New Englanders, a Yankee is a Vermonter.
And in Vermont, a Yankee is somebody who eats apple
   pie for breakfast.
And to a Vermonter who eats apple pie for breakfast,
A Yankee is someone who eats it with a knife.
—Variously attributed to E. B. White, Robert Frost, and
"Yankees"

In the few short centuries since the rocky, verdant land of Algonkin speakers was renamed "New England" by European colonists, some foods have gone from being everyday foods to being symbols of the region, then mere memories. Pie has become a food you buy at the supermarket instead of an everyday dessert stashed in the back pantry. Gingerbread has almost vanished, while doughnuts reign triumphant.

Once upon a time dessert in New England was pie, at least according to newspapers. In the late nineteenth century, columnists enthusiastically proclaimed that New Englanders and a good chunk of New York State composed the Pie Belt—a region whose residents ate pie for breakfast, dinner, supper, and midnight snacks and as a general cure for climate-induced ennui. Gingerbread was so common that poor mill workers ate it for breakfast.

Now, day-to-day New England life is more likely to include Dunkin' doughnuts than pie or gingerbread, or at least Dunkin' coffee. The Dunkin' chain, which boasts 1,150 stores in Massachusetts alone, sells 1.9 billion cups of hot or cold coffee a year and 2.7 billion doughnuts—but that figure includes Munchkins, which are small, so the total volume of coffee and doughnuts is probably similar.[48] In a 2018 survey, almost half of the adults in Manchester, New Hampshire, Boston, and Providence had bought something at Dunkin' Donuts in the past 30 days.[49] Not everyone bought doughnuts, but few of them were buying gingerbread or pie.

Pie En Vogue

There is some basis for this Yankee pie identification, at least in colonial times. Compared to colonists in New York and the Chesapeake Bay colonies, seventeenth-century Bostonians apparently baked more pies—or at least they threw a lot more pie-sized cooking pans into their privies (ah, the wild parties of Puritan forebears).[50]

After the Revolutionary War, New Englanders were definitely making pies as well. Martha Ballard's famous diary of her life as a midwife in Maine's Kennebec Valley from 1785 to 1812 includes dozens of references to baking apple, pumpkin, and mince pies, but no meat pies apart from mince. If meat pies were being prepared, they were beneath notice.[51] Despite Ballard's vegetarian dessert predilections, there are plenty of meat pies in both southern and northern cookbooks from the federal period, such as Amelia Simmons's *American Cookery* (published in Connecticut in 1796) and Mary Randolph's 1824 *The Virginia Housewife*. Both books feature several savory pies made of meat and seafood, but Randolph's book has a single dessert pie recipe, while Simmons's book has six, and a 1763 Massachusetts manuscript cookbook contains nine dessert pies.[52]

Several of these "dessert" pies in the Simmons book are for various meats mixed with sugar and spices, in that curious amalgam called "mincemeat." Mincemeat is yet another example of a once-universal American food that is being rapidly forgotten, much like anchovy pizza and diner-menu beef liver and onion plates. It's hard to compete with modern flavors like chocolate, barbecue, and cool ranch. When mincemeat is served, it is generally restricted to holiday meals at home at Christmas or Thanksgiving.

Pies became popular in New England in the nineteenth century partly because wheat flour became widely available, making it easy to bake pies with crusts that would stay edible for a long time, and because sugar became cheaper over the course of the century. By midcentury, some women with large kitchens and capacious pantries baked dozens if not hundreds of pie in the weeks before Thanksgiving, ensuring that their families would have old half-frozen pastry to eat any time they wished in the coming months.[53]

Another reason pie became so common in New England is because of a key piece of equipment: the stove. Most New England families, urban and rural, switched from cooking over a fire to stovetop cooking in the first half of the nineteenth century, which made pie the Dessert Most Likely to Succeed.

It's hard to cook a pie over a fire in a hearth. Where do you put the pie plate? Can you keep the fire or embers at the right temperature for long enough to bake the pie but not burn it? You can bake a pie in the same bake oven you use for bread, but it takes time and attention to stoke the fire for baking and check that it will not burn your pie. Stoves kept temperatures more constant over a longer period of time, and it was far easier to heat or cool an oven to the right temperature for a pie.[54]

New England cookbook authors reacted by including more and more recipes for pies and fewer and fewer for boiled puddings, the easiest dessert to make over an open fire.[55] Cookbook recipes for *steamed* puddings— which are cooked in a "pudding mold" in a pot of water, not boiled in a bag in a kettle—increased at the same time, but never took up as much print as pie, probably because they're often mushy and just don't taste as good.

By the nineteenth century, pie wasn't just for dinner. In 1832, Samuel Goodrich wrote that a New England breakfast included "ham, beef, sausages, pork, bread, butter, boiled potatoes, pies, coffee and cider."[56] That was probably a hotel breakfast, though. In the cities, poor folks and people with desk jobs got most of their energy from bread or pastry and hot tea or coffee with sugar, just like today's workers.[57] Apple pie was omnipresent in nineteenth-century New England, but blueberry, cherry, pumpkin, strawberry, rhubarb, and mince pie and even plain custard could carry the day in a pinch.

Ralph Waldo Emerson was half crazed by pie, foisting enormous slices on unsuspecting women in railway carriages, if Oliver Wendell Holmes is to be believed.[58] Pies weren't always loved, though. All sorts of pies, especially meat pies, were blamed for Yankee disease, and health concerns undoubtedly contributed to their disappearance from cookbooks. Authors Sarah Josepha Buell Hale and Catharine Beecher were highly suspicious of pies in the 1840s. Hale declared that fruit pies were "harmless compared with *meat pies, which should never be made*"—the animal fat in the mince and the crust combining for ill health. Beecher said that rich piecrust was deathly because it combined "the three evils of animal fat, *cooked* animal fat, and heavy bread," rendering it completely indigestible. Beecher went on to suggest using bread dough or what appear to be recipes for biscuits, not piecrust, as they are "sweetened with saleratus," that is, chemical leavening.[59]

Fifty years later, city-slicker tourists vacationing on Vermont farms in the 1890s complained that their hosts served too many pies (and biscuits and doughnuts) and not enough vegetables, pretty little berries, and cream.[60]

Pies Makes a Yankee

Rudyard Kipling is generally blamed for introducing the notion of the Pie Belt to credulous journalists. Kipling was purportedly interviewed in 1894 by the *St. James' Gazette* about his time living in Vermont, and allegedly made the following observation:

> "Now the Yankee does not seem to be able to sleep o' night, or laugh out loud, or assimilate his food in peace. I thought that last was mainly due to the kind of food he tried to assimilate. No doubt that has a good deal to do with it. I speak with knowledge, for I live on the borders of the Great Pie Belt!" "The Great Pie Belt?" echoed our appalled interviewer. "Yes," replied Mr. Kipling; "the Pie Belt, which extends through the New England States and across Northern New York. Pie is a habit all over the Eastern States; in the Belt it is a debauch. Have you considered the physiological condition of a people which eats pie for breakfast, pie for dinner, and pie for supper, and takes ice-water and sweetstuffs between whiles?"[61]

Some self-proclaimed experts opined that pie's indigestibility created Yankee character. In an article appealingly titled "Pie, Progress, and Ptomaine Poisoning," a researcher opined that pie destroyed the digestion—all for the good.

> Now it is well known to all that the average New England Yankee is in appearance lean lank and cadaverous, but he is possessed of indomitable perseverance never failing strength and don't-know-when-you're-beaten courage. The farmers who dwell within the limits of the great North American "pie belt" live upon cream of tartar biscuit and revel in pie at least three times a day, and that, too, the year around. They are as a class dyspeptics—begnawn by indigestion—and they try a new kind of patent medicine every week, yet these same ill-nourished Yankee farmers are tougher than wild cats, and so surcharged with nervous energy that their thrift and enterprise has made New England proverbial as that part of our land which is known as God's Country, and from this vigorous stock sprung a large proportion of those hardy pioneers who cleared and settled the great Western States. . . .

Now the history of the old Puritan stock seems to show that people can develop and maintain an enormous amount of physical energy on a diet which is very poor in nutritious principles. Medical men may hurl their thunder against the indigestible pie but the mighty work which the pastry fed Pilgrim Fathers and their pie eating descendants wrought in our own land is proof positive that there are many worse things in this world than food which is deficient in nutritive principles.[62]

And yet, there were always doubts. A 1902 Chicago newspaper column gave credit to an entirely different pastry: "It will always be question whether it was the pie or the doughnut that gave the sons of Massachusetts, Vermont, Connecticut, New Hampshire, Maine, and Rhode Island their strength, energy, and intellectuality. Some contend that it was the pie and the doughnut, the one neutralizing the effects of the other. The pancake had doubtless something to do with it."[63]

Despite all this Yankee certitude, the word "Pie Belt" was quickly usurped. Yankees were never the only people interested in pies. An 1872 article in *Scientific American* titled "A Gigantic Pie Bakery" boasts that the New York Pie Baking Company was manufacturing 50,000 pies a day and consuming 60,000 pounds of pumpkins and squashes and 800 pounds of mince beef to slake the endless appetites of New York City's pie fiends.[64] In 1905, *Scientific American* reported on Philadelphia pie-making machines that could produce 16 pies per minute.[65]

By 1894, the *Boston Globe* was reporting that the Pie Belt had expanded: "The south still may cling to its puddings, but long ago it surrendered to the Yankee pie without conditions or any reservation whatsoever."[66] A 1909 Kansas paper claimed the Pie Belt "begins where New York leaves off, climbs the Appalachian range, meanders across Pennsylvania, Ohio, Indiana, Illinois, takes in Iowa and Missouri, and spreads out fanwise until the whole of the great golden west is shielded by it."[67]

Gingerbread, Fashion Victim

The same molasses obsession that made baked beans sticky after the Civil War may be one reason why gingerbread has gradually disappeared from

New England cookbooks, where it once dominated baking chapters. For example, N. K. M. Lee's 1832 *The Cook's Own Book*, by "A Boston House-keeper," featured 11 different types of gingerbread with enigmatic names including gingerbread, American gingerbread, Indian gingerbread, and Lafayette gingerbread, sweetened with various combinations of sugar, brown sugar, molasses and "treacle."[68] Only one recipe is made without sugar, and that one specifies treacle, not molasses. ("Treacle" is a problematic ingredient. Most culinary authorities declare that it's just a British term for molasses—but some nineteenth-century American cookbook writers seem to have thought there was some kind of difference between them.) New England cookbooks published up to 1880 continue to mix sugar and molasses in gingerbread recipes, and generally contain more sugar than molasses.[69]

Then gingerbread changed, accepting molasses as its One True Sweetener. The process was well under way by 1900. The 1896 *Boston Cooking-School Cook Book*, also known as the *Fannie Farmer Cookbook*, has eight recipes for gingerbread, but sweeteners have been strictly separated. Four recipes have molasses and four have sugar—and the sugar-based recipes have effete names like "Fairy Gingerbread" and "Gossamer Gingerbread," as though turn-of-the-century sugar was too light, airy, and delicate a substance to be included in any meal sturdier than an elegant lady's tea.[70]

By 1900, sugar had become the fuel of the industrial economy. Between 1850 and 1900, despite a rise in prices during the Civil War, the cost of sugar in the United States dropped from more than 370 percent of the price of molasses to just over 10 percent more—and sugar didn't have to be stored in heavy, breakable bottles or jars.[71] Sugar was cheap and easy to ship and store, and workers ate more and more of it each year. An 1886 survey of the diets provided by boarding houses in Lowell, Massachusetts, indicates that the mill workers were consuming an average of a pound and a half of sugar per week, but just three ounces of molasses.[72] These same workers ate less than an ounce of cornmeal per week, and four and a half pounds of flour.

The 1896 *Boston Cooking-School Cook Book* had 8 recipes for gingerbread and five recipes for cakes that were made or frosted with chocolate. The most recent edition of the book—now called the *Fannie Farmer Cookbook*—has just two recipes for gingerbread but 14 different chocolate cakes. The 2012 *New Boston Globe Cookbook: More Than 200 Classic New England Recipes, from Clam Chowder to Pumpkin Pie* has just one gingerbread but five chocolate cakes.[73] Molasses's bitter edge is too challenging, too pedestrian for palates accustomed to the dull, bland sweetness of white sugar.

Even in 1909, gingerbread was a common New England food—at least among the poor. A 1912 study of poor immigrants in Lowell lists the following diets, which contain no fruit and very few vegetables, but all feature gingerbread in at least one meal a day.

SHOEMAKER, FRENCH . . .

Food

Breakfast, bread, butter, sometimes salt fish or pork, coffee.

Dinner, bread, meat three days per week, salt fish or pork the remainder, potatoes, sometimes pie, water.

Supper, bread, sometimes brown or oatmeal bread, butter, tea, occasionally gingerbread. Cannot afford luxuries.

WEAVER (SKILLED) ENGLISH . . .

Food

Breakfast, butter, cold meat or eggs, cake, tea.

Dinner, meat, potatoes, vegetables, pickles, bread, pie or pudding.

Supper, bread, butter, cheese or fish, gingerbread, tea.

LABORER IN MILL FRENCH CANADIAN (UNSKILLED) . . .

Food

Breakfast, bread, butter, cold meat, gingerbread and coffee.

Dinner, bread, butter, meat, potatoes, vegetables and pie.

Supper, bread, butter, sauce, cake, tea. Soup once a week.

Doughnuts Triumphant

And then the twentieth century happened to breakfast. Even rural New Englanders stopped eating pie in the morning, as their city cousins had done decades before—or stopped eating breakfast at home altogether.

Fortunately, William Rosenberg stepped into the breach. In 1955 Rosenberg founded Dunkin' Donuts, while his brother-in-law Harry Winouker founded Mr. Donut the same year. Speculations on forbidden conversation topics at Rosenberg family dinners aside, both chains prospered through the wonders of franchising, a new method of organizing business in the 1950s. While Mr. Donut has become a favorite in East Asia, Dunkin' Donuts is the one true donut chain in New England; the *Boston Globe*'s map of its domination of Massachusetts is breathtaking.[74]

Rosenberg was one of the leaders in the franchise movement. He probably could have sold lint and toothpaste in a bun and made money. There have been charges that Dunkin' Donuts are not much better; modern management means that most of today's Dunkin' Donuts are trucked to most stores from faraway bakeries, not made fresh in the shop. As it is, Dunkin' Donuts is so closely identified with coffee in New England that in 2009 the firm ran a $10 million advertising campaign to remind consumers that they could buy doughnuts at Dunkin' Donuts.[75]

Pie for Now

Pies went the way of most home baking in the twentieth century, gradually dwindling from neglect except during ethnic holidays like Thanksgiving. There have been attempts to revive pie, including Frankenstein monsters like "New England Breakfast Pie," which includes canned apples, sausages, brown sugar, and cheddar cheese in a prefab piecrust.[76]

There is one pie that has become more popular throughout the twentieth century: the whoopie pie. In all honesty it isn't really a pie at all; it consists of a pair of soft chocolate cookie cakes sandwiched around marshmallow filling. In a 2011 debate on whether the whoopie pie should be designated Maine's official dessert, one state representative rightly declared, "Whoopie pie, it's not even a pie . . . it's two pieces of cake with frosting in the middle."[77]

In the end, there was a compromise between the real pie and whoopie pie contingents. In a 107–34 vote, the whoopie pie was declared the Maine state treat, while blueberry pie was named the state's dessert.[78]

This pastry sandwich probably originated in the 1920s, when marshmallow concoctions like Fluff, the industrial-age sweetener from Somerville, Massachusetts, became widely available. Despite various Pennsylvanian claims and counterclaims, the first documented whoopie pies were sold in Lewiston, Maine, in 1925, with the Berwick Baking Company of Roxbury, Massachusetts, following suit by 1931.[79]

Today you can attend an annual Maine Whoopie Pie Festival in Dover-Foxcroft in June.[80] If you'd like a mouthful of marshmallow in some other month, the easiest place to find a whoopie pie is any New England gas station quickie mart. You can find the classic chocolate marshmallow whoopie pies everywhere, and flavors like pumpkin, strawberry, banana, peanut butter, and raspberry show up in cake and filling.[81] No one objects to all these odd variations because although people can and do make them at home, whoopie pies have always been made by bakeries. They're regional and impersonal—part of the scenery, but not part of anyone's identity, and they're cheap enough than anyone can eat them. Perhaps that's why they're more popular than actual pie.

Sours

Cranberries! You can eat them raw, if you're the sort of person who likes to chew lemon wedges, but most people eat them with turkey (as sauce) or vodka (as souse). Originally a regional oddity, cranberries have become one of the unlikely symbols of Thanksgiving, along with turkey and pumpkin pie—although cranberry pie graced more Thanksgiving tables than sauce in the nineteenth century.[82]

It's a little strange that anyone ever bothered eating cranberries at all. The Narragansett collected cranberries in the seventeenth century, but that was before the Europeans introduced apple trees.[83] Cranberries are sour and bitter, unlike other New England native fruits, like blueberries, strawberries, and beach plums. Only about 5 percent of cranberries are eaten as fresh fruit, compared to 51 percent of blueberries.[84] Part of the reason for that is that most cranberries are harvested using the cheap, low-labor "wet" method that makes them unusable for fresh or frozen use.

The "wet" method or harvesting cranberries is simple. Water is pumped into cranberry bogs, and the floating cranberries are "corralled," scooped out of the water, and shipped off for processing.[85] About 90 percent of cranberries are harvested this way.[86] Only dry-harvested cranberries plucked from vines are sold fresh—and dry harvesting requires much more labor.[87]

The other reason is that fresh cranberries don't taste very good without being coated with sugar, and preferably cooked. There's a reason why 20 percent of the US cranberry crop—roughly 80 million pounds—is eaten during Thanksgiving week,[88] and so little the rest of the year. Cranberries have become part of the ritual of Thanksgiving, but why? Why not blueberry compote, or apple chutney, or pear sauce? Why take a small, sour fruit that grows only in ocean-side bogs in five states and make it the center of the all-American meal?

Cranberries' Growing Reputation

Beginning in Dennis, Massachusetts, in 1816, cranberry farming was a sleepy business at first.[89] That year, Henry Hull transplanted "crane-berries" from a marsh in Dennis to sandy soil and discovered that they grew just fine outside of bogs.

Despite Hull's success, cranberry farming took a while to catch on. An 1890 history of Barnstable County, Massachusetts, claims that most of the prominent local growers started farming in the 1840s. It was an easy way to make money from land that was economically worthless (though undoubtedly very valuable to the local ecosystem). Local historians credited marketing campaigns for making the cranberry a viable crop instead of merely a sour, bitter Cape curiosity.

> To the product of this berry a vast number of bogs and lowlands have been transformed from a condition of seeming worthlessness to the most valuable land of the county. . . . Probably the men who brought the berry to the attention of the public outside of the districts to which it was indigenous and created a demand for it, were potent factors in the development of this

industry. That change of taste, which we have noticed as continually going on, has brought this little waif of the swamp lands into notice, and made it a favorite with the epicures of every country.[90]

It's not clear what produced this change of taste; perhaps the New England societies stimulated distant demand. Whatever the reason, cranberries boomed in New England after the Civil War. They'd already become more popular as sugar got cheaper through the 1850s, making it more economical to make cranberries edible—although sugar prices quadrupled during the Civil War, making sour fruit far less attractive. By the 1870s, though, sugar prices fell back to antebellum levels, then continued to dwindle, and more and more Americans used more and more sugar. The amount of sugar sold in the United States went up by a factor of 8 between 1866 and 1896, and US per capita sugar consumption rose by a third from 1880 and 1900, reaching 64 pounds per person per year.[91]

Cranberries also became popular because there were a lot of Cape Cod residents with no other career options. After the Civil War the whaling industry collapsed due to international competition and whale extinction, and railroads, not ships, started transporting most goods up and down the coast. What few wooden ships remained were rapidly being replaced by iron steamships. Hundreds of shipbuilders and fishermen were searching for any kind of income, and cranberries fortuitously grew on bogs and marshes near where these unemployed seamen used to work.[92] Women picked most of the harvest in the early days, though, as this 1875 observer noted:

> It is pleasant to see the pickers busily gathering the for market, a labor performed almost wholly by females. An instrument called a cranberry rake was formerly used, but as it bruised the fruit, it been discarded for hand picking. Very little outlay is necessary in the preparation of a cranberry bed, and much less labor than is usual with ordinary farm crops, while the return is much greater. Here the visitor is astonished at seeing the vine producing abundantly in what appears to be pure white sand.[93]

The market value of cranberries increased in the 1870s, and production gradually shifted from small family-owned bogs to large businesses with hired hands.[94] On Cape Cod, cranberry picking shifted from a part-time job for local women to work for Portuguese and Finnish immigrants, much the same way jobs at the Lowell Mills had shifted from Yankee farmers' daughters to immigrants. A 1903 study of Massachusetts immigrants paints an astonishingly insensitive portrait of Portuguese immigrants performing dawn-to-dusk stoop labor and Portuguese child workers—who certainly weren't in school during this charming September ritual.

> With the early autumn comes the yearly exodus to the cranberry bogs of Cape Cod. This is a season of work and pleasure, looked forward to with the greatest delight. It is like a great family reunion, for here they meet their kinsfolk who have settled on the Cape, as well as many relatives and friends from the city whom they rarely see in their cruelly over-worked lives. And after the busy day of picking, screening and measuring the cranberries is over—which begins with the drying off of the dew on the vines and ends with the setting of the sun—they are ready for an evening of genuine relaxation. The great frame shanties, where many workers are housed, afford opportunities for the exchange of many a bit of gossip and for many a game and dance.[95]

To be fair, the author does go on to say in the next paragraph, "The great poverty of the Portuguese prohibits many gayeties; indeed, it almost prevents the simplest hospitality."

Ocean Spray, Cranberry Pushers

The Cape Cod Cranberry Growers' Association was formed in 1888, but the true engine of cranberry world domination wasn't founded until 1930. Of the worldwide cranberry crop today, 70 percent is sold through Ocean Spray, the cooperative headquartered in Lakeville-Middleboro, Massachusetts.[96]

In 1930, cranberry growers in Hanson, Massachusetts, formed the Ocean Spray cooperative to market cranberries. Originally named Cranberry Canners, Inc., Ocean Spray comprises more than 600 cranberry growers in all five cranberry-growing regions of the United States: Wisconsin,

Massachusetts, New Jersey, Oregon, and Washington.[97] As *Modern Farmer* recently put it, "Around 65 percent of the cranberry industry is controlled by the Ocean Spray Cooperative, a figure so high that only an obscure exemption for agriculture has allowed it to exist in the face of antitrust laws."[98] The Capper-Volstead Act of 1922 exempts "associations" making agricultural products from antitrust laws.[99]

Ocean Spray's first project was to dominate the turkey-condiment universe with the most popular cranberry product in the world: canned jellied cranberry sauce.[100] This purplish-red gel was Ocean Spray's first product. It was reportedly developed by Marcus Urann, an Ocean Spray founder, as far back as 1912 as a way to sell excess cranberries that were left over after the Thanksgiving-to-Christmas season.[101]

As of 2017, Americans were gobbling up 70 million cans of Ocean Spray canned, sugared cranberry jelly each year, and 76 percent of Americans served jellied canned cranberry goop at their Thanksgiving dinners.[102] The state where canned cranberry logs are most popular is Georgia, where cranberries don't grow.[103] That does make some sense, as the jiggly cylinders are basically cranberry-flavored corn syrup—and corn does grow in Georgia. As one YouTube commenter put it, "It's like Koolaid in juicy jello form."[104]

Cranberricide

Cranberries might have just continued as an ingredient in canned holiday gloop indefinitely if it hadn't been for the 1959 aminotriazole crisis, when the entire industry was threatened by a pesticide contamination scandal. The herbicide aminotriazole, which causes thyroid tumors in rats, was detected in cranberries in the Pacific Northwest.[105]

Berries contaminated with aminotriazole in 1957 and 1958 were voluntarily impounded by growers, then later destroyed. The United States didn't suffer a cranberry crisis then, partly because US cranberry growers have been growing far more cranberries than anyone wants for decades. Cranberry growers "carried over" between 7 and 31 percent of the cranberry crop to the next year every year between 1949 and 2010, and in 2018 a quarter of the new cranberry crop was destroyed to get rid of surplus berries.[106] Because of this eternal oversupply, the USDA has become a major buyer of cranberries.

In 1959, USDA inspectors seized thousands of barrels of cranberries from all over the country to inspect them for the contaminant. "It was a disaster," said Link Thatcher, a Cape Cod cranberry grower. "We went from $13 a barrel to $3, overnight. I laid off six men and went into carpentry."[107]

Eventually the FDA tested and released 99 percent of US cranberries back to the market a few days before Thanksgiving. As you might expect, even the thought of exposing your family to carcinogenic chemicals—whether or not any were actually in the barrel—wasn't a popular holiday sentiment, and cranberry sales collapsed. Mamie Eisenhower served applesauce with the unlucky, unpardoned White House turkey. Cranberry growers were granted some money to make up for their losses, but not until the following May.[108]

Cranberries Wet and Dry

The market rebounded within a year of the aminotriazole scandal, but Ocean Spray was on guard. Cranberry growers needed to persuade more people to eat more cranberries beyond Thanksgiving.[109] The growers had been unleashing new products on Americans for years before the scandal, but they needed a new flagship product. Ocean Spray brought out sweetened cranberry juice cocktail in 1933 and marketed juices, jams, and dried berries, increasing US consumptions of processed cranberries from 17 percent of the crop in 1934 to 57 percent by 1954.[110] Now, with cancer stalking their dreams, Ocean Spray committed itself to one goal: to get Americans to consume cranberries in as many forms as possible.

The first great innovation was a new Frankenstein-like concoction named for a fruit that does not exist in nature: the cran-apple. In 1964, Ocean Spray introduced to the world Cran-Apple and Cran-Grape—two "juice cocktails" loaded with extra sugar. Today's Cran-Apple has 32 grams of sugar per cup, compared to 9 grams in a cup of unsweetened cranberry juice.[111]

At about the same time, someone realized that cranberry juice masked the taste of vodka even better orange juice, and the Cape Codder cocktail was born. New England's most puritanical fruit had learned to party, and Ocean Spray's expansion was driven by liquor-fueled sales.[112] By the 1970s, the Ocean Spray cooperative controlled more than 90 percent of the American cranberry crop.

Judging by sales, Cran-Apple juice was an enormous improvement over actual cranberries. Today, New Englanders drink far more cranberries than they ever ate in sauce, and Americans consume eight times as much cranberry stuff as they did in 1944. Cranberry production has gone up by more than 1,000 percent since the 1940s.[113]

Forty years later, cranberries received their second great marketing boost with the leftovers from making cranberry juice. Craisins are fruit-like objects that are made with cranberry skins (or "hulls"), but no actual cranberry pulp.[114] In 2003, Randy Papadellis, president and CEO of Ocean Spray, decided to make sugar-coated cranberry skins into the best snack ever.

As Papadellis put it in 2010, "In the mid '90s, we'd extract juice from the cranberry and then leave behind what we call the hulls. And we paid people to come and haul away the hulls. Our first breakthrough was realizing that by reinfusing a little bit of cranberry juice back into that cranberry hull, we could create something that we now call a sweet and dried cranberry, and we've branded it as Craisins."[115] Of course, Ocean Spray adds plenty of sugar along with that little bit of juice. Raw cranberries have 4.3 grams of sugar per 100 grams; Craisins pack 7.25 grams.[116]

The technology to dry cranberries on an industrial scale was first developed during World War II to help feed the troops, to the extent that dehydrated cranberries can be considered food and not merely flavoring.[117] Ocean Spray first sent sweetened dried cranberry skins to grocery store baking aisles in 1983, but they languished as an inferior substitute for raisins—the fruit that ruins oatmeal cookies.

Ocean Spray needed a different approach to market its little sour skins. Papadellis decided to market Craisins as a snack food that was "healthier" than potato chips and candy bars at a time when Americans were becoming a little touchy about their collective weight problems. The result: "[Craisins] grew from a tiny little $20 million business to a $400 million business."[118] In 2016, Ocean Spray turned 250 million pounds of cranberries into Craisins.[119]

Farmers noticed and responded by growing even more cranberries than ever for Craisins, creating a new and different cranberry glut. The problem with growing cranberries for Craisins is that Craisins leave most of the cranberry behind. Americans gobbled down the wizened husks of sugar-coated cranberry skins, but they didn't drink all the cranberry juice that had been drained from the fruit. Cranberry processors ended up with thousands of gallons of excess juice.

In 2009, Ocean Spray began public auctions to dispose of all that juice, and prices fell from $54 to $34 a barrel. Prices have stayed low, prompting a series of lawsuits against Ocean Spray for alleged price fixing.[120] In the meantime, the 2016 Massachusetts Cranberry Revitalization Task Force final report offers pages of comments on "exit strategies" for farmers who want to stop growing cranberries altogether.[121] At least one farmer put up solar panels on his bog instead of relying on the cranberry crop.[122]

Cranberries have been going through boom-and-bust cycles for more than two decades. The inflation-adjusted price of cranberries went up by more than 6 percent a year on average between 1970 and the mid-1990s, hitting $65 per barrel in 1996, then fell to $17.20 per barrel in 1999. Craisins saved the day for about a year, briefly driving cranberry prices up to $70 per barrel in 2008, but by 2015 prices had shrunk to a mere $8 per barrel, about a quarter of the $30 to $34 growers need to break even.[123]

In 2017, the USDA ordered cranberry farmers to "move 15% of the crop away from consumers" (that is, destroy it) to protect prices. At that time, the price per 100-pound barrel of processed cranberries was $29.10. Americans consumed 7.3 million pounds of cranberries in 2017, but cranberry processors had almost 9.5 million barrels of inventory—more than a year's supply.[124]

Part of the problem is that cranberries, like grapes, grow on vines, which take time to mature. They can't just be planted each season to keep up with demand; some cranberry plantings are a century old. Some cranberries are also biennial bearers, which means that they produce fruit only every other year.

The major quandary facing cranberry farmers is that their bogs can't grow anything else. That is the major reason that people started growing cranberries in them in the first place—they were revitalizing land that was economically dead. You can't plow up a bunch of muck and plant soybeans or graze cattle or charge tourists to roll in the mud. Cranberry bogs are a sunk investment, so to speak.

Despite the fact that they're called bogs, cranberry-growing land is more akin to an in-ground swimming pool than a swamp. Here's a 2007 description of how new cranberry bogs are born:

The land is cleared of vegetation, scalped, and leveled approximately two feet below the existing grade of the soil. A layer of sand is laid to create an acidic surface optimum for vine growth, and sand is periodically added to maintain the beds. The vines take root in the sand, forming a monoculture that takes three to five years to produce commercial quantities of fruit. Water is added to irrigate, to flood the beds for frost protection, and for harvest.[125]

And what of aminotriazole? Cranberry growers don't use it anymore, but they spray plenty of other poisons on their land. Cranberries are fickle fruit. They don't grow as quickly as lots of grasses, sedges, and other weeds that appreciate damp, acidic, sandy soil, and a lot of cranberries are biennial bearers—which means you have to protect them through two growing seasons just to start to get fruit.[126] Damp soil and flooded bogs can lead to fungal diseases, and insects love to suck juice from berries and their vines as well.[127] Cranberry farmers use enormous amounts of water to flood bogs for harvest, to control weeds, and to protect vines from early frosts, which means that there are many opportunities for cranberry farms' pesticides, herbicides, and fertilizers to contaminate local waterways.[128]

Just 0.3 percent of the US cranberry crop was organic as of 2016, so more than 99 percent is sprayed with some type of pesticide, herbicide, or both. When bogs are flooded with water for harvesting, as 90 percent of cranberry bogs are, any lingering toxic residues float off to poison insects and plants in nearby wetlands. Since the Clean Water Act doesn't regulate runoff from watery crops like rice and cranberries, the growers don't have to ensure the water they return to nearby streams, rivers, and wetlands is clean.[129]

Samples tested by the USDA in 2017 contained 18 different pesticides, including diazinon, which was found in 5 percent of cranberries in 2016. Diazinon is an insecticide and neurotoxin, and it was banned from home use in 2005 due to health risks, but farmers are still allowed to use it on edible crops.[130]

Most US cranberries are grown in Wisconsin, Massachusetts, New Jersey, Oregon, and Washington state, in that order; Canadian cranberries come from British Columbia and Quebec.[131] Maine produces less than 1 percent of the US cranberry total.[132] That second place trophy is impressive for Massachusetts, which harvests about 27 percent of the annual cranberry crop.[133] The Commonwealth has a hard time breaking the top ten for any other farm product thanks to long winters and an even longer history of luring farmers away to work in cities. All of these places have the cool winters that cranberries need to enter dormancy and freshen up for spring, and sandy, acidic soil that keeps the plants perky.

Peak Cranberry?

We may be living at the time of peak cranberry. The New England climate is changing, and the new combination of shorter, warmer winters combined with more intense rainstorms and hotter summers is poised to drastically reduce cranberry production in Massachusetts. Warmer winters reduce cranberry plant blooms by 50 percent and help vile pests like the cranberry weevil and army worm survive. More pests mean most cranberry farmers use more pesticides, which can kill the honey bees that pollinate plants, and heavy spring rains keep bees from coming out to pollinate the blooms. In 2014, the Maine cranberry harvest dropped by half largely due to storms pouring down as much as three inches of rain a day when the cranberries were in bloom. Hot weather scalds cranberries, damaging them and keeping them pale and greenish instead of ruddy—the opposite of the human skin response to the sun. Coastal growers may also fall victim to rising oceans, which can make local groundwater too salty for sour fruit.[134]

Whatever happens to cranberries, Ocean Spray intends to survive. When the CEO was asked "What's next for Ocean Spray?" in 2010, he responded, "Blueberries. There are only three fruits indigenous to America: the cranberry, the Concord grape and the blueberry. Our next step is to do with blueberries what we've done with cranberries."[135]

This statement is ridiculous of course—there are plenty of other fruits that are native to the United States, including strawberries, beach plums, pawpaws, persimmons, mayapples, and elderberries. But given what's happened to Massachusetts cranberry farmers, maybe it's just as well if these other fruits escape Papadellis's attention.

Spirits

Apples have a very long history of being drunk in New England, perhaps drunk even before they were first eaten. The Reverend William Blaxton was growing apples in what is now Boston by 1630, but no one knows when or how he got them or what he used them for. A decade later, he planted the first apple orchard in Rhode Island and grew "yellow sweetings." When he preached, supposedly "to encourage his young hearers [, he] gave them the first apples they ever saw."[136] Trees Blaxton supposedly grew still bore fruit two centuries later in Cumberland, Rhode Island.[137]

By 1628, though, two years before Reverend Blaxton's orchard was observed, some older hearers in the colony at the time were hankering after cider, based on their orders for apple seeds, not trees. Governor Samuel Endicot had men plant New England's first apple orchard on his land in Salem in 1628, and the Massachusetts Bay Colony put in an order for apple seeds from England that same year.[138] It's not clear what sort of apples Endicot grew from this Transatlantic seed order, and the seeds the Massachusetts Bay Colony received would have been a very mixed bag.

Apples do not breed true from seeds. To reproduce apple varieties, breeders don't plant apple trees but graft branches from an existing apple tree on to another tree's root stock. Plant a Red Delicious apple's seed and you may get a sweet, crisp red apple—or you may get a shriveled, bitter, green little grinch fruit. No one then, and no one since, has discovered how to foretell the future apple from a seed.

If you're planning to make cider, though, it's much better to have a variety of apples on hand, not just sweet stuff. Apples eaten fresh are "sweet" or "dessert" apples—but as any beer drinker knows, sweetness isn't always the best flavor for alcohol. Beer makers use hops to add a balanced bitterness to their brews. To create a tastier drink, traditional hard cider makers include not only sweet but also bitter and sharp apples.

Bitter apples are full of tannins, the harsh-tasting chemicals that make your mouth feel dry when you drink black tea or oaky wines or chew acorns. Bitter apples can contain 0.2 percent tannins by weight—which is a lot. Sharp apples are sour, like lemon juice or crabapples, and have at least 0.45 percent acid by weight.[139]

The most entertaining cider apples are "bitter sharps," which are sour and bitter and confusing to people who've been eating Red Delicious apples all their lives. Hideously awful for eating fresh, bitter sharp apples enhance ciders with their complex flavors, making them more palatable to adults and more repugnant to children.

Of course, colonists did grow dessert apples too—just not nearly as many of them. By 1649, one Henry Wolcott of Windsor, Connecticut, had established a grand orchard containing several named varieties of sweet apple trees, including Summer Pippin, Holland Pippin, Pearmain, London Pippin, and Belly Bond, a garbling of the French "Belle et Bonne."[140]

Although apples can thrive in New England, they are also prey to an astonishing number of pests and pestilences. In 1641, a despondent George Fenwick wrote to Massachusetts Bay governor Winthrop, "I am pretty well storred with chirries and peach trees, and did hope I had had a good nurserie of Aples of you sent me last yeare, but the worme haue in a manner distroyed them all as they came vp." The governor was kind enough to send Fenwick apples to replace the trees the worm "distroyed," and Fenwick said, "I hartile thanke yow."[141]

Six years after Endicot's orchard project, bargain shopper William Wood reported from Boston, "I have been here in season to have seen a prodigious quantity of apples from which they make a marvelously good cider. One hundred and twenty pots cost only eight shillings, and at the inn it is sold twopence the pot, twopence the pot for beer."[142]

Cider wasn't always New England's favorite beverage. Englishman Daniel Gookin, describing the Algonkin speakers who lived in the region before colonists arrived, wrote in 1674, "Their drink was formerly no other but water, and yet it doth continue, for their general and common drink. But of late years some of them planted orchards of apples, and make cider: which some of the worst of them are too prone to abuse unto drunkenness."[143]

In the seventeenth century, colonists were used to drinking beer, not cider, back in England. Unfortunately, all the extra barley for making beer was also back in England. After a series of miserable wheat harvests, including the disaster of 1644 when "the blast took hold of Connecticut and New England," barley became more valuable as an ingredient for bread and broth, not beer. Apple cider was the next best thing to beer.[144]

Almost a century later, in 1734, the honorable Paul Dudley of Roxbury, chief justice of Massachusetts, boasted about the sheer amount of fruity alcohol being produced.

Our people of late Years have run so much upon Orchards that in a village near Boston consisting of about forty Families they made near three Thousand Barrels of Cyder. This was in the Year 1721. And in another Town of two Hundred Families in the same year, I am credibly informed they made near ten Thousand Barrels. Some of our Apple Trees will make six, some have made seven Barrels of Cyder, but this is not common, and the Apples will yield from seven to nine Bushels for a Barrel of Cyder.[145]

Cider was largely a "home brew" drink in America from the earliest settlement onward. Apples grew abundantly in New England and the Mid-Atlantic, and cider could be made from wormy, scabby apples that couldn't be stored for winter eating. Cider was so cheap that it wasn't worth shipping to distant cities to sell. Farm families would keep a few barrels of cider in the cellar along with cabbages and potatoes, and up until the 1830s Americans were downing an average of 15 gallons of hard cider a year, along with 5 gallons of distilled spirits (mostly whiskey) and 2 gallons of beer.[146] Homemade hard cider was relatively low in alcohol (approx. 5–7 percent), but when hard cider was shipped to cities it was fortified with stronger liquors until it was at least 20 proof to keep it from spoiling.[147]

Americans were consuming an average of 4 gallons of pure alcohol apiece per year in the 1830s, which is all the more mind-boggling when you consider that a large proportion of Americans were children. Although women did drink (and sometimes concealed their drinking in "stomach-ache elixirs"), most alcohol was consumed by men, and the heaviest drinking half of men—one-eighth of the population—drank two-thirds of the alcohol in the nation.[148] That's the equivalent of guzzling 20 gallons of alcohol per year, or about five shots of whiskey per day.

After 1830, cider drinking started to decline in New England. More people were living in cities, had no place to keep cider barrels, and relied on commercially prepared libations—and beer and whiskey were much easier to make on a commercial scale than cider. Wheat for beer and corn for whiskey were cheap, abundant, and faster and easier to grow than mature apple trees, and these grains fermented faster and more reliably than apples.[149] Also, in 1826, two Boston preachers founded the American Temperance Society to stop New Englanders from drinking the hard cider and apple jack. Reputable New England families who dabbled in horticulture bred pears instead of apples to show that they had the true health of the nation at heart.

Hard cider began evaporating from the American diet altogether around the Civil War, when beer became more popular. When the American alcohol industry became industrialized on a large scale after the Civil War, drinking habits changed. German immigrants in the Midwest and beyond built breweries, not cider mills, and shipped their products on railroads. Drinking Americans increased their annual consumption of beer from 2 gallons per person per year before the Civil War to 10.5 gallons by 1885 and to an astonishing 20 gallons by 1910.[150] New England Yankees never bothered building hard cider factories on the same scale.

By the end of the nineteenth century, apple cider drinking drastically declined and had almost disappeared 20 years before Prohibition outlawed alcoholic drinks. Drinking hard cider had gone out of fashion. It had the aura of a rustic "poor man's drink." As early as 1840, William Henry Harrison campaigned for president by recalling that he had drunk hard cider in a log cabin when he was a youth as proof of his common, folksy roots.[151] By 1900, very few people wanted to drink grandma's favorite tipple. Better to try some of that newfangled Coca-Cola, which was also fizzy and stimulating—but not alcoholic—and marketed as a modern, up-to-date drink.[152]

Hard cider was also primarily drunk by rural white Yankee Protestant northeasterners—the same people who most strongly supported the temperance movement from the 1820s onward.[153] Drinks like beer and whiskey survived the movement, the theory goes, because they were drunk by large urban populations that didn't support temperance.

Some farmers were troubled by the temperance movement's assertion that their hard cider could be contributing to drunkenness and destroyed their orchards. Henry David Thoreau lamented the loss of New England's cheering trees in 1859, longing for a long-past age "when men both ate and drank apples, when the pomace heap was the only nursery, and trees cost nothing but the trouble of setting them out."[154]

Although there are many internet rumors about the FBI burning apple orchards during Prohibition, none of the sources that mention the destruction cite a year or place where these conflagrations occurred. They seem even more unlikely given that farm-brewed hard cider was specifically exempt from the Volstead Act, enacted in 1919 to enforce the Eighteenth Amendment establishing Prohibition.[155] Specifically, the act said that the restrictions "shall not apply to a person manufacturing nonintoxicating cider and fruit juice exclusively for use in his home"—but it didn't specify that cider makers had to keep their ciders from fermenting.[156] Farmers couldn't legally sell the fermented cider, but they had never sold that much of it in the first place.

From Cider to Appleseed

After they started making cider, New Englanders made Johnny Appleseed. Johnny Appleseed, née John Chapman, supposedly spent his time gently planting apples, soothingly civilizing the western frontier, providing nourishing food for pioneers. Even though Johnny Appleseed planted most of his apples between what is now Toledo, Ohio, and Fort Wayne, Indiana, his apples—and his fame—are the result of New England's ongoing efforts to define America.

John Chapman was born in 1774 in Leominster, Massachusetts. Drive by Leominster on MA Route 2 today and you'll see a sign reading,

> *Welcome to* LEOMINSTER
> *Pioneer Plastic City*
> *The Birthplace of Johnny Appleseed*

This sign simultaneously honors both Chapman's spunk and Leominster's status as the home of the first manufacturer of pink plastic lawn flamingoes.

By the 1790s, Chapman had left Massachusetts for northwestern Pennsylvania. His life was a mixed bag of business dealings, wandering, and proselytizing. He spent his time creating apple nurseries in the unclaimed wilderness in Ohio and Indiana, planting and selling apple trees, and buying, defaulting on, and losing property. His apples were never meant for pies. John Appleseed (as he called himself) would collect apples from pressings at cider mills and throw them on the ground in a semicleared thicket, coming back a year later to see which saplings had survived.[157] Historians assert that he did this from 1800 to 1814 in an attempt to stake claims to land out in the pioneer territories by "improving" the lots. In the end, all his claims were jumped by other settlers.

Although he did plant plenty of apple trees, Chapman was not the first person to plant apples in the Midwest. Contemporary observers spotted apple orchards in Native American villages in Hardin County, Ohio, in 1800, and apple nurserymen were shipping apple scion wood for grafting back east from Cincinnati in 1804.[158] As historian William Kerrigan observed, "When I traveled around the Midwest to gather material in my research, I regularly encountered local historians who claimed Johnny Appleseed must have planted the wild apple trees the first settlers of their town found when they arrived. It did not occur to them to consider that native peoples could have planted them."[159]

Chapman wasn't far ahead of the nursery business. The first nursery selling grafted, named varieties of apple trees was set up in Marietta, Ohio, in 1794 and was selling more than 16,000 apple trees a year by 1821.[160] An 1818 catalog published by Silas Wharton, a nurseryman in Waynesville, Ohio—an area John Chapman wouldn't reach for another decade—lists 79 varieties of apples for sale, including 58 "winter keepers" for storing through spring.[161] Pioneers who traveled on any major roads or waterways in Ohio had plenty of opportunities to purchase seedlings of Maiden's Blush, Golden Pippins, Rhode Island Greenings (allegedly the same apple planted by Reverend Blaxton in Cumberland), Royal Pearmains, and even the infelicitously named Skunk Apple.[162]

Unlike the professional nurserymen, Appleseed reportedly refused to plant or propagate grafted seedlings because grafting was "wicked."[163] How kind was it of John Chapman to scatter weedy trees with bitter fruit across land that didn't belong to him? Did he simply continue to mark his territory, like a bear scratching on a convenient oak, as his businesses failed?

Chapman didn't spend all his time as a fruit pusher. He also proselytized for the New Church, also known as the Swedenborgian Church, which held (and still holds) a variety of radical beliefs for Christians, including rejecting the trinity for a single God, asserting that Judgement Day had already taken place, and claiming that people create their own heaven or hell in the afterlife depending on how well they loved others on earth.[164] From the 1830s onward, Chapman wandered the Midwest dressed in tattered clothes and carrying just a few New Church books and a bag of apple seeds. He traveled endlessly, sleeping on floors and in barns, planting apple trees and spreading the good news about Swedenborgianism wherever he went.[165]

Early accounts of Johnny Appleseed in Ohio county histories dating from the 1860s told tall tales about the tree hugger's ability to chop twice as many trees in a day as other men or how he could withstand extreme heat and cold. Many mentioned his meekness and humility. Some sneered at his planting apple trees in the wilderness with no protection, leaving them to be devoured by hungry deer and cattle.[166]

By the 1870s, though, Appleseed was being rehabilitated as "A New England Kind of Saint," as the poet Vachel Lindsay later put it, a man who epitomized piety, charity, and frugality.[167] Unitarian minister W. D. Haley published a paean to Johnny Appleseed in the *Atlantic* magazine in 1871, praising Chapman's compassion and gentleness: "He was never known to hurt any animal or to give any living thing pain—not even a snake. The Indians all liked him and treated him very kindly. They regarded him, from his habits, as a man above his fellows."[168] Haley never explained how he knew that "the Indians" had any particular feelings toward this man, who wasn't planting apple trees for them—the trees were for the white settlers. No first-person accounts of Native Americans' reactions to Chapman have been reported.[169]

Lydia Maria Francis Child, the Massachusetts author whose poem "Over the River and Through the Wood" helped to entrench Thanksgiving in American culture, published a poem titled "Apple Seed John" that sparked Appleseed's fame. In 1881, Child wrote about how humble and devoted Appleseed was.

> In cities, some said the old man was crazy;
> While others said he was only lazy;
> But he took no notice of gibes and jeers,
> He knew he was working for future years.
>
> . . .
>
> So he kept on traveling far and wide,
> Till his old limbs failed him, and he died.
> He said at last, "T'is a comfort to feel
> I've done good in the world, though not a great deal."[170]

The poem was immensely popular. Appleseed was a new kind of national hero for post–Civil War Americans exhausted by violence and tired of war. Unlike gun-toting Davy Crockett and Daniel Boone, who made space for new settlements by slaughtering the existing Native American residents, Johnny Appleseed simply planted trees to improve the land, something that Child and her peers repeatedly claimed the Native Americans didn't do. This was odd, given the unending Victorian repetition of the story of Squanto's gift of corn agriculture to the Pilgrims. How is it that Native Americans taught the Pilgrims how to grow corn but couldn't understand the importance of planting fruit trees? And yet Child wrote,

> Sometimes an Indian of sturdy limb
> Came striding along and walked with him;
> And he who had food shared with the other,
> As if he had met a hungry brother.
> When the Indian saw how the bag was filled,
> And looked at the holes that the white man drilled,
> He thought to himself 'twas a silly plan
> To be planting seed for some future man.[171]

Appleseed's reputation took off after Child's poem was published, and through the 1930s he was offered up as the incarnation of the American spirit, tramping across the hinterlands, peacefully planting seeds in meadows in a state whose land was ceded to white settlers by Shawnee, Chippewa, Ojibwa, Wyandot, and many other tribes.[172] In these stories, the Native Americans simply vanish the same way the friendly Native Americans were supposed to have evaporated from New England history after the first Thanksgiving instead of dying from disease, enslavement, and King Philip's War—or even continuing to live in New England, as their descendants do today.

In latter-day poems, children's books, and Disney cartoons produced in the 1920s and 1930s, Chapman's Swedenborgian beliefs become a generic benevolent Christianity. Instead of a colonizer roaming a ravaged landscape, he's a faithful, benevolent seed planter, a Pomona of the prairie. Chapman also made a difference as an individual. He didn't try to actually change how society worked by, say, joining the abolitionists or unionizing farmworkers.[173]

Cider production slowed as New Englanders fled their cold, rocky farms in the late nineteenth century and beer brewed from Midwestern grain became cheaper than apples—but in the last two decades, New England has seen a resurgence of hard cider makers and drinkers, with events like Franklin County Cider Days promoting the historic drink.[174] Apples grow well in New England, unlike wheat, which pouts in New England's humid, fickle climate. And the joy of growing apples for cider is that the drinkers never see the apples—just the cider. Farmers don't need to endlessly spray insect-poisoning chemicals or prune apple trees to create plump, beautiful apples suitable for tempting Snow White. Ugly, lumpy apples make cider just as well as pretty fruits and take a lot less work.

Hard cider apples can have skin covered with grayish-brown scab spots or be half dissolved into fruity bags of bruised brown mush or have a few strategic holes chewed by hungry worms. It doesn't matter; their juice will look the same.[175] They can be fully ripened to their maximum sweetness because they don't have to be transported while they're firm and crisp (i.e., underripe) and can stand up to the rigors of travel. Cider apples can also be mechanically harvested after they drop from the tree instead of pains-takingly handpicked. Consumers never see the bruises, and the fermen-tation process kills any *E. coli* contamination that may infest unsanitary grounds.[176]

Today, paying the cost of labor is a challenge for New England farmers—just as finding any workers at all was a challenge for New Eng-land's seventeenth-century colonists. And once again, the easiest way to get a hard drink is apples.

As for those juicy, sweet dessert apples: as of 2001, consumers in the Northeast drank more apple juice and ate more apple desserts per capita than any other area of the county, but lagged the West in consuming fresh apples.[177] As is our regional tradition, New Englanders prefer packaged, processed foods over fruit that is simple, primitive, and fresh.

Cheese and Taste

NEW ENGLAND's artisan cheese makers are a perfect microcosm of New England food invention. The overwhelming majority of cheese makers left New England for larger pastures in Wisconsin more than a century ago. Although a few loyal cheddarers remained, local cheese became a charming relic, like hand-tatted doilies or grosgrain hat ribbons, not an industry. The "traditions" surrounding artisan cheese in New England were largely learned elsewhere or invented out of whole cheesecloth.

In the early nineteenth century, cheese was a big deal in New England—a very large and ponderous deal. On New Year's Day 1802, industrious farmers from Cheshire, Massachusetts, presented President Thomas Jefferson with a wheel of cheese weighing 1,450 pounds.[1] At the time of the Revolutionary War, there were clusters of cheese makers in Narragansett, Rhode Island, Braintree, Massachusetts, and many towns in southern Connecticut. More than 130,000 pounds of cheese were shipped to the West Indies per year.[2]

Eighteenth- and nineteenth-century Yankees throughout western Massachusetts, Connecticut, and Vermont made astonishing quantities of cheese, cheese, cheese! In 1850, Litchfield County, Connecticut, alone produced close to three million pounds of the stuff at a time when just 45,253 people lived there.[3] That's 60 pounds of cheese per person—and heaven knows how much crackers you'd need to eat it.

But Litchfield's dairy-saturated citizens were not the champions of cheesiness. In 1860, a few proud Vermonters personally produced 5,000 pounds of cheese.[4] That figure becomes even more impressive in light of the fact that around 1850, Americans ate an average of only four pounds of cheese per year.[5] In the 1850s, New Englanders were producing 11 pounds of cheese and 18 pounds of butter per person per year (27 million and 43 million pounds, respectively).[6]

After the Civil War, though, cheese left with the railroads. Connecticut cheese making is a case study in cheese's departure for the hinterlands. In the 1820s, Goshen, Connecticut, alone made more than 400,000 pounds of cheese, and in 1845, Litchfield County made 2.75 million pounds of cheese—partly thanks to Lewis Norton's Pineapple Cheese factory in Goshen.[7]

Beginning in 1808, Lewis Norton produced a commodity called pineapple cheese, which was simply cheddar cheese hung so that net marks were impressed on the rind, then painted with linseed oil or shellac to look yellow.[8] That shellacking made the cheese last an extraordinarily long time, although the rind was not edible. (It was too pretty to eat anyway.) A popular housewarming present, the cheese was a spectacle of conspicuous consumption, almost designed for Victorian middle-class households aspiring to gentility. Eating them properly required several frivolous appurtenances with no other culinary purpose, as this author noted in the 1955 *The Complete Book of Cheese:*

> Always an ornamental cheese, it once stood in state on the side-board under a silver bell also made to represent a pineapple. You cut a top slice off the cheese, just as you would off the fruit, and there was a rose-colored, fine-tasting, mellow-hard cheese to spoon out with a special silver cheese spoon or scoop. Between meals the silver top was put on the silver holder and the oiled and shellacked rind kept the cheese moist. Even when the pineapple was eaten down to the rind, the shell served as a dunking bowl to fill with some salubrious cold fondue or salad.[9]

Alas, the pineapple season could not go on forever in a cruel northern climate. Lewis Norton built a Connecticut pineapple cheese factory in 1844, but his son Edward Norton moved pineapple cheese making to upstate New York around 1851—when Connecticut milk was becoming more valuable as fresh butter for New York City and Boston than as aged cheese. The Connecticut factory finally closed in 1904, and the New York Nortons sold the whole concern to Kraft, which shuttered the business in 1931.[10]

The entire Connecticut dairy industry gradually became a butter business after the Civil War, then collapsed altogether. Connecticut has 63 butter factories in 1889, and a Lebanon, Connecticut, creamery sent "tons of butter to Providence," but almost none of these creameries were left by

1926. The Lebanon creamery even went back to making cheese! A Connecticut state agricultural report blamed "ruinous western competition in butter and the introduction of butter substitutes"—but Vermont farmers faced the same competition and their creameries thrived,[11] probably due to lower land costs. Connecticut's cows turned to providing fresh milk for city folk, and by 1900 three-fourths of the milk produced in Connecticut was sold fresh.[12]

Cheese moved west with the railroads. The center of American cheese making in 1800 was a thick swath of Massachusetts, Connecticut, and Rhode Island—but as transportation and refrigeration improved, farmers began producing fresh milk and butter for city dwellers to eat today, not to store for future hard times.

While butter stayed near the cities, by 1850 most American cheese production had moved west from the New England coast to the Connecticut River Valley in Massachusetts, Vermont, and western New York. Enterprising cheese makers built enormous factories where the milk of dozens if not hundreds of farms could be combined, where land and grain were cheap, and where cities were far, far away.

Following the Civil War, cheese consolidated even more. Far from being a homey "artisan" food mostly made by women on their own farms, cheese became a standardized mass-market commodity made in factories. As one author wrote, "By 1880 farm-made cheese comprised less than 5 percent of the total United States output, which shot up from 103 million pounds in 1860 to 243 million pounds in 1880 and 298 million in 1900."[13] Contemporary accounts from the late 1860s talk about the advantages of bringing milk to mass cheese-making operations, saying that having factories make cheese would "greatly relieve the farmer's wife" and that "the flesh and blood of our wives and daughters are of too much consequence to be worn out by this ceaseless toil."[14] An 1864 song from "Cheesedom"—an area of Ohio's Western Reserve largely settled by migrants from Connecticut—contained this lament:

> My baking is spoiling,
> My clothes must be boiling
> And beef must be broiling
> And cheese to make too![15]

Much of American cheese in the post–Civil War era was exported to Britain, where there was a greedier appetite for cheese. Americans ate only about 4 pounds of cheese per capita per year in the late nineteenth to early twentieth centuries, while the British were eating 12 pounds apiece by 1905.[16]

As cheese became a commodity, cheese making moved to places where land and grain were cheap. In 1880, *Scientific American* declared, "The Mohawk Valley [western Massachusetts / Vermont] has lost its rank as the center of the cheese industry of the United States. The new head center is at Wellington, Ohio."[17] By 1900, cheese making had moved to Vermont, western New York, Ohio, and Wisconsin; and by 1950, cheese had just about vanished from New England. Cheese was primarily produced on the western end of New York bordering Lake Erie and in Wisconsin, with scattered cheese outposts in Ohio, Missouri, and Tennessee.[18]

In 1922, Wisconsin made 71 percent of US cheese, but America's cheesy center has continued to move west.[19] The United States makes 25 percent of the world's cheese, and today more than a quarter of US cheese is made in Wisconsin, America's cheesiest state.[20] California comes in second at about 20 percent, followed by Idaho and New York, New Mexico, and Minnesota. Together, these states make about 75 percent of US cheese production. Vermont's share comes to slightly more than 1 percent.[21]

Wisconsin isn't necessarily the land of milk and honey, though. Cheese making there has consolidated, with the number of factories falling from more than 2,700 in 1922 to just 126 in 2009. In a recapitulation of cheese's American past, Wisconsin production has moved away from small businesses in rural communities to a few dozen factories that produce more than a million pounds of cheese per year.[22]

In the late twentieth century, Vermont became the anti-Wisconsin, the center of a new, very small-scale artisanal cheese movement. The new New England cheese makers didn't move back east from Wisconsin. Instead, they moved north from New York and Boston, and many of them weren't cheese makers to begin with at all. Over the past four decades, Vermont has witnessed several culture clashes between the nouveau fromage cheese makers and longtime Vermont residents who have other, more local concerns than supplying Manhattan cheesemongers and their ilk.

Cheese, Wheels, and Vermont

It can be tempting to assert that Vermont farmers concentrated on cheese thanks to a cultural fascination with culturing pure, innocent white milk, into something that is more golden and eternal, like the enduring Yankee soul. In fact, Vermonters didn't have a choice about what to make. Vermont's grassy hillsides (grassy thanks to farmers' cutting all the trees down to raise Merino sheep ca. 1810–1840) are terrible for raising corn, but provide excellent grass for cows. In the era before refrigerated railroad cars, the only way to preserve cream and milk for sale was to convert it into cheese. Unlike milk, cheese could be shipped in most weather by wagon or train and arrive in urban markets in much the same condition as when it started its journey.

Vermont's cheese industry gradually slumped into obscurity as improvements in transportation and refrigeration and urban consumer demand made shipping fresh milk and butter to Boston more profitable than waiting for cheddar to age. In 1851, Vermont railroads began providing refrigerator cars (really, giant ice chests on wheels) for shipping butter, cheese, and meat.[23] Between 1852 and 1871, butter shipments from Saint Albans, Vermont, alone tripled from over 1 million to more than 3 million pounds. Cheese shipments rose too, from 600,000 to 2 million pounds, then dropped to 400,000 pounds as Bostonians began to slurp up Vermont's milk in liquid and butter form.

Dozens of creameries were built in Vermont from 1870 onward, allowing farmers to bring their milk to central dairies so that it could be cooled, separated into milk and cream, and packed onto railroads cars.[24] In 1890, Vermont produced five times as much butter as cheese.[25]

Vermont farmers had a ready market in milk-mad Boston. By 1911, Bostonians were consuming 90 million quarts of milk a year; by 1921, 180 million quarts.[26] A 1922 poll showed that Bostonians drank more milk than the residents of any other major US city, an average of a pint per person per day.[27] By 1938, this totaled 250 million quarts—69 percent of it delivered by rail. That year, Vermont was producing more than half of Boston's milk and shipping 270 million pounds of milk to Boston and 125 million pounds of milk to New York.[28] Boston's "milkshed" of dairy suppliers extended to Maine, New Hampshire, New York, and Pennsylvania, and even beyond Vermont to Sherbrooke, Quebec.[29]

Between 1900 and 1950, Vermont's cheese making dwindled. As Boston and New York's thirsty denizens guzzled millions of gallons of milk, it didn't make economic sense for dairies to withhold their profitable milk to make cheese, so they didn't.

The energy of the Vermont dairy industry did not impress the jaded city folks who wrote the 1937 *WPA Guide to Vermont*. One writer described Colchester thus: "Here again a creamery furnishes the basic industry of the community. The general atmosphere of rural lethargy is enlivened each morning by the farmers bringing in their milk and loitering to buy groceries and supplies, or to exchange stories and political opinions."[30] The town of Burke was more reputable as the Mountain View Farm's cows provided milk to "a creamery, where the milk from the farm's great herd is daily turned into 150 pounds of American cheese."[31] That's as specific as the WPA guide got about Vermont cheese. Who would be interested in cheese from Vermont? You could get cheap American cheese anywhere, so why not get the Wisconsin brand at the local Piggly Wiggly?

Today, the reason to buy Vermont cheese is to experience exquisite, locally made, artisanal delicacies—if you can afford them. Vermont's emerging cheese makers over the past four decades have had very different economic and cultural priorities than the local farmers who loaded milk cans onto Boston-bound trains.

Flatlander Food

Vermont's latter-day cheese revival is the result of sincere efforts by cheese makers and their very wealthy backers. A 2006 article quotes Ihsan Gurdal, the owner of Boston's Formaggio Kitchen, who built his own cheese-aging cave in the 1990s:

> Gurdal grew animated talking about new American cheese makers, and he revealed that the majority are *not* traditional farmers making the transition to market production but successful business people who retired early, bought land in the country, and started making cheese.
>
> Among the earliest are Miles and Lilian Cahn, former owners of Coach Leather, who bought farmland in New York's Hudson River Valley. . . . The majority of New England's artisanal cheese makers are college graduates

who have either returned to family land with new class dispositions and business sensibility, or have adopted Vermont as a land of ecologically sound business opportunity.[32]

In other words, Vermont cheese is made by people who aren't from Vermont. And these people have different ideas about how Vermont land should be used than people who grew up there. As Heather Paxson put it, "What crosses borders are not only residents but also ideas about place and place-making—as well as tastes cultivated in other foodscapes."[33]

People who were already living in Vermont haven't always been happy with the newcomers and their fancy cheese. A 1984 book title read *Real Vermonters Don't Milk Goats*. A Vermont state representative at a 2004 Vermont Farm Summit expanded on the theme: "Real Vermonters don't milk goats and real Vermonters don't post signs [prohibiting hunting or snowmobiling]!"—two activities popular with "eco-conscious" urbanites.[34]

Another writer explored class attitudes toward cheese in Vermont with his taxi driver in 2015:

> In Wisconsin, I would always tell taxi drivers I was a cheese buyer visiting cheese makers and farms. Then, without fail, they would tell me about their favorite cheeses, where to get the best curds, and what cheese factories had tragically gone out of business. . . . In Vermont, the conversation went like this: . . . "I'm a cheese buyer, visiting Vermont cheese makers." Cabdriver: "Did you hear what Rush Limbaugh said about illegal immigrants?"[35]

The question remains, if most Vermont cheese is made by and for "flatlanders"—the Vermont term for migrants from low-lying Boston, New York, New Jersey, and their ilk—in what sense is Vermont cheese part of Vermont? Vermont artisanal cheese makers are a little like the Mainers catching glass eels in the Penobscot River and shipping them to East Asia. They're practitioners of an extractive industry, like oilmen and lumberjacks, exploiting local resources to support cuisine favored by wealthier people who live far away.

Versions of Vermont

Although local residents may complain about city folk, Vermonters have been carefully curating the state's image to "flatlander" city dwellers for profit for more than a century. In the 1890s, the Vermont Board of Agriculture began to promote an idealized vision of farm life to both Boston tourists and farmers. In an attempt to help struggling farmers in areas that were rapidly losing population, the board began issuing pamphlets to urbanites with titles like "A List of Desirable Vermont Farms at Low Prices"—the title soon changed to "Vermont: Its Fertile Farms and Summer Homes." The board also published advice to farmers like "there is no crop more valuable than this [tourist] crop from the city."[36]

Critics objected that catering to tourists would take up too much of a farm's resources, and keep farmers from modernizing their dairy operations. However, the Board of Agriculture understood that Vermont was making a lot of money from its reputation as a source of pure maple syrup, fresh butter, and sweet milk—and that farmers could make even more by selling firsthand experiences of clean air and sunshine (which farmers got for free). In lieu of Maine's craggy coastlines or Nantucket's heroic whaling past, Vermont offered nostalgia—for some city dwellers, a return to their rural childhoods; for others, an antidote to hot cities full of immigrants.[37] Vermont welcomed city folk who wished to escape "the heat, the dust, and disease of the cities, and become strong by close communion with nature, surrounded with her richest privileges."[38]

That yearning included dreams of wholesome farm breakfasts with fresh milk, eggs, and berries. Unfortunately, those products are what the farmers packed onto Boston-bound trains, not what they ate themselves. Farmers ate pretty much the same thing as every other working-class New England family: a lot of pork, biscuits, doughnuts, and pies.[39] Snooty summer boarders complained about being served tough beef and pies made of dried apples and prunes, not fresh summer berries.[40]

In response, the farm magazines gave kindly advice on how to feed these odd, demanding, yet profitable people. Many ran articles about how to rotate meals and vary desserts, and supply enough chicken eggs, fresh cream, and fruit to mollify city folks. As a 1918 article published by the Vermont commissioner of agriculture put it,

Since the garden is so important the man who starts out to keep summer boarders must carefully consider what kind of a garden *summer boarders would like*. He must not plan on planting a garden growing only the things that he himself likes, or that he thinks that other people *ought to like*, but he must rather consider wholly what fruits and vegetables his *guests will like*. . . .

He must learn first of all that city people, though they have to buy them in the market, eat three times as many vegetables as do the farmers who may have them growing right at the kitchen door. Also, they eat three or four times as many sorts.[41]

This writer also gave some blunter advice: "The city people are fond of salads. In the summer boarding house, the salad platter should be the garbage pail for the left-over vegetables."

The Vermonters were becoming urban market gardeners, like the suburban farmers who supplied Boston and New York from the earliest European settlements—but instead of trucking their produce to the city, the city came to them.

Tinkering with Terroir

Since the 1980s, aspiring Vermont cheese makers have flown to Europe to witness small-scale cheese making and order custom copper kettles for their artisan farmstead cheese-creating operations. Ironically, these cheese makers were flying east when they could have driven west. Small-scale cheese makers in Wisconsin, where boutique operators call their production facilities "factories," used the same copper kettles up through the 1980s.

Wisconsin's smaller cheese makers are more likely to make American specialties like brick cheese than camembert, and they generally use pasteurized cow's milk instead of goat's milk straight from the pasture, but several firms still produce the traditional cheese they have made for generations. Wisconsin's Chalet Cheese, the only US producer of notoriously stinky Limburger cheese, was founded in 1885; Widmer's Cheese Cellars of Wisconsin produces brick cheese in a factory the current owner's grandfather bought in 1922.[42] Vermont does have a few long-standing cheese makers—the production facilities of Crowley Cheese and Plymouth Cheese date back to 1882 and 1890, respectively—and they use the term "factory" for their cheese production too, and sell wax-encased cow's milk cheddars made from the milk of dozens if not hundreds of farms, not delicate goat's milk cheeses in handcrafted boxes.[43]

Instead of apprenticing with Plymouth Cheese, Vermont's nouveau fromage farmers have been "reverse engineering terroir," as Heather Paxson writes, coming up with cheese that will make the local environment seem special rather than seeking out special cheeses created by the existing farmers and their environment. These cheese enthusiasts are adopting cheese making traditions from Europe or even creating new practices in lieu of having centuries-old traditions—or even decades-old traditions.

They don't have much choice. Vermont's artisanal cheeses cost more than five times as much to make as a brick of Velveeta, and no one can argue that Jasper Hill's exquisite aged milk products are essential to human nutrition. They *need* to be special to justify the price.

As Paxson puts it, "Reverse engineering terroir may work to naturalize entrepreneurial innovation, making it seem a part of nature and therefore as legitimate, inevitable, and even morally good."[44] It's a story that allows, even encourages retired Coach handbag executives to make exquisite natural cheese. Vermont's pure country air inspires all sorts of spending and conspicuous consumption—that is, appreciation for fine food and craftsmanship.

Another researcher cites the "cheese stories" that are sold with Vermont's pricey cheddars and tommes. The cheese story "functions as the main vehicle for communicating the embedded qualities of artisan cheese. Cheese stories contain information about where and how the cheese was made—for example, information about the people, the animals, the farm, and the handcrafted nature of the cheese." Whether these tales are told by cheese makers on frigid farms or by cheesemongers in charming, well-heated Boston shops, the stories sell the cheese.[45]

You don't have to look very far for examples of "cheese stories." The website for award-winning, high-priced Jasper Hill's cheeses sports the title "A Taste of Place: Greensboro, Vermont."[46]

Jasper Hill's website also says, "Jasper Hill's mission is to make the highest possible quality products in a way that supports Vermont's working landscape. We are driven to be the standard bearer of quality and innovation in the artisan cheese industry while promoting our regional taste of place." Historically, farmers haven't worried about preserving a "working landscape" because they didn't spend their time looking at landscapes. They ran farms, dairies, butteries, and cheese factories. Office workers don't worry about preserving the "working landscape" of accounting firms or pharmaceutical manufacturing facilities.

A "landscape" sounds like a place you admire, not a place where you live and work. A "working landscape" is presumably a landscape where you admire other people working, like those quaint farmers who aren't making cheese.

The text on Thistle Hill Farm's site shows how Vermont cheese entrepreneurs would like their customers to think about "terroir": "An important aspect of the taste of Tarentaise is that our cows eat from our pastures and hay grown, and harvested, by us on the farm. 'One place, one cheese' is a phrase we have heard again and again. This is the concept of 'terroir.' Our cheese has a flavor and characteristics exclusive to our farm. If we bought milk, or brought in feed from elsewhere, it would taste like it came from elsewhere."

But what does elsewhere taste like? And is it really that different from Thistle Hill Farm? Would the Tarentaise be noticeably different if the cows moved across the property line to the hay field next door?

Paxson observes that in France, the idea of *terroir*—the environment that gives a unique flavor to wine, cheese, and other foods—applies to entire regions, not individual farms. Vermont cheese makers talk about the sun, animals, and delicious meadow flowers growing on their individual farms, not in, say, Vermont's Northeast Kingdom.[47] According to cheese makers at Jasper Hill, Thistle Hill Farm, and many other similar Vermont outfits, terroir isn't something that's shared with your community. It's private property, and jealously kept.

Part of the problem is that Vermonters also don't have ancient communal cheese making traditions. Look back beyond 1850 for the roots of preindustrial cheese making in Vermont and you won't find cheese dynasties or even much milk. From 1810 to 1840, Vermonters raised far more Merino sheep for their profitable wool than high-maintenance cows. About 70 percent of Vermont's land was deforested during that period by ovine greed. Once the railroads opened, cheap wool from the West reached eastern mills and Vermonters abandoned raising sheep on rugged hillsides for the valleys preferred by clumsy cows, rumors of one-sided "wampahoofus" beasts notwithstanding.[48]

The USDA has even passed rules that specifically bar the sort of hyperlocal cheese making French farmers indulge in every day. A 1950 rule barred cheese makers from using raw milk to make cheese that was aged less than 60 days.[49] All of the milk that's legally made into cheese in Vermont spends more time in an aging room than it ever did in a cow.

Local Cheese, Faraway Fans

Today, US residents annually gorge on more than 30 pounds of cheese per person.[50] Most of that cheese is produced in efficient consolidated factories far from Vermont's gentle hill-town cows.

With roughly one professional cheese maker per 13,000 residents, Vermont has the highest ratio of artisan cheese makers per capita in the US.[51] That's a pretty easy number to reach in a state with a population of under 650,000 people. As of 2019, Vermont had roughly 49 local cheese makers, compared to 24 in Massachusetts, 21 in New Hampshire, and 87 in Maine.[52] Still, in 2006, a single farm in Modesto, California, produced 400,000 pounds of raw-milk farmstead cheddar cheese—or roughly the 2005 cheese production of the entire state of Vermont (475,000 pounds)—or the cheese production of Goshen, Connecticut, population 1,585, ca. 1820.[53]

It's getting harder to even get the milk to make cheese in New England; from 2000 to 2010, one-third of New England's dairy farms closed.[54] Larger herds with lower costs in California, Wisconsin, even Pennsylvania and New York State are undercutting Massachusetts dairy farms,[55] and New England's market share of national dairy production is declining.[56] The United States even created a sort of "milk cartel" called the Northeast Dairy Compact to protect New England farmers from price fluctuations— but the compact provoked bitter criticism from producers in other states and was allowed to expire in 2001.

While dairy farms are disappearing, small-scale artisan cheese making has broken out all over New England. The Vermont Cheese Council alone produces a "cheese trail" map listing 42 producers selling more than 150 varieties of cheese. How long can New England dairy farmers sustain themselves on hand-shaped tomme rounds costing $20 a pound?

Conclusion

GIVING THANKS FOR NEW ENGLAND FOOD

A NY BOOK on New England food must include Thanksgiving, the New England–branded meal that has compelled the nation to eat squash and cranberries, more or less willingly. This invented holiday draws from two conflicting and competing traditions—official Thanksgiving days declared by state governments, celebrated in nineteenth-century New England with church services and family reunions, and Forefathers' Day feasts celebrated by New England Society men's clubs around the country, complete with punch and cigars. Both piety and gluttony have been a part of Thanksgiving for a very long time. However, Pilgrims and their alleged foods were not part of Thanksgiving celebrations until after an 1889 novel titled *Standish of Standish: A Story of the Pilgrims* made the novel-reading public excited about Pilgrim traditions—traditions that were largely invented by the author.

In the end though, most New England residents don't pop a turkey and ten pies in the oven on a daily or even monthly basis. Instead of re-creating an imaginary seventeenth-century meal, imagine a Thanksgiving made up of the foods New England's residents actually ate.

Thanksgiving: A Day of Dull Food

New Englanders celebrated Thanksgiving and Forefathers' Day for decades before Thanksgiving became a national holiday, creating a regional ethnic food for a day or two each year. Forefathers' Day, December 22, was celebrated as the day when the Pilgrims supposedly first alighted on Plymouth's shores and was a sort of practice Thanksgiving. Below is the menu at the Plymouth Old Colony Club for the first Forefathers' Day feast in 1769:

1 a large baked Indian whortleberry [blueberry] pudding

2 a dish of . . . succatach corn and beans boiled together

3 a dish of clams

4 a dish of oysters and a dish of cod fish

5 a haunch of venison, roasted by the first Jack brought to the colony

6 a dish of sea fowl [!]

7 a dish of frost fish and eels [!!]

8 an apple pie

9 a course of cranberry tarts and cheese made in the Old Colony

These articles were dressed in the plainest manner (all appearance of luxury and extravagance being avoided, in imitation of our ancestors, whose memory we shall ever respect).[1]

Note that there is no turkey. Cranberries appear only at dessert, and the menu specifies that the food was "dressed in the plainest manner"—as though the Pilgrims *wanted* to live without wheat, sugar, butter, and other comforts.

The invented tradition of Forefathers' Day was adopted by New England Societies all around the country. These societies were founded by native Yankee men who had left for warmer climes. The New England Society of New York celebrated a Forefathers' Day in 1805, and between 1815 and 1860 New England Societies were founded in locales as disparate as Charleston, South Carolina, New Orleans, Detroit, Cincinnati, and San Francisco.[2] These dinners were men's club entertainments, not family reunions like today's Thanksgivings. The menu for a 1900 Forefathers' Day dinner at the New England Society in Brooklyn lists one of the meal's courses as "Cigars."[3]

While the Forefathers' Day dinners were spreading around the nation, New England states started celebrating Thanksgiving as a regional holiday. During the seventeenth century, local governments would proclaim days of thanksgiving in response to fortunate events—a good harvest, peace after a war—or sometimes just to express gratitude, and celebrants would spend most of their day in church services, not visiting far-flung relatives. These feast days were balanced by spring fast days, which also involved attending lengthy church services, but no feasting.[4]

The first documented Thanksgiving in New England was just two weeks after the first documented fast day. On a Wednesday in July 1623, after six weeks of drought had shriveled their corn, the Pilgrims spent a day in prayer in the hopes that God would be "hereby moved in mercy to look down upon us and grant the request of our dejected souls," as Pilgrim Edward Winslow wrote. The next morning, clouds "distilled such soft, sweet, and moderate showers of rain, continuing some fourteen days . . . it was hard to say whether our withered corn or drooping affections were most quickened or revived."

The local Wampanoag weren't invited to this fast day, but at least one man was curious about what was going on. According to Winslow, Hobbamock, an emissary sent to the colonists by the Wampanoag, asked the Pilgrims why they had spent all day in church when they had just done the same thing on Sunday, three days before—an excessive amount of church even for Pilgrims. Upon learning that the colonists had prayed for rain, Winslow claimed that Hobbamock was impressed and commented that when his people performed "conjuration" for rain, they might get a storm that knocked their corn down, not gentle rain.[5] Apparently, rain making was a competitive business for deities in old New England.

Two weeks later, at the end of July, the Pilgrims celebrated a "solemn day . . . wherein we returned glory, honor and praise, with all thankfulness, to our good God, which dealt so graciously with us."[6] This was the first recorded thanksgiving in the New World—which is not the same thing as what is called the "first thanksgiving" today.

American elementary schoolchildren don't draw Thanksgiving pictures of people sitting on benches in a cabin; they scribble in outlines of Pilgrims and Wampanoag sitting at picnic tables, staring at a roasted turkey the size of an underfed velociraptor. That version is based on a single paragraph from a letter from Edward Winslow to a friend in England that was printed in an obscure pamphlet titled *Mourt's Relation*. That pamphlet was lost entirely from ca. 1700 until 1820, when a copy was discovered in Philadelphia. Here's the entire account of the event:

> Our harvest being gotten in, our governor sent four men on fowling that so we might after a special manner rejoice together after we had gathered the

fruit of our labors. They four in one day killed as much fowl as with a little help beside, served the company almost a week. At which time amongst other recreations, we exercised our arms, many of the Indians coming amongst us and among the rest their greatest king, Massasoyt with some ninety men, whom for three days we entertained and feasted; and they went out and killed five deer, which they brought to the plantation, and bestowed on our governor and upon the captain and others.[7]

The only "traditional" Thanksgiving food that might be mentioned in this description is the fowl. "Fowling" might have yielded turkeys or ducks or something else; Pilgrim William Bradford mentioned both water fowl and wild turkeys as being birds "wherewith this place abounds."[8]

This 100+-person three-day party sounds more like a medieval feast than a family celebration of hearth and home. By the time this description was republished in a book titled *Chronicles of the Pilgrim Fathers* in 1841, New Englanders were already regularly celebrating Thanksgivings in the early winter, having post-harvest family reunions in chilly weather in late fall or early autumn. Lydia Maria Francis Child's famous 1844 Thanksgiving poem, "Over the River and Through the Woods," talks about driving a sleigh through "white and drifted snow."[9] Pilgrims weren't mentioned in state Thanksgiving proclamations or Abraham Lincoln's Thanksgiving proclamation of 1863—and the "First Settlers" got only a passing mention from Theodore Roosevelt in 1905. The Pilgrims weren't mentioned by name until Franklin Delano Roosevelt's Thanksgiving proclamation in 1939.[10]

The whole idea that the holiday might have something—anything!—to do with Pilgrims seems to have emerged in 1889, when a popular novel titled *Standish of Standish: A Story of the Pilgrims* was published, complete with pretty descriptions of the imaginary meal, like this:

The oysters in their scallop shells were a singular success, and so were the mighty venison pasties, and the savory stew compounded of all that flies the air and all that flies the hunter in Plymouth woods, no longer flying now but swimming in a glorious broth cunningly seasoned by Priscilla's anxious hand and thick bestead with dumplings of barley flour, light, toothsome, and satisfying.

Beside these were roasts of various kinds, and thin cakes of bread or man-chets, and bowls of salad set off with wreaths of autumn leaves laid around them, and great baskets of grapes, white and purple, and of the native plum so delicious when fully ripe in its three colors of black, white, and red.[11]

This literary classic also features a lengthy description of Priscilla fussing about how to properly cook and serve oysters, which she apparently had never bothered to eat in the entire time she had lived in Plymouth, next to the ocean.

Twenty-eight printings later, the *Standish of Standish* Thanksgiving dinner was thoroughly imprinted on Americans' brains, and printed pictures of Pilgrim picnics appeared in the *Ladies Home Journal* and *Thanksgiving Souvenir* pamphlets printed for teachers to give out to schoolchildren.[12]

The Feast That Replaced Church

In the eighteenth century, Thanksgiving gradually turned into an annual holiday, and most celebrants went to only one church service, not two, leaving a lot more time for eating. Between the Revolutionary War and 1863, Thanksgiving dates were set by state-by-state proclamations. The governor would proclaim a day of thanksgiving two to four weeks ahead of the date—generally in late fall.[13] After Abraham Lincoln's first proclamation in 1863, national Thanksgiving proclamations replaced New England's state-by-state celebrations.

The Thanksgiving menu that evolved over time was a little more forgiving than the first Forefathers' Day "plain" food, but not entirely. Pies became acceptable, even mandatory—although nineteenth-century New England cooks would include a chicken pie along with the main courses.[14] Churchgoing dropped away in the twentieth century as the holiday became more about feasting and family than faith (and when was the last time your family came together to observe a Christian fast day?).

Cranberries cropped up in Thanksgiving menus fairly early on, as this 1845 Thanksgiving menu from *The New England Economical Housekeeper, and Family Receipt Book* demonstrates:

Roast Turkey stuffed

A Pair of Chickens stuffed and boiled with cabbage and a piece of lean pork

A Chicken Pie

Potatoes; turnip sauce; squash; onions; gravy and gravy sauce; apple and cranberry sauce; oyster sauce; brown and white bread

Plum and Plain Pudding with sweet sauce

Mince, Pumpkin, and Apple Pies

Cheese[15]

Nearly a century later, World War II troops overseas in 1944 were served a more familiar-looking Thanksgiving dinner. The military's "master Thanksgiving menu" listed grapefruit juice, roast turkey with sage dressing (stuffing cooked outside the bird), cranberry sauce, mashed potatoes, string beans, corn, celery, pumpkin pie, candy, nuts, and coffee.[16]

In between, though, cranberries weren't guaranteed at Thanksgiving dinner. Menus generally included turkey, but that fowl might be accompanied by currant jelly or oyster sauce for a fancier dinner with invited guests.[17] An 1893 magazine writer commented, "The Thanksgiving Dinner would hardly seem perfect without our national dishes turkey, succotash, and pumpkin pie, but the rest of the menu can be changed ab libitum."[18]

Of course, perhaps the take-it-or-leave-it attitude toward cranberry sauce comes from the author's estrangement from properly coagulated fruit juice. The recipe included in the article states, "Cranberry sauce should not jelly."[19] Mary J. Lincoln's 1895 recipe for cranberry sauce from the Boston-based *American Kitchen Magazine* deplored poorly cooked cranberry sauce:

CRANBERRIES: How seldom we find cranberry sauce in perfection either in private families hotels or restaurants! It is usually purple, either too sour, or sweetened with molasses, or it is a mass of tough skins and seeds in a thin syrup, or, if sifted, it is a thin, dark-colored, uninviting-looking and tinny-tasting mixture, neither a sauce nor a marmalade, and surely ought never to be called a jelly. . . . [In good sauce] the skins will be soft and tender and yet the berries will be nearly whole and the syrup clear and sometimes almost a jelly.[20]

Even the turkey was up for grabs in some quarters. In 1895, *Christian Work* had Nancy Larkin opine on the topic of serving roast duck at a Thanksgiving dinner hosted by someone "not *very* rich, but just rich enough to have a cook who knew how to prepare everything to a turn and waitresses enough to serve the dinner well."

> The turkey, you see, is omitted, because between ourselves, the turkey is not a particularly toothsome bird. The "fixins," as the children say, are what make a turkey dinner so much appreciated. Almost any other roast bird tastes better. Turkey and Thanksgiving are indissolubly connected only in the popular, not in the fashionable mind, an inheritance—this belief—from the days of our Pilgrim and Puritan forefathers, who did not have a great variety of food, and who killed a turkey on feast days as the greatest treat they could make ready.[21]

For years, the most essential element in New England Thanksgivings celebrations wasn't cranberry sauce or turkey but chicken pie. Sarah Josepha Buell Hale, the author and human dynamo who almost single-handedly made Thanksgiving into a national holiday, agreed. Here is her description of the role of chicken pie in the Thanksgiving celebration at a comfortable New Hampshire farmer's home in her 1827 novel *Northwood*.[22] Hale doesn't mention cranberries at all.

> The roasted turkey took precedence on this occasion, being placed at the head of the table, and well did it become its lordly station, sending forth the rich odor of its savory stuffing and finely covered with the froth of the basting . . . the middle being graced, as it always is, on such occasions by that rich burgomaster of the provisions called a chicken pie. This pie, which is wholly formed of the choicest parts of fowls enriched and seasoned with a profusion of butter and pepper and covered with an excellent puff paste, is like the celebrated pumpkin pie an indispensable part of a good and true Yankee Thanksgiving, the size of the pie usually denoting the gratitude of the party who prepares the feast.

Pumpkins: A Thanksgiving Aside

*Instead of Apples and Peares they had Pomkins and Squashes
of divers kinds.*[23]

Pumpkins, the fruit of the Pilgrims, are the lowliest and lowest-growing of American Indians' "three sisters" crops of corn, beans, and squash. For most Americans, pumpkins are useful on two days a year: Halloween, when they are carved, and Thanksgiving, when they are mashed, sweetened, spiced, baked in a crust, and then smothered in whipped cream until they are edible. That makes them twice as popular as cranberries, which are ingested only at Thanksgiving—but that isn't saying much.

Like corn, pumpkins originated in Central America and traveled to New England by the same trade routes. Squash seeds and rinds dating back 8,000 to 10,000 years have been discovered in caves in Oaxaca, Mexico. These dried remnants had larger seeds than wild squash, indicating that the ancient Mexicans had already domesticated the squash and begun to cultivate it for food, not simply gather it in the wild.[24] Seeds of *Cucurbita pepo* species reached eastern Pennsylvania and Maine by 5,000 BC—3,000 years before corn and 2,000 years before the earliest traces of beans.[25] The "three sisters" cultivation of corn, beans, and squash in a single field is a fairly late development, and probably didn't reach New England until AD 1300 or later.[26]

Seeds from plants of the genus *Cucurbita pepo*—pumpkin, squash, and gourds—were some of the first new seeds brought back to Europe, where the fast-growing pleasingly shaped vegetables rapidly spread. New World gourds were lovingly drawn in a prayer book in Touraine, France, ca. 1508 and painted on the charmingly named festoons at the Villa Farnesina, Rome, between 1515 and 1518.[27] Half a century after Columbus's first voyage, a variety of squashes sprang up in European herbals: field pumpkins, summer squash, acorn squashes, scallops, and ornamental gourds.[28]

The local Wampanoag and other tribes cooked their "pompions" in pottage along with corn, beans, and meats, according to Daniel Gookin's 1674 *Historical Collections of the Indians in New England*:

Their food is generally boiled maize, or Indian corn, mixed with kidney-beans, or sometimes without. Also they frequently boil in this pottage fish and flesh of all sorts. . . they mix with the said pottage several sorts of roots; as Jerusalem artichokes, and ground nuts, and other roots, and pompions, and squashes, and also several sorts of nuts or masts, as oak acorns, chestnuts, walnuts: these husked and dried, and powdered, they thicken their pottage therewith.[29]

Unlike cranberries, though, pumpkins can be grown by home gardeners who do not live in a bog. Every year, proud gardeners exhibit swollen squashy specimens weighing more than half a ton at the Topsfield Fair. Why? Because they can. The reason they can is that companies like Pinetree Garden Seeds of New Gloucester, Maine, and Johnny's Selected Seeds of Winslow, Maine, sell seeds for Dill's Atlantic Giant pumpkins, the homeliest, hugest variety of pumpkins ever to displace a perennial bed.

By the nineteenth century, jokesters were writing poems about dear old pumpkin's culinary dominance.[30] This particular ode was undoubtedly written in 1824, but its credits read, "FOREFATHERS SONG, Composed about the year 1630 taken memoriter in 1791 from the lips of an old lady at the advanced age of 92."

> If fresh meat be wanting to fill up our dish,
> We have carrots and pumpkins and turnips and fish
> And is there a mind for a delicate dish?
> We repair to the clam banks and there we catch fish
> Instead of pottage and puddings and custards and pies
> Our pumpkins and parsnips are common supplies
> We have pumpkins at morning and pumpkins at noon
> If it was not for pumpkins we should be undone
>
> If barley be wanting to make into malt
> We must be contented and think it no fault
> For we can make liquor to sweeten our lips
> Of pumpkins and parsnips and walnut tree chips.

Can We Give Thanks for New England Food?

Staged, ritual Thanksgiving meals were deliberately created and promoted in the nineteenth century. Today, this invented tradition is even less connected to New Englanders' everyday eating than convention center chowder-and-Craisin catering options. The solid majority of "New England" cookbooks, magazines, websites, and social media posts about food all describe an imagined, ahistorical place that has little to do with how most New England residents ate in the past and even less with what people actually eat in New England today.

Given all the many histories, geographies, and peoples in this vast space, is something called "New England food" even possible? Maybe. Here are some ideas for selecting true New England foods—not what Ye Olde Wealthee Bostonians might have had their servants prepare, but what people living in the region actually eat today.

— They are commonly available in large areas of New England—the entire coastline, inland supermarkets, or a large category of restaurants. Clam cakes at Newport, Rhode Island, beaches are delightful, but someone in Burlington, Vermont, probably hasn't had them.

— They are accessible to people of all income levels. Lobsters are wonderful, but a lot of people won't pay more than $7 a pound for an ocean insect that you have to kill and dissect yourself. Even lobster rolls—chopped lobster with mayonnaise on a bun—top $15 apiece. Seasonally, New Englanders can buy lobster rolls for under $10 at McDonald's, which uses defrosted frozen lobster, producing the same old lobster experience available at a Red Lobster franchise in Sioux City, Iowa.[31] Maple syrup is iffy, given that it costs $15 or more per quart away from maple-tapping communities.

— They are eaten on an everyday basis, not just on holidays. Vacation food like fried dough and Christmas and Easter treats like ricotta pie are not part of New England's everyday diet.

— The product must either originate in New England, be grown or made in New England, or be strongly associated with New England, preferably both. Grinders are eaten all over New England, but these sandwiches are also eaten all over the eastern seaboard under names like "subs" and "hoagies." Apple pies are delightful, but they're baked all over the United States. The phrase is "as American as apple pie," not "as Connecticutian as apple pie."

The best example of a food that fits all these criteria is Durkee-Mower's Marshmallow Fluff. Invented in Somerville, Massachusetts, in 1917, Fluff wasn't the first marshmallow spread in the history of the world—Fannie Farmer mentioned a "marshmallow creme" in her 1896 *Boston Cooking-School Cook Book*—but thanks to aggressive multimedia marketing, Durkee-Mower's Fluff is the most well-known marshmallow spread in New England. The Fluffernutter sandwich, a gooey, dessert-like concoction of peanut butter and Fluff on white bread, is eaten for lunch throughout New England, but remains incomprehensible to visitors from other regions.[32] Somerville holds an annual Fluff Festival each September, featuring odd canapes, games, and performances by the Flufferettes.[33]

Baked beans and clam chowder might qualify as New England foods, but only the canned varieties. Very few New England cooks are willing to shuck clams or wait near a stove for 8 to 10 hours for beans to bake, assuming they could actually find salt pork at the supermarket to make the beans at all. Fish sticks might qualify as well. They were invented in and are still largely manufactured in Gloucester, Massachusetts, though the fish is imported from around the world.

Cranberries are a near miss. About 73 percent of the US cranberry crop is grown outside New England, mostly in Wisconsin, and thanks to Ocean Spray's heroic decades-long efforts, cranberry sauce has become an American food, not a New England regional food.[34]

Whoopie pies make the cut, but Boston cream pie (a cake with custard filling and topped with chocolate icing) does not, due to decreasing observations in the wild of New England bakeries and supermarkets. New England's Greek-style pizza, with a pan-baked crust and mixed mozzarella and cheddar topping, does, unfortunately.

None of these foods are made by loving grandmothers laboring over pastry boards or carefully deboning delicate fish fillets. Most New England grandmothers haven't done that sort of work since the dawn of Pop-Tarts (1964). If we want New England's regional culinary traditions to consist of something other than industrialized, prepackaged fast food, we need to change our culture.

There is some hope. In some areas, local and recent immigrant traditions are creating vibrant culinary innovations, at least for affluent restaurant goers. As a *Boston Globe* article noted in 2017,

> That today less than 30 percent of North End residents are of Italian descent doesn't change the fact that Italian food is the main draw for outsiders. . . . If you listen to the kitchen staff doing the cooking, you will hear, as you do now in Italy, new voices, many of them Spanish. Jose Duarte, from Peru, runs Taranta. And, famously, some of the North End's best pasta, at Bricco, was long made by a Russian woman. That's amore. That's America.[35]

Dozens of local organizations are working to make New England more resilient, make food production more local, help immigrants grow and sell new crops, and help consumers adopt new foods. Programs like the New Entry Sustainable Farming Project, the University of Massachusetts Ethnic Crops Program, and Food Solutions New England are offering alternatives to a future of food grown in algae vat farms. But they're small. Companies like Conagra and Kraft are much, much bigger.

In 1899, scientist and social reformer Ellen Swallow Richards wrote.

> We began to ask, what are the national dishes of Americans? It is astonishing how few still partake of the simple fare known as New England. It seems to be a part of the restless and hurried life of this generation in large cities to have abandoned the cheap and simple foods that need long cooking and a little skill to make them palatable. This reduces the fare to chops and steaks, and tea with bread and cakes to be picked up at the bake shop. Are these our national foods? It would almost seem so. Certain it is that home cookery is decreasing in amount and not improving in quality more and more dependence being placed on the bakeshop and restaurant.[36]

Today, that dependence is placed on fast-food chains and supermarket prepared foods. The national dishes of New England may be takeout pizza and rotisserie chicken, not baked beans or clam chowder or even hasty pudding. They may not be glamorous, but they reflect who we are. The question is, who do we want to be?

ACKNOWLEDGMENTS

DOZENS OF people helped me write and research this book. I owe a special debt to my agent, Alfred LaFarge, who offered an empty house on an island where I could sit and write when I needed to concentrate on my book. My husband Scott has been kind throughout this process, and I am eternally grateful that he married me.

Faith Ferguson and Carolyn Goldstein reassured me that my historical research was worthwhile and interesting, and Geoff Cohen, Robert Mela, and Lydia Swan sent me historical tidbits to help me write. Thanks to Kathleen Wall for patiently answering some very basic questions. Thanks to the staff of the Schlesinger Library, especially Sarah Hutcheon, for their help and cheer. I also am grateful for help over the course of my research from Peter Benes, Rachel Black, Frank Clark, Robert Dirks, Mark Essig, David Lambert, Martha Mayo, John J. McCusker, James McWilliams, Ian Mosby, Patrick Munson, John Pollack, and Mildred Rahn, all of whom answered my questions out of the goodness of their hearts.

NOTES

INTRODUCTION

1. M. Groening, *School Is Hell* (New York: Pantheon, 1987).

2. G. Hepting, "Death of the American Chestnut," *Journal of Forest History* 18, no. 3 (July 1974): 60–67.

3. See, for example, the discerning discussion of the historical record in Katherine Neustadt, *Clambake: A History and Celebration of an American Tradition* (Amherst: University of Massachusetts Press, 1992).

4. See Frederick Douglass Opie, *Hog and Hominy: Soul Food from Africa to America Frederick Douglass* (New York: Columbia University Press, 2010).

5. Lyn Hey, "Children's Civic Lesson Fires Up Age-Old Debate over Barbecue," *USA Today*, May 29, 2005.

6. M. K. Bennett, "The Food Economy of the New England Indians 1605–75," *Journal of Political Economy* 63, no. 5 (1955): 369–397.

7. Virginia DeJohn Anderson, "King Philip's Herds: Indians, Colonists, and the Problem of Livestock in Early New England," *William and Mary Quarterly*, 3rd ser., 51, no. 4 (1994): 601–624.

8. Charles D. Cheek, "Massachusetts Bay Foodways: Regional and Class Influences," *Historical Archaeology* 32, no. 3 (1998): 153–172.

9. Governing, "Population Density for U.S. Cities Statistics" (November 2017), www.governing.com.

10. IndexMundi, "Maine Population per Square Mile, 2010 by County," www.indexmundi.com.

11. B. Washuk, "Lewiston Makes Strides towards Embracing Its Immigrant Population," *Portland Press Herald*, January 14, 2018.

CHAPTER 1: WHO IS A YANKEE?

1. B. D. Wortham-Galvin, "The Fabrication of Place in America: The Fictions and Traditions of the New England Village," *Traditional Dwellings & Settlements Review* 20, no. 11 (2010): 21–34, 25.

2. Wortham-Galvin, "Fabrication of Place in America," 25.

3. Boston Redevelopment Authority and Mayor's Office for New Bostonians, "Imagine All the People: Foreign Born Immigrants in Boston" (2009), www.bostonplans.org; A. Filindra and S. Pearson-Merkowitz, *Immigrants and Immigration in the Ocean State: History, Demography, Public Opinion and Policy Responses* (Kingston: University of Rhode Island Urban Initiative, 2014).

4. Wortham-Galvin, "Fabrication of Place in America," 25.

5. James A. Kindraka, "Milk Run! The Story of Milk Transportation by Rail," *Dispatch* 12, no. 1 (1990): 19.

6. Dona Brown, *Inventing New England: Regional Tourism in the Nineteenth Century* (Washington, DC: Smithsonian Institution Press, 1995), 135–167, "That Dream of Home," 159.

7. Wortham-Galvin, "Fabrication of Place in America," 25.

8. Roger N. Parks, "Comments on Change in Agriculture 1790–1840," *Agricultural History* 46, no. 1 (January 1972): 173–180, 174.

9. David R. Meyer, "The Transition from Agriculture to Manufacturing in the East before 1860," in *The Changing American Countryside: Past, Present and Future. Proceedings of a Conference Sponsored by the W.K. Kellogg Foundation* (November 30–December 1, 1995), 13.

10. Meyer, "Transition from Agriculture to Manufacturing," 13.

11. Meyer, "Transition from Agriculture to Manufacturing," 13.

12. Parks, "Comments on Change in Agriculture," 174.

13. E. H. Jenkins, *A History of Connecticut Agriculture* (New Haven: Connecticut Agricultural Experiment Station, 1926), 346; www.census.gov.

14. Jenkins, *History of Connecticut Agriculture*, 352–353.

15. C. Merchant, *Ecological Revolutions: Nature, Gender, & Science in New England*, 2nd ed. (Chapel Hill: University of North Carolina Press, 1989), 244.

16. N. DePaoli et al., *Historic & Archaeological Resources of Southeast Massachusetts: A Framework for Preservation Decisions* (Boston: Massachusetts Historical Commission, 1982).

17. T. M. Rittentour, "Late Glacial Paleo-Ecology of New England" (2012), www.bio.umass.edu.

18. B. D. Smith, "Origins of Agriculture in Eastern North America," *Science*, New Series 246, no. 4937 (December 22, 1989): 1566–1571.

19. E. D. Chilton, "Towns They Have None: Diverse Subsistence and Settlement Strategies in Native New England," in *Northeast Subsistence-Settlement Change: AD 700–1300*, ed. J. P. Hart and C. B. Rieth (Albany: State University of New York, State Education Department, 2002), 289–300.

20. Virginia DeJohn Anderson, "King Philip's Herds: Indians, Colonists, and the Problem of Livestock in Early New England," *William and Mary Quarterly*, 3rd ser., 51, no. 4 (1994): 601–624.

21. Anderson, "King Philip's Herds."

22. Jerusalem artichokes have a messy genetic lineage, but evidence suggests that they originated in the east-central United States. See D. G. Bock, N. C. Kane, D. P. Ebert, and L. H. Rieseberg, "Genome Skimming Reveals the Origin of the Jerusalem Artichoke Tuber Crop Species: Neither from Jerusalem nor an Artichoke," *New Phytology* 201, no. 3 (2014): 1021–1030; S. Tushingham, C. M. Snyder, K. J. Brownstein, W. J. Damitio, and D. R. Gang, "Biomolecular Archaeology Reveals Ancient Origins of Indigenous Tobacco Smoking in North American Plateau," *PNAS* 115, no. 46 (2018): 11742–11747.

23. A. Mendelson, "The Lenapes: In Search of Pre-European Foodways in the Greater New York Region," in *Gastropolis: Food and New York City*, ed. A. Hauck-Lawson and J. Deutsch (New York: Columbia University Press, 2009), 15–33, 29.

24. E. Peacock, "Historical and Applied Perspectives on Prehistoric Land Use in Eastern North America," *Environment and History* 4, no. 1 (February 1998): 1–29; Mendelson, "The Lenapes," 19; J. P. Hart and W. A. Lovis, "Reevaluating What We Know about the Histories of Maize in Northeastern North America: A Review of Current Evidence," *Journal of Archaeological Research* 21, no. 2 (June 2013): 175–216, 203.

25. M. Kurlansky, *Cod: A Biography of the Fish That Changed the World* (New York: Penguin, 1998).

26. H. C. Kraft, "Sixteenth and Seventeenth Century Indian/White Trade Relations in the Atlantic and Northeast Regions," *Archaeology of Eastern North America* 17 (1989): 1–29, 7; D. Gabaccia, *We Are What We Eat: Ethnic Foods and the Making of Americans* (Cambridge, MA: Harvard University Press, 1998), 21.

27. J. S. Marr and J. T. Cathey, "New Hypothesis for Cause of Epidemic among Native Americans, New England, 1616–1619," *Emerging Infectious Diseases* 16, no. 22 (2010): 281–286.

28. K. J. Bowers, "Native Interactions and Economic Exchange: A Re-evaluation of Plymouth Colony Collections" (thesis, University of Massachusetts Boston, 2015), 44; L. Turgeon, "The Tale of the Kettle: Odyssey of an Intercultural Object," *Ethnohistory* 44, no. 1 (1997): 1–29, 10.

29. M. K. Bennett, "The Food Economy of the New England Indians, 1605–75," *Journal of Political Economy* 63, no. 5 (1955): 369–397, 379.

30. C. Chartier, "Wampanoag Foodways" (Plymouth Archaeological Rediscovery Project, n.d.), 1, www.plymoutharch.com.

31. Chartier, "Wampanoag Foodways," 7–9.

32. Bennett, "Food Economy of the New England Indians," 379.

33. Gabaccia, *We Are What We Eat*, 21; J. Winthrop, R. Dunn, and L. Yeandle, *The Journal of John Winthrop, 1630–1649* (Cambridge, MA: Harvard University Press, 1996), 73; Mendelson, "The Lenapes," 30.

34. Marr and Cathey, "New Hypothesis."

35. W. Bradford, *History of Plymouth Plantation, 1620–1647*, ed. Worthington Chauncey Ford (Boston: Massachusetts Historical Society, 1912), 220–221; M. Laskey, "The Great Dying: New England's Coastal Plague, 1616–1619," *CVLT Nation*, July 15, 2014, www.cvltnation.com.

36. Marr and Cathey, "New Hypothesis."

37. M. E. Newell, *Brethren by Nature: New England Indians, Colonists, and the Origins of American Slavery* (Ithaca, NY: Cornell University Press, 2015), 75–78.

38. North American Indian Center of Boston, "Tribes in New England," www.niacob.org.

39. B. Feintuch and D. H. Watters, eds., *The Encyclopedia of New England* (New Haven, CT: Yale University Press, 2005), 811.

40. Feintuch and Watters, *Encyclopedia of New England*, 363.

41. Virginia DeJohn Anderson, "The Origins of New England Culture," *William and Mary Quarterly*, 3rd ser., 48, no. 2 (April 1991): 231–237, 232.

42. Rev. Francis Higginson as quoted in G. F. Dow, *Everyday Life in the Massachusetts Bay Colony* (Boston: Society for the Preservation of New England Antiquities, 1935), 3; Benjamin Blom as quoted in Gabaccia, *We Are What We Eat*, 19.

43. American Antiquarian Society, "Records of the Company of the Massachusetts Bay to the Embarkation of Winthrop and His Associates for New England as Contained in the First Volume of the Archive of the Commonwealth of Massachusetts," *Transactions and Collections of the American Antiquarian Society* 3 (1857): 12–13; J. Brown, *The Carpenter's Rule* (London: Fisher, and R. Mount, 1688), chap. 10.

44. E. Johnson, *Johnson's Wonder-Working Providence 1628–1651*, ed. J. Franklin Jameson (New York: Charles Scribner's Sons, 1910), 65; C. Lee, "Public Poor Relief and the Massachusetts Community, 1620–1715," *New England Quarterly* 55, no. 4 (December 1982): 564–585, 570; T. L. Bratton, "The Identity of the New England Indian Epidemic of 1616–1619," *Bulletin of the History of Medicine* 62, no. 3 (1988): 351–383, 351.

45. K. Stavely and K. Fitzgerald, *America's Founding Food* (Chapel Hill: University of North Carolina Press, 2004), 39–43.

46. Stavely and Fitzgerald, *America's Founding Food*, 23–28.

47. Stavely and Fitzgerald, *America's Founding Food*, 67, 260–266.

48. R. Wilk, "The Extractive Economy: An Early Phase of the Globalization of Diet," *Review (Fernand Braudel Center)* 27, no. 4 (2004): 285–306, 292–293; Anderson, "King Philip's Herds," 607.

49. S. McMahon, "A Comfortable Subsistence: The Changing Composition of Diet in Rural New England, 1620–1840," *William and Mary Quarterly*, 3rd ser., 42, no. 1 (1985): 26–65, 39–41.

50. D. S. Shields, *The Culinarians: Lives and Careers from the First Age of American Fine Dining* (Chicago: University of Chicago Press, 2017), 25–28, 29–33.

51. New England Historical Society, "Before the Famine Ships, the Irish Made Their Mark in New England" (2018), www.newenglandhistoricalsociety.com.

52. New England Historical Society, "Before the Famine Ships."

53. F. D. Cogliano, "Deliverance from Luxury: Pope's Day, Conflict and Consensus in Colonial Boston, 1745–1765," *Studies in Popular Culture* 15, no. 2 (1993): 15–28, 16.

54. Cogliano, "Deliverance from Luxury."

55. J. C. Fitzpatrick, "George Washington and Religion," *Catholic Historical Review* 15, no. 1 (1929): 23–42, 28.

56. New England Historic Genealogical Society, *The Irish in New England* (Cambridge, MA: Crimson Printing, 1985).

57. M. Feeney, "When the Irish Came to Boston," *Boston Globe*, March 15, 2017, www.bostonglobe.com; F. J. Turner, "New England 1830–1850," *Huntington Library Bulletin*, no. 1 (May 1931): 153–198, 186; Feintuch and Watters, *Encyclopedia of New England*, 330.

58. P. Jackson, "Women in 19th Century Irish Emigration," *International Migration Review* 18, no. 4 (1984): 1004–1020, 1007.

59. H. Diner, *Erin's Daughters in America: Irish Immigrant Women in the Nineteenth Century* (Baltimore: Johns Hopkins University Press, 1983), 89; O. Handlin, *Boston's Immigrants: A Study in Acculturation* (Cambridge, MA: Belknap, 1959), 61.

60. L. Clarkson and M. Crawford, *Feast and Famine: Food and Nutrition in Ireland 1500–1920* (Oxford: Oxford University Press, 2001), "Potatoes, Population, and Diet, circa 1650 to circa 1845," 59–87.

61. N. Kissane, *The Irish Famine: A Documentary History* (Syracuse, NY: Syracuse University Press, 1996).

62. Kissane, *Irish Famine*, 16.

63. Clarkson and Crawford, *Feast and Famine*, 61.

64. R. Dirks, *Food in the Gilded Age: What Ordinary Americans Ate* (Lanham, MD: Rowman & Littlefield, 2016), 24–30.

65. H. R. Diner, *Hungering for America: Italian, Irish, and Jewish Foodways in the Age of Migration* (Cambridge, MA: Harvard University Press, 2001), 103–106; M. F. Wack, "Recipe-Collecting, Embodied Imagination, and Transatlantic Connections in an Irish Emigrant's Cooking," *Canadian Journal of Irish Studies* 41 (2018): 100–123, 112; Clarkson and Crawford, *Feast and Famine*, 23.

66. W. R. Wilde, "On the Introduction and Period of the General Use of the Potato in Ireland," *Proceedings of the Royal Irish Academy* 6 (1856): 356–372, 359; H. O'Connell, "Bleak Food: William Wilde, Famine, and Gastronomy," *Canadian Journal of Irish Studies* 41 (2018): 156–177.

67. Wilde, "On the Introduction and Period," 359.

68. For example, "Irishmen Can't Live Like Cameleopards upon Air No More Than an Englishman on Potato and Point!," *Spirit of the English Magazines*, 1825, 300.

69. O'Connell, "Bleak Food."

70. Kissane, *Irish Famine*, 13.

71. Wilde, "On the Introduction and Period," 357.

72. P. Lysaght, "Women and the Great Famine: Vignettes from the Irish Oral Tradition," in *The Great Famine and the Irish Diaspora in America*, ed. A. Gribben (Amherst: University of Massachusetts Press, 1999), 31.

73. Diner, *Hungering for America*, 31.

74. Feintuch and Watters, *Encyclopedia of New England*, 330.

75. Handlin, *Boston's Immigrants*, 243.

76. T. J. Archdeacon, *Becoming American* (New York: Simon & Schuster, 1984), 47.

77. Feintuch and Watters, *Encyclopedia of New England*, 647.

78. J. C. G. Kennedy, *The Eighth Census of the United States: Population, Manufactures, Agriculture, Statistics, Including Mortality, Property, Etc.*, vol. 3 (US Census Bureau, 1860).

79. Feintuch and Watters, *Encyclopedia of New England*, 375.

80. M. M. Con Iomarie, "Recognizing Food as Part of Ireland's Intangible Cultural Heritage," *Folk Life* 56 (2018): 93–115.

81. N. Foner, "Immigrant Women and Work in New York City, Then and Now," *Journal of American Ethnic History* 18, no. 3 (1999): 95–113.

82. For a description of living conditions, see, for example, G. Kenngott, *The Record of a City: A Social Survey of Lowell Massachusetts* (Boston: Macmillan, 1912), 117.

83. M. Peel, "On the Margins: Lodgers and Boarders in Boston, 1860–1900," *Journal of American History* 72, no. 4 (1986): 813–834.

84. J. L'Heureux, "Why They Came: Franco-American Immigration," *Bangor Daily News*, January 24, 2018, http://francoamerican.bangordailynews.com.

85. B. J. Ancelet, J. Edwards, and G. Pitre, *Cajun Country* (Jackson: University Press of Mississippi, 1991), 140–141.

86. M. Bienvenu, C. A. Brasseaux, and R. A. Brasseaux, *Stir the Pot: The History of Cajun Cuisine* (New York: Hippocrene Books, 2005), 28–30, 40.

87. D. Bélanger and C. Bélanger, "Readings in Quebec History: French Canadian Emigration to the United States, 1840–1930," *Quebec History*, August 23, 2000, http://faculty.marianopolis.edu.

88. Feintuch and Watters, *Encyclopedia of New England*, 331.

89. Massachusetts Department of Labor and Industries, Division of Statistics, "Annual Report on the Statistics of Labor" (Boston: Rand Avery, 1881), 469.

90. R. L. Gentilcore, *Historical Atlas of Canada* (Toronto: University of Toronto Press, 1987), vol. 2, plate 12.

91. R. L. Jones, "French-Canadian Agriculture in the St. Lawrence Valley, 1815–1850," *Agricultural History* 16, no. 3 (1942): 137–148, 144–145; J. Isbister, "Agriculture, Balanced Growth, and Social Change in Central Canada since 1850: An Interpretation," *Economic Development and Cultural Change* 25, no. 4 (1977): 673–697, 680–682.

92. Feintuch and Watters, *Encyclopedia of New England*, 331.

93. Feintuch and Watters, *Encyclopedia of New England*, 332.

94. Bélanger and Bélanger, "Readings in Quebec History"; J. P. Allen, "Society Migration Fields of French Canadian Immigrants to Southern Maine," *Geographical Review* 62, no. 3 (1972): 366–383.

95. Bélanger and Bélanger, "Readings in Quebec History."

96. B. Beattie, "Migrants and Millworkers: The French Canadian Population of Burlington and Colchester, 1860–1870," *Proceedings of the Vermont Historical Society* 60, no. 2 (1992): 95–117.

97. F. M. Waldron, "To Be an Homme de Famille in Petit-Canada: Ethnicity and National Identity among New England's Working-Class Migrant Men from Quebec, 1880–1920" (paper, Historical Society 2008 Conference, Baltimore, June 5–8, 2008).

98. C. Bélanger, "Rapatriement," *Quebec History*, August 23, 2000, http://faculty.marianopolis.edu.

99. B. Ramirez, "French Canadian Immigrants in the New England Cotton Industry: A Socioeconomic Profile," *Labour Le Travailleur* 11 (1983): 125–142.

100. Bélanger and Bélanger, "Readings in Quebec History."

101. R. Daniels, *Coming to America: A History of Immigration and Ethnicity in American Life*, 2nd ed. (New York: Perennial/HarperCollins, 2002), 264.

102. G. Gerstle, *Working-Class Americanism: The Politics of Labor in a Textile City, 1914–1960* (Princeton, NJ: Princeton University Press, 2002), 48.

103. See, for example, New England Historical Society, "Pass the Tourtiere, C'est Le Reveillon!," www.newenglandhistoricalsociety.com.

104. E.g., "One of the most common memories of Franco-Americans raised in this neighborhood is the smell of pork cooking in almost every kitchen as mothers and grandmothers worked to feed large families on limited budgets. Franco-American culinary traditions include a meat pie, called tourtière, and a pork spread called cretons or gorton." E. Blood and E. Duclos-Orsello, "Franco-American Salem: A Brief History," http://di.salemstate.edu.

105. "Canadian Folk Life and Folklore," *Nation* 67 (1898): 337–338; W. P. Greenough, *Canadian Folk-Life and Folk-Lore* (New York: G.H. Richmond, 1897), 151.

106. Greenough, *Canadian Folk-Life and Folk-Lore*, 169–170.

107. P. Marchand, *Ghost Empire: How the French Almost Conquered North America* (Toronto: McClelland & Stewart, 2009), 185.

108. K. Merrill, "The Habitant and the Hamsteak: The Preservation of Historic French-Canadian Foodways and New England Migration" (master's thesis, Boston University, 2012).

109. See, for example, J. L'heureux, "Pate Chinois and the Franco-American Cuisine," *Bangor Daily News*, February 22, 2019, http://francoamerican.bangordailynews.com.

110. "Acadian Culture in Maine," http://acim.umfk.maine.edu; also published as North Atlantic Region National Park Service, *Acadian Culture in Maine* (Boston: National Park Service, 1992), 32–34; M. Corbin, "Acadian Food" (2008), http://umaine.edu.

111. I. S. Podea, "Quebec to 'Little Canada': The Coming of the French Canadians to New England in the Nineteenth Century," *New England Quarterly* 23, no. 3 (1950): 365–380, 377."

112. Massachusetts Bureau of Statistics of Labor, "Annual Report of the Bureau of Statistics of Labor," vol. 17 (Boston: Wright & Potter, 1886), 312.

113. Massachusetts Bureau of Statistics of Labor, "Annual Report," 237–328.

114. Kenngott, *Record of a City*, 115.

115. Kenngott, *Record of a City*, 116.

116. Kenngott, *Record of a City*, 133–135.

117. Kenngott, *Record of a City*, 133–135.

118. Merrill, "Habitant and the Hamsteak"; Y. Takai, *Gendered Passages: French-Canadian Migration to Lowell, Massachusetts, 1900–1920* (New York: Peter Lang, 2008), 168–171.

119. Takai, *Gendered Passages*, 168–171.

120. G. L. Sharrow, "African American History in New England," www.vermontfolklifecenter.org; New England Historical Society, "How the Slave Trade Took Root in New England" (2019), www.newenglandhistoricalsociety.com.

121. L. E. Horton, "From Class to Race in Early America: Northern Post-Emancipation Racial Reconstruction," *Journal of the Early Republic* 19, no. 4 (1999): 629–649, 630.

122. Feintuch and Watters, *Encyclopedia of New England*, 327; C. M. Clark-Pujara, "Slavery, Emancipation and Black Freedom in Rhode Island, 1652–1842" (PhD diss., University of Iowa, 2009), 3.

123. Clark-Pujara, "Slavery, Emancipation and Black Freedom," 41.

124. R. K. Fitts, "The Landscapes of Northern Bondage," *Historical Archaeology* 30, no. 2 (1996): 54–73, 55.

125. Horton, "From Class to Race in Early America," 639.

126. Feintuch and Watters, *Encyclopedia of New England*, 328.

127. Feintuch and Watters, *Encyclopedia of New England*, 329; Clark-Pujara, "Slavery, Emancipation and Black Freedom," 93–94.

128. Horton, "From Class to Race in Early America," 639, 630, 643.

129. M. A. Way, "Beef, Mutton, Pork, and a Taste of Turtle: Zooarchaeology and Nineteenth-Century African American Foodways at the Boston-Higginbotham House, Nantucket, Massachusetts" (master's thesis, University of Massachusetts Boston, 2010), 26.

130. R. D. Rohrs, "Exercising Their Right: African American Voter Turnout in Antebellum Newport, Rhode Island," *New England Quarterly* 84, no. 3 (2011): 402–421, 402.

131. M. Sammons and V. Cunningham, *Black Portsmouth: Three Centuries of African-American Heritage* (Durham, NH: University Press of New England, 2004), 26.

132. C. Adams and E. H. Pleck, *Love of Freedom: Black Women in Colonial and Revolutionary New England* (Oxford: Oxford University Press, 2010), 40–41.

133. Fitts, "Landscapes of Northern Bondage," 60.

134. W. J. Brown, *The Life of William J. Brown, of Providence, R.I.: With Personal Recollections of Incidents in Rhode Island* (Providence: Angell & Co., 1883), 11–12.

135. Brown, *Life of William J. Brown*, xix–xx.

136. A. Chan, "Archaeology and the Unexpected Revelation," *Royall House & Slave Quarters News*, Fall 2013, www.royallhouse.org.

137. J. F. Deetz, *In Small Things Forgotten: An Archaeology of Early American Life*, rev. ed. (New York: Anchor, 1996), 199–200; K. A. Hutchins-Keim, "Parting Ways Revisited: Archaeology at a Nineteenth-Century African-American Community in Plymouth, Massachusetts," *Journal of African Diaspora Archaeology & Heritage* 4, no. 2 (2015): 115–142.

138. D. B. Landon et al., "Investigating the Heart of a Community: Archaeological Excavations at the African Meeting House, Boston, Massachusetts" (Andrew Fiske Memorial Center for Archaeological Research Publications, 2007), 2.

139. Way, "Beef, Mutton, Pork, and a Taste of Turtle," 94.

140. Landon et al., "Investigating the Heart of a Community," 122–123.

141. Landon et al., "Investigating the Heart of a Community," 177.

142. New England Historical Society, "The Secret History of New England's Sundown Towns" (2018), www.newenglandhistoricalsociety.com; J. W. Lowen, *Sundown Towns: A Hidden Dimension of American Racism* (New York: New Press, 2018); A. Burke, "America Was All Abuzz about Ashby: Recalling March 1973 Day When a Resolution Calling on the Town to Endorse Freedom, Equality for Minority Groups . . . Was Defeated," *Lowell Sun Enterprise*, March 6, 2018, www.lowellsun.com.

143. H. A. Whitfield, "African Americans in Burlington, Vermont, 1880–1900," *Vermont History* 75, no. 2 (2007): 101–123.

144. W. C. Fowler, *The Historical Status of the Negro in Connecticut* (Charleston, SC: Walker, Evans & Cogswell, 1901), 25.

145. G. De Paola, "Foodways to Freedom through the Kitchen," *Edible Rhody*, September 6 2017, http://ediblerhody.ediblecommunities.com; G. G. Channing, *Early Recollections of Newport, R.I.: From the Year 1793 to 1811* (Newport, RI: A. J. Ward, C. E. Hammett, Jr., 1868), 46–47; Adams and Pleck, *Love of Freedom*, 179–180; Rhode Island Historical Society, "Foodways to Freedom: African Heritage Entrepreneurs in 18th- and 19th-Century Rhode Island" (2017), www.rihs.org; W. D. Piersen, *Black Yankees: The Development of an*

Afro-American Subculture in Eighteenth-Century New England (Amherst: University of Massachusetts Press, 1988), 101.

146. W. B. Weeden, *Early Rhode Island: A Social History of the People* (New York: Grafton Press, 1910), 116–117.

147. Adams and Pleck, *Love of Freedom*, 179–180.

148. Shields, *Culinarians*, 29–33.

149. National Park Service, "African American Heritage Sites in Salem: A Guide to Salem's History" (Salem, MA: Salem Maritime National Historic Site, 2008).

150. Shields, *Culinarians*, 145–149.

151. M. Bishop, "Cape Verdean-American Story with Marilyn Halter," *Afropop Worldwide*, May 8, 2009, http://afropop.org.

152. Bishop, "Cape Verdean-American Story."

153. Bishop, "Cape Verdean-American Story."

154. City of Boston, Mayor's Office for Immigrant Advancement, and Boston Redevelopment Authority, "Imagine All the People: Cape Verdeans" (2016), www.boston-plans.org.

155. W. J. Bolster, ed., "Maritime New England," in Feintuch and Watters, *Encyclopedia of New England*, 1082–1084.

156. L. Batalha and J. Carling, eds., *Transnational Archipelago: Perspectives on Cape Verdean Migration and Diaspora* (Amsterdam: Amsterdam University Press, 2008), 18.

157. City of Boston, Mayor's Office for Immigrant Advancement, and Boston Redevelopment Authority, "Imagine All the People"; J. F. Smith, "Cape Verde, Rising, with Emigres' Help," *Boston Globe*, April 26, 2009.

158. M. Twitty, "The Untold Story of African-American Dishes That Defined the American Palate," *First We Feast*, October 27, 2016, http://firstwefeast.com.

159. See, for example, the comments on G. Allen, "Manchup: Cape Verde's National Dish Is a Savory Mix," *Leite's Culinaria*, October 15, 2018, http://leitesculinaria.com.

160. L. M. Long, *Ethnic American Food Today: A Cultural Encyclopedia* (New York: Rowman & Littlefield, 2015), 106; M. H. Zanger, "Iberian Influences on American Food," in *The Oxford Encyclopedia of Food and Drink in America*, vol. 1, ed. A. F. Smith (New York: Oxford University Press, 2013), 303–307, 306; "Culinária de Cabo Verde (Receitas com Fotos)," December 7, 2006, http://caboindex.com.

161. Nuala, "Auntie Laura's Gufong (a Cape Verdean Favorite!)," *The Cool Cook*, September 21, 2010, https://thecoolcook.wordpress.com.

162. M. E. Lee, *Black Bangor: African Americans in a Maine Community, 1880–1950* (Durham, NH: University Press of New England, 2005), 73–74.

163. Migration Policy Institute, "U.S. Immigrant Population by Metropolitan Area" (2013–2017), www.migrationpolicy.org.

164. Migration Policy Institute, "Caribbean Immigrants in the United States" (February 13, 2019), www.migrationpolicy.org; Migration Policy Institute, "U.S. Immigrant Population by Metropolitan Area."

165. L. Beaulieu, *The New England Orchard Cookbook—Harvesting Dishes & Desserts from the Region's Bounty* (Guilford, CT: Globe Pequot Press, 2016); P. Anderson, "The Migrant Life: Work in Orchards, Farms Is Annual Rite," *Sun Chronicle*, September 18, 2011, www.thesunchronicle.com; M. McKee, "Farmers Upset by Delays in Getting Foreign Workers," *Boston Globe*, October 30, 2011, http://archive.boston.com; "Guest Workers in Maine Picking Apples," http://uniquemainefarms.com; E. Reed, "Can America's Documented, Foreign Guest Worker Program Keep Up with Demand?," *Concord Monitor*, March 20, 2017, www.concordmonitor.com.

166. S. Puleo, "From Italy to Boston's North End: Italian Immigration and Settlement, 1890–1910" (master's thesis, University of Massachusetts Boston, 1994), 1.

167. Puleo, "From Italy to Boston's North End," 4.

168. New England Historical Society, "How the Italian Immigrants Came to New England," www.newenglandhistoricalsociety.com; Puleo, "From Italy to Boston's North End," 4.

169. Puleo, "From Italy to Boston's North End," 116.

170. Puleo, "From Italy to Boston's North End," 116.

171. Feintuch and Watters, *Encyclopedia of New England*, 332.

172. New England Historical Society, "How the Italian Immigrants Came to New England."

173. New England Historical Society, "How the Italian Immigrants Came to New England."

174. Puleo, "From Italy to Boston's North End," 8.

175. New England Historical Society, "Italians in New England Declared Enemy Aliens in WWII," www.newenglandhistoricalsociety.com.

176. Puleo, "From Italy to Boston's North End," 120; M. H. Zanger, "Italian American Food," in Smith, *Oxford Encyclopedia of Food and Drink in America*, 303–307, 306.

177. R. A. Woods, ed., *Americans in Process: A Settlement Study by the Residents and Associates of the South End House* (Cambridge, MA: Houghton Mifflin/Riverside Press, 1903), 107–108.

178. Woods, *Americans in Process*.

179. Woods, *Americans in Process*, 107–108.

180. E. Lord, J. J. D. Trenor, and S. J. Barrows, *The Italian in America* (New York: B.F. Buck, 1905), 121–122; A. Bennett, "Italians as Farmers and Fruit Growers," *Outlook* 90 (September 12, 1908): 87–88.

181. Marini Farm, "The Marini Farm Story" (2019), http://marinifarm.com/history; G. Anderson and D. D. Kricker, "A New Way of Farming in Waltham," *Farm News*, March 31, 2005, http://communityfarms.org; M. Daly, "Saving Arrigo Farm," *Waltham Land Trust Journal*, Fall 2013, https://walthamlandtrust.org/wp-content/; "Agriculture," www.winchester. us; G. Garrelick, "Frank Palumbo," Concord Oral History Program, http://con5635.verio. com.

182. Zanger, "Italian American Food," 350.

183. J. J. Wallah, *How America Eats: A Social History of US Food and Culture* (New York: Rowman & Littlefield, 2013), 76–77.

184. See discussion in Diner, *Hungering for America*, 48–83.

185. Mark Zanger expresses similar thoughts in his article "Italian American Food."

186. J. Lovell, "The Amato's Maine Italian Sandwich, A Portland Classic," *New England Today*, November 7, 2018, http://newengland.com.

187. See, for example, J. F. Carafoli, *Great Italian American Food in New England: History, Traditions, and Memories* (Guildford, CT: Globe Pequot Press, 2016).

188. S. A. Blejwas, "Puritans and Poles: The New England Literary Image of the Polish Peasant Immigrant," *Polish American Studies* 42, no. 2 (1985): 46–88, 47.

189. New England Historical Society, "Flashback Photo: The 1912 Bread and Roses Strike," www.newenglandhistoricalsociety.com; New England Historical Society, "How the Polish Immigrants Came to New England," www.newenglandhistoricalsociety.com; D. Stacom, "As Many Ethnic Neighborhoods Falter, New Britain's Little Poland Is on the Rise," *Hartford Courant*, August 16, 2015, www.courant.com; "Late 19th-Century Immigration in Connecticut," October 17, 2015, http://connecticuthistory.org; Sister Lucille, C.R., "Polish

Farmers and Workers in the United States to 1914," *Polish American Studies* 15, nos. 1–2 (1958): 1–9.

190. M. Hoberman, *Yankee Moderns: Folk Regional Identity in the Sawmill Valley of Western Massachusetts, 1890–1920* (Knoxville: University of Tennessee Press, 2000), xxxiv.

191. Blejwas, "Puritans and Poles," 47.

192. E. S. Tyler, "The Poles in the Connecticut Valley," *Smith College Monthly* 16 (1910): 579–585; E. Ross, *The Old World in the New: The Significance of the Past and Present Immigration to the American People* (New York: Century Co., 1914), 126; "Aliens in New England," *Greenfield Gazette and Courier*, December 7, 1912, www.memorialhall.mass.edu; Hoberman, *Yankee Moderns*, 37–39.

193. Blejwas, "Puritans and Poles," 48.

194. Blejwas, "Puritans and Poles," 47, 49.

195. E. K. Titus, "The Pole in the Land of the Puritan," *New England Magazine* 29, no. 2 (October 1903): 162–166.

196. Kenngott, *Record of a City*, 126.

197. R. Forrant and C. Strobel, "Ethnicity in Lowell" (Boston: National Park Service, 2011), 100–101.

198. Vermont Country Store, "Baked Goods," www.vermontcountrystore.com.

199. E. L. Cohen, "Polish American Food," in Smith, *Oxford Encyclopedia of Food and Drink in America*, 25–28.

200. "Patti's Pierogis," www.pattispierogis.com.

201. Feintuch and Watters, *Encyclopedia of New England*, 334.

202. New England Historical Society, "How Portuguese Immigrants Came to New England," www.newenglandhistoricalsociety.com.

203. "Portuguese American Food," in Smith, *Oxford Encyclopedia of Food and Drink in America*, 45–47; L. M. Long, *Ethnic American Food Today*, 519–525.

204. D. Leite, "Malassadas | Portuguese Doughnuts," *Leite's Culinaria*, March 5, 2019, http://leitesculinaria.com; "Portuguese American Food," 45–47.

205. K. C. Meyers, "Portuguese Festival Honors Tradition, Culture of Town's Vital Families," *Cape Cod Times*, June 27, 2015, www.capecodtimes.com.

206. "Cities with the Highest Percentage of Portuguese in the United States" (2019), http://zipatlas.com.

207. L. Ruckstuhl, "8 Cookbooks from New England Authors for Everyone on Your Gift List," *ARTery*, November 20, 2018, www.wbur.org.

208. Greek Boston, "20th Century Greek Immigration to Massachusetts," www.greekboston.com.

209. Kenngott, *Record of a City*, 125.

210. C. Robb, "Pizza—Who's Got the Best?," *Boston Globe*, November 10, 1977, 78; J. Gutierriez, "You Asked, We Answered: Why Are There SO Many 'Houses of Pizza' in New Hampshire?," New Hampshire Public Radio, February16, 2018, www.nhpr.org.

211. M. Karagianis, "Greek Pizza King Gives Recipe for Reaching to the Top," *Boston Globe*, April 3, 1976, 3.

212. Gutierriez, "You Asked"; T. Doyle, "Greek Pizza Is the Best Mediocre Food You've Never Eaten," *Vice*, June 7, 2017, http://munchies.vice.com.

213. J. Denker, *The World on a Plate: A Tour through the History of America's Ethnic Cuisine* (Lincoln: University of Nebraska Press, 2007), 62.

214. See, for example, the Lynnwood pizza made by Frank Kurlitis in A. Tucker, "South Shore Bar Pizza: Lynwood Cafe in Randolph, MA," *New England Today*, October 9, 2018, http://newengland.com.

215. Denker, *World on a Plate*, 62; New London Style Pizza, "FAQ," www.newlondon-stylepizza.com.

216. Karagianis, "Greek Pizza King," 3; A. Spinazzola, "Greek Pizza: It's a Many Splendored Thing," *Boston Globe*, January 2, 1980, 40.

217. J. K. López-Alt, "The Pizza Lab: How to Make New England Greek-Style Pizza at Home," The Pizza Lab, February 28, 2019, http://slice.seriouseats.com; L. Barrett, *Pizza: A Slice of American History* (Minneapolis: Voyageur Press, 2014); M. J. Patrone, "Cheap Eats: The Greek Variety of Pizza Is Not Like the Other Ones," *Boston Globe*, March 14, 1985, 77.

218. Doyle, "Greek Pizza."

219. New England Historical Society, "How the Greek Immigrants Came to New England," www.newenglandhistoricalsociety.com/greek-immigrants-came-new-england.

220. A.W. Lee, *A Shoemaker's Story: Being Chiefly about French Canadian Immigrants, Enterprising Photographers, Rascal Yankees, and Chinese Cobblers in a Nineteenth-Century Factory Town* (Princeton, NJ: Princeton University Press, 2008).

221. Feintuch and Watters, *Encyclopedia of New England*, 332.

222. M. White, "How Boston's Chinatown Dining Scene Came to Be: An Anthropologist on 150 Years of Asian Food," *Boston Globe*, June 10, 2015, www.bostonglobe.com.

223. Puleo, "From Italy to Boston's North End," 102; C. S. Lee, "Debunking the Myth of Ethnic Solidarity in Three Franco-American Texts," *French Review* 80, no. 6 (May 2007): 1293–1302, 1301.

224. Boston College, Department of History, "Global Boston: Chinese," http://globalboston.bc.edu.

225. University of Massachusetts Boston, Institute for Asian Studies, "Population of Asian American Subgroups in Massachusetts" (2019), www.umb.edu.

226. Randall, "Asian Americans Are Hard to Find in New Hampshire, One of the Whitest States in the Country," *AsAmNews*, February 10, 2016, http://multimedia.scmp.com.

227. Dirks, *Food in the Gilded Age*, 143–147.

228. M. Lo, "'Authentic' Chinese Food: Chinese American Cookbooks and the Regulation of Ethnic Identity" (paper, Association for Asian American Studies, March 2001), www.malindalo.com; M. S. Johnson, "Boston's New Immigrants and New Economy, 1965–2015," *Historical Journal of Massachusetts* 46, no. 2 (2018): 2–37, 20.

229. M. Singh, "Boston Chinese: A Fusion Food Cooked Up in a Melting Pot City," *Salt*, March 30, 2017, www.npr.org; J. Cui, "The Americanization of Chinese Food: How Chinese Restaurateurs Adapted 'Authentic' Cuisine That Sells," *Ruggles Media*, December 7, 2017, www.northeastern.edu.

230. I. L. Lim, "The Chow Mein Sandwich: American as Apple Pie," *Radcliffe Culinary Times* 3, no. 2 (1993): 4–5.

231. Lim, "Chow Mein Sandwich."

232. I. L. Lim and J. Eng-Wong, "Chow Mein Sandwiches: Chinese American Entrepreneurship in Rhode Island," in *Origins and Destinations: 41 Essays on Chinese America*, ed. M. A. Kwok and E. Y. Quan (Los Angeles: Chinese Historical Society of Southern California, UCLA Asian American Studies Center, 1978), 417–436, 428.

233. N. O'Malley, "Old-School Massachusetts Foods: Chow Mein Sandwich & Coffee Milk (I Ate It So You Don't Have To)," *Mass Live*, April 16, 2015, www.masslive.com; J. Stern and M. Stern, "Mill Town Meals: The Massachusetts City of Fall River Boasts Uncommon—and Uncommonly Good—Regional Foods," *Saveur*, February 23, 2013, www.saveur.com; A. M. Lopes, "Interview with Dorothy Lopes," November 11, 2010, 19, www.nps.gov.

234. White, "How Boston's Chinatown Dining Scene Came to Be"; D. Polan, "Joyce Chen Cooks and the Upscaling of Chinese Food in America in the 1960s" (2015), http://openvault.wgbh.org.

235. C. R. Venator-Santiago, "Are Puerto Ricans American Citizens?," *U.S. News & World Report*, March 3, 2017, www.usnews.com.

236. Nuestras Raíces, "Latinos in Rhode Island: Puerto Ricans | Los Puertorriqueños" (2019), www.nuestraraicesri.org.

237. M. Schlecter, *New England* (Westport, CT: Greenwood, 2004), 119.

238. A. Torres, *Latinos in New England* (Philadelphia: Temple University Press, 2006), 293; A. Forsyth, H. Lu, and P. McGirr, "Plazas, Streets, and Markets: What Puerto Ricans Bring to Urban Spaces in Northern Climates," *Landscape Journal* 20, no. 1 (2001): 62–76, 62.

239. Hunter College Center for Puerto Rican Studies, "Puerto Ricans in Connecticut, the United States, and Puerto Rico, 2014" (April 2016), http://centropr.hunter.cuny.edu; Boston Planning & Development Agency Research Division, "Puerto Ricans in Massachusetts, the United States, and Puerto Rico 2016" (November 2017), www.bostonplans.org.

240. US Census Bureau, http://factfinder.census.gov.

241. N. Morris, *Puerto Rico: Culture, Politics, and Identity* (Santa Barbara, CA: Praeger/Greenwood, 1995), 138; "History of Puerto Rican Food," *El Boricua*, http://elboricua.com.

242. C. M. Ortiz Cuadra, *Eating Puerto Rico: A History of Food, Culture, and Identity* (Chapel Hill: University of North Carolina Press, 2013), 200; D. Charles, "How Puerto Rico Lost Its Home-Grown Food, but Might Find It Again," *Salt*, May 13, 2017, http://npr.org.

243. O. Rivera, "Puerto Rican Food," in *The Oxford Companion to American Food and Drink*, ed. A. F. Smith (Oxford: Oxford University Press, 2007), 482; K. Albala, *Food Cultures of the World Encyclopedia*, vol. 2 (Santa Barbara, CA: ABC-CLIO, 2011), 273–281, 275.

244. Morris, *Puerto Rico*, 87–88.

245. D. W. Taylor and G. J. Anderson, "Key Plants Preserve Elements of Culture: A Study over Distance and Time of Fresh Crops in Puerto Rican Markets in Hartford, Connecticut, a 'Moveable Feast,'" *American Journal of Botany* 101, no. 4 (2014): 624–636.

246. Albala, *Food Cultures of the World Encyclopedia*, 273–281.

247. H. Lin, O. I. Bermudez, and K. L. Tucker, "Dietary Patterns of Hispanic Elders Are Associated with Acculturation and Obesity," *Journal of Nutrition* 133, no. 11 (2003): 3651–3657.

248. A. Lopez-Cepero et al., "Comparison of Dietary Quality among Puerto Ricans Living in Massachusetts and Puerto Rico," *Journal of Immigrant and Minority Health* 19, no. 2 (2017): 494–498; J. De Leon, "Household Composition, Acculturation and Diet among Low-Income Puerto Ricans in Hartford, Connecticut" (PhD diss., University of Florida, 2000).

249. S. E. Noel et al., "A Traditional Rice and Beans Pattern Is Associated with Metabolic Syndrome in Puerto Rican Older Adults," *Journal of Nutrition* 139, no. 7 (2009): 1360–1367; M. I. Van Rompay et al., "Acculturation and Sociocultural Influences on Dietary Intake and Health Status among Puerto Rican Adults in Massachusetts," *Journal of the Academy of Nutrition and Dietetics* 112, no. 1 (2012): 64–74.

250. "Race and Ethnicity in New England," *Statistical Atlas*, September 14, 2018, http://statisticalatlas.com.

251. L. Schuster, "Powering Greater Boston's Economy: Why the Latino Community Is Critical to Our Shared Future" (Boston Indicators, June 7, 2017), http://bostonindicators.org.

252. Feintuch and Watters, *Encyclopedia of New England*, 333.

253. Feintuch and Watters, *Encyclopedia of New England*, 332.

254. Feintuch and Watters, *Encyclopedia of New England*, 336.

255. Kenngott, *Record of a City*, 12.

256. H. S. Wright, *The New England Cook Book* (New York: Duffield, 1912), 50.

257. Feintuch and Watters, *Encyclopedia of New England*, 336–337.

258. Feintuch and Watters, *Encyclopedia of New England*, 337.

259. Feintuch and Watters, *Encyclopedia of New England*, 337–338.

260. Feintuch and Watters, *Encyclopedia of New England*, 337.

261. Feintuch and Watters, *Encyclopedia of New England*, 338.

262. E. M. Grieco et al., "The Size, Place of Birth, and Geographic Distribution of the Foreign-Born Population in the United States:1960 to 2010" (Population Division Working Paper 96, US Census Bureau, 2012), Figure 12, www.census.gov.

263. City of Boston, "Imagine All the People New Bostonians Series October 2007: Foreign Born" (2007), www.bostonredevelopmentauthority.org.

264. Calculated from figures in S. A. Camerota, *Immigrants in the United States: A Profile of America's Foreign-Born Population* (Center for Immigration Studies, 2012), www.cis.org, Table 2: Number and Growth of Immigrant Populations by State, 2010, 2000, 1990.

265. Angela A. Brittingham and G. P. de la Cruz, "Ancestry: 2000" (US Census Bureau, 2004), 6–8, www.census.gov.

CHAPTER 2: THE TRUTH ABOUT BAKED BEANS

1. J. T. Ehler, "Baked Beans," www.foodreference.com.

2. R. Williams, *A Key to the Language of America* (1643), 182, as quoted in C. Chartier, "Wampanoag Foodways" (Plymouth Archaeological Rediscovery Project, n.d.), www.plymoutharch.com.

3. Chartier, "Wampanoag Foodways."

4. Chartier, "Wampanoag Foodways."

5. Maine Folklife Center, "Bean Hole Beans," http://umaine.edu; Patten Lumbermen's Museum, www.lumbermensmuseum.org; D. A. Wilson, *Logging and Lumbering in Maine* (Charleston, SC: Arcadia, 2001), 14; C. Johnson, *New England and Its Neighbors* (London: Macmillan, 1912), 45.

6. M. K. Bennett, "The Food Economy of the New England Indians, 1605–75," *Journal of Political Economy* 63, no. 5 (1955): 369–397, 384.

7. W. Reed, *The History of Sugar and Sugar Yielding Plants* (London: Longmans, Green, 1866).

8. E. Oertel, "History of Beekeeping in the United States," in *Agricultural Handbook*, no. 535 (Washington, DC: US Department of Agriculture, 1980).

9. K. Wall, colonial foodways culinarian, Plimoth Plantation, personal communication.

10. E. Ogintz, "Debunking Thanksgiving Myths at Plimoth Plantation," *CNN Travel*, November 21, 2008, http://articles.cnn.com.

11. J. A. Goodwin, *The Pilgrim Republic: An Historical Review of the Colony of New Plymouth, with Sketches of the Rise of Other New England Settlements, the History of Congregationalism, and the Creeds of the Period* (Boston: Houghton Mifflin, 1888).

12. E. Wolf, *Europe and the People without History* (Berkeley: University of California Press, 1982).

13. J. R. Music, *The Pilgrims: A Story of Massachusetts* (London: Funk & Wagnalls, 1893).

14. W. A. Green, "Supply versus Demand in the Barbadian Sugar Revolution," *Journal of Interdisciplinary History* 18, no. 3 (1988): 403–418.

15. J. J. McCusker and R. R. Menard, *The Economy of British America, 1607–1789, with Supplemental Bibliography* (Chapel Hill: University of North Carolina Press, 1991), 151.

16. J. Hersh and H.-J. Voth, "Sweet Diversity: Colonial Goods and the Rise of European Living Standards after 1492" (Economics Working Papers 1163, 2011), 15, http://ssrn.com.

17. R. R. Menard, "Plantation Empire: How Sugar and Tobacco Planters Built Their Industries and Raised an Empire," *Agricultural History* 81, no. 3 (2007): 309–332.

18. R. B. Sheridan, *Sugar and Slavery: An Economic History of the British West Indies, 1623–1775* (Barbados: Canoe Press, 2000).

19. G. M. Ostrander, "The Colonial Molasses Trade," *Agricultural History* 30, no. 2 (1956): 77–84.

20. Ostrander, "Colonial Molasses Trade."

21. Ostrander, "Colonial Molasses Trade."

22. A. Barr, *Drink: A Social History of America* (New York: Carroll & Graf, 1999); Sheridan, *Sugar and Slavery*; "Estimated Population of US Colonies 1610 to 1780," http://web.viu.ca.

23. N. Shoemaker, "Whale Meat in American History," *Environmental History* 10, no. 2 (2005): 269–294.

24. K. Bragdon, *Native People of Southern New England, 1500–1650* (Norman: University of Oklahoma Press, 1999), 59.

25. E. A. Little and M. J. Schoeninger, "The Late Woodland Diet on Nantucket Island and the Problem of Maize in Coastal New England," *American Antiquity* 60, no. 2 (1995): 351–368.

26. Bragdon, *Native People of Southern New England*, 63.

27. Little and Schoeninger, "Late Woodland Diet."

28. Little and Schoeninger, "Late Woodland Diet."

29. Bragdon, *Native People of Southern New England*, 86.

30. L. Cecil, "Squanto and the Pilgrims," *Society* 27, no. 4 (1990): 40–44.

31. W. Bradford, E. Winslow, R. Cushman, and J. Robinson, *The Journal of the Pilgrims at Plymouth in New England 1620* (New York: John Wiley, 1848), spelling and punctuation modernized.

32. W. Wood, *New England's Prospect* (Boston: John Wilson and Sons, 1865), 75.

33. S. McMahon, "A Comfortable Subsistence: The Changing Composition of Diet in Rural New England, 1620–1840," *William and Mary Quarterly*, 3rd ser., 42, no. 1 (1985): 26–65, 45.

34. Virginia DeJohn Anderson, "King Philip's Herds: Indians, Colonists, and the Problem of Livestock in Early New England," *William and Mary Quarterly*, 3rd ser., 51, no. 4 (1994): 601–624.

35. D. Gookin, *Historical Collections of the Indians in New England*, as excerpted in *Collections of the Massachusetts Historical Society for the Year 1792*, vol. 1 (Boston: Munroe & Francis, 1806).

36. E. Johnson, *Johnson's Wonder-Working Providence 1628–1651*, ed. J. Franklin Jameson (New York: Charles Scribner's Sons, 1910), 162.

37. T. Lechford, *Plain Dealing, or Newes from New England*, as cited in Bennett, "Food Economy of the New England Indians," 384.

38. McMahon, "Comfortable Subsistence," 40.

39. K. Stavely and K. Fitzgerald, *America's Founding Food* (Chapel Hill: University of North Carolina Press, 2004), 51.

40. G. Marks, *The World of Jewish Holiday Cooking* (New York: Simon & Schuster, 1996), 122.

41. K. Albala, *Beans: A History* (New York: Berg, 2007), 163.

42. "The Gossip," *Boston Weekly Magazine* 1, no. 37 (July 9, 1803), 1.

43. J. M. Scott, *Blue Lights, or the Convention: A Poem in Four Cantos* (Chatham, NY: Charles M. Baldwin, 1817), 142.

44. "Sarse" meant "vegetables," or at least the sorts of vegetables that could be convinced to emerge from New England's rocky soil in the 1820s: carrots, beets, turnips, parsnips, and potatoes. "Innards" were, well, the insides of whatever animal happened to be moving slowly

nearby. J. Neal, *Randolph: A Novel* (Pennsylvania, 1823), 289. H. Colburn, *The London Literary Gazette of Belles Letters, Arts, Sciences, etc.*, no. 442 (July 19, 1825): 435.

45. S. Judah, *The Buccaneers: A Romance of Our Own Country, in Its Ancient Day* (Boston: Munroe & Francis, 1827), 11.

46. Anonymous, "Centennial Celebration at Farmington," *Supplement to the Hartford Courant*, 6, no. 23 (November 14, 1840), as published in *Supplements to the Hartford Courant for the years 1840 and 1841*, vol. 6 (Hartford: John L. Boswell, 1840), 177.

47. E. S. Thomas, *Reminiscences of the Last Sixty-Five Years: Commencing with the Battle of Lexington* (Hartford, CT: Case, Tiffany and Burnham, 1840), 272.

48. *New England Farmer* 4 (November 11, 1825): 127.

49. US Department of Agriculture Economic Research Service, "A History of Sugar Marketing" (Agricultural Economic Report no. 193, USDA, February 1971), 5.

50. US Department of Agriculture Economic Research Service, "History of Sugar Marketing," 5; W. E. H. Lecky, *A History of England in the Eighteenth Century*, vol. 4 (London: Longmans, Green, 1878, 1917), http://oll.libertyfund.org.

51. Lecky, *History of England*.

52. US Department of Agriculture Economic Research Service, "History of Sugar Marketing," 5.

53. J. W. Redway, *Commercial Geography* (New York: Charles Scribner's Sons, 1903), 185.

54. V. Mescher, "How Sweet It Is! A History of Sugar and Sugar Refining in the United States Including a Glossary of Sweeteners" (2005), www.raggedsoldier.com; US Department of Agriculture Economic Research Service, "History of Sugar Marketing," 7.

55. US Bureau of the Census, "Table 11. Population of the 100 Largest Urban Places: 1880" (June 15, 1998), www.census.gov.

56. M. Rawson, *Eden on the Charles: The Making of Boston* (Cambridge, MA: Harvard University Press, 2010), 234. For a fuller discussion of Bostonian identity and the Colonial Revival, see Rawson's chapter "Recreating the Wilderness," 233–276.

57. Rawson, *Eden on the Charles*.

58. *Aunt Mary's New England Cook Book* (1881), as quoted in Stavely and Fitzgerald, *America's Founding Food*, 251.

59. F. L. Branchard, "Unadvertised Industries: Molasses," *Printers' Ink* 52, no. 2 (1905): 46–47.

60. Branchard, "Unadvertised Industries."

61. "When War Alters the Market Former Favorite Comes Back," *Printer's Ink* 102, no. 8 (1918): 48–52.

62. US Census Bureau, "Statistical Abstract of the United States: 2012," Table 217, www.census.gov.

CHAPTER 3: THE LIMITS OF NEW ENGLAND FOOD

1. Calculated from US Census Bureau stats at www.gilderlehrman.org.

2. See chapter 6 discussion of pie.

3. See the discussion of gingerbread in chapter 6.

4. See the discussion of Polish Immigrants in chapter 1, "Who Is a Yankee?" and of Italian immigrants in chapter 5, "From River and Sea."

5. M. Rawson, *Eden on the Charles: The Making of Boston* (Cambridge, MA: Harvard University Press, 2010), 268.

6. Rawson, *Eden on the Charles*, 233–276.

7. As reported in "1940 Census of Population: Volume 1. Number of Inhabitants. Total Population for States, Counties, and Minor Civil Divisions; for Urban and Rural Areas; for Incorporated Places; for Metropolitan Districts; and for Census Tracts," www.census.gov.

For a discussion of what "urban" and "rural" meant, see "Urban—Description" (Integrated Public Use Microdata Series), http://usa.ipums.org.

8. F. M. Farmer, *The Boston Cooking-School Cook Book* (Boston: Little, Brown, 1896), 33.

9. Farmer, *Boston Cooking-School Cook Book*, 298.

10. L. Gvion, "What's Cooking in America? Cookbooks Narrate Ethnicity: 1850–1990," *Food, Culture & Society* 12, no. 1 (2009): 53–76, 64.

11. F. B. Goodrich, *The Tribute Book, a Record of the Munificence [&c.] of the American People during the War for the Union* (1865), 195–196.

12. "Brooklyn and Long Island Fair in Aid of the United States Sanitary Commission," in *History of the Brooklyn and Long Island Fair, February 22, 1864* (Brooklyn: "The Union," Steam Presses, 1864), 74.

13. Goodrich, *Tribute Book*, 195–196.

14. "Brooklyn and Long Island Fair," 75.

15. R. Roth, "The New England, or 'Olde Tyme,' Kitchen Exhibit at Nineteenth-Century Fairs," in *The Colonial Revival in America: A Winterthur Book*, ed A. Axelrod (New York: Norton, 1985), 179.

16. C. E. Beecher and H. B. Stowe, *The American Woman's Home: or, Principles of Domestic Science; Being a Guide to the Formation and Maintenance of Economical, Healthful, Beautiful, and Christian Homes* (New York: J.B. Ford, 1869), 124.

17. K. J. Carpenter, "The Discovery of Vitamin C," *Annals of Nutrition and Metabolism* 61 (2012): 259–264.

18. K. J. Carpenter, "Nutritional Studies in Victorian Prisons," *Journal of Nutrition* 136, no. 1 (2006): 1–8.

19. H. Levenstein, "The New England Kitchen and the Origins of Modern American Eating Habits," *American Quarterly* 32, no. 4 (1980): 369–386.

20. W. O. Atwater, "The Pecuniary Economy of Food," *Century Magazine* 35, no. 3 (1888): 437–447, 442.

21. Levenstein, "New England Kitchen," 372.

22. Levenstein, "New England Kitchen," 371–372.

23. L. Shapiro, *Perfection Salad: Women and Cooking at the Turn of the Century* (New York: Farrar, Straus, and Giroux, 1986), 154.

24. Shapiro, *Perfection Salad*, 38–39.

25. Shapiro, *Perfection Salad*, 148–149.

26. Shapiro, *Perfection Salad*, 149.

27. E. Atkinson, *The Science of Nutrition: Treatise upon the Science of Nutrition* (Boston: Damrell & Upham, 1896), 13.

28. Atkinson, *Science of Nutrition*, 26.

29. Atkinson, *Science of Nutrition*, 174.

30. M. H. Abel, *Practical Sanitary and Economic Cooking Adapted to Persons of Moderate and Small Means* (Rochester, NY: American Public Health Association/E. R. Andrews, 1889), 153.

31. Abel, *Practical Sanitary and Economic Cooking*, 149.

32. Levenstein, "New England Kitchen," 386.

33. E. S. Richards, "Scientific Cooking: Studies in the New England Kitchen," *Forum* 15 (1893): 355–361.

34. Levenstein, "New England Kitchen," 385.

35. Shapiro, *Perfection Salad*, 150.

36. Richards, "Scientific Cooking."

37. H. Levenstein, *Revolution at the Table: The Transformation of the American Diet* (New York: Oxford University Press, 1988), 24.

38. D. Gabaccia, *We Are What We Eat: Ethnic Food and the Making of Americans* (Cambridge, MA: Harvard University Press, 1998), 128.

39. Bertha Wood, quoted in Gabaccia, *We Are What We Eat*, 128.

40. Quoted in Gabaccia, *We Are What We Eat*, 122.

41. E. R. Richards, *The Rumford Kitchen Leaflets* (Boston: Rockwell and Churchill Press, 1899), 15.

42. Richards, *Rumford Kitchen Leaflets*, 130.

43. US Department of Labor and US Bureau of Labor Statistics, "100 Years of U.S. Consumer Spending: Data for the Nation, New York City, and Boston" (Report 991, May 2006–August 3, 2006), 3, www.bls.gov; "CPI Inflation Calculator," www.in2013dollars.com.

44. Gabaccia, *We Are What We Eat*, 127.

45. Levenstein, "New England Kitchen," 382.

46. Shapiro, *Perfection Salad*, 175.

47. Shapiro, *Perfection Salad*, 133; M. J. Lincoln, *Boston School Kitchen Text-Book: Lessons in Cooking for the Use of Classes in Public and Industrial Schools* (Boston: Roberts Brothers, 1890), xxvi–xxvii.

48. Gabaccia, *We Are What We Eat*, 129.

49. Shapiro, *Perfection Salad*, 137.

50. J. H. Kellogg, "Recent Dietetic Experiments," in *Proceedings of the Ninth Annual Conference, 1–6 July 1907, Lake Placid Conference on Home Economics* (Essex County, NY: Lake Placid Club, 1907), 118.

51. Brochure, New England Society of New York, www.nesnyc.org.

52. D. T. Knobel, *Paddy and the Republic: Ethnicity and Nationality in Antebellum America* (Middletown, CT: Wesleyan University Press, 1986), 70–71.

53. M. Hopkins, *The Central Principle: An Oration Delivered before the New England Society of New York, December 22, 1853* (New York: E. French, 1954); Knobel, *Paddy and the Republic*, 73.

54. M. Lynch-Brennan, *The Irish Bridget: Irish Immigrant Women in Domestic Service in America, 1840–1930* (Syracuse, NY: Syracuse University Press, 2009), 11.

55. A. Yentsch, "Applying Concepts from Historical Archaeology to New England's Nineteenth-Century Cookbooks," *Northeast Historical Archaeology* 42 (2013): 121–123.

56. H. Diner, *Erin's Daughters in America: Irish Immigrant Women in the Nineteenth Century* (Baltimore: Johns Hopkins University Press, 1983), 31.

57. Lynch-Brennan, *Irish Bridget*, 84.

58. O. Handlin, *Boston's Immigrants: A Study in Acculturation* (Cambridge, MA: Belknap, 1959), 60.

59. US Decennial Census 1860, www.census.gov.

60. T. Dublin, *Transforming Women's Work: New England Lives in the Industrial Revolution* (Ithaca, NY: Cornell University Press, 1995), 161.

61. A. Salcedo, T. Schoellman, and T. Tertilt, "Families as Roommates: Changes in U.S. Household Size from 1850 to 2000" (Working Paper 15477, National Bureau of Economic Research, 2009), www.nber.org.

62. Calculations from W. C. Hunt, *Occupations at the Twelfth Census*, vol. 1 (Washington, DC: US Census Office, 1900), 498–499.

63. A. T. Urban, "An Intimate World: Race, Migration, and Chinese and Irish Domestic Servants in the United States, 1850–1920" (PhD diss., University of Minnesota, 2009), http://conservancgy.umn.edu.

64. H. R. Diner, *Hungering for America: Italian, Irish, and Jewish Foodways in the Age of Migration* (Cambridge, MA: Harvard University Press, 2001), 98.

65. R. S. Cowan, *More Work for Mother: The Ironies of Household Technologies from the Hearth to the Microwave* (New York: Basic Books, 1985), 122.

66. US Census Office, *Twelfth Census of the United States Volume IV: Population* (Washington, DC: Government Printing Office, 1880), 864.

67. Statistics derived from Dublin, *Transforming Women's Work*, 243, and US Census Office, *Twelfth Census of the United States*, 606–620.

68. US Census Office, *Fourteenth Census of the United States Volume IV: Population* (Washington, DC: US Government Printing Office, 1920), 149.

69. See, for example, Diner, *Hungering for America*, 117.

70. "The Morals and Manners in the Kitchen," *Nation* 16 (January 2, 1873): 6.

71. Diner, *Hungering for America*, 194.

72. F. Kellor, *Out of Work: A Study of Employment Agencies, Their Treatment of the Unemployed, and Their Influence upon Home and Business* (New York: Putnam, 1904), 129–130.

73. Diner, *Erin's Daughters in America*, 90.

74. Diner, *Hungering for America*, 113–145.

75. A. Vilesis, *Kitchen Literacy* (Washington, DC: Island Press/Shearwater Books, 2008), 48.

76. Vilesis, *Kitchen Literacy*, 48–49.

77. Vilesis, *Kitchen Literacy*, 49.

78. Vilesis, *Kitchen Literacy*, 47.

79. S. Graham, *A Treatise on Bread Making* (Boston: Light & Stearns, 1837), 42–44.

80. Massachusetts Commission on the Cost of Living, "Report of the Commission on the Cost of Living" (Boston: Wright and Potter, 1910), 259; US Census Bureau, "Urban and Rural Population: 1900 to 1990" (1995), www.census.gov.

81. J. R. Wilkie, "The United States Population by Race and Urban-Rural Residence 1790–1860: Reference Tables," *Demography* 31, no. 1 (1976): 139–148.

82. US Census Bureau, "Urban and Rural Population."

83. Levenstein, *Revolution at the Table*, 25.

84. Cowan, *More Work for Mother*, 165.

85. C. S. Devas, *Political Economy* (London: Longmans, Green, 1901), 142.

86. Shapiro, *Perfection Salad*, 45.

87. Shapiro, *Perfection Salad*, 48–49.

88. Shapiro, *Perfection Salad*, 53.

89. Shapiro, *Perfection Salad*, 59.

90. Student of Fanny Farmer as quoted in Shapiro, *Perfection Salad*, 111; Gabaccia, *We Are What We Eat*, 127.

91. H. Levenstein, "The 'Servant Problem' and American Cookery," *Revue Française d'Etudes Américaines*, nos. 27–28 (1986): 127–137, 128–129.

92. See, for example, J. Corson Dodd, *Miss Corson's Practical American Cookery and Household Management* (New York: Mead & Company, 1885), 337.

93. A New England Mother, *Aunt Mary's New England Cook Book: A Collection of Useful and Economical Cooking Receipts* (Boston: Lockwood, Brooks & Company, 1881), 8.

94. Farmer, *Boston Cooking-School Cook Book*, 183.

95. J. Stern and M. Stern, "In Praise of the New England Boiled Dinner," *New England Today*, March 16, 2018, http://newengland.com.

96. See comments on "New England Boiled Dinner Recipe," *Yankee Magazine*, March 12, 2018, http://newengland.com; "How to Prepare a Real New England Boiled Dinner," *Boston Globe*, June 21, 1930, 16.

97. M. Kurlansky, ed., *The Food of a Younger Land: A Portrait of American Food from the Lost WPA Files* (New York: Penguin, 2009); H. Blits, *Canning Fruits and Vegetables by Hot Air and Steam and Berries by the Compounding of Syrups and the Crystallizing and Candying of Fruits Etc Etc with New Edition and Supplement* (Pittsburgh, 1890), 197.

98. See, for example, M. Standish, *Cooking Maine Style: Tried and True Recipes from Down East*, ed. Sandra Oliver (Camden, ME: Down East Books, 2018), 46.

99. "A Chapter on Eating," *Knickerbocker* 31 (March 1848): 221–225, 225.

100. B. Dojny, *The New England Cookbook: 350 Recipes from Town and Country, Land and Sea, Hearth and Home* (Boston: Harvard Common Press, 1999) 274.

101. Michigan State Prison, *Biennial Report of the Board of Control and Officers of the Michigan State Prison for the Two Years Ending June 30, 1908* (Lansing, MI: Wynkoop, Hallenbeck Crawford, 1908), 116.

102. "What to Do with Corned Beef?," *Cultivator & Country Gentleman* 56L (November 25, 1891): 965.

103. J. Whitehead, *Whitehead's Family Cook Book and Book of Breads and Cakes* (Chicago: Jessup Whitehead, 1891), 5.

104. M. Parloa, *The Appledore Cook Book: Containing Practical Receipts for Plain and Rich Cooking* (Boston: DeWolfe, Fiske, 1884), 35. See also the Chicago version in Whitehead, *Whitehead's Family Cook Book*, 5.

105. "An Old Connecticut Boiled Dinner," *Good Housekeeping*, October 27, 1888, ii.

106. C. A. Moore, "Vermont Foods," in Kurlansky, *Food of a Younger Land*.

107. W. De Lue, "Random Notes of an Epicurean Vagabond: Corned Beef and . . . ," *Boston Globe*, May 5, 1933, 20.

108. See the discussion in chapter 1, "Who Is a Yankee?"; Dona Brown, *Inventing New England: Regional Tourism in the Nineteenth Century* (Washington, DC: Smithsonian Institution Press, 1995), 135–167, "That Dream of Home," 163.

109. J. R. Garrison and J. H. Hall, "Stats in Market Regulations and Agricultural Change in Suffolk County, Massachusetts, 1675–1725," *Pioneer America* 13, no. 2 (1981): 29–42, 37–38.

110. H. Misson, *M. Misson's Memoirs and Observations in His Travels over England* (London: D. Browne, 1719), 314.

111. Misson, *M. Misson's Memoirs*, 314.

112. J. J. Henry, "An Accurate and Interesting Account of the Hardships and Sufferings of That Band of Heroes Who Traversed the Wilderness in the Campaign against Quebec in 1775," *Pennsylvania Archives*, vol. 15, ed. W. H. Egle, 59–192, 120–121, as cited in "New England Boiled Dinner," www.pbs.org.

113. W. J. Davey and R. P. MacKinnon, *Dictionary of Cape Breton English* (Toronto: University of Toronto Press, 2016), 18; P. Smith, "Jiggs Dinner Is Not Sunday Dinner," *Telegram*, November 18, 2016, www.thetelegram.com.

114. G. U. Harn, *Memorial Manual of the Congregational Church, Mansfield, Ohio* (Mansfield, OH: Congregational Church, 1882), 202.

115. M. J. Lincoln, *Boston Cook Book* (Boston: Roberts Brothers, 1891), 229.

116. Farmer, *Boston Cooking-School Cook Book*, 183.

117. Farmer, *Boston Cooking-School Cook Book*, 183.

118. W. Brown, "Conditions in the Town in the Decade from 1840 to 1850," in *History of the Town of Hampton Falls, New Hampshire from the Time of the First Settlement within Its Borders*, vol. 2 (Concord, NH: Rumford Press, 1918), 241.

119. L. M. Lyons and M. A. Lyons, eds., *Pause to Copy: Memoir of Louis M. Lyons—Journalist with Conscience and Integrity*, vol. 4 (Xlibris Corporation, 2008), 58.

120. Boston MA City Council, *Documents of the City of Boston* 4, nos. 102–130 (1904): 1084–1088, 1180–1181.

121. A. Sarah, "A Boiled Dinner," *New England Farmer*, reprinted in *Canada Farmer* 1 (March 1, 1864): 62.

122. W. H. White, "The Garden," *New England Farmer*, March 1867, 143.

123. J. C. Nylander, *Our Own Snug Fireside: Images of the New England Home, 1760–1860* (New Haven, CT: Yale University Press, 1994), 190.

124. Nylander, *Our Own Snug Fireside*, 190.

125. G. W. Henry, *Trials and Triumphs (for Half a Century) in the Life of G.W. Henry: As Experienced while Sojourning Forty Years in Egypt, One Year in the Slough of Despond, Three Years in Twilight, and Six Years in the Land of Beulah: Together with the Religious Experience of His Wife: To Which Are Added One Hundred Spiritual Songs, with Music* (New York, 1853), 51.

126. L. A. Kebler, "Sixty Years Ago: Recollections of New England Country Life," *New England Magazine* 6, no. 12 (1892): 48–59.

127. C. King, "Milwaukee," *New England Magazine* 6, no. 12 (1892): 110–133, 133.

128. I. B. Scott, "The Craze for Pewter," *House Furnishing Review* 17, no. 3 (March 1900): 146.

129. I. H. Harper, *The Life and Work of Susan B. Anthony: Including Public Addresses, Her Own Letters and Many from Her Contemporaries during Fifty Years*, vol. 1 (Indianapolis: Bowen-Merrill, 1898), 14.

130. O. Edson, *History of Chautauqua County, New York* (Boston: W.A. Fergusson, 1894), 306.

131. S. Robinson, *Me-won-i-toc: A Tale of Frontier Life and Indian Character; Exhibiting Traditions, Superstitions, and Character of a Race That Is Passing Away. A Romance of the Frontier* (New York: New York News Company, 1867), 53.

132. W. Bottrell, *Stories and Folk-Lore of West Cornwall* (Penzance, 1880), 51.

133. I. Whitney, "Old Time Cookery," in *Wide Awake*, vol. 16 (Boston: D. Lothrop & Company, 1883), 82–91, 84.

134. See, for example, Whitney, "Old Time Cookery," 82–91; E. S. Bowles and D. S. Towle, *Secrets of New England Cooking* (1947; repr., New York: Dover, 2000), 76; L. Whitney, "Madame Whitney's Housekeeping," in *Grandfather's Stories* (New York: American Book Company, 1889), 64–69.

135. See, for example, *Handbook of Domestic Cookery* (London: William Collins & Sons, 1882), 190; *English Cookery, Containing Practical Directions for Dressing Family Dinners, etc.* (London: Cradock & Co, 1843), 23; S. Tickeltooth (pseud. Charles Silby), *The Dinner Question: Or, How to Dine Well and Economically* (London: Routledge Warne and Routledge, 1860), 74; A. G. Payne, "How to Cook a Sucking Pig," *Cassell's Family Magazine*, 1880, 242–244; N. M. K. Lee, *The Cook's Own Book, and Housekeeper's Register: Being Receipts for Cooking of Every Kind of Meat, Fish, and Fowl; and Making Every Sort of Soup, Gravy, Pastry, Preserves, and Essences. With a Complete System of Confectionery; Tables for Marketing; a Book of Carving; and Miss Leslie's Seventy-five Receipts for Pastry, Cakes, and Sweetmeats* (Boston: Munroe and Francis, 1842), 137; L. C. Draper and W. A. Croffut, *A Helping Hand for Town and Country: An American Home Book of Practical and Scientific Information . . .* (Cincinnati: Moore, Wilstach & Moore, 1870), 674.

136. C. J. Murphy, *Lecture Delivered by Charles J. Murphy . . . : Before the National Agricultural Society of France, at the International Congress of Millers, Held at Paris in August, 1889, on American Indian Corn (Maize) as a Cheap, Wholesome, and Nutritious Human Food . . .* (Edinburgh: R. Grant & Son, Edinburgh, 1890), 58.

137. F. J. Pratt, "Our Grandmother's Dishes," *Spirit of '76*, no. 24 (August 1896): 317.

138. W. Mason, "The Boiled Dinner," *Farm Journal* 39 (October 1915): 542(6).

139. See, for example, *Aunt Mary's New England Cook Book*, 8. See also "A Genuine New England Boiled Dinner," *American Kitchen Magazine*, October 1902, 193–196.

140. Compare A. Sarah, "A Boiled Dinner," *New England Farmer*, as reprinted in *Canada Farmer* 1 (March 1, 1864): 62, vs. the version in Bowles and Towle, *Secrets of New England Cooking*, 113.

141. Bowles and Towle, *Secrets of New England Cooking*, 107.

142. "How to Prepare a Real New England Boiled Dinner," 16.

143. K. Stavely and K. Fitzgerald, *America's Founding Food* (Chapel Hill: University of North Carolina Press, 2004), 181.

144. "Classic Boiled Dinner in Decline as More Maine Youth Discover Flavor," *New Maine News*, December 17, 2017, http://newmainenews.com.

CHAPTER 4: CORN AND PREJUDICE

1. E. Blasco, "5 Questions with a Colonial Culinarian" (National Museum of American History, November 19, 2012), http://americanhistory.si.edu.

2. W. Bradford, *Bradford's History of Plymouth Plantation, 1606–1646*, ed. William T. Davis (New York: Charles Scribner's Sons, 1908); Blasco, "5 Questions."

3. J. P. Hart and W. A. Lovis, "Reevaluating What We Know about the Histories of Maize in Northeastern North America: A Review of Current Evidence," *Journal of Archaeological Research* 21, no. 2 (June 2013): 175–216, 203.

4. Hart and Lovis, "Reevaluating What We Know," 183.

5. Hart and Lovis, "Reevaluating What We Know," 197.

6. Hart and Lovis, "Reevaluating What We Know," 179.

7. K. Stavely and K. Fitzgerald, *America's Founding Food* (Chapel Hill: University of North Carolina Press, 2004), 39.

8. Stavely and Fitzgerald, *America's Founding Food*, 41.

9. Stavely and Fitzgerald, *America's Founding Food*.

10. E. Johnson, *Johnson's Wonder-Working Providence 1628–1651*, ed. J. Franklin Jameson (New York: Charles Scribner's Sons, 1910), 115.

11. Stavely and Fitzgerald, *America's Founding Food*.

12. D. P. Kelsey, "Early New England Farm Crops: Small Grains—Barley, Rye, Oats, Buckwheat and Wheat" (Old Sturbridge Village Research Paper, 1980), www.osv.org.

13. E. J. Perkins, *The Economy of Colonial America* (New York: Columbia University Press, 1988), 62.

14. K. J. Friedmann, "Victualling Colonial Boston," *Agricultural History* 47, no. 3 (1973): 189–205, 190.

15. Friedmann, "Victualling Colonial Boston."

16. D. C. Hsiung, "Food, Fuel, and the New England Environment in the War for Independence, 1775–1776," *New England Quarterly* 80, no. 4 (December 2007): 614–654, 622.

17. E. Risch, *Supplying Washington's Army* (Washington, DC: US Army Center of Military History, 1981), 190.

18. E. H. Jenkins, *A History of Connecticut agriculture* (New Haven: Connecticut Agricultural Experiment Station, 1926), 327.

19. Friedmann, "Victualling Colonial Boston," 195.

20. B. C. Smith, "Food Rioters and the American Revolution," *William and Mary Quarterly* 51, no. 1 (1994): 3–38.

21. A. Yentsch, "Applying Concepts from Historical Archaeology to New England's Nineteenth-Century Cookbooks," *Northeast Historical Archaeology* 42 (2013): 121–123.

22. T. Frisch, "A Short History of Wehat," *Valley Table* (2008), www.valleytable.com.

23. "Samuel Hopkins Granted First Patent in the United States," *Philadelphia Inquirer*, July 31, 2013, www.philly.com.

24. J. Townsend, "Grocer Advertisement from Boston 1732" (Savoring the Past, September 27, 2012), http://savoringthepast.net.

25. "Quick Bread Primer," King Arthur Flour, www.kingarthurflour.com.

26. L. Civitello, *Baking Powder Wars: The Cutthroat Food Fight That Revolutionized Cooking* (Champaign: University of Illinois Press, 2017); A. L. Meyer and J. A. Wilson, *Baking Across America* (Austin: University of Texas Press, 1998), 8–9; S. Schmidt, "Emptins" (Manuscript Cookbooks Survey, May 2017), www.manuscriptcookbookssurvey.org.

27. A. Simmons, *American Cookery* (Hartford, CT: Hudson & Goodwin, 1796), 64.

28. S. Lohman, "The History Dish: Pearlash, The First Chemical Leavening," *Four Pounds Flour*, May 23, 2012, www.fourpoundsflour.com.

29. Friedmann, "Victualling Colonial Boston"; Jenkins, *History of Connecticut Agriculture*, 340.

30. J. R. Garrison and J. H. Hall, "Market Regulations and Agricultural Change in Suffolk County, Massachusetts, 1675–1725," *Pioneer America*, Vol. 13, no. 2 (September 1981), 29–42, 39.

31. Garrison and Hall, "Market Regulations and Agricultural Change," 39, 36.

32. Garrison and Hall, "Market Regulations and Agricultural Change," 39.

33. R. Briggs, "The Hominy Foodway of the Historic Native Eastern Woodlands," *Native South* 8 (2015): 112–146.

34. P. McGovern, "Out of the Ashes: A Brief Local History of Potash and Pearlash," *Vermont's Local Banquet*, June 1, 2012, http://localbanquet.com.

35. R. V. Briggs, "Hominy Foodway of the Native Eastern Woodlands" (paper, 71st Annual SEAC Conference, November 12–15, 2014, Greenville, SC), http://allthingshominy. com; P. Adams, "Transforming Corn," *Cooks Illustrated*, August 14, 2016, www.cooksillus-trated.com.

36. Briggs, "Hominy Foodway of the Historic Native Eastern Woodlands," 119; K. Clay, E. Schmick, and W. Troesken, "The Rise and Fall of Pellagra in the American South" (NBER Working Paper 23730, August 2017, May 2018), www.nber.org; H. M. Marks, "Epidemiologists Explain Pellagra: Gender, Race, and Political Economy in the Work of Edgar Sydenstricker," *Journal of the History of Medicine and Allied Sciences* 58, no. 1 (2003): 34–55.

37. McGovern, "Out of the Ashes."

38. Civitello, *Baking Powder Wars*.

39. Andrew F. Smith, ed., *The Oxford Encyclopedia of Food and Drink in America*, vol. 1 (New York: Oxford University Press, 2013), 358.

40. Stavely and Fitzgerald, *America's Founding Food*, 242; "Quick Bread Primer."

41. American Chemical Society, "Development of Baking Powder," June 12, 2006, www. acs.org; What's Cooking America, "Baking Powder" (2016), http://whatscookingmaerica.net.

42. "Saleratus in Bread," *Scientific American* 10, no. 21 (February 3, 1855): 165.

43. B. Panko, "The Great Uprising: How a Powder Revolutionized Baking," *Smithsonian*, June 20, 2017, www.smithsonianmag.com.

44. *Congressional Record—House*, April 17, 1911, 350.

45. J. H. Mitchell, *The Paradise of All These Parts: A Natural History of Boston* (Boston: Beacon, 2009), 150.

46. "Wheat: Background" (USDA Economic Research Service Briefing Room Wheat Background Page, July 2010), www.ers.usda.gov.

47. L. Walsh, "Consumer Behavior, Diet, and the Standard of Living in Late Colonial and Early Antebellum America, 1770–1840," in *American Economic Growth and Standards of*

Living before the Civil War, ed. R. E. Gallman and J. J. Wallis (Chicago: University of Chicago Press, 1992), 217–264, 239.

48. P. Bidwell, "The Agricultural Revolution in New England," *American Historical Review* 26, no. 4 (1921): 683–702, 689.

49. S. McMahon, "A Comfortable Subsistence: The Changing Composition of Diet in Rural New England, 1620–1840," *William and Mary Quarterly*, 3rd ser., 42, no. 1 (1985): 26–65, 52.

50. McMahon, "Comfortable Subsistence," 52.

51. See, for example, Roger N. Parks, "Comments on Change in Agriculture 1790–1840," *Agricultural History* 46, no. 1 (January 1972): 173–180, 174–175.

52. W. Rothenberg, "The Productivity Consequences of Market Integration: Agriculture in Massachusetts, 1771–1801," in Gallman and Wallis, *American Economic Growth*, 311–344, 335.

53. J. B. Harris, *High on the Hog: A Culinary Journey from Africa to America* (New York: Bloomsbury, 2011), 96–97.

54. J. Fisher, "Feeding the Million: Markets, Metabolism, and the Transformation of the Food System in New York City 1800–1860" (PhD diss., Pennsylvania State University Graduate School, College of Earth and Mineral Sciences, 2012), 157–158; J. Bell, *On Regimen and Longevity: Comprising Materia Alimentaria, National Dietetic Usages, and the Influence of Civilization on Health and the Duration of Life* (Philadelphia: Haswell & Johnson, 1842), 92.

55. A. Nicholson, *Annals of the Famine in Ireland, in 1847, 1848, and 1849* (New York: E. French, 1851), 30–31.

56. N. Kissane, *The Irish Famine: A Documentary History* (Dublin: National Library of Ireland, 1995), 38.

57. Nicholson, *Annals of the Famine*, 161.

58. Massachusetts Commissioner for the Agricultural Survey of the State, *Third Report* (Boston, 1840), 51–52.

59. W. W. Hall, *Hall's Journal of Health for 1854*, vol. 1, no. 12 (New York: December 1854), 280–281.

60. "Corn Bread," *American Farmers' Magazine* 11 (1858): 187. See also M. Essig, "The Myth of Cornbread Fingerprints" (Southern Foodways Alliance Fall Symposium 2016), www.southernfoodways.org.

61. *The Farmer's Cabinet* (Amherst, NH, February 13, 1851), as quoted in Essig, "Myth of Cornbread Fingerprints."

62. Jenkins, *History of Connecticut Agriculture*, 399.

63. Jenkins, *History of Connecticut Agriculture*, 414–415, 419.

64. "Count Rumford and the New England Kitchen," *New England Kitchen* 1, no. 1 (April 1894): 7–11, 10; E. M. Howe, "Women's Council Table: The New England Kitchen," in *The Chautauquan* (Chautauqua Press, 1892), 223–224, 223.

65. E. R. Richards, *The Rumford Kitchen Leaflets* (Boston: Rockwell and Churchill Press, 1899).

66. M. Frankel, "How Does the Average American Spend Their Paycheck? See How You Compare," *USA Today*, May 8, 2018, www.usatoday.com.

67. H. Levenstein, "The New England Kitchen and the Origins of Modern American Eating Habits," *American Quarterly* 32, no. 4 (1980): 369–386, 384.

68. R. Horowitz, *Putting Meat on the American Table: Taste, Technology, Transformation* (Baltimore: Johns Hopkins University Press, 2006), 12.

69. Levenstein, "New England Kitchen," 371–372.

70. M. E. Green, "The New Era in Food Supplies," *New England Kitchen* 2, no. 5 (1895): 242.

71. A. Aubrey, "Reviving an Heirloom Corn That Packs More Flavor and Nutrition," *Salt*, August 22, 2013, www.npr.org; D. Barber, *The Third Plate: Field Notes on the Future of Food* (New York: Penguin, 2015), 1.

72. S. Graham, *A Treatise on Bread, and Bread-Making* (Boston: Light & Stearns, 1837), 36–37.

73. M. S. Kideckel, "Anti-intellectualism and Natural Food: The Shared Language of Industry and Activists in America since 1830," *Gastronomica*, Spring 2018, 44–54, 46–47.

74. S. J. B. Hale, *The Good Housekeeper* (Boston: Weeks, Jordan and Company, 1839), 12–13, 21.

75. Friedmann, "Victualling Colonial Boston," 191.

76. S. L. Oliver, *Saltwater Foodways: New Englanders and Their Food at Sea and Ashore, in the Nineteenth Century* (Mystic, CT: Mystic Seaport Museum, 1995), 78; Stavely and Fitzgerald, *America's Founding Food*, 28.

77. T. R. Hazard and R. Hazard, *The Johnny-Cake Papers of "Shepard Tom": Together with Reminiscences of Narragansett Schools of Former Days* (Boston: "Printed for the Subscribers," 1915), 28. See also Stavely and Fitzgerald, *America's Founding Food*, 29.

78. *New England Magazine: An Illustrated Monthly Review of New England Life and Achievement* 27, no. 2 (October 1903): 19. See also *Public Opinion: A Comprehensive Summary of the Press throughout the World on All Important Current Topics*, vol. 33 (Public Opinion Company, September 11, 1902), 351.

79. J. C. O'Connell, *Dining Out in Boston* (Hanover, NJ: University Press of New England, 2016), 143.

80. T. B. Doyle, "Durgin-Park Is Closing Next Week, after Nearly 200 Years," *Boston Eater*, January 4, 2019, http://boston.eater.com.

81. Menu, Jacob Wirth restaurant, www.jacobwirth.com; M. Hurwitz, "Jacob Wirth Restaurant in Boston's Theater District Closed after Fire in Building," *Boston Restaurant Talk*, June 9, 2018, http://bostonrestaurants.blogspot.com.

82. *The Ruth D. Gates Digital Scrapbook*, 25, http://slis.simmons.edu.

83. H. S. Wright, *The New England Cook Book* (New York: Duffield, 1912), 181.

84. Royal Baking Powder Company, *My Favorite Receipt* (New York: Royal Baking Powder Company, 1886), 48–49.

85. "A Chapter on Eating," *Knickerbocker* 31 (March 1848): 225.

86. A. Miller, "Cornbread," in *Soul Food: The Surprising Story of an American Cuisine, One Plate at a Time* (Chapel Hill: University of North Carolina Press Books, 2013), 186–207.

87. K. Purvis, "Why Does Sugar in Cornbread Divide Races in the South?," *Charlotte Observer*, March 29, 2016, www.charlotteobserver.com.

88. Miller, "Cornbread," 202.

89. Purvis, "Why Does Sugar in Cornbread Divide Races in the South?"

90. M. Russell, *A Domestic Cook Book: Containing a Careful Selection of Useful Receipts for the Kitchen* (Pawpaw, MI: The Author, 1866), 26.

91. D. Beard, "Good Things to Eat: Exercise Your Appetite on These Home, Camp, and Trail Dishes," *Boy's Life*, March 1925, 14.

92. S. Rutledge, *The Carolina Housewife* (Charlotte, SC: W.R. Babcock, 1847), 21, 23.

93. *The Picayune Creole Cookbook*, 2nd ed. (New Orleans: Times-Picayune, 1901), 402–403.

94. US Department of Agriculture, Work Projects Administration, *Family Food Consumption and Dietary Levels: Five Regions* (1941), 35, 45–46, www.ars.usda.gov.

95. Essig, "Myth of Cornbread Fingerprints."

96. C. V. Woodward, *Origins of the New South, 1877–1913: A History of the South* (Baton Rouge: Louisiana State University Press, 1981), 318–319; M. Essig, "The Mistaken Case of the Killer Cornbread," Atlas Obscura, January 24, 2017, www.atlasobscura.com.

97. Essig, "Mistaken Case of the Killer Cornbread"; US Department of Commerce, "Statistical Abstract of the United States: 1916" (Washington, DC: Government Printing Office, 1917), 527.

98. C. R. Wilson, "Biscuits," in *The Encyclopedia of Southern Culture Volume 7: Foodways*, ed. John T. Edge (Chapel Hill: University of North Carolina Press, 2009), 122–125.

99. A. Torres, *Latinos in New England* (Philadelphia: Temple University Press, 2006).

RECIPES

1. Plimoth Plantation, "Recipes: Taste the Past" (2019), http://plimoth.org.

2. S. J. B. Hale, *The Good Housekeeper* (Boston: Weeks, Jordan and Company, 1839), 18.

3. A. Simmons, *American Cookery* (Hartford, CT: Hudson & Goodwin, 1796), 33; M. E. Rundell, *A New System of Domestic Cookery* (Philadelphia: Benjamin C. Buzby, 1807), 189.

4. M. F. Wack, "Recipe-Collecting, Embodied Imagination, and Transatlantic Connections in an Irish Emigrant's Cooking," *Canadian Journal of Irish Studies* 41 (2018): 100–123.

5. D. Pare-Watson, "French Canadian Yellow Split Pea Soup—A Historical Perspective," *Urbnspice*, 2018, http://urbnspice.com; D. Leveille, "Canadian Chef Traces Habitant Pea Soup 400 Years Back to French Explorer Samuel de Champlain," *PRI Arts, Culture & Media*, October 10, 2012, http://pri.org.

6. Nuala, "Auntie Laura's Gufong (A Cape Verdean Favorite!)," *The Cool Cook*, September 21, 2010, http://thecoolcook.wordpress.com.

7. *Specialita Culinarie Italiane: 137 Tested Recipes of Famous Italian Foods* (Boston: North Bennet Street Industrial School, 1936), 34.

8. R. Strybel, "Who Likes Pierogi? Recipes, Fillings, and Fun Facts," *Polish American Journal*, http://polamjournal.com; "Pierogi," http://polishplate.com.

9. J. K. López-Alt, "New England Greek Style Pizza," *The Pizza Lab*, August 19, 2011, http://seriouseats.com; T. Doyle, "Greek Pizza Is the Best Mediocre Food You've Never Eaten," *Vice*, June 7, 2017, http://vice.com.

10. C. M. Steele, "Tillie's Kale Soup," *Provincetown Portuguese Cookbook*, http://iamprovincetown.com.

11. L. M. F. Child, *The American Frugal Housewife*, 12th ed. (Boston: Carter and Hendee, 1832), 51.

12. P. Mayotte, "French Canadian Baked Beans," in *History of Franco Americans in Lowell, Massachusetts*, http://francolowellma.wordpress.com.

13. M. Lyons, "Beans Offer Variety, Good Nutrition," *Lowell Sun*, March 28, 1979.

14. Pot Shop of Boston, "Baked Beans," http://potshopofboston.com.

15. *Massachusetts Woman's Christian Temperance Union Cuisine* (Boston: E.B. Stillings & Company, 1878), 49.

16. E. Atkinson et al., *The Science of Nutrition* (Boston: Damrell & Upham, 1895), 51.

17. M. H. Abel, *Practical Sanitary and Economic Cooking Adapted to Persons of Moderate and Small Means* (Rochester, NY: American Public Health Association, 1890), 92–93.

18. "Miscellaneous Cooking," *Godey's Lady's Book and Magazine* 90, no. 539 (1875): 471.

19. M. J. Lincoln, *Boston School Kitchen Text-Book* (Boston: Roberts Brothers, 1890), 199.

20. C. E. Beecher, *Miss Beecher's Domestic Receipt Book*, 3rd ed. (New York: Harper & Bros., 1846), 86–87.

21. M. Parloa, *Miss Parloa's New Cook Book and Marketing Guide* (Boston: Estes and Lauriat, 1880), 311.

22. "Chafing Dishes," *New England Kitchen Magazine*, April 1894, 37.

23. Parloa, *Miss Parloa's New Cook Book*, 272, 281.

24. A. Sarah, "A Boiled Dinner," *New England Farmer*, as reprinted in *Canada Farmer* 1 (March 1, 1864): 62.

25. Woodman's, "New England Boiled Dinner," http://woodmans.com, September 17, 2014.

26. "Pork Shoulder Boiled Dinner (Cozido)," *Portuguese American Mom*, February 24, 2016, http://theportugueseamericanmom.com.

27. Child, *American Frugal Housewife*, 65.

28. Lincoln, *Boston School Kitchen Text-Book*, 144.

29. J. Stern and M. Stern, *The Durgin-Park Cookbook: Classic Yankee Cooking in the Shadow of Faneuil Hall* (Nashville: Rutledge Hill Press, 2002), 29.

30. A. Fisher, *What Mrs. Fisher Knows about Old Southern Cooking, Soups, Pickles, Preserves Etc.* (San Francisco: Women's Cooperative Printing Office, 1881), 11.

31. "Cheese and Loroco Pupusas," http://extenstion.umass.edu; L. Rivera, "Latinos in Greater Boston: Migration, New Communities, and the Challenge of Displacement," *Changing Faces of Greater Boston*, May 2019, 49, http://bostonindicators.org.

32. F. M. Farmer, *The Boston Cooking-School Cook Book* (Boston: Little, Brown, 1896), 298–299.

33. N. Meads, "Portuguese Clams and Rice," *Provincetown Portuguese Cookbook* (1999), www.iamprovincetown.com.

34. "Winning Stuffed Quahogs," *Providence Journal*, February 3, 1999, as attributed to "Barbara from Bristol," http://quahog.org.

35. Hale, *Good Housekeeper*, 70.

36. *625 Choice Recipes from the Ladies of the Second Cong. Church, of Holyoke, Mass.* (Holyoke, MA: Transcript, 1886), http://holyokemass.com.

37. M. Silsby, "One Crust Blueberry Pie," *Peninsula Gazette* 4, no. 27 (July 2, 1957): 4.

38. Maine Historical Society, "Washington Pie Recipe ca. 1875," http://mainememory.net.

39. Women's Educational and Industrial Union, *The Kirmess Cook-Book* (Boston: Alfred Mudge & Son, 1887), 47.

40. M. J. Lincoln, *Mrs. Lincoln's Boston Cook Book* (Boston: Roberts Brothers, 1884), 104.

41. D. G. Parenteau, "Les Repas de Mon Enfance: Growing Up Franco-American," June 9, 2019, http://facebook.com.

42. *Tried Recipes Collected by the Ladies of the Mission Circle of the First Church* (Woodbury, CT: First Church, 1912), 65; Farmer, *Boston Cooking-School Cook Book*, 476.

43. F. M. Farmer, *The Boston Cooking-School Cook Book*, 3rd ed. (Boston: Little, Brown, 1901), 559.

44. Maine Historical Society, "Six Household Suggestions and Recipe for Champaign Cider, ca. 1890," http://mainememory.net.

45. *Fish, Flesh, and Fowl: A Book of Recipes for Cooking Compiled by Ladies of State Street Parish* (Portland: J.S. Staples, 1877), 28, 34.

46. S. T. Rorer, *My Best 250 Recipes* (Philadelphia: Arnold and Company, 1907), 115.

47. Vermont Creamery, "Shaved Asparagus Salad with Goat Cheese" (2019), http://vermontcreamery.com.

48. Must Be the Milk, "Kimchi Grilled Cheese," http://mustbethemilk.com.

49. Simmons, *American Cookery*.

50. E. A. Howland, *The New England Economical Housekeeper, and Family Receipt Book* (Worcester, MA: S. A. Howland, 1845), 43.

51. L. Beaulieu, *The Providence and Rhode Island Cookbook* (Guilford, CT: Insider's Guide/Globe Pequot Press, 2006), 176.

1. T. McLeish, "Limited Availability of Local Seafood in New England," *Eco RI News*, July 6, 2018, www.ecori.org.

2. S. Oliver, "The Truth about Spices, Lobsters, and Flaming Ladies," *Debunk House*, May 22, 2018, http://archive.li; see also Sandra Oliver, "What You Hear about Lobsters, and What's True," *Working Waterfront*, July 20, 2015, www.islandinstitute.org.

3. Edmund Delaney (1983), quoted in D. Foster, "Two Cautionary Notes re Conservation," personal communication.

4. Townsend, *Birds of Essex County, MA* (1905), quoted in Foster, "Two Cautionary Notes."

5. F. Day, *British and Irish Salmonidæ* (London: Williams and Norgate, 1887), 113–114.

6. R. C. Hoffman, "A Brief History of Aquatic Resource Use in Medieval Europe," *Helgoland Marine Research* 59 (2005): 22–30.

7. Hoffman, "Brief History of Aquatic Resource Use."

8. S. Oliver, "What You Hear about Lobsters, and What's True," July 20, 2015, www.islandinstitute.org.

9. As quoted in C. C. Carlson, "The [In]Significance of Atlantic Salmon," *History through a Pinhole* 8, nos. 3/4 (1996), www.nps.gov.

10. Gulf of Maine Research Institute, "Lobstering History," February 24, 2012, www.gma.org.

11. F. Higginson, *New England's Plantation; or, A Short and True Description of the Commodities and Discommodities of That Country* (London: Printed by T.C. and R.C. for Michael Sparke, 1680), 9; S. L. Oliver, *Saltwater Foodways: New Englanders and Their Food at Sea and Ashore, in the Nineteenth Century* (Mystic, CT: Mystic Seaport Museum, 1995), 380–381.

12. Gulf of Maine Research Institute, "Lobstering History."

13. K. Korneski, "Development and Degradation: The Emergence and Collapse of the Lobster Fishery on Newfoundland's West Coast, 1856–1924," *Acadiensis* 41, no. 1 (2012): 21–48, 33.

14. R. A. Carey, *Against the Tide: The Fate of the New England Fisherman* (New York: Houghton Mifflin Harcourt, 2000), 112.

15. Carey, *Against the Tide*, 112.

16. G. Turim, "From Humble to Haute: Lobster's Climb to the Top," May 31, 2013, www.history.com.

17. P. Freedman and J. Warlick, "High-End Dining in the Nineteenth-Century United States," *Gastronomica* 11, no. 1 (Spring 2011): 44–52.

18. S. J. B. Hale, *Mrs. Hale's New Cook Book* (Philadelphia: T. B. Peterson and Brothers, 1857).

19. Carey, *Against the Tide*, 112.

20. Carey, *Against the Tide*, 112.

21. Korneski, "Development and Degradation," 31.

22. G. S. Pearson, "The Democratization of Food: Tin Cans and the Growth of the American Food Processing Industry, 1810–1940" (PhD diss., Lehigh University, 2016), 375–376, http://preserve.lehigh.edu; P. Smith, "Black Lobster and the Birth of Canning," *Smithsonian*, March 8, 2012, www.smithsonianmag.com.

23. Carey, *Against the Tide*, 168.

24. Carey, *Against the Tide*, 169.

25. N. Jenkins, "Fare of the Country: In Maine, Lobster on a Roll," *New York Times*, July 14, 1985, as cited in Food History Timeline, www.foodtimeline.org.

26. J. Whitaker, "Find of the Day: Moody's Diner Cookbook," September 7, 2015, http://restaurant-ingthroughhistory.com.

27. Carey, *Against the Tide*, 170.

28. J. Kehoe, "Uncle Lobster: Maine Gained a Culinary Icon, They Say, the Day John D. Rockefeller Was Served a Stew Meant for the Help," August 29, 2007, www.saveur.com.

29. Kehoe, "Uncle Lobster."

30. Gulf of Maine Research Institute, "Lobstering History."

31. Gulf of Maine Research Institute, "Lobstering History."

32. P. Overton, "Size and Value of Maine Lobster Haul Fell Sharply in 2017. Will the Industry Survive One Bad Year? Yes. Will It Hurt Individual Lobstermen? Yes," *Augusta Press Herald*, March 2, 2018, www.pressherald.com.

33. Lobster Institute Working Group, "A New Vision for the Lobster Institute," June 12, 2018, http://umain.edu.

34. R. Rathbun, "The Lobster Fishery," in *The Fisheries and Fishery Industries of the United States: Section V. History and Methods of the Fisheries*, ed. George Brown Goode (Washington, DC: Government Printing Office, 1887), 704.

35. G. H. Lewis, "Shell Games in Vacationland: *Homarus americanus* and the State of Maine," in *Usable Pasts*, ed. T. Tuleja (Logan: Utah State University Press, 1997), 249–273, 252.

36. Lewis, "Shell Games in Vacationland," 252.

37. K. Mulhere, "This Map Shows the Average Income in Every State—and What It's Really Worth," *Time*, March 15, 2018, http://time.com; P. Davidson, "Median U.S. Household Income Rises 1.8 Percent to Record $61,400 in 2017," *USA Today*, September 12, 2018, www.usatoday.com.

38. Lewis, "Shell Games in Vacationland."

39. Lewis, "Shell Games in Vacationland."

40. P. McGuire, "See a Lot of Tourists in Maine Last Year? Total Visits Rose to 36.7 Million. That's a Five-Year High, but the Rate of Growth Slowed to 2.5% and Tourists' Spending Barely Changed Despite Their Increased Presence," *Augusta Press Herald*, April 4, 2018, www.pressherald.com.

41. Lewis, "Shell Games in Vacationland."

42. Gulf of Maine Research Institute, "Lobstering History."

43. Gulf of Maine Research Institute, "Are We Farming Lobster in the Gulf of Maine?," www.gmri.org.

44. Gulf of Maine Research Institute, "Are We Farming Lobster in the Gulf of Maine?"

45. New England Fishery Management Council, "Council Reaffirms Current Approach for River Herring/Shad; Launches Work on 2019–2021 Atlantic Herring Specifications" (June 4, 2018), http://nefmc.org; "Bait Shortage Puts Squeeze on Maine's Lobstering Fleet" (July 2, 2018), www.mainebiz.com; N. McCrea, "Maine Lobster Industry Braces for Looming Bait Shortage," *Bangor Daily News*, June 30, 2018, http://bangordailynews.com.

46. Gulf of Maine Research Institute, "Are We Farming Lobster in the Gulf of Maine?"

47. "Bait Shortage."

48. E. Greenhalgh, "Climate & Lobsters," October 6, 2016, www.climate.gov.

49. D. Abel, "Losing Hope for Lobster South of Cape Cod," *Boston Globe*, December 2, 2017, www.bostonglobe.com.

50. Greenhalgh, "Climate & Lobsters"; Overton, "Size and Value of Maine Lobster."

51. S. Schmidt, "The Feast-or-Famine Life of Lobstering in Maine," *Living on Earth*, July 8, 2018, www.pri.org.

52. Schmidt, "Feast-or-Famine Life."

53. D. Abel, "Fish Wars Loom as Climate Change Pushes Lobster, Cod, and Other Species North," *Boston Globe*, June 21, 2018, www.bostonglobe.com.

54. P. Whittle, "Climate Change Threatens to Sink Gulf of Maine Fishing Industry," *Augusta Press Herald*, June 27, 2016, www.pressherald.com.

55. S. Julian, "This Buoy's for You," *Boston Globe*, June 30, 2010, www.boston.com.

56. Greenhalgh, "Climate & Lobsters."

57. Greenhalgh, "Climate & Lobsters."

58. T. Waring and J. Acheston, "Evidence of Cultural Group Selection in Territorial Lobstering in Maine," *Sustainability Science* 13 (2018): 21–34.

59. C. P. Magra, "'Soldiers . . . Bred to the Sea': Maritime Marblehead, Massachusetts, and the Origins and Progress of the American Revolution," *New England Quarterly* 77, no. 4 (2004): 531–562, 534.

60. W. H. Lear, "History of Fisheries in the Northwest Atlantic: The 500-Year Perspective," *Journal of Northwest Atlantic Fishery Science* 23 (1998): 41–73.

61. Charles D. Cheek, "Massachusetts Bay Foodways: Regional and Class Influences," *Historical Archaeology* 32, no. 3 (1998): 53–172, 155.

62. Massachusetts Historical Commission, "Cross Street Backlot Katherine Nanny Naylor: A Personal Story from Colonial Boston" (2014), Mass Historical Commission Exhibits online, www.sec.state.ma.us.

63. Cheek, "Massachusetts Bay Foodways," 155, 163.

64. S. E. Roberts, "'Esteeme a Little of Fish': Fish, Fishponds, and Farming in Eighteenth-Century New England and the Mid-Atlantic," *Agricultural History* 82, no. 2 (2008): 143–163, 155.

65. Roberts, "'Esteeme a Little of Fish,'" 155.

66. Oliver, *Saltwater Foodways*, 333.

67. J. L. Blake, *The Parlor Book: Or, Family Encyclopedia of Useful Knowledge and General Literature . . . Ornamented with Fine Colored Engravings* (New York: J.L. Piper, 1837), 356.

68. Blake, *Parlor Book*, 356.

69. Quoted in Oliver, *Saltwater Foodways*, 334.

70. Oliver, *Saltwater Foodways*, 333.

71. Oliver, *Saltwater Foodways*, 344; K. Q. Seelye, "In Maine, Last Sardine Cannery in the U.S. Is Clattering Out," *New York Times*, April 3, 2010.

72. C. S. Devas, *Political Economy* (London: Longmans, Green, 1901), 84–85.

73. D. Boeri and J. Gibson, *Tell It Goodbye Kiddo: The Decline of the New England Offshore Fishery* (Camden, ME: International Marine, 1976), 7.

74. P. B. Doeringer and D. G. Terkla, *Troubled Waters: Economic Structure, Regulatory Reform and Fisheries Trade* (Toronto: Toronto University Press, 1996), 21.

75. G. M. Grasso, "What Appeared Limitless Plenty: The Rise and Fall of the Nineteenth-Century Atlantic Halibut Fishery," *Environmental History* 13, no. 1 (2008): 66–91, 74.

76. Oliver, *Saltwater Foodways*, 336–337.

77. Oliver, *Saltwater Foodways*, 338.

78. "Message from the President of the United States Transmitting a Letter of the Secretary of State with the Correspondence Relative to the Proposed Fisheries Treaty" (Senate Doc 113, 50th Congress, 1st Session, 1888), 635.

79. Grasso, "What Appeared Limitless Plenty," 68.

80. Grasso, "What Appeared Limitless Plenty," 68–69.

81. Oliver, *Saltwater Foodways*, 346.

82. Grasso, "What Appeared Limitless Plenty," 74.

83. Grasso, "What Appeared Limitless Plenty," 77.

84. H. Deese, "Hail the Mighty Halibut! A Familiar Fish Story with a Surprise Ending," June 20, 2016, www.islandinstitute.org.

85. Grasso, "What Appeared Limitless Plenty," 66–91, 79.

86. Grasso, "What Appeared Limitless Plenty," 66–91, 74.

87. Grasso, "What Appeared Limitless Plenty," 66–91, 80.

88. Grasso, "What Appeared Limitless Plenty," 66–91, 82.

89. Grasso, "What Appeared Limitless Plenty," 66–91, 83.

90. Grasso, "What Appeared Limitless Plenty," 66–91, 68–69.

91. Grasso, "What Appeared Limitless Plenty," 66–91, 83.

92. R. Kipling, *Captains Courageous: A Story of the Grand Banks* (New York: Century Company, 1919), 75.

93. Grasso, "What Appeared Limitless Plenty," 66–91, 83.

94. NOAA National Marine Fisheries Service, "Species of Concern: Atlantic Halibut" (May 22, 2013), www.greateratlantic.fisheries.noaa.gov.

95. NOAA National Marine Fisheries Service, "Species of Concern."

96. P. Whittle, "US Says Number of Overfished Fish Stocks at All-Time Low," *Boston Globe*, May 17, 2018, www.bostonglobe.com; Deese, "Hail the Mighty Halibut!"

97. Whittle, "US Says Number of Overfished Fish Stocks at All-Time Low"; S. Rappaport, "Are Maine Halibut Headed for Trouble?," *Mount Desert Islander*, January 10, 2017, www.mdislander.com.

98. W. J. Bolster, "Putting the Ocean in Atlantic History: Maritime Communities and Marine Ecology in the Northwest Atlantic, 1500–1800," *American Historical Review* 113, no. 1 (2008): 19–47, 30.

99. Bolster, "Putting the Ocean in Atlantic History," 32.

100. Bolster, "Putting the Ocean in Atlantic History," 32.

101. Bolster, "Putting the Ocean in Atlantic History," 33.

102. C. C. Carlson, "The [In]Significance of Atlantic Salmon," *History Through a Pinhole* 8, nos. 3/4 (1996), www.nps.gov.

103. Carlson, "[In]Significance of Atlantic Salmon."

104. Carlson, "[In]Significance of Atlantic Salmon."

105. Carlson, "[In]Significance of Atlantic Salmon."

106. Carlson, "[In]Significance of Atlantic Salmon."

107. Carlson, "[In]Significance of Atlantic Salmon."

108. D. R. Foster, "Challenges and Opportunities for the Application of Historical Studies to Conservation" (July 30, 2004), foresthistory.org.

109. M. Latti, "Ready for Another Fight: With Its Population Stable, Shad Promise a Challenge for Anglers as They Fight, Run and Leap Like Salmon," *Portland Press Herald*, May 18, 2013, www.pressherald.com; C. Woodard, "Maine's River Herring Making Dramatic Comeback, a Godsend for the Food Chain," *Portland Press Herald*, July 17, 2017, www.pressherald.com; C. Woodside, "A Tale of Shad, the State Fish," April 4, 2019, connecticuthistory.org; D. L. Deen, "American Shad: Our Iconic Fish," February 1, 2013, www.ctriver.org.

110. Bolster, "Putting the Ocean in Atlantic History."

111. Bolster, "Putting the Ocean in Atlantic History."

112. Bolster, "Putting the Ocean in Atlantic History."

113. As quoted in D. Vickers, "Those Dammed Shad: Would the River Fisheries of New England Have Survived in the Absence of Industrialization?," *William and Mary Quarterly*, 3rd ser., 61, no. 4 (2004): 685–712. See also S. Judd and L. M. Boltwood, *History of Hadley:*

Including the Early History of Hatfield, South Hadley, Amherst and Granby, Massachusetts (Amherst, MA: Metcalf, 1863), 313–314.

114. R. Judd, *Second Nature: An Environmental History of New England* (Amherst: University of Massachusetts Press, 2014), 181.

115. Vickers, "Those Dammed Shad."

116. Vickers, "Those Dammed Shad."

117. Vickers, "Those Dammed Shad."

118. Vickers, "Those Dammed Shad."

119. Vickers, "Those Dammed Shad."

120. Vickers, "Those Dammed Shad."

121. Vickers, "Those Dammed Shad."

122. Judd, *Second Nature*, 182.

123. Vickers, "Those Dammed Shad."

124. Judd, *Second Nature*, 184.

125. Vickers, "Those Dammed Shad."

126. L. Konkel, "On the Rebound, New England Oysters Face Climate Change Threat," *Daily Climate*, April 17, 2013, www.scientificamerican.com; J. Bolster, "Clamming and Oystering," in *The Encyclopedia of New England*, ed. B. Feintuch and D. H. Watters (New Haven, CT: Yale University Press, 2005), 1060–1062.

127. K. Stavely and K. Fitzgerald, *America's Founding Food* (Chapel Hill: University of North Carolina Press, 2004), 106.

128. Oliver, *Saltwater Foodways*, 388.

129. F. M. Farmer, *The Boston Cooking-School Cook Book* (Boston: Little, Brown, 1896), 177, 132.

130. Oliver, *Saltwater Foodways*, 386.

131. J. C. O'Connell, *Dining Out in Boston* (Hanover, NJ: University Press of New England, 2016); Oliver, *Saltwater Foodways*, 386; Stavely and Fitzgerald, *America's Founding Food*, 107.

132. Stavely and Fitzgerald, *America's Founding Food*, 107.

133. Oliver, *Saltwater Foodways*, 385.

134. Oliver, *Saltwater Foodways*, 385.

135. Oliver, *Saltwater Foodways*, 385.

136. Konkel, "On the Rebound."

137. E. Pillsbury, "All At Last Returns to the Sea: Land Use and Water Quality on Southern New England's Shore," in *Landscape History of New England*, ed. B. Harrison and R. W. Judd (Cambridge, MA: MIT Press, 2011).

138. Pillsbury, "All at Last Returns to the Sea"; Bolster, "Clamming and Oystering," in Feintuch and Watters, *Encyclopedia of New England*, 1060–1062.

139. R. Rheault, "Rhode Island Shellfish Initiative Launch," *East Coast Shellfish Growers Association Newsletter*, no. 2 (June 2017), 7; University of Maine Aquaculture Research Institute, "Assessment of Oyster Production in Maine and New England" (June 28, 2018), umaine.edu; Konkel, "On the Rebound."

140. Connecticut Department of Agriculture, "Connecticut Shell Fishing Industry Profile" (January 10, 2011), www.ct.gov; Bureau of Aquaculture, "Connecticut's Shellfish Industry," December 5, 2018, www.ct.gov.

141. C. Brooks, "As Lobsters Dwindle in Long Island Sound, Oysters Thrive," *New York Times*, September 10, 2015, www.nytimes.com.

142. A. Shea, "Bacteria That Thrive in Warmer Waters Keep Mass. Oyster Fisheries on High Alert," *WBUR*, August 30, 2017, www.wbur.org.

143. Oliver, *Saltwater Foodways*, 385.

144. Oliver, *Saltwater Foodways*, 370; Stavely and Fitzgerald, *America's Founding Food*, 306.

145. N. H. Jenkins, "The Deep-Fried Truth about Ipswich Clams; No Matter the Source of the Harvest, the Secret to a Classic Seaside Meal May Be the Mud," *New York Times*, August 21, 2002, www.nytimes.com.

146. United Nations Food and Agriculture Organization, "Species Fact Sheets: *Spisula solidissima* (Dillwyn, 1817)" (2019), www.fao.org.

147. Stavely and Fitzgerald, *America's Founding Food*, 88.

148. Oliver, *Saltwater Foodways*, 372.

149. As quoted in Stavely and Fitzgerald, *America's Founding Food*, 91.

150. M. Rawson, *Eden on the Charles: The Making of Boston* (Cambridge, MA: Harvard University Press, 2010), 117.

151. Oliver, *Saltwater Foodways*, 282–283; Katherine Neustadt, *Clambake: A History and Celebration of an American Tradition* (Amherst: University of Massachusetts Press, 1992), 28.

152. Oliver, *Saltwater Foodways*, 283.

153. Neustadt, *Clambake*, 49.

154. Oliver, *Saltwater Foodways*, 288.

155. Oliver, *Saltwater Foodways*, 283.

156. Neustadt, *Clambake*, 55.

157. E. D. Reese, "Clambake," in *The Oxford Companion to American Food and Drink*, ed. A. F. Smith (Oxford: Oxford University Press, 2007), 132.

158. As quoted in Stavely and Fitzgerald, *America's Founding Food*, 91.

159. Stavely and Fitzgerald, *America's Founding Food*, 95.

160. Oliver, *Saltwater Foodways*, 296.

161. Legal Sea Foods Boston Terminal C all-day menu (April 2019), http://files.legalseafoods.com.

162. C. Canfield, "Moon Snails Decimate Clam Harvest," *Portland Press Herald*, June 24, 2010, www.pressherald.com.

163. S. Bishop, "Harvest Halted by Red Tide," *Boston Globe*, May 23, 2009, www.boston.com.

164. M. Bonner, "Vital Surf Clam Harvesting Grounds Closed by New England Fisheries Management Council," *South Coast Today*, December 6, 2018, www.southcoasttoday.com.

165. P. Whittle, "As Clam Harvesting Declines, Could Farming Be the Answer?," *Portland Press Herald*, June 3, 2018, www.pressherald.com.

166. New England Historical Society, "When Sardines Were Bigger Than Lobsters, Maine Women Had Good Jobs," www.newenglandhistoricalsociety.com.

167. Gee R. Robert, "Villages, Towns, and Cities: New England's Legacy Landscape," in Harrison and Judd, *Landscape History of New England*, 238.

168. Harrison and Judd, *Landscape History of New England*, 241.

169. E. Russell, "Nation's Last Sardine Cannery Closing," *Bangor Daily News*, April 14, 2014, http://bangordailynews.com.

170. Russell, "Nation's Last Sardine Cannery Closing."

171. New England Historical Society, "When Sardines Were Bigger Than Lobsters."

172. Robert, "Villages, Towns, and Cities," 245.

173. P. Josephson, "The Ocean's Hot Dog: The Development of the Fish Stick," *Technology and Culture* 49, no. 1 (2008): 41–61.

174. Josephson, "Ocean's Hot Dog."

175. Josephson, "Ocean's Hot Dog."

176. Josephson, "Ocean's Hot Dog."

177. Josephson, "Ocean's Hot Dog," 60.

178. Josephson, "Ocean's Hot Dog," 53.

179. Josephson, "Ocean's Hot Dog," 56.

180. R. Schweid, "Consider the Eel," *Gastronomica: The Journal of Food and Culture* 2, no. 2 (Spring 2002): 14–19.

181. "Learn about the American Eel," www.mass.gov.

182. K. Pinchin, "The Epic Fight Over the Enigmatic Eel: The Slippery Fish Is at the Center of a Canadian National Debate about Economics, Conservation and Indigenous Rights," *Smithsonian*, February 5, 2018, www.smithsonianmag.com; A. Kuffner, "Everywhere in R.I.: The Elusive American Eel," *Providence Journal*, June 8, 2018, www.providencejournal.com.

183. K. Okamoto, "When an Endangered Species Endangers a Culture: Eel Farming Is at the Core of One Japanese City's Identity—But Overconsumption Threatens Both the Animal and a Centuries-Old Tradition," *Atlantic*, January 12, 2016, www.theatlantic.com.

184. "Concern Grows among Japan's Glass Eel Farmers as Catch Slips Away," *Japan Times*, January 22, 2018, www.japantimes.co.jp.

185. J. Hunt, "Japan Copes with the Disappearing Eel," *New Yorker*, January 2, 2017, www.newyorker.com.

186. "Will 'Unagi' Vanish from the Dinner Table?," *Japan Today*, September 30, 2016, http://japantoday.com.

187. B. Trotter, "With 3 Weeks to Go, Maine's Baby Eel Harvest Tops $20M," *Bangor Daily News*, May 19, 2018, http://bangordailynews.com.

188. Atlantic States Marine Fisheries Commission, "American Eel," www.asmfc.org.

189. N. Flaherty, "Why Maine Is the Only State in the US with a 'Significant' Elver Fishery," *Maine Public*, May 1, 2018, www.mainepublic.org.

190. Flaherty, "Why Maine Is the Only State."

191. A. Kuffner, "Feeding a Black Market, Poachers Have Trapped Eels in R.I.," *Providence Journal*, June 18, 2018, www.providencejournal.com; "2 Indicted for Illegal Eel Harvesting in Massachusetts, New Jersey Waters," *WMUR*, January 18, 2018, www.wmur.com; Associated Press, "NH Police Arrest Two Suspected in International Eel-Smuggling Operation," *CBS Boston,* May 3, 2015, http://boston.cbslocal.com; R. Ebersole, "Inside the Multimillion-Dollar World of Eel Trafficking," *National Geographic*, June 7, 2017, http://news.nationalgeographic.com.

192. P. Whittle, "Lucrative Baby Eel Fishery Shut Down over Illegal Sales," *U.S. News & World Report*, May 23, 2018, www.usnews.com; P. Whittle, "Eels Break Records in Maine, Where They Sell for Big Money," *AP News*, May 20, 2018, www.apnews.com.

193. ASMFC American Eel Stock Assessment Subcommittee, "2017 American Eel Stock Assessment Update October 2017," Atlantic States Marine Fisheries Commission, October, 2017, www.asmfc.org.

194. M. Barr, "Baby Eels Have Changed Fortune for Maine's Fishermen—and Brought Trouble," *Boston Globe*, July 5, 2017, www.bostonglobe.com.

195. P. Whittle, "Regulators Keep Lid on Nation's Only Eel Fishery, in Maine," *Providence Journal*, August 12, 2018, www.providencejournal.com; R. Ebersole, "19 Eel Smugglers Sentenced, but Lucrative Trade Persists," *National Geographic*, June 2018, http://news.nationalgeographic.com.

196. Flaherty, "Why Maine Is the Only State."

197. D. Struck, "Maine's Most Mysterious Catch," *Christian Science Monitor*, June 7, 2017, www.csmonitor.com.

198. Atlantic States Marine Fisheries Commission, "American Eel," www.asmfc.org.

199. Struck, "Maine's Most Mysterious Catch."

200. Flaherty, "Why Maine Is the Only State."

201. "Maine Elver Fishermen Association," www.facebook.com.

202. P. Whittle, "New England Clam Harvest Continues to Dwindle," *Boston Globe*, April 7, 2018, www.boston.com; "Soft-Shell Clam Aquaculture," www.manomet.org; "A Changing Climate in Our Mud Flats: Ribbon Worms," September 28, 2016, www.mainecoastfishermen.org; J. M Hagan and E. Wilkerson, "How to Install a Soft-Shell Clam Farm" (Manomet Sustainable Economies Program, October 2018), www.manomet.org.

203. Christopher Paul Magra, "The New England Cod Fishing Industry and Maritime Dimensions of the American Revolution" (PhD diss., University of Pittsburgh, 2006), 102.

204. Magra, "New England Cod Fishing Industry," 235.

205. Magra, "New England Cod Fishing Industry," 237.

206. Magra, "New England Cod Fishing Industry," 235.

207. Magra, "New England Cod Fishing Industry," 291.

208. Magra, "New England Cod Fishing Industry," 217.

209. Magra, "New England Cod Fishing Industry," 288.

210. R. Kunzig, "Twilight of the Cod," *Discover*, April 1, 1995, http://discovermagazine.com.

211. Kunzig, "Twilight of the Cod."

212. Kunzig, "Twilight of the Cod."

213. As quoted in Lear, "History of Fisheries," 44.

214. Lear, "History of Fisheries," 44.

215. Lear, "History of Fisheries," 45.

216. Lear, "History of Fisheries," 45.

217. Magra, "'Soldiers . . . Bred to the Sea,'" 534–535.

218. Magra, "'Soldiers . . . Bred to the Sea,'" 534–535.

219. Lear, "History of Fisheries," 49.

220. Lear, "History of Fisheries," 49.

221. W. J. Bolster, ed., "Maritime New England," in Feintuch and Watters, *Encyclopedia of New England*.

222. A. Roland, W. J. Bolster, and A. Keyssar, *The Way of the Ship: America's Maritime History Reenvisioned, 1600–2000* (Hoboken, NJ: John Wiley, 2008), 84–85.

223. D. B. Rutman, "Governor Winthrop's Garden Crop: The Significance of Agriculture in the Early Commerce of Massachusetts Bay," *William and Mary Quarterly* 20, no. 3 (1963): 396–415, 403.

224. Magra, "'Soldiers . . . Bred to the Sea,'" 536.

225. Magra, "'Soldiers . . . Bred to the Sea,'" 533.

226. Magra, "New England Cod Fishing Industry," 217.

227. Magra, "New England Cod Fishing Industry," 217.

228. W. B. Rothenberg, "The Invention of American Capitalism: The Economy of New England in the Federal Period," in *Engines of Enterprise: An Economic History of New England*, ed. P. Temin (Cambridge, MA: Harvard University Press, 2002), 69–108, 103.

229. Lear, "History of Fisheries," 52.

230. Lear, "History of Fisheries," 60.

231. Lear, "History of Fisheries," 60.

232. Judd, *Second Nature*, 107–108; J. R. Blasi, "George Washington, Thomas Jefferson, and Alexander Hamilton and an Early Case of Shared Capitalism in American History: The Cod Fishery" (Working paper, Rutgers University School of Management and Labor Relations, 2012), 26, http://smlr.rutgers.edu; J. B. C. Jackson, K. E. Alexander, and E. Sala, eds., *Shifting Baselines: The Past and the Future of Ocean Fisheries* (Washington, DC: Island

Press, 2011); B. J. Payne, "Fishing the Borderlands: Government Policy and Fishermen on the North Atlantic" (master's thesis, University of Maine, 2001), 196, 41.

233. Payne, "Fishing the Borderlands," 196, 41.

234. Payne, "Fishing the Borderlands," 196, 41.

235. *New England Magazine* (1896), quoted by M. McKenzie, "Iconic Fishermen and the Fates of New England Fisheries Regulations, 1883–1912," *Environmental History* 17, no. 1 (2012): 3–28, 21.

236. Rothenberg, "Invention of American Capitalism," 106.

237. Bolster, "Maritime New England."

238. Bolster, "Maritime New England."

239. L. S. Parsons and W. H. Lear, "Perspectives on Canadian Marine Fisheries Management," *Canadian Bulletin of Fisheries and Aquatic Sciences*, no. 26 (1993): 12.

240. Lear, "History of Fisheries," 60.

241. F. M. Serchuk and S. E. Wigley, "Assessment and Management of the Georges Bank Cod Fishery: An Historical Review and Evaluation," *Journal of Northwest Atlantic Fishery Science* 13 (1992): 25–52, 28.

242. Serchuk and Wigley, "Assessment and Management," 28.

243. Serchuk and Wigley, "Assessment and Management," 28.

244. J. Hubbard, "In the Wake of Politics: The Political and Economic Construction of Fisheries Biology, 1860–1970," *Isis* 105, no. 2 (June 2014): 364–378, 376.

245. Hubbard, "In the Wake of Politics," 374.

246. Lear, "History of Fisheries," 66–67.

247. Lear, "History of Fisheries," 67.

248. Lear, "History of Fisheries," 67.

249. Kunzig, "Twilight of the Cod."

250. Kunzig, "Twilight of the Cod."

251. Kunzig, "Twilight of the Cod."

252. Lear, "History of Fisheries," 67; statistics from NOAA Fisheries, "Annual Commercial Landing Statistics," www.stnmfs.noaa.gov.

253. Lear, "History of Fisheries," 70.

254. Lear, "History of Fisheries," 70.

255. Lear, "History of Fisheries," 71.

256. Kunzig, "Twilight of the Cod."

257. NOAA Fisheries, "Atlantic Cod," www.fisheries.noaa.gov.

258. NOAA Fisheries, "Landings," http://foss.nmfs.noaa.gov.

259. As quoted in J. M. Acheson, "Anthropology of Fishing," *Annual Review of Anthropology* 10 (1981): 275–316, 282, 292.

260. Magra, "'Soldiers . . . Bred to the Sea,'" 559.

261. J. A. Conforti, *Saints and Strangers: New England in British North America* (Baltimore: Johns Hopkins University Press, 2006), 77.

262. Conforti, *Saints and Strangers*, 78.

263. McKenzie, "Iconic Fishermen," 8.

264. McKenzie, "Iconic Fishermen," 18.

265. S. A. Murawski, "A Brief History of the Groundfishing Industry of New England" (Northeastern Fisheries Science Center), www.nefsc.noaa.gov.

266. McKenzie, "Iconic Fishermen," 21.

267. McKenzie, "Iconic Fishermen," 17.

268. McKenzie, "Iconic Fishermen," 14.

269. McKenzie, "Iconic Fishermen," 14.

270. McKenzie, "Iconic Fishermen," 22.

271. McKenzie, "Iconic Fishermen," 22.

272. McKenzie, "Iconic Fishermen," 23.

273. US Department of Justice, "Report to the Congress of the United States A Review of the Restrictions on Persons of Italian Ancestry during World War II" (November 2001), www.schino.com.

274. P. B. Doeringer, P. I. Moss, and D. G. Terkla, "Capitalism and Kinship: Do Institutions Matter in the Labor Market?," *ILR Review* 40, no. 1 (1986): 48–60.

275. Doeringer, Moss, and Terkla, "Capitalism and Kinship," 55.

276. Doeringer, Moss, and Terkla, "Capitalism and Kinship," 53.

277. Doeringer, Moss, and Terkla, "Capitalism and Kinship," 53.

278. Acheson, "Anthropology of Fishing," 278.

279. Doeringer, Moss, and Terkla, "Capitalism and Kinship," 57.

280. Doeringer, Moss, and Terkla, "Capitalism and Kinship," 58.

281. D. Wilson et al., "Social and Cultural Impact Assessment of the Highly Migratory Species Fisheries Management Plan and the Amendment to the Atlantic Billfish Fisheries Management Plan" (New Brunswick, NJ: Ecopolicy Center for Agriculture, Environmental, and Resource Issues New Jersey Agricultural Experiment Station Cook College, July 1998).

282. M. Hall-Arber et al., "Gloucester/North Shore Sub-region" (New England's Fishing Communities, MIT Sea Grant), http://seagrant.mit.edu.

283. Hall-Arber et al., "Gloucester/North Shore Sub-region."

284. P. Whittle, "Why New England's Cod Catch Is at an All-Time Low," *Boston Globe*, January 14, 2018, www.boston.com; Statistics from National Marine Fisheries Service, "Commercial Landings," www.st.nmfs.noaa.gov.

285. A. J. Pershing et al., "The Future of Cod in the Gulf of Maine" (Gulf of Maine Research Institute, June 2013), 6, www.gmri.org.

286. D. Abel, "A Milestone in the War over the True State of Cod," *Boston Globe*, April 3, 2017, www.bostonglobe.com.

287. Abel, "Milestone in the War over the True State of Cod."

288. Abel, "Milestone in the War over the True State of Cod."

289. E. Horowitz, "Does Fishing Have a Future in New England?," *Boston Globe*, December 22, 2015, www.bostonglobe.com.

290. Horowitz, "Does Fishing Have a Future in New England?"

291. Kunzig, "Twilight of the Cod."

292. D. McDonald, "Fishing Regulators Approve Measures to Conserve Atlantic Herring," *Boston Globe*, September 26, 2018, www.bostonglobe.com.

293. McDonald, "Fishing Regulators Approve Measures."

294. D. Abel, "The 'Codfather' Is Behind Bars, and New Bedford's Economy Is Paying the Price," *Boston Globe*, May 7, 2018, www.bostonglobe.com; M. J. Valencia, "'The Codfather,' a New Bedford Fishing Mogul, Pleads Guilty," *Boston Globe*, March 30, 2017, www.bostonglobe.com.

295. Valencia, "'The Codfather.'"

296. Abel, "'Codfather' Is Behind Bars."

297. Abel, "'Codfather' Is Behind Bars."

298. D. Abel, "Fishing Officials Ease Restrictions in Waters Off New England," *Boston Globe*, January 7, 2018, www.bostonglobe.com.

299. J. Cote, "Former Captain of New Bedford Fishing Boat Pleads Guilty to Interfering with Coast Guard Inspection," *Boston Globe*, August 24, 2018, www.bostonglobe.com.

300. R. Rattigan, "Something Fishy in the Quotas?," *Boston Globe*, September 8, 2017, www.bostonglobe.com.

301. Rattigan, "Something Fishy in the Quotas?"

302. Abel, "Fish Wars Loom"; J. W. Morley et al., "Projecting Shifts in Thermal Habitat for 686 Species on the North American Continental Shelf," *PLOS ONE* 13, no. 5 (2018): e0196127, http://journals.plos.org; B. Berwyn, "Fish Species Forecast to Migrate Hundreds of Miles Northward as U.S. Waters Warm," *Inside Climate News*, May 16, 2018, http://insideclimatenews.org.

303. Morley et al., "Projecting Shifts in Thermal Habitat."

304. M. Finucane, "Hundreds of Fish Species Will Be Forced to Shift North Due to Climate Change, Study Says," *Boston Globe*, May 16, 2018, www.bostonglobe.com.

305. A. J. Pershing et al., "Slow Adaptation in the Face of Rapid Warming Leads to Collapse of the Gulf of Maine Cod Fishery," *Science* 350, no. 6262 (November 13, 2015): 809–812, http://science.sciencemag.org; M. Lavelle, "Collapse of New England's Iconic Cod Tied to Climate Change," *Science*, October 29, 2015, www.sciencemag.org.

306. Abel, "Fish Wars Loom."

307. Judd, *Second Nature*, 112.

308. Bolster, "Maritime New England."

309. Bolster, "Maritime New England."

310. P. Whittle, "US Imported More Seafood in 2017 Than Any Year," *Boston Globe*, June 24, 2018, www.bostonglobe.com.

CHAPTER 6: SWEETS, SOURS, AND SPIRITS

1. "Quebec Maple Syrup Production Plummeted by 22.4% in 2018," *Montreal Gazette*, December 12, 2018, http://montrealgazette.com; National Agricultural Statistics Service, "Maple Syrup 2010," *New England Agricultural Statistics*, July 2010, www.nass.usda.gov; Fédération de producteurs acérocles du Québec, "An Average Maple Syrup Harvest for the 2010 Season" (July 2010), www.siropderable.ca; National Agricultural Statistics Service, "United States Maple Syrup Production" (June 13, 2018), www.nass.usda.gov.

2. See, for example, Leader Evaporator, "Plastic Tubing/Pipeline Systems for Collecting Maple Sap," www.leaderevaporator.com.

3. P. Gregg, "Going Underground: Michigan Sugarmakers Bury Their Mainlines," *Maple News*, March 2015, www.themaplenews.com.

4. J. M. Lawrence and R. Martin, *Sweet Maple: Life, Lore & Recipes from the Sugarbush* (Darby, PA: Diane, 1999).

5. P. J. Munson, "Still More on the Antiquity of Maple Sugar and Syrup in Aboriginal Eastern North America," *Journal of Ethnobiology* 9, no. 2 (1989): 159–170; P. J. Munson, "The Antiquity of Maple Sucrose Concentrates: Reply to Holman and Mason," *Journal of Ethnobiology* 13, no. 9 (1989): 292–299.

6. B. Heinrich, "Maple Sugaring by Red Squirrels," *Journal of Mammalogy* 73, no. 1 (1992): 51–54.

7. C. V. Cogbill, J. Burk, and G. Motzkin, "The Forests of Presettlement New England, USA: Spatial and Compositional Patterns Based on Town Proprietor Surveys," *Journal of Biogeography* 29 (2002): 1279–1304.

8. W. M. Ciesla, "Non-wood Forest Products from Temperate Broad-Leaved Trees," in *Non-Wood Forest Products 15* (Rome: Food and Agriculture Organization of the United Nations, 2002).

9. Munson, "Antiquity of Maple Sucrose Concentrates"; R. Boyle, *Some Considerations Touching the Usefulness of Experimental Natural Philosophy*, 2nd ed. (Oxford: Henry Hall, 1664), 102, as cited in H. A. Schuette and A. J. Ihde, "Maple Sugar: A Bibliography of Early Records, II," *Transactions of the Wisconsin Academy of Sciences, Arts and Letters* 37 (1946): 89–184.

10. M. K. Bennett, "The Food Economy of the New England Indians, 1605–75," *Journal of Political Economy* 63, no. 5 (1955): 369–397.

11. L. Raleigh, "Land-Use History of Long Point" (Trustees of Reservations, 2000), www.thetrustees.org.

12. Raleigh, "Land-Use History of Long Point."

13. USDA Natural Resources Conservation Service, "Sugar Maple" (US Department of Agriculture, Natural Resources Conservation Service, 2006), http://plants.usda.gov; G. J. Nowacki and M. D. Abrams, "The Demise of Fire and 'Mesophication' of Forests in the Eastern United States," *Bioscience* 58, no. 2 (2008): 123–138.

14. R. S. Walter and H. W. Yawney, "Red Maple," in *Silvics of North America*, vol. 2, ed. R. M. Burns and B. H. Honkala (Washington, DC: US Department of Agriculture Forest Service Agriculture Handbook 654, 1990).

15. W. D. Ely, "The Sap and Sugar of the Maple-Tree," *Garden and Forest* (New York) 164 (April 15, 6, 1891): 171–172; Bennett, "Food Economy of the New England Indians," 385.

16. M. B. Holman and K. C. Egan, "Processing Maple Sap with Prehistoric Techniques," *Journal of Ethnobiology* 5 (1985): 61–75.

17. Holman and Egan, "Processing Maple Sap."

18. Holman and Egan, "Processing Maple Sap," 64.

19. Holman and Egan, "Processing Maple Sap," 70.

20. Holman and Egan, "Processing Maple Sap," 70; C. I. Mason, "Prehistoric Maple Sugaring Sites," *Midcontinental Journal of Archaeology* 10, no. 1 (1985): 149–152.

21. Munson, "Still More on the Antiquity of Maple Sugar."

22. Munson, "Still More on the Antiquity of Maple Sugar," 166.

23. E. Oertel, "History of Beekeeping in the United States," in *Agricultural Handbook*, no. 535 (Washington, DC: US Department of Agriculture, 1980).

24. A. Taylor, *American Colonies* (New York: Penguin, 2002), 211.

25. R. R. Menard, "Plantation Empire: How Sugar and Tobacco Planters Built Their Industries and Raised an Empire," *Agricultural History* 81, no. 3 (2007): 309–332.

26. J. E. McWilliams, "New England's First Depression: Beyond an Export-Led Interpretation," *Journal of Interdisciplinary History* 33, no. 1 (2002): 1–20, 6–7.

27. Menard, "Plantation Empire."

28. J. Hersh and H.-J. Voth, "Sweet Diversity: Colonial Goods and the Rise of European Living Standards after 1492" (Economics Working Papers 1163, 2011), 15, http://ssrn.com; "Currency, Coinage and the Cost of Living: Pounds, Shillings & Pence, and Their Purchasing Power, 1674–1913," *Proceedings of the Old Bailey*, March 2018, www.oldbaileyonline.org.

29. Hersh and Voth, "Sweet Diversity," 12, 15.

30. C. Holman, "A Sweet Small Something: Maple Sugaring in the New World," in *The Invented Indian: Cultural Fictions and Government Policies*, ed. J. A. Clifton (New Brunswick, NJ: Transaction, 1990).

31. R. B. Sheridan, *Sugar and Slavery: An Economic History of the British West Indies, 1623–1775* (Barbados: Canoe Press, 2000).

32. K. Stavely and K. Fitzgerald, *America's Founding Food* (Chapel Hill: University of North Carolina Press, 2004), 216.

33. Mason, "Prehistoric Maple Sugaring Sites?," 150.

34. H. S. Russell, *A Long, Deep Furrow: Three Centuries of Farming in New England* (Hanover, NH: University Press of New England, 1982), 305–306.

35. N. B. Wilkinson, "The Philadelphia Free Produce Attack upon Slavery," *Pennsylvania Magazine of History and Biography* 66, no. 3 (1942): 294–313, 295–296.

36. Russell, *Long, Deep Furrow*, 458.

37. L. M. F. Child, *The American Frugal Housewife* (Boston: Carter, Hendee, & Company, 1835). There is a single mention of maple in a section titled "cheap dye stuffs": "White maple bark makes a good light brown slate color. This should be boiled in water set with alum. The color is reckoned better when boiled in brass instead of iron" (9). See also M. Parloa, *The Appledore Cook Book: Containing Practical Receipts for Plain and Rich Cooking* (Boston: DeWolfe, Fiske, 1884), 103.

38. F. M. Farmer, *The Boston Cooking-School Cook Book* (Boston: Little, Brown, 1896).

39. B. Dojny, *The New England Cookbook: 350 Recipes from Town and Country, Land and Sea, Hearth and Home* (Boston: Harvard Common Press, 1999).

40. V. Barlow and S. Long, "Rediscovering a Long-Gone Forest: An Interview with Charlie Cogbill," *Northern Woodlands Magazine*, Spring 2007, http://nothernwoodlands.org; Cogbill, Burk, and Motzkin, "Forests of Presettlement New England."

41. A. Kekacs, "Tom Wessels Reads Complex Stories Written into the Forested Landscape," *Forests for Maine's Future*, October 15, 2010, www.forestsformainesfuture.org.

42. T. Wessels, *Reading the Forested Landscape* (Woodstock, VT: Countryman Press, 2005).

43. K. Levine, "In New England, Concern Grows for Sugar Maple," *Morning Edition* (National Public Radio, October 29, 2007), www.npr.org.

44. B. Donohue, "Sugar Maples, and a Bit of Needed Rain," *Boston Globe*, June 21, 2010, www.boston.globe.com.

45. M. Thomas, "Marketing Maple in the 1930s: The Pierce County Maple Syrup Producers Association," *Wisconsin Maple News* 20, no. 2 (2004): 7; M. Rogers, "Guide to Maple Syrup Grades," *New England Today*, March 1, 2019, http://newengland.com.

46. Rogers, "Guide to Maple Syrup Grades"; US Department of Agriculture Agricultural Marketing Service, "United States Standards for Grades of Maple Syrup Effective March 2, 2015," www.ams.usda.gov.

47. B. Daley, "A Forest of Change," *Boston Globe*, March 17, 2008, www.bostonglobe.com; S. Geisler, "Warm Weather Creates a Sticky Situation for Maple Syrup Famers," *Boston Globe*, March 25, 2010, www.bostonglobe.com; C. B. Skinner, A. T. DeGaetano, and B. F. Chabot, "Implications of Twenty-First Century Climate Change on Northeastern United States Maple Syrup Production: Impacts and Adaptations," *Climatic Change* 100, nos. 3–4 (2010): 685–702.

48. "Facts about Dunkin' Donuts," *Newsday*, July 21, 2018, www.newsday.com.

49. G. Balk, "New England's Love for Dunkin' Donuts Flows Deeper Than Seattle's Love for Starbucks," *Seattle Times*, March 14, 2018, www.seattletimes.com; S. Storrs, "Dunkin's Run: A Love Story," *Boston Magazine*, August 30, 2010, www.bostonmagazine.com.

50. Charles D. Cheek, "Massachusetts Bay Foodways: Regional and Class Influences," *Historical Archaeology* 32, no. 3 (1998): 153–172.

51. N. Jenkins, "Martha Ballard: A Woman's Place on the Eastern Frontier," in *From Betty Crocker to Feminist Food Studies: Critical Perspectives on Women and Food*, ed. A. V. Avakian and B. Haber (Amherst: University of Massachusetts Press, 2005), 109–119.

52. M. Randolph, *The Virginia Housewife: Or, Methodical Cook* (Washington, DC: Davis and Force, 1824); A. Simmons, *American Cookery: The Art of Dressing Viands, Fish, Poultry, and Vegetables* (Hartford, CT: Hudson & Goodwin, 1796); A. Gardiner, *Mrs. Gardiner's Receipts from 1763* (Hallowell, ME: White & Horne, 1938).

53. Stavely and Fitzgerald, *America's Founding Food*, 227–228; S. L. Oliver, *Saltwater Foodways: New Englanders and Their Food at Sea and Ashore, in the Nineteenth Century* (Mystic, CT: Mystic Seaport Museum, 1995), 244–245.

54. A. Yentsch, "Applying Concepts from Historical Archaeology to New England's Nineteenth-Century Cookbooks," *Northeast Historical Archaeology* 42 (2013): 121–123.

55. Yentsch, "Applying Concepts from Historical Archaeology," 122.

56. J. Larkin, "Dining Out in the 1830s," *Old Sturbridge Village Visitor*, Spring 1999, http://resources.osv.org.

57. Hersh and Voth, "Sweet Diversity," 11; H. A. Anderson, *Breakfast: A History* (Lanham, MD: Rowan & Littlefield, 2013), 89. See also chapter 1, "Who Is a Yankee?"

58. O. W. Holmes, *Ralph Waldo Emerson* (New York: Houghton Mifflin, 1886), 269.

59. Quotes as featured in Stavely and Fitzgerald, *America's Founding Food*, 225. See also C. E. H. Beecher, *Miss Beecher's Domestic Receipt Book* (New York: Harper & Brothers, 1850), 127–128.

60. Dona Brown, *Inventing New England: Regional Tourism in the Nineteenth Century* (Washington, DC: Smithsonian Institution Press, 1995), 159.

61. "The Great Pie Belt," *Star* (Christchurch), July 28, 1894, 2.

62. F. W. Searle, "Pie, Progress, and Ptomaine Poisoning," *Journal of Medicine and Science* 4, no. 9 (August 1898): 353–355.

63. "A Voice from the Pie Belt," *Inter Ocean* (Chicago), May 14, 1902, 6.

64. "A Gigantic Pie Bakery," *Scientific American* 27, no. 20 (November 16, 1872): 305.

65. "Pie-Making by Machinery," *Scientific American* 93, no. 14 (September 30, 1905), 256.

66. Uncle Dudley, "One Man's Food Is Another Man's Poison," *Boston Globe*, November 4, 1894, 20.

67. "The Pie Belt," *Barber County Index* (Barber, KS), November 17, 1909, 3.

68. N. K. M. Lee, *The Cook's Own Book* (Boston: Munroe and Francis, 1832).

69. Stavely and Fitzgerald, *America's Founding Food*, 249–252.

70. Farmer, *Boston Cooking-School Cook Book*, 402–404.

71. D. S. Brady, "Relative Prices in the Nineteenth Century," *Journal of Economic History* 24, no. 2 (1964): 145–203, 193.

72. M. C. Beaudry and S. A. Mrozowski, *Interdisciplinary Investigations of the Boott Mills, Lowell, Massachusetts: Volume I: Life at the Boarding Houses* (Boston: National Park Service North Atlantic Regional Office, 1987), 127.

73. S. Julian, *New Boston Globe Cookbook: More Than 200 Classic New England Recipes, from Clam Chowder to Pumpkin Pie* (Guilford, CT: Globe Pequot Press, 2012).

74. M. Carroll, "Snapshot: Dunkin' Donuts vs. Starbucks: Where Do You Stand?," *Boston Globe*, June 17, 2010, www.boston.com.

75. "New Dunkin' Donuts Ad Campaign: You Know, We Also Sell Doughnuts," *New York Daily News*, March 18, 2009, www.nydailynews.com.

76. Cooks.com, "New England Breakfast Pie," May 25, 2007, www.cooks.com.

77. R. S. Cox, *New England Pie: History under a Crust* (Charleston, SC: American Palate, 2015), 59.

78. "Maine House Votes for Whoopie Pie as State Treat, Blueberry Pie as State Dessert," *Bangor Daily News*, March 23, 2011, http://bangordailynews.com.

79. Cox, *New England Pie*, 58; N. Griffin, *Making Whoopies: The Official Whoopie Pie Book* (Camden, ME: Down East Books, 2010), 15–17.

80. Maine Whoopie Pie Festival, www.mainewhoopiepiefestival.com.

81. "One Bakery Owner's Dream: Taking Whoopies to the World," *New York Times*, December 26, 2005, www.nytimes.com.

82. Stavely and Fitzgerald, *America's Founding Food*, 342.

83. E. D. Chilton, "Towns They Have None: Diverse Subsistence and Settlement Strategies in Native New England," in *Northeast Subsistence-Settlement Change: AD 700–1300*, ed. J. P. Hart and C. B. Rieth (Albany: State University of New York, State Education Department, 2002), 9.

84. E. A. Evans and F. H. Ballen, "An Overview of US Blueberry Production, Trade, and Consumption, with Special Reference to Florida" (Food and Resource Economics Department, UF/IFAS Extension, October 2017), http://edis.ifas.ufl.edu; L. Kratochwill, "What's the Deal with Cranberry Sauce?," *Popular Science*, November 26, 2015, www.popsci.com.

85. Ocean Spray, "About the Harvest," www.oceanspray.com; H. C. Brown, "Going Rogue: Farmers Will Destroy One in Four Cranberries This Year," *New Food Economy*, November 23, 2018, http://newfoodeconomy.org.

86. K. A. Smith, "This Man Made the First Canned Cranberry Sauce: How Marcus Urann's Idea Revolutionized the Cranberry Industry," *Smithsonian*, November 27, 2013, www.smithsonianmag.com.

87. Ocean Spray, "About the Harvest."

88. Ocean Spray, "Cranberry Sauce Stats" (September 30, 2017), www.oceanspray.com.

89. M.-A. Rea, "Early Introduction of Economic Plants into New England," *Economic Botany* 29, no. 4 (1975): 333–356, 345.

90. S. L. Deyo, *History of Barnstable County, Massachusetts, 1620–1890* (New York: Blake, 1890), 147–148.

91. R. A. Ballinger, "A History of Sugar Marketing through 1974" (US Department of Agriculture Economics, Statistics, and Cooperatives Service Agricultural Economic Report no. 382, 1978), 10, 16; W. A. Woloson, *Refined Tastes: Sugar, Confectionery, and Consumers in Nineteenth-Century America* (Baltimore: Johns Hopkins University Press, 2003), 8.

92. D. Thompson, "The Spectacular Rise and Fall of U.S. Whaling: An Innovation Story," *Atlantic*, February 22, 2012, www.theatlantic.com; F. Burrow, *Cannonballs & Cranberries* (Taunton, MA: William S. Sullwold, 1976), 55, 64, 71.

93. S. A. Drake, *Nooks and Corners of the New England Coast* (New York: Harper & Brothers, 1875), 317.

94. W. Francis, "Historic & Archaeological Resources of Cape Cod & the Islands: A Framework for Preservation Decisions" (Massachusetts Historical Commission, 1986), 235, 372, www.sec.state.ma.us.

95. R. A. Woods, ed., *Americans in Process: A Settlement Study by the Residents and Associates of the South End House* (Cambridge, MA: Houghton Mifflin/Riverside Press, 1903), 245–246; Drake, *Nooks and Corners*, 317.

96. A. Coyle, "7 Juicy Facts about Cranberries," *Wicked Local Hull*, November 16, 2018, http://hull.wickedlocal.com.

97. Agricultural Resource Marketing Center, "Cranberries" (revised April, 2019), www.agmrc.org.

98. D. Nosowitz, "There Really Is a 'Congressional Cranberry Caucus,' And Here's What It Does," *Modern Farmer*, December 1, 2016, http://modernfarmer.com.

99. Smith, "This Man Made the First Canned Cranberry Sauce."

100. Fairland Farms, "A Little Cranberry History," http://fairlandfarm.net; Ocean Spray, "Our Story," www.oceanspray.com; Smith, "This Man Made the First Canned Cranberry Sauce."

101. Ocean Spray, "Cranberry Sauce Stats."

102. Fairland Farms, "A Little Cranberry History"; Ocean Spray, "Our Story"; Ocean Spray, "Cranberry Sauce Stats."

103. R. Sugar, "Canned Cranberry Sauce Explained," *Vox*, November 21, 2018, www.vox.com.

104. Jackassletters, "Ocean Spray Jellied Cranberry Sauce in a Can!," YouTube, January 22, 2012, www.youtube.com.

105. M. R. Janzen, "The Cranberry Scare of 1959: The Beginning of the End of the Delaney Clause" (PhD diss., Texas A&M University, December 2010), 86–87.

106. Janzen, "Cranberry Scare of 1959," 86; Brown, "Going Rogue."

107. "Cancer Scare Forgotten, Cranberry Farms Thrive," *New York Times*, November 18, 1979, www.nytimes.com.

108. Janzen, "Cranberry Scare of 1959," 173.

109. M. Tortorello, "The Great Cranberry Scare of 1959," *New Yorker*, November 24, 2015, www.newyorker.com.

110. Janzen, "Cranberry Scare of 1959," 94; Smith, "This Man Made the First Canned Cranberry Sauce."

111. USDA Nutrition Database, "USDA Branded Food Products Database Release July 2018," http://ndb.nal.usda.gov.

112. C. Sweeney, "Can Ocean Spray CEO Randy Papadellis Save the Cranberry Business?," *Boston Magazine*, April 17, 2016, www.bostonmagazine.com.

113. V. Amanour-Boadu, M. Boland, and D. Barton, "Ocean Spray Cranberries at the Crossroads" (Arthur Capper Cooperative Center Case Study no. 03-01, 2003, Department of Agricultural Economics, Kansas State University).

114. M. Carroll, "More Tart Words for Cranberry Product," *Boston Globe*, December 6, 2009, www.boston.com.

115. R. Reiss, "Ocean Spray's Secrets of Co-op Success," *Forbes*, September 15, 2010, www.forbes.com.

116. USDA Nutrition Database, "USDA Branded Food Products."

117. E. V. Jesse and R. T. Rogers, "The Cranberry Industry and Ocean Spray Cooperative: Lessons in Cooperative Governance" (FSRG Monograph Series no. 19, Food System Research Group, Department of Agricultural and Applied Economics, University of Wisconsin–Madison, January 2006), 4.

118. Sweeney, "Can Ocean Spray CEO Randy Papadellis Save the Cranberry Business?"; "Northland Sells Cranberry Processing Business to Ocean Spray; Drops Lawsuit," *Milwaukee Business Journal*, September 24, 2004, www.bizjournals.com.

119. B. Goggin, "The Cranberry's Bitter History," *Digg*, November 21, 2017, http://digg.com.

120. Goggin, "Cranberry's Bitter History."

121. Goggin, "Cranberry's Bitter History"; Massachusetts Cranberry Revitalization Task Force, "Final Report: A Review of the Massachusetts Cranberry Industry, the Complex Challenges Ahead, and Recommendations Geared towards Stabilizing and Revitalizing This Critical Sector of Agricultural Production" (Massachusetts Department of Agricultural Resources, May 20, 2016).

122. J. E. Spiegel, "Cranberry Farmer Grows New 'Crop': Solar Energy," *Yale Climate Connections*, May 8, 2017, www.yaleclimateconnections.org.

123. M. Carolan, "Can Cranberries Conquer the World? A US Industry Depends on It," *The Conversation*, December 10, 2017, http://theconversation.com.

124. F. Kloosterman, "15 Percent of Cranberry Crop Restricted; 25 Percent Proposed for 2018," *Fruit Growers News*, May 2, 2018, http://fruitgrowersnews.com; Agricultural Marketing Resource Center, "Cranberries" (October 2018), www.agmrc.org; Brown, "Going Rogue"; Cranberry Marketing Committee, "Per Capita Cranberry Consumption" (2017), http://reports.uscranberries.com.

125. A. C. Hanson and D. C. Bender, "Irrigation Return Flow or Discrete Discharge? Why Water Pollution from Cranberry Bogs Should Fall within the Clean Water Act's NPDES Program," *Lewis & Clark Environmental Law Review* 37, no. 2 (2007), http://elawreview.org.

126. L. Konkel, "Why Are Organic Cranberries So Hard to Find?", *Civil Eats*, November 23, 2015, http://civileats.com.

127. Konkel, "Why Are Organic Cranberries So Hard to Find?"

128. Massachusetts Clean Water Toolkit, "Introduction to Nonpoint Source Pollution: What Is Nonpoint Source Pollution?," http://prj.geosyntec.com; H. A. Sandler and K. M. Ghantous, "Weed Management 2018–220" (University of Massachusetts Cranberry Station), http://ag.umass.edu; Buzzards Bay Coalition, "Issues: Cranberry Bogs," www.savebuzzards-bay.org.

129. Carolan, "Can Cranberries Conquer the World?"

130. M. Cone, "EPA Takes Pest Killer Diazinon Off the Shelves," *Los Angeles Times*, January 1, 2005, http://articles.latimes.com; US Department of Agriculture Agricultural Marketing Service, USDA Pesticide Data Program Database, http://apps.ams.usda.gov; T. Laylin, "Looking for Organic Cranberries This Thanksgiving? Here's Why They're Hard to Find," *NBC News*, November 21, 2018, www.nbcnews.com.

131. Sugar, "Canned Cranberry Sauce Explained."

132. M. Miliken, "Maine Food Insider: State's Cranberry Industry Striving to Stay above Water," *Mainebiz*, November 22, 2017, www.mainebiz.biz.

133. US Department of Agriculture National Agricultural Statistics Service, Agricultural Statistics Board, "Cranberries," August 10, 2017, http://downloads.usda.library.cornell.edu.

134. C. Armstrong, "Cranberries and a Changing Climate" (University of Maine Cooperative Extension, 2016), http://extension.umaine.edu; C. Kummer, "Thanksgiving's Moveable Feast," *New York Times*, November 23, 2006, www.nytimes.com.

135. Reiss, "Ocean Spray's Secrets."

136. S. G. Arnold, *History of the State of Rhode Island and Providence Plantations* (New York: Appleton, 1859), 99.

137. Russell, *Long, Deep Furrow*, 50.

138. Rea, "Early Introduction of Economic Plants," 337. See also M. P. Wilder, "The Horticulture of Boston and Vicinity," in *The Memorial History of Boston: The Last Hundred Years, pt. II, Special Topics*, ed. J. Winsor (Boston: James R. Osgood, 1881), 607–640, 608.

139. A. Lea, "Cider-making: An Overview," *Food Science and Technology* 18 (2004): 14–17; "What Is a Cider Apple?," www.ciderschool.com.

140. Rea, "Early Introduction of Economic Plants," 340.

141. As quoted in Rea, "Early Introduction of Economic Plants," 338.

142. W. Wood, *New England's Prospect* (Boston: John Wilson and Sons, 1865), as quoted in Winsor, *Memorial History of Boston*, 492.

143. As quoted in Bennett, "Food Economy of the New England Indians," 382.

144. Russell, *Long, Deep Furrow*, 42.

145. As quoted in Wilder, "Horticulture of Boston and Vicinity," 609.

146. W. J. Rorabaugh, *The Alcoholic Republic: An American Tradition* (Oxford: Oxford University Press, 1979), 9–10, 110–111.

147. Rorabaugh, *Alcoholic Republic*, 111; M. E. Lender and J. K. Martin, *Drinking in America: A History* (New York: Simon & Schuster, 1987), 9; S. C. Brown, "Beers and Wines of Old New England: Under Harsh Conditions in A Country Very Different from the Fatherland, the Early Settlers Gradually Evolved Beverages Which They Came to Appreciate for Their Own Qualities," *American Scientist* 66, no. 4 (1978): 460–467, 465.

148. Rorabaugh, *Alcoholic Republic*, 13, 9–10.

149. K. Rowles, "Processed Apple Product Marketing Analysis: Hard Cider & Apple Wine" (SP 2000-06, Department of Agricultural, Resource, and Managerial Economics. Cornell University, June 2000).

150. Rorabaugh, *Alcoholic Republic*, 9–10; M. H. Stack, "A Concise History of America's Brewing Industry" (Economic History Association), http://eh.net; Stack, "Concise History."

151. W. H. Kerrigan, "The Fall and Rise of Hard Cider," *American Orchard*, August 31, 2014, http://americanorchard.wordpress.com; W. H. Kerrigan, "Hard Cider and the Election of 1840," *American Orchard*, March 11, 2015, http://americanorchard.wordpress.com.

152. D. R. Williams, "Cider," http://mason.gmu.edu.

153. Williams, "Cider."

154. Kerrigan, "War on the Cider Apple."

155. W. J. Rorabaugh, *Prohibition: A Concise History* (Oxford: Oxford University Press, 2018).

156. T. Pinney, *A History of Wine in America, Volume 2: From Prohibition to the Present* (Berkeley: University of California Press, 2007), 22–23; see also *Congressional Record (Senate)*, February 16, 1931, 5007, www.govinfo.govf.

157. D. H. Diamond, "Pioneer Apple Orchards in the American West: Random Seeding versus Artisan Horticulture," *Agricultural History* 84, no. 4 (2010): 423–450, 431; *History of Crawford County and Ohio* (Chicago: Baskin & Battey, 1881), 219.

158. Diamond, "Pioneer Apple Orchards," 445; A. Leeson, ed., *History of Seneca County, Ohio* (Chicago: Warner, Beers & Co., 1886), 202; Letter sent by John Armstrong to President Jefferson, in D. D. Jackson, ed., *Letters of the Lewis and Clark Expedition, with Related Documents, 1783–1854*, 2 vols. (Urbana: University of Illinois Press, 1978), 2:685.

159. W. Kerrigan, "The Invention of Johnny Appleseed," *Antioch Review* 70, no. 4 (Fall 2012): 608–625, 617.

160. Diamond, "Pioneer Apple Orchards," 433.

161. Diamond, "Pioneer Apple Orchards," 434.

162. Diamond, "Pioneer Apple Orchards," 435.

163. Diamond, "Pioneer Apple Orchards," 430.

164. Swedenborgian Church of North America, "Tenets of Swedenborgianism" (2017), http://swedenborg.org. Kerrigan, "Invention of Johnny Appleseed," 610.

165. Kerrigan, "Invention of Johnny Appleseed," 610.

166. Kerrigan, "Invention of Johnny Appleseed," 610.

167. Kerrigan, "Invention of Johnny Appleseed," 611–612.

168. Kerrigan, "Invention of Johnny Appleseed," 614.

169. Kerrigan, "Invention of Johnny Appleseed," 616.

170. Kerrigan, "Invention of Johnny Appleseed," 615.

171. Kerrigan, "Invention of Johnny Appleseed," 617.

172. Ohio History Connection, "American Indians," www.ohiohistorycentral.org.

173. See analysis in Kerrigan, "Invention of Johnny Appleseed."

174. Franklin County Chamber of Commerce, "Franklin County Cider Days," www.ciderdays.org.

175. See, for example, C. Jolicoeur, "Apple Blending for Cider," www.cjoliprsf.ca.

176. Rowles, "Processed Apple Product Marketing Analysis," 26.

177. A. Perez, B.-H. Lin, and J. Allshouse, "Demographic Profile of Apple Consumption in the United States" (Economic Research Service/USDA, Fruit and Tree Nuts S&O/FTS-292 September 2001), 37–47.

CHAPTER 7: CHEESE AND TASTE

1. E. V. Mitchell, *It's an Old New England Custom* (New York: Vanguard Press, 1946).

2. L. Durand, "The Migration of Cheese Manufacture in the United States," *Annals of the Association of American Geographers* 42, no. 4 (1952): 263–282, 265.

3. K. Stavely and K. Fitzgerald, *America's Founding Food* (Chapel Hill: University of North Carolina Press, 2004); US Census 1850, www2.census.gov.

4. Stavely and Fitzgerald, *America's Founding Food.*

5. US Agricultural Research Service, "Experiment Station Record #42" (Washington, DC: Government Printing Office, 1921), 378.

6. C. Merchant, *Ecological Revolutions: Nature, Gender, & Science in New England*, 2nd ed. (Chapel Hill: University of North Carolina Press, 1989), 234.

7. T. Dwight, *Travels in New-England and New-York*, vol. 2 (New Haven, CT: Timothy Dwight, 1821), 374; E. H. Jenkins, *A History of Connecticut Agriculture* (New Haven: Connecticut Agricultural Experiment Station, 1926), 395.

8. "Pineapple Cheese," *Victorian Passage into Time*, April 15, 2014, www.victorianpassage. com; G. Mangan, "The Story of Pineapple Cheese," *Connecticut History*, http://connect-icuthistory.org.

9. B. Brown, *The Complete Book of Cheese* (New York: Gramercy, 1955), 56.

10. H. J. W. Gilbert, *Rushford and Rushford People* (Chautauqua, NJ: Helen Josephine White Gilbert, 1910), 501; P. R. Eisenstadt, *The Encyclopedia of New York State* (Syracuse, NY: Syracuse University Press, 2005), 1205; C. Donnelly, ed., *The Oxford Companion to Cheese* (Oxford: Oxford University Press, 2016), 569; Mangan "Story of Pineapple Cheese."

11. Jenkins, *History of Connecticut Agriculture*, 397.

12. Jenkins, *History of Connecticut Agriculture*, 398.

13. S. McMurry, "Women's Work in Agriculture: Divergent Trends in England and America, 1800 to 1930," *Comparative Studies in Society and History* 34, no. 2 (1992): 248–270, 259.

14. McMurry, "Women's Work in Agriculture," 260.

15. Durand, "Migration of Cheese Manufacture," 271.

16. McMurry, "Women's Work in Agriculture," 260.

17. "Facts about Cheese," *Scientific American* 43, no. 9 (1880): 138.

18. Durand, "Migration of Cheese Manufacture."

19. J. A. Cross, "Changing Patterns of Cheese Manufacturing in America's Dairyland," *Geographical Review* 102, no. 4 (2012): 525–538, 525.

20. CLAL, "US: Cheese Production," www.clal.it.

21. US Department of Agriculture, National Agricultural Statistics Service, "Dairy Products: 2017 Summary" (April 2018), http://downloads.usda.library.cornell.edu.

22. Cross, "Changing Patterns of Cheese Manufacturing," 536–537.

23. J. H. White, *The American Railroad Freight Car: From the Wood-Car Era to the Coming of Steel* (Baltimore: Johns Hopkins University Press, 1993), 272.

24. Federal Writers' Project, *The WPA Guide to Vermont: The Green Mountain State* (San Antonio, TX: Trinity University Press, 2013).

25. S. M. Babcock, *The Cheese Industry: Its Development and Possibilities in Wisconsin* (Madison: University of Wisconsin Agricultural Experiment Station, 1897), 14.

26. James A. Kindraka, "Milk Run! The Story of Milk Transportation by Rail," *Dispatch* 12, no. 1 (1990): 19.

27. Kindraka, "Milk Run!," 19.

28. Federal Writers' Project, *WPA Guide to Vermont.*

29. Kindraka, "Milk Run!," 19.

30. Federal Writers' Project, *WPA Guide to Vermont*, 279.

31. Federal Writers' Project, *WPA Guide to Vermont*, 207.

32. H. Paxson, "Artisanal Cheese and Economies of Sentiment in New England," in *Fast Food / Slow Food: The Cultural Economy of the Global Food System*, ed. R. Wilk (Lanham, MD: AltaMira Press, 2006), 201–218, 206–207.

33. H. Paxson, "Placing the Taste of Vermont Cheese," *Diffusion* 2, no. 2 (2010), http://id.erudit.org.

34. Paxson, "Placing the Taste of Vermont Cheese."

35. G. Edgar, *Cheddar: A Journey to the Heart of America's Most Iconic Cheese* (White River Junction, VT: Chelsea Green, 2015).

36. Dona Brown, *Inventing New England: Regional Tourism in the Nineteenth Century* (Washington, DC: Smithsonian Institution Press, 1995), 144.

37. Brown, *Inventing New England*, 135–167.

38. Vermont State Board of Agriculture, Resources and Attractions (1892 ed.), as quoted in A. Rebek, "The Selling of Vermont: From Agriculture to Tourism, 1860–1910," *Proceedings of the Vermont Historical Society* 44, no. 1 (1976).

39. Brown, *Inventing New England*, 159.

40. Brown, *Inventing New England*, 159.

41. Brown, *Inventing New England*, 159; G. W. Perry, "Managing the Summer Boarder Garden," in *Fifteenth Annual Report of the Vermont State Agricultural Society* (Saint Albans, VT: Saint Albans Messenger Company, 1917), 60–70.

42. H. Paxson, "Cheese Cultures: Transforming American Tastes and Traditions," *Gastronomica* 10, no. 4 (2010): 35–47, 42–45.

43. "Plymouth Artisan Cheese," www.plymouthartisancheese.com; "Crowley Cheese," www.crowleycheese.com.

44. H. Paxson, "Locating Value in Artisan Cheese: Reverse Engineering Terroir for New-World Landscapes," *American Anthropologist*, New Series, 112, no. 3 (2010): 444–457, 445.

45. R. DiStefano and A. Trubek, "Cheese Stories: Cheesemongers, Vermont Artisan Cheese and the Value of Telling Stories," *Cuizine* 6, no. 1 (2015); Shaping Foodways and Food Decisions, www.erudit.org.

46. "Jasper Hill Farm," www.jasperhillfarm.com.

47. Paxson, "Locating Value in Artisan Cheese," 447; Paxson, "Placing the Taste of Vermont Cheese."

48. Paxson, "Locating Value in Artisan Cheese," 453.

49. B. Marler, "Publisher's Platform: '60-Day Rule': The Facts," *Food Safety News*, February 6, 2001, www.foodsafetynews.com.

50. J. Buzby, "Cheese Consumption Continues to Rise," *Amber Waves* (USDA Economic Research Service, February 2005), www.ers.usda.gov.

51. Based on data from Vermont Cheese Council, "Members," www.vtcheese.com; Vermont Cheesemakers Festival, vtcheesefest.com; and "Vermont: Quickfacts," www.census.gov.

52. Massachusetts Cheese Guild, "Meet the Cheesemakers," macheeseguild.org; "Granite State Dairy Promotion," www.nhdairypromo.org; Maine Cheese Guild, "All Maine Cheesemakers Map," mainecheeseguild.org.

53. H. Paxson, "Post-Pasteurian Cultures: The Microbiopolitics of Raw-Milk Cheese in the United States," *Cultural Anthropology* 23, no. 1 (2008): 15–47, 35; Census for 1820, www.census.gov.

54. American Farmland Trust, "New England Milkshed Assessment" (2013), www.farmland.org.

55. P. Duffey, "Making Its Mark," *Rural Cooperative Magazine*, May/June 2000, www.rurdev.usda.gov.

56. E. Ladue, B. Gloy, and C. Cykendall, "Future Structure of the Dairy Industry: Historical Trends, Projections, and Issues" (Research Bulletin 01, Department of Applied Economics and Management, Cornell University 2003), http://aede.osu.edu.

CONCLUSION

1. J. Thacher, *History of the Town of Plymouth, from Its First Settlement in 1620, to the Present Time: With a Concise History of the Aborigines of New England, and Their Wars with the English, &c* (Boston: Marsh, Capen & Lyon, 1835), 181–182.

2. J. W. Baker, *Thanksgiving: The Biography of an American Holiday* (Durham, NH: University Press of New England, 2010), 63–64.

3. The New England Society, *Proceedings at the Twentieth Annual Meeting and Twentieth Annual Festival of the New England Society in the City of Brooklyn* (1900), 23.

4. K. Curtin and S. L. Oliver, *Giving Thanks: Thanksgiving Recipes and History from Pilgrims to Pumpkin Pie* (New York: Clarkson Potter, 2005), 29–30; Baker, *Thanksgiving*, 22–23.

5. E. Winslow, *Good Newes from New England* (Bedford, MA: Applewood Books, 1996), 54–55; Plimoth Planation, "Plimoth Plantation's Wampanoag Homesite," www.plimoth.org.

6. Winslow, *Good Newes from New England*, 56.

7. A. Young, *Chronicles of the Pilgrim Fathers of the Colony of Plymouth: From 1602–1625* (Boston: C. C. Little and J. Brown, 1841), 231; Baker, *Thanksgiving*, 12–14.

8. Young, *Chronicles of the Pilgrim Fathers*, 229.

9. Baker, *Thanksgiving*, 12–14.

10. Baker, *Thanksgiving*, 14.

11. J. G. Austin, *Standish of Standish: A Story of the Pilgrims* (Boston: Houghton, Mifflin, 1889), 286.

12. Baker, *Thanksgiving*, 15.

13. Baker, *Thanksgiving*, 39–41.

14. S. L. Oliver, *Saltwater Foodways: New Englanders and Their Food at Sea and Ashore, in the Nineteenth Century* (Mystic, CT: Mystic Seaport Museum, 1995), 242–245; Baker, *Thanksgiving*, 46; Curtin and Oliver, *Giving Thanks*, 30–32.

15. E. A. Howland, *The New England Economical Housekeeper, and Family Receipt Book* (Worcester, MA: S. A. Howland, 1845), 72; B. A. Twomey, "Plain Cooking: The Emergence of the Community Cookbook after the Civil War" (thesis proposal, San Jose State University, Department of Library and Information Science, November 2007).

16. A. M. Schlesinger, "A Dietary Interpretation of American History," *Proceedings of the Massachusetts Historical Society*, 3rd ser., 68 (1944–1947): 199–227, 216.

17. "Thanksgiving Menus," *Demorest's Family Magazine* 28 (November 1891): 47; "The Housekeeper," *Ballou's Monthly Magazine* 64 (1886): 432; Aunt Babette, *Aunt Babette's Cook Book: Foreign and Domestic Receipts for the Household* (New York: Bloch, 1889), 495.

18. H. L. Johnson, "Thanksgiving," *Table Talk* 8, no. 11 (November 1893): 374–376, 374.

19. Johnson, "Thanksgiving," 375.

20. M. J. Lincoln, "Thanksgiving, Our American Festival," *American Kitchen Magazine* 4 (1895): 84–92, 91–92.

21. "A Thanksgiving Dinner," *Christian Work: Illustrated Family Newspaper* 59 (1895): 796.

22. S. J. B. Hale, *Northwood: A Tale of New England* (Boston: Bowles & Dearborn, 1827), 109.

23. E. Johnson, *Johnson's Wonder-Working Providence 1628–1651*, ed. J. Franklin Jameson (New York: Charles Scribner's Sons, 1910).

24. B. D. Smith, "The Initial Domestication of Cucurbita pepo in the Americas 10,000 Years Ago," *Science*, New Series 276, no. 5314 (May 9, 1997): 932–934.

25. J. P. Hart and N. A. Sidell, "Additional Evidence for Early Cucurbit Use in the Northern Eastern Woodlands East of the Allegheny Front," *American Antiquity* 62, no. 3

(1997): 523–537, 523; J. B. Petersen and N. A. Sidell, "Mid-Holocene Evidence of Cucurbita Sp. from Central Maine," *American Antiquity* 61, no. 4 (1996): 685–698; D. S. Decker, "Origin(s), Evolution, and Systematics of Cucurbita pepo (Cucurbitaceae)," *Economic Botany* 42, no. 1 (1988): 4–15, 4; E. Peacock, "Historical and Applied Perspectives on Prehistoric Land Use in Eastern North America," *Environment and History* 4, no. 1 (February 1998): 1–29.

26. Peacock, "Historical and Applied Perspectives," 10; J. P. Hart and C. M. Scarry, "The Age of Common Beans (Phaseolus vulgaris) in the Northeastern United States," *American Antiquity* 64, no. 4 (1999): 653–658, 657; C. H. Brown, "Prehistoric Chronology of the Common Bean in the New World: The Linguistic Evidence," in *Pre-Columbian Foodways: Interdisciplinary Approaches to Food, Culture, and Markets in Ancient Mesoamerica*, ed. J. Staller and M. Carrasco (New York: Springer, 2009), 273–292, 280.

27. H. S. Paris et al., "First Known Image of Cucurbita in Europe, 1503–1508," *Annals of Botany* 98, no. 1 (July 2006): 41–47; J. Janick and H. S. Paris, "The Cucurbit Images (1515–1518) of the Villa Farnesina, Rome," *Annals of Botany* 97, no. 2 (February 2006): 165–176.

28. Decker, "Origin(s), Evolution, and Systematics," 5; H. S. Paris, "Historical Records, Origins, and Development of the Edible Cultivar Groups of Cucurbita pepo (Cucurbitaceae)," *Economic Botany* 43, no. 4 (1989): 423–443, 426.

29. D. Gookin, *Historical Collections of the Indians in New England* (1792), Special Collections Publications (Miscellaneous) Paper 13, 150.

30. J. B. Moore, *Collections, Historical & Miscellaneous, and Monthly Literary Journal*, vol. 3 (Concord, MA: J. B. Moore, 1824), 230.

31. Mike Urban, "The McDonald's Lobster Roll Experience," *New England Today*, June 21, 2018, http://newenglandtoday.com.

32. Nik DeCosta-Klipa, "For 100 Years, Fluff Has Stuck to Its Somerville Roots. But the Story Isn't That Simple," September 22, 2017, www.boston.com; Mimi Graney, *Fluff: The Sticky Sweet Story of an American Icon* (Boston: Union Park Press, 2017), 96–97.

33. www.flufffestival.com.

34. National Agricultural Statistics Service, Agricultural Statistics Board, US Department of Agriculture, "Cranberries ISSN: 1948–9013" (August 10, 2017).

35. Merry White and Gus Rancatore, "How the North End Became Boston's Little Italy and Why, Just Like in the Big Italy, Its Cuisine Is More Diverse Than You Might Think," *Boston Globe*, January 23, 2017, www.bostonglobe.com.

36. Quoted in Laura Shapiro, *Perfection Salad: Women and Cooking at the Turn of the Century* (Berkeley: University of California Press, 2008), 151.

INDEX

Abel, Mary Hinman, 71–74, 76, 137
Abenaki, 49, 105, 156, 220–21
Acadian immigrants
    arrival and diet of, 18–19, 22, 25, 156
    Beignets recipe of, 156
African Americans
    arrival of, 25–26
    Cape Verdean immigrants' arrival impact
        for, 30–32
    as caterers and restaurateurs, 30
    Civil War regiment, 30
    cookbooks, 118, 146
    cornbread recipes, 118, 146–47
    foods and culinary influences of, 25, 26–31
    Great Migration, 29
    home economics menus exclusion of foods
        of, 77
    malnourishment of, slaves, 27
    New England slavery and discrimination
        of, 25–28
    Plymouth mystery jars of, 28
    population data for, 26
Aladdin Oven, 70–71, 137
Albala, Ken, 55
alcoholic beverages
    beer brewing and consumption, 12, 51, 104,
        108, 139, 246, 248
    Champaign Cider, 158
    Civil War and consumption of, 248
    cranberry juice popularity and, 240–41
    1830s consumption data for, 247
    rum production and consumption, 51, 102,
        223, 224
    Temperance movement/Prohibition
        impact on, 247–49
American Cookery (Simmons), 104, 123–24, 144,
    148, 162, 228
The American Frugal Housewife (Child), 133,
    144–45, 224–25
American Home Economics Association, 76
American Kitchen Magazine, 272–73

American Revolution. *See* Revolutionary War
Anchovy Toast with Eggs, 140–41
Anthony, Susan B., 94
Appledore Cook Book (Parloa), 87
apples
    Apple Pie, Sarah Josepha Buell Hale's, 152
    Champaign Cider, 158
    contemporary consumption of fresh, 253
    early evidence of growing, 244–45, 249–50
    hard cider history and evolution, 12, 104,
        158, 219, 245–49, 253
    Johnny Appleseed plantings of, 249–50
    Native American, orchards, 249–50
    Nice Apple Pie, 153
    varieties, bitter compared with sweet, 245–
        46, 253
Appleseed, Johnny. *See* Johnny Appleseed
Apricot Sauce, 141–42
ashes, cooking with, 105–7
ASMFC. *See* Atlantic States Marine Fisher-
    ies Commission
Asparagus Salad with Goat Cheese, Shaved,
    160
Atkinson, Edward, 69, 70–71, 114
Atlantic States Marine Fisheries Commis-
    sion (ASMFC), 198, 199
Atwater, W. O., 68–69
Aunti Laura's Gufong/Fungine, 128
Aunt Mary's New England Cook Book (1881),
    61, 86
Austin, J. G., 267, 270–71
Azoreans, 31, 38, 39

baked beans. *See also* Boston baked beans
    canned, consumption of, 277
    common false history for, 48
    early reputation of, 56–58
    1832 Baked Beans (original and adapta-
        tion), 133
    of French Canadian immigrants, 21–22,
        55, 134

Lowell's Famous Rochette's Baked Beans, 134

Paul Mayotte's French Canadian American Baked Beans, 134

Pilgrims version of, 1, 12, 55

in publications from 1800s, 1, 55–58

sugar in, origins of, 1, 55, 58, 61–62

wood-fire, logistics for, 49

Baker, Charlie, 214

baker's ammonia, 104

baking powder, 103–4, 106, 107

baking soda, 106, 107

beans. *See also* baked beans; Boston baked beans

in Puerto Rican diet, 44

Tillie's Portuguese American Sausage, Kale, and Potato Soup, 132

Wampanoag cultivation and use of, 51–55

Beecher, Catharine, 82, 139, 229

beef

French Canadian Turkey Stuffing, 162–63

middle class views on, 88

New England Boiled Dinner, 142

New England Kitchen Beef Broth, 137

beer

consumption, 12, 51, 246, 248

yeasts for bread making from making, 104, 108, 139

beets, 86–88, 90, 94–97, 142

Beignets, Acadian, 156

bell peppers, stuffed, 128–29

Bernoon, Emmanuel "Manna," 30

berries. *See* blueberries; cranberries

beverages. *See* alcoholic beverages

Bisquick, 32, 128

Blackburn, Howard, 209

Blaxton, William, 244–45

blueberries

cranberry consumption contrasted with, 235

Native American use of, 9, 13, 121

Ocean Spray intentions for, 244

One-Crust Blueberry Pie, Myrle Sylsby's, 154

Blue Lights, or the Convention (Scott), 56

Bolster, Jeffrey, 199

Boston

African American discrimination in, 26

Brahmins/elites, 14, 60, 69

dairy consumption in 1920s, 258

food riots in, 103, 105

immigrant population in 2007 by country of origin, 46

Irish immigrant population in, 14, 17, 79–80

Native American names for locations in, 64

Pot Shop of, 135

servant population statistics in, 80

soup kitchens in late 1880s, 69–70

Boston, Seneca, 29

Boston baked beans

molasses obsession and origins of, 231

Native Americans attributed to origins of, 1, 2, 48–49

origins, myths and realities of, 1–2, 12, 48–49, 231

Pilgrims and origin stories of, 1, 12, 48

Pot Shop of Boston recipe for, 135

sugar-bean ratio increase from 1880 to 2017, 61–62, *62*

Boston Cook Book (1891) (Lincoln, M.), 90

Boston Cooking School

educators and celebrity cooks at, 76, 84–85, 87, 140

founding and intentions of, 83–84

Boston Cooking-School Cook Book (1896) (Farmer), 85–86, 90, 150, 156–57, 225, 232–33, 277

Boston cream pie, 154, 277

Boston Gingerbread, 158

Boston Globe, 40, 61, 97–98, 231, 234, 278

Boston School Kitchen Text-Book (Lincoln, M.), 76, 138, 145

Boston Weekly Magazine, 55–56

Bottrell, W., 95

Bradford, William, 10, 50, 53, 99, 182, 270

Bragdon, Kathleen, 52

Brainard, Newton C., 168

Bran Biscuits, 126

bread

advice contrasted with realities of 1800s, making, 75–76, 78–79, 81–83, 115–16

Bread Pancakes, Mary Hinman Abel's, 137

cornbread compared with wheat, 100–101

corn criticized for making, 100–101

Corn Egg Bread, 147

for English settlers, 12, 103–5, 116

molasses in colonial, 116

Rye and Indian/Cornmeal Bread (Hale's and adaptation), 122–23

rye in colonial, 12, 103, 116

Victorian food science menus dominance of, 71–72, 75–76, 78–79

wheat, making logistics and costs, 100–101, 102–3, 105

Wheat Bread of Distillery or Brewer's Yeast, Catharine Beecher's, 139
yeasts for making, 82, 101, 104, 108, 139
Bread and Roses Strike (1912), 36
Brooklyn and Long Island Fair (1864), 65–66
broth, beef, 137
Brown, Moses, 27
Brown, William J., 27
The Buccaneers (Judah), 56
Burnham, George, 169
Bushnell, Horace, 78
butter making, 16, 255–56, 258

cabbage
French Canadian immigrants use of, 22, 25
Irish immigrants use of, 23
New England boiled dinner history and, 86–92, 94–98
New England Boiled Dinner recipe, 142–43
Polish immigrants use of, 38
Cabot, John, 202
Cajun people and culture, 3, 18–19
cake
icings, Rundell's, 123, 125
"pies" that are, 154, 277
Plum Cake (Simmons' and adaptation), 123–25
Canada. *See* French Canadian immigrants
Cape Cod
Cape Verdeans settlements on, 31, 33, 39
cranberry industry in, 237–38, 240
maritime industry decline in, 218, 219
Portuguese Americans in, 39
shellfish history and culture on, 42, 52–53
whales, 182
Cape Verdean immigrants, 30–32, 33, 39, 128
Captains Courageous (Kipling), 2, 181, 205, 210
Caribbean
immigrants, 32
sugar production, 223–24
Carlson, Catherine, 183
Carolina Housewife (Rutledge), 118
celery curls, 150
Champaign Cider, 158
Chapman, John. *See* Johnny Appleseed
cheese
Cheese and Loroco Pupusas, 147
current-day consumption of, 265
Herb and Cheddar Easter Tomatoes, 159
Kimchi Grilled Cheese, 161
pineapple, about, 255
pineapple, how to stuff, 159

Shaved Asparagus Salad with Goat Cheese, 160
cheese making/industry
butter making shift from, 255–56, 258
current-day, 257, 265
dairy industry decline relation to, 265
factories, 159, 255, 256–57, 262–63
history and evolution, 254–65
imports, 257
mass marketing shift with, 256–57
pineapple, 255
post–Civil War, 255–57
railroads impact on, 255, 256, 258
"reverse engineering terroir" tactic in, 262–65
shellacking and preservation in, 255
states dominant in contemporary, 257
Vermont, 159, 257–65
Vermont, newcomers and elites role in, 259–60
Vermont, prior to 1850, 264–65
Chen, Joyce, 43
chestnuts, 2, 54–55
chicken pie
recipe, 162
Thanksgiving tradition inclusion of, 272, 273
Child, Lydia Maria Francis, 133, 144–45, 224–25, 251–52, 270
Chinese Exclusion Act of 1882, 41
Chinese immigrants, 22, 41–43
chowder
canned, consumption of, 277
Fish Chowder recipe (original and adaptation), 149
origins, 177–78, 193
parties, 192
Chow Mein Sandwich, 42, 132
Christian Work (Larkin), 273
Chronicles of the Pilgrim Fathers (Young), 270
cider, hard
apple varieties for, 245–46, 253
Champaign Cider, 158
decline in, factors behind, 247–48
history and evolution of, 12, 104, 158, 219, 245–49, 253
Temperance movement/Prohibition impact on, 247–49
Civil War
African American regiment in, 30
alcohol consumption shift with, 248
cheese making after, 255–57
corn consumption and, 112, 118

Johnny Appleseed reputation relation to
aftermath of, 251–52
maple syrup and, 2, 224–25
sugar prices during, 232, 237
clams
clambake tradition and history, 49, 191–
93
current-day realities of consumption of,
276, 277
at Forefathers' Day feasts, 192
Native American use of, 49, 191, 192
Portuguese Clams and Rice, 150–51
quahog, 151, 191
threats to, 193–94, 199
types of, 190–91
Wampanoag baking, early evidence of, 49
Winning Stuffed Quahogs, 151
climate change
cranberries impacted by, 244
fish and seafood impacted by, 174–75, 184,
193–94, 199, 208, 217
cod
climate change impact for, 208, 217
Codfish and Cod Fish Cakes, 148
decline in, 199, 207, 208, 214–16, 215
fishermen, about, 202–4
fishing method for, 201–2, 206
history and industry, 165, 166, 174, 175–80,
182, 200–204, 207–8
illegal fishing of, 216–17
Revolutionary War and, 200–201, 203–4
Colonial Revival
about, 78
food budgets and choices, 78–79
immigrants viewed under, 78
maple syrup promotion with, 219
molasses boost during, 60–61
New England foods influenced by, 56, 64,
78–79, 117, 219
Columbian Exposition in Chicago, Rumford Kitchen at, 74–75, 138
Connecticut
African American discrimination in, 26
baked beans evidence in early, 57
community cookbook, 156–57
dairy industry shift to butter, 255–56
farming to manufacturing shift in early
1800s, 7
pineapple cheese factory in, 255
Polish immigrant population in, 36
Connolly, James B., 211–12
cooking equipment
Aladdin Oven, 70–71, 137

of 1880s, 70–71, 82–83, 103, 137
Native Americans early, 49
pie making increase relation to, 228–29
urbanization impacts for, 82–83
The Cook's Own Book (Lee), 232
cornbread, 99
African American, 118, 146–47
baking powder in contemporary, 103–4,
107
Corn Egg Bread, 147
decline of, factors behind, 107–16, 119
Durgin-Park Cornbread, 146
Johnny Cake/Hoe Cake recipe, 144
New England adoption of, 116–17
northern and southern, distinctions, 111,
118, 119–20
Plantation Corn Bread or Hoe Cake, 147
southern style, 111, 118, 119–20, 146–47
with sugar, introduction of, 118–19
wheat bread compared with, 100–101
wheat in, rise in use of, 117
corn/cornmeal
ashes used in cooking, 105–7
in bread making, criticisms of, 100–101
for cattle, 107, 112
Civil War and consumption of, 112, 118
Corn Cake, 145
Corn Egg Bread, 147
as currency in Massachusetts, 101
declining use of, 110–12
Durgin-Park Cornbread, 146
English immigrants use and criticisms of,
10, 52, 99, 100–101, 107, 108
growing, suitability of, 101, 117
Gufong/Fungine, Aunti Laura's, 128
Hasty Pudding, 144–45
hoe cakes and, 99, 112, 144, 146–47
introduction of, 52, 99–100
Italian use and love of, 114
Johnny Cake/Hoe Cake recipe, 144
Latinx use of, 120, 147
Nasaump, 121
Native American cultivation and use of, 8,
10, 52, 53, 99–100, 105
Plantation Corn Bread or Hoe Cake, 147
poverty and low income associations with,
102–3, 109–10, 111–12, 119
processing of, industrial, 114
Rye and Indian/Cornmeal Bread (Hale's
and adaptation), 122–23
Samp, 122
slaves associated with, 109
southerners use of, 118–20

Wampanoag storage of, 53
white to yellow shift, factors behind, 117–18
cranberries
    beverage consumption, 240–41
    boom-bust cycles for, 219, 241–44
    Cape Cod production of, 237–38, 240
    climate change impacts for, 244
    Craisins popularity impact for, 241–42
    Cranberry Sauce and Cranberry Jelly, 157
    Forefathers' Day consumption of, 268
    growing/harvesting of, 235–36, 242–44,
        275
    Massachusetts, industry, 243–44
    Native American use of, 235
    Ocean Spray, 238–39, 244, 277
    pesticides and, 243
    reputation and consumption evolution for,
        236–38, 277
    Thanksgiving tradition and, 235, 236, 271–73
Cream Meringues, Maria Parloa's, 140
Cromwell, Oliver, 14
Crowley Cheese factory, 159, 262–63
Cultivator & Country Gentleman, 158
Curried Lobsters, 169

dairy/dairy industry, 16, 161. See also cheese;
    cheese making/industry
    Boston consumption in 1920s of, 258
    cheese making role in decline of, 265
    cheese to butter shift in, 255–56, 258
    chowder origins and, 193
Daniell, Maria, 137
Davis, Frank E., 179
Dean, Micah, 214–15
Delicate Pie, 152
Devasm, Charles Stanton, 83
A Domestic Cook Book (1866) (Russell), 118,
    146
doughnuts
    consumption, current-day, 227, 234
    Dunkin' Donuts founding and popularity
        and, 227, 234
    Sour Milk Doughnuts—Mrs. Henderson,
        155
Dudley, Paul, 246–47
Durgin-Park, 116–17, 146
Durgin-Park Cornbread, 146
Dutch immigrants, 50, 106

eels, 196–99
eggs
    Anchovy Toast with Eggs, 140–41
    Bread Pancakes, Mary Hinman Abel's, 137

Corn Egg Bread, 147
Cream Meringues, Maria Parloa's, 140
Kisses, 140
Maple Mousse, 156–57
1832 Baked Beans (original and adaptation),
    133
elites/elitism
    on beef over pork, 88
    Boston Brahmins, 14, 60, 69
    Boston Cooking School and, 84–85
    recipes and, 159–60
    serving arrangements and, 93
    Vermont artisan cheese making and,
        259–60
    Yankees, 14, 60, 64, 65
The Eliza Cookbook (1936), 118
El Salvadoran Americans, 46, 147, 214
Emerson, Ralph Waldo, 229
Endicot, Samuel, 245, 246
English immigrant/settlers. See also Pilgrims
    arrival and population data for, 11–12, 45
    bread for, 12, 103–5, 116
    corn use and criticisms from, 10, 52, 99,
        100–101, 107, 108
    current-day population of, 47
    diet for early, 11–13, 58
    leaveners used by, 103–4
    pottage in diet of, 12, 13, 31, 53–54, 98, 121
    sugar usage by, 58
    wheat preference of, 100–103, 105

Fall River Chow Mein Sandwich, 132
Fannie Farmer Cookbook. See Boston Cooking-
    School Cook Book (1896)
Farmer, Fanny, 84–86, 90, 150, 156–57, 225,
    232–33, 277
Federal Writers' Project, 74, 86, 88
Fish, Flesh, and Fowl, 158
fish and seafood. See also clams; cod; her-
    ring; lobster; oysters; shellfish
    boneless, 178
    Cajun immigrants use of, 19
    canned, adoption of, 178, 194–95
    climate change impacts for, 174–75, 184,
        193–94, 199, 208, 217
    corruption in, industry, 198–99, 216–17
    dams impact for, 165, 183–84, 186–87, 199
    eels consumption and, 196–99
    farming, 217–18
    Fish Balls, 138
    Fish Chowder (original and adaptation),
        149
    fish sticks, 1, 165, 195–96

fresh, early consumption of, 175–79
Georges Bank, 180–81, 201, 203, 206–8, 211
Gorton's, 195–96, 213
halibut history and industry, 179–82, 206
immigrant diet and, 15, 16, 19, 179
import data, 218
industrialization impacts on, 165, 187
Massachusetts 1763 exports of, 176
Massachusetts surveys of, 214–15
methods of catching, evolution in, 205–6
Newfoundland coast and, 9, 200, 202, 204, 205, 209, 217
nutrition and beliefs about, 177
overfishing threats for, 167, 174, 179, 181–82, 184, 187, 194, 197–98, 199, 206–8
post-war industry "free-for-all" on, 206–8
refrigeration and, 176, 178–79, 195
regulation, 207–8, 209, 210–12, 216
salmon, 167, 168, 183–84, 217–18
sardines, 178, 194–95
Scalloped Fish, 138
shad significance in, 167, 183, 184, 185–87
slaves fed "refuse," 176
southern species and quotas for, 217–18
stories and myths about, 166–68
sturgeon history and industry, 184–85
whale meat, 182
Fisher, Abby, 146–47
fishermen
    cod, about, 202–4
    family business and kinship boats of, 212–14
    fishing methods evolution impact for, 205–6
    government handouts for, 204–5
    government regulation conflicts with, 210–12
    immigrants as, 33, 205, 212–13
    Italian immigrant, 33, 212–13
    longevity for, 203
    Native American early contact with European, 9, 52
    reputation and lifestyle, 2, 202, 205, 208–10
    ship owners and, 203
Fitzgerald, Kathleen, 55, 60
food budgets and choices
    Atkinson on, 70–71
    Colonial Revival approach to, 78–79
    Richards on low-income, 69–76, 112–14
food science, Victorian
    bread prevalence in menus based on, 71–72, 75–76, 78–79
    on fruits, 67–68

home economics and racial discrimination under, 76–77
immigrants' diets and, 69–70, 73–74
New England foods/foodways impacted by, 2–3, 63, 67–74, 76–77
on vegetables, 67–68, 70, 73–74
food storage, 16, 28, 53, 232
Forefathers' Day feasts, 192, 267–68
French Canadian immigrants
    arrival and population data for, 18, 19, 20–21, 45
    baked beans of, 21–22, 55, 134
    Baked Beans recipe, Paul Mayotte's, 134
    current-day population of, 47
    diet and culinary influences of, 18–19, 21–25, 55, 61, 143, 156
    maple syrup in diet of, 61, 156
    poverty and living conditions for, 23–24, 45
    railroads role for, 20, 22, 108
    Raisin Pie recipe, 153
    recipes, 127, 134, 153, 156, 162–63
    Turkey Stuffing recipe of, 162–63
    Yellow Split Pea Soup recipe, 127
Frozen Cabinet Pudding with Apricot Sauce, Maria Parloa's, 141–42
fruits. See also apples; blueberries; cranberries
    Italian immigrant use of, 33–34
    New England Kitchen menus absence of, 66–67
    Victorian food science on, 67–68
fungine recipe, 128

Galarza, Emmie, 164
Garcelon, William F., 211–12
Gardner, Augustus P., 211
Georges Bank fishing, 180–81, 201, 203, 206–8, 211
German immigrants, 79, 113, 248
gingerbread
    Boston Gingerbread, 158
    decline, factors behind, 231–33
    Gingerbread 2, Sugar, 158
    low-income and immigrant population consumption of, 233
    molasses revolution and, 60–61, 231–32
    pearl ash as leavener for, 104
    Soft Gingerbread (original and adaptation), 136
    sugar compared with molasses, 232
Godey's Lady's Book and Magazine, 138, 177
The Good Housekeeper (Hale), 115, 122, 152
Goodwin, John, 196

Gookin, Daniel, 54, 246, 274–75
Gorton's, 195–96, 213
Gould, Edwin W., 211
Graham, Sylvester, 82, 115
grains. *See also* corn/cornmeal; rice; rye;
   wheat
   consumption in 1941, 119
   Native Americans use of native, 100
   New England growing season and, 108–9
   railroads and mill towns for, 108
Greek immigrants
   arrival and population data for, 39
   diet and culinary influences of, 39–41
   as grocery owners, 41
   New England Greek Pizza recipe, 131
   pizza of, 40, 41, 131, 277
Green, Mary E., 114
grinders, 35, 276
gufong
   about, 32
   recipe, 128
Gurdal, Ihsan, 259–60

Hale, Sarah Josepha Buell, 115–16, 122, 152,
   169, 177, 273
Haley, W. D., 251
halibut, 179–82, 206
Hall, Prince, 26
Hall, W. W., 111
Hall's Journal of Health (Hall, W.), 111
Harrison, William Henry, 193, 248
   hasty pudding
   about, 95, 99, 112, 114
   recipe, 144–45
heath hen, 167
Heffernan, Agnes McCloskey, 126
Hemenway, Mary, 76
Herb and Cheddar Easter Tomatoes, 159
herring
   as bait fish, 171, 173, 216
   canned as "sardines," 178, 194
   Irish immigrant consumption of, 15, 16
   threats and decline, 173, 207, 216
Historical Collections of the Indians in New
   England (Gookin), 274–75
hoe cake
   about, 99, 112, 146–47
   recipe, 144
Holmes, Oliver Wendell, 229
Holyoke, Massachusetts, pie recipes from,
   152–53
home economics, Victorian, 76–79
honey, 50, 221, 223, 244

Hopkins, Mark, 78
Horsford, Eben, 107
Howland, Esther, 162, 271–72

ice cream, 156–57
icings, cake, 123, 125
immigrants, 152. *See also specific immigrants*
   in Boston in 2007 by country of origin,
   46
   Colonial Revival views on, 78
   current-day culinary innovations, 278
   discrimination against, 14, 18, 60, 64, 76–78,
   213
   fish and seafood habits with, 15, 16, 19, 179
   in fishing business, 33, 205, 212–13
   gender ratio of early, 14–15, 45, 79
   gingerbread consumption by, 233
   home economics exclusion of foods of, 77
   New England foodways role of, 1–4, 6, 63,
   278
   New England Society propaganda against,
   78
   population growth from 1990 to 2010, 47
   population in 2010, 46–47
   population in late 1800s, 6
   poverty of early, 18, 23–24, 45
   restrictions and legislation on, 41, 46
   urbanization impact on foodways of, 65,
   83, 113
   Victorian food science views on diet of,
   69–70, 73–74
industrialization
   farming shifts to, 7
   fish impacted by, 165, 187
   New England foodways impacted by, 65,
   74
   New England Kitchen movement and,
   112–13
Irish immigrants
   arrival and population data for, 13–14, 17
   in Boston, 14, 17, 79–80
   diet and culinary influence of, 14–18, 23,
   143
   discrimination toward, 14, 18, 60, 64, 78
   potato blight history for, 14–15, 17, 20,
   109–10
   potato cultivation and use by, 15–17
   poverty of, 18, 45
   recipes, 126
   servant population of, 79–81
   women percentage of, 14–15, 45, 79
Irish potato blight and famine, 14–15, 17, 20,
   109–10

Italian immigrants
   arrival and population data for, 32–33, 35
   current-day population of, 47
   diet and culinary influences of, 33–36,
      114
   discrimination of, 213
   farms of, 34
   fishing businesses of, 33, 212–13
   pizza of, 35–36
   produce consumption and businesses of,
      33–34
   recipes, 128–29

Jacobs, Paul, 195–96
Janoplis, Maria, 148
Jefferson, Thomas, 254
Jigg's Dinner, 89, 95
Johnny Appleseed (née John Chapman)
   apple plantings of, 249–50
   birth/birthplace of, 249
   religious beliefs of, 250, 252
   reputation and legacy of, 251–52
Johnny Cake/Hoe Cake recipe, 144
Johnson, Edward, 54, 100
Journal of Home Economics, 76
Judah, S., 56

kale
   Portuguese immigrants use of, 38–39, 132
   Tillie's Portuguese American Sausage,
      Kale, and Potato Soup, 132
Kellogg, J. H., 77
Kimchi Grilled Cheese, 161
King Philip's War, 4, 10, 54, 252
Kipling, Rudyard, 2, 181, 205, 210, 230
Kisses, 140
kitchens. *See also* cooking equipment; New
   England Kitchens
   conditions in mid-to-late 1800s, 81–83
   soup, in late 1880s, 69–70
Knickerbocker, 86, 117

Lagasse, Emeril, 132
Larkin, Nancy, 273
Latham bill, 210–11
Latinx
   arrival and population data for, 44–45, 46,
      120, 147
   corn use by, 120, 147
   recipes, 147
leavening agents, 103–4, 106–7, 136
Lechford, Thomas, 54
Lee, N. K. M., 232

Levenstein, Harvey, 69, 72, 114
Lincoln, Abraham, 270, 271
Lincoln, Mary, 76, 84, 90, 138, 145, 155,
   272–73
lobster
   canning industry, 169–69
   consumption, myth and reality of, 166–71,
      276
   current-day consumption of, 276
   Curried Lobsters, 169
   history and industry in Maine, 2, 168–75
   Lobster Salad, 150
   threats and protections, 174–75
   tourism and, 173
   traps, 173–75
   during World War II, 170–71
Lohman, Sarah, 104
loroco, 147
Lowell's Famous Rochette's Baked Beans,
   134
low-income population. *See* poverty/low-
   income population

Maine
   clam decline in, 199
   community recipes from, 158
   eel industry, 197–98
   lobster history and industry in, 2, 168–75
   sardine industry, 194–95
   whoopie pie role in, 234–35
maple syrup
   Acadian Beignets, 156
   Civil War and, 2, 224–25
   Colonial Revival promotion of, 219
   contemporary industry and costs for, 225–
      26, 276
   current-day consumption realities of, 276
   extraction and processing, 220, 221, 222
   French Canadian immigrants use of, 61,
      156
   grades, 226
   increased use of, evidence of, 224–25
   Maple Mousse, 156–57
   maple sugar contrasted with, 222–23, 224
   Native American use of, myth and reali-
      ties of, 49, 156, 219, 220–23
   preciousness of, 49
   reputation, evolution of, 219
   Vermont share of, 220
Marshmallow Fluff, 277
Mashpee tribe, 10, 192
Mason, Walt, 96–97
Massachusetts

African American slavery and discrimination in, 26, 27–28
corn as currency in, 101
cranberry industry in, 243–44
farm-city connection in, 6–7
fish exports in 1763, 176
fish health surveys in, 214–15
French Canadian population in, 19
Irish immigrant population in, 14, 17
Johnny Appleseed birth in, 249
molasses market in early, 51, 59
Native American roots in naming of, 5
pie recipes from Holyoke, 152–53
rum production in 1700s, 51
urban population in late 1800s, 5
Massachusetts Division of Marine Fisheries (MDMF), 214–15
Massachusetts Woman's Christian Temperance Union Cuisine, 136
Mayflower, 11–12, 53, 58
Mayotte, Paul, 134
McMahon, Sarah, 53–54, 55
MDMF. *See* Massachusetts Division of Marine Fisheries
Mead, Nancy, 150
Memoirs (Misson), 89
Menhaden Oil and Guano Association, 211
Meringues, Maria Parloa's Cream, 140
Me-won-i-toc (Robinson), 94–95
Micmac people, 221
Minuit, Peter, 50
Miss Beecher's Domestic Receipt Book (Beecher), 139
Misson, Henri, 89
Miss Parloa's New Cook Book and Marketing Guide (Parloa), 136, 140, 141
Mock Mince Pie, 153
Mohegan tribe, 10
molasses
    Boston baked beans origins with popularity of, 231
    branding and marketing of, 61
    Caribbean production of, 223
    in colonial bread, 116
    Colonial Revival boost for, 60–61
    gingerbread relation to production of, 60–61, 231–32
    Pilgrims production of, 51
    popularity of, 59–61, 63–64, 126, 224
    Soft Gingerbread (original and adaptation), 136
    sugar consumption contrasted with, 232–33

traditional recipes substituted with, 63–64
    treacle compared with, 232
Molasses Act in 1733, 59
Mourt's Relation, 269–70
Mrs. Hale's New Cook Book (Hale), 169
Mrs. Lincoln's Boston Cook Book (1884) (Lincoln, M.), 155
Myrle Sylsby's One-Crust Blueberry Pie, 154

Narragansett people, 9, 49, 54, 221, 235, 254
Nasaump, 121
National Oceanic and Atmospheric Administration (NOAA), 181–82, 208, 214–15, 216
National Origins Act of 1924, 46
Native Americans. *See also* Wampanoag
    Abenaki, 49, 105, 156, 220–21
    ancient regional history for, 8
    apple orchards of, 249–50
    blueberries use by, 9, 13, 121
    in Boston baked beans origin stories, 1, 2, 48–49
    clam consumption of, 49, 191, 192
    cooking equipment for early, 49
    corn cooked with ash by, 105
    corn cultivation and use by, 8, 10, 52, 53, 99–100, 105
    enslavement of, 10
    epidemics of 1600s impact on, 10
    European fishermen, pre-Pilgrim contact with, 9, 52
    grains for, pre-European contact, 100
    in Johnny Appleseed stories, 252
    King Philip's War between Pilgrims and, 4, 10, 54, 252
    maple syrup usage, myth and realities of, 49, 156, 219, 220–23
    Micmac, 221
    Mohegan, 10
    Narragansett, 9, 49, 54, 221, 235, 254
    New England adoption of names from, 5, 64
    New England foods influence from, myths and realities of, 1, 2, 3–4, 8–10, 48
    Pequot, 10, 49, 54
    Pilgrims impact on food sources of, 4, 8, 10, 54
    population, current-day, 10
    salmon consumption and, 183–84
Naylor, Katherine Nanny, 176
NEFMC. *See* New England Fishery Management Council
Negro Culinary Arts Club, 118

New Boston Globe Cookbook, 233
New Cook Book (Parloa), 85
New England. *See also specific locations and topics*
    grain consumption in 1941, 119
    grain growing conditions in, 108–9
    identity crisis impact on foodways, 63–64
    immigrant population data, current-day, 46–47
    maritime economy decline in, 218, 219
    Native American names adoption in, 5, 64
    in 1910, a snapshot of, 45–46
    population make-up and densities in, 4
    reputation contrasted with realities, 2, 5–6, 7–8
    rural to urban population shift in, 5–6, 82, 108
    servant population statistics in, 80
    slavery, 25–28
    urban population in 1900s, 65
New England boiled dinner
    cabbage and, 86–92, 94–98
    contemporary, 98
    criticism of, 90–92
    decline of, 96–98
    ingredients and instructions for, 86, 87–88, 89, 97–98, 142–43
    Jigg's Dinner version of, 89, 95
    naming of, 89
    origins of, 86, 88
    pudding with, 90, 93, 94, 95–96
    recipes, 142–43
    reputation of, 2, 63, 87, 89–92, 96–97
    serving arrangement for, 92–95
    for sick patients, 91–92
    women's marriageability and, 96
New England Cook Book (1999), 87, 225
The New England Cook Book (1912), 46, 117
The New England Economical Housekeeper, and Family Receipt Book (Howland), 162, 271–72
New England Farmer, 92, 142
New England Fishery Management Council (NEFMC), 207, 208, 216
New England foods/foodways. *See also specific topics and foods*
    Colonial Revival influence on, 56, 64, 78–79, 117, 219
    current-day, realities and factors behind, 276–78
    factors stunting, overview of, 63–64
    in first Thanksgiving myths and realities, 2–3, 50, 99, 267, 269–71

immigrants' role in, 1–4, 6, 63, 64, 278
industrialization impacts on, 65, 74
myths and realities about, 1–4, 8–10, 48–50, 63, 117, 267, 276–78
Native American influence on, myths and realities of, 1, 2, 3–4, 8–10, 48
New England Kitchen movement impact on, 65–67, 69–70
organizations for resilience of, 278
servants' role in, 79–83
urbanization relation to, 13, 65, 82–83, 108
Victorian ideals and food science impact on, 2–3, 63, 67–74, 76–77
New England Greek Pizza, 131, 277
New England Kitchen Magazine, 84, 114, 140
New England Kitchens
    collapse of, 73, 74
    on food for working class and poor, 69–70, 112–13
    food science behind, 69–70
    industrialization relation to, 112–13
    New England foodways impacted by, 65–67, 69–70
    recipes, 137
    Richards leadership of, 69–75, 138
    vegetables absence in menus of, 66–67, 71
New England Society, 78, 237, 267, 268
New England's Prospect (Wood), 53
Newfoundland, 9–10, 89, 200, 202, 204–5, 209, 217
A New System of Domestic Cookery (Rundell), 123, 125
Nice Apple Pie, 153
Nicholson, Asenath, 109
Nipmuc tribe, 10
NOAA. *See* National Oceanic and Atmospheric Administration
Northwood (Hale), 273
Norton, Lewis and Edward, 255
nutrition
    corn with ash and, 105–6
    fish beliefs and, 177
    New England boiled dinner and, 91–92
    pie popularity and, 229, 230
    scurvy and ignorance of, 11–12, 67–68
    slaves lack of, 27
    Victorian understanding of, 67–68, 70–74
    vitamins understanding and, 67–68, 72

Ocean Spray cranberries, 238–39, 244, 277
ovens
    Aladdin, 70–71, 137
    evolution of, 103

"Over the River and Through the Wood"
(Child), 251–52, 270
oysters
consumption of, 188–89
decline, history and factors behind, 188,
189–90
first Thanksgiving stories and, 270–71

Palfrey (doctor), 57–58
Papadellis, Randy, 241, 244
Parenteau, Daniel G., 156
Parloa, Maria, 84, 85, 87, 126, 136, 140, 141–42
The Parlor Book, 177
Paul Mayotte's French Canadian American
Baked Beans, 134
Paxson, Heather, 263, 264
pearl ash, 104, 106
peas, 12, 53, 55
Penn, William, 51
Pequot people, 10, 49, 54
pierogi
about, 38
recipe, 129–30
pies
Amelia Simmons' Pumpkin Pies, 162
cakes called, 154, 277
current-day realities of consumption of,
276–77
Delicate Pie, 152
Holyoke, Massachusetts recipes for, 152–53
homemade, evidence and evolution of,
227–30, 234
Mock Mince Pie, 153
Myrle Sylsby's One-Crust Blueberry Pie,
154
Nice Apple Pie, 153
nutrition criticisms with popularity of,
229, 230
Raisin Pie, French Canadian American, 153
reputation myths and realities, 219, 227–28,
231
Sarah Josepha Buell Hale's Apple Pie, 152
savory, popularity of, 228
Thanksgiving tradition and, 271
Washington Pie, 154
whoopie, 154, 234–35, 277
Yankee identification with, 227–28, 230–31
The Pilgrim Republic (Goodwin), 196
Pilgrims
arrival and population data for, 11–12
baked beans for, 1, 12, 55
in Boston baked beans origins stories, 1,
12, 48

clambakes and, 192
corn cultivation and use by, 10, 52, 99, 100,
107
corn cultivation taught by Native Americans to, 10, 52, 99
European contact with Native Americans
prior to, 9, 52
first Thanksgiving myths and realities for,
2–3, 50, 99, 267, 269–71
Forefathers' Day feasts in celebration of,
192, 267–68
King Philip's War between Native Americans and, 4, 10, 54, 252
Mayflower arrival and foods for, 11–12, 53,
58
Native American food sources impacted
by, 4, 8, 10, 54
in New England foods origin stories,
1–3
in New England reputation, 5
peas use by, 12, 53, 55
religious culture, 269
Standish of Standish story of Thanksgiving
tradition of, 267, 270–71
sugar availability for, 50–51
in Thanksgiving holiday proclamations,
absence of, 270
pineapple cheese, 159, 255
pizza
of Greek immigrants, 31, 40, 41, 277
of Italian immigrants, 35–36
New England Greek Pizza, 131
Plain Dealing (Lechford), 54
plantains
Plantain Stuffing, 164
Puerto Ricans use of, 44, 164
Plantation Corn Bread or Hoe Cake, 147
plum cake, 30, 123–25
Plymouth mystery jars, 28
Polish immigrants
arrival and population data of, 36
Bread and Roses Strike and, 36
diet and culinary influences of, 36–38
farms of, 36–37
pierogi of, 38, 129–30
Pollard, Othello, 30
Pompkin Pies, Amelia Simmons', 162
Pope's Day, 14
pork
Baked Beans, Paul Mayotte's French
Canadian American, 134
1832 Baked Beans (original and adapta-
tion), 133

Fish Chowder (original and adaptation), 149

French Canadian immigrants use of, 21

French Canadian Turkey Stuffing, 162–63

Lowell's Famous Rochette's Baked Beans, 134

middle class views on, 88

New England Boiled Dinner, 142–43

New England boiled dinner instructions and, 88, 98

Pork Shoulder Boiled Dinner, 143

Tillie's Portuguese American Sausage, Kale, and Potato Soup, 132

Portuguese immigrants

  arrival and population data for, 38, 39

  Clams and Rice recipe of, 150–51

  diet and culinary influences of, 38–39

  kale consumption by, 38–39, 132

  recipes, 132, 143, 148, 150–51

  religious culture of, 38

  Sausage, Kale, and Potato Soup recipe of, 132

potash, 105–6

potatoes

  blight and famine in Ireland, 14–15, 17, 20, 109–10

  Cod Fish Cakes, 148

  Fish Balls, 138

  Irish cultivation and use of, 15–17

  New England Boiled Dinner, 142–43

  Potato Pierogi Filling, 130

  Tillie's Portuguese American Sausage, Kale, and Potato Soup, 132

Pot Shop of Boston, 135

pottage

  in English settler diet, 12, 13, 31, 53–54, 98, 121

  ingredients, 12, 53

  in Wampanoag diet, 54, 55, 121

poultry, 165, 167, 270

poverty/low-income population

  corn associated with, 102–3, 109–10, 111–12, 119

  of French Canadian immigrants, 23–24, 45

  gingerbread consumption and, 233

  of Irish immigrants, 18, 45

  maple syrup early association with, 219

  Richards advice on food choices for, 69–76, 112–14

Practical Sanitary and Economic Cooking Adapted to Persons of Moderate and Small Means (Abel), 71–72, 137

Prohibition, 247–49

The Providence and Rhode Island Cookbook, 162–63

Provincetown Portuguese Cookbook, 132, 148, 150–51

pudding

  Frozen Cabinet Pudding with Apricot Sauce, Maria Parloa's, 141–42

  hasty, 95, 99, 112, 114, 144–45

  New England boiled dinner, 90, 93, 94, 95–96

Puerto Rican Americans

  arrival and population data for, 43, 44–45, 46

  diet and culinary influences for, 43–44

  Plantain Stuffing, 164

  Thanksgiving Turkey recipe, 163

pumpkin/pumpkin

  growing, 275

  Native American use of, 274–75

  origins, 274

  Pompkin Pies, Amelia Simmons', 162

  Thanksgiving tradition and, 274–75

Pupusas, Cheese and Loroco, 147

Puritans/Puritan-era beliefs, 107, 231, 273. *See also* English immigrant/settlers; Pilgrims

beer production and, 51

  fishermen lifestyle contrasted with, 209

  Irish immigrant arrival conflicts with, 13, 60

  Yankees and, 60

quahogs, 151, 191

Quamino (duchess), 30, 123

Rafael, Carlos, 216–17

railroads

  cheese making market impacted by, 255, 256, 258

  Chinese immigrant work on, 22, 41

  French Canadians immigration and, 20, 22, 108

  grain industry impacted by, 108

raisins

  Mock Mince Pie, 153

  Raisin Pie, French Canadian American, 153

Randolph, Mary, 228

Rawson, Michael, 64

Real Vermonters Don't Milk Goats, 260

recipes

  Acadian Beignets, 156

  Anchovy Toast with Eggs, 140–41

  Apple Pie, Sarah Josepha Buell Hale's, 152

Baked Beans, Paul Mayotte's French Canadian American, 134
Beef Broth, New England Kitchen, 137
Boston Baked Beans, Pot Shop of Boston's, 135
Boston Gingerbread, 158
Bran Biscuits, 126
Bread Pancakes, Mary Hinman Abel's, 137
Champaign Cider, 158
Cheese and Loroco Pupusas, 147
Chicken Pie, 162, 272
Clams and Rice, Portuguese, 150–51
Codfish and Cod Fish Cakes, 148
Corn Cake, 145
Corn Egg Bread, 147
Cranberry Sauce and Cranberry Jelly, 157
Cream Meringues, Maria Parloa's, 140
Curried Lobsters, 169
Delicate Pie, 152
Durgin-Park Cornbread, 146
1832 Baked Beans (original and adaptation), 133
Fall River Chow Mein Sandwich, 132
Fish Balls, 138
Fish Chowder (original and adaptation), 149
Frozen Cabinet Pudding with Apricot Sauce, Maria Parloa's, 141–42
Gingerbread 2, Sugar, 158
Gufong/Fungine, Aunti Laura's, 128
Hasty Pudding, 144–45
Herb and Cheddar Easter Tomatoes, 159
Johnny Cake/Hoe Cake, 144
Kimchi Grilled Cheese, 161
Kisses, 140
Lobster Salad, 150
Lowell's Famous Rochette's Baked Beans, 134
Maple Mousse, 156–57
Mock Mince Pie, 153
Myrle Sylsby's One-Crust Blueberry Pie, 154
Nasaump, 121
New England Boiled Dinner, 142–43
New England Greek Pizza, 131
Nice Apple Pie, 153
Pierogi, 129–30
Plantain Stuffing, 164
Plantation Corn Bread or Hoe Cake, 147
Plum Cake (Simmons' and adaptation), 123–24

Plum Cake Icing, 125
Pompkin Pies, Amelia Simmons', 162
Pork Shoulder Boiled Dinner, 143
Puerto Rican Thanksgiving Turkey, 163
Raisin Pie, French Canadian American, 153
Rye and Indian/Cornmeal Bread (Hale's and adaptation), 122–23
Samp, 122
Sausage, Kale, and Potato Soup, Tillie's Portuguese American, 132
Scalloped Fish, 138
Shaved Asparagus Salad with Goat Cheese, 160
Soft Gingerbread (original and adaptation), 136
Sour Milk Doughnuts—Mrs. Henderson, 155
Stuffed Peppers, 128–29
Turkey Stuffing, French Canadian, 162–63
Washington Pie, 154
Wheat Bread of Distillery or Brewer's Yeast, Catharine Beecher's, 139
Winning Stuffed Quahogs, 151
Yellow Split Pea Soup, French Canadian, 127
religious culture. See also Puritans/Puritan-era beliefs
fertility rates and, 7
Irish immigrants, discrimination and, 14, 60, 78
Johnny Appleseed and, 250, 252
pie recipes and, 152–53
of Portuguese immigrants, 38
Thanksgiving tradition and, 267, 268–69, 271
Wampanoag on Pilgrims, 269
Reminiscences of the Last Sixty-Five Years (Thomas), 57–58
Remond, John, 30
Revolutionary War
Boston food riots during, 103
cheese making during, 254
cod and, 200–201, 203–4
fishing rights after, 204
Irish immigrants in, 14
pie making after, 228
Rhode Island
apple growing history in, 244–45
chowder origins and, 193
clams, 151
slavery in, 25–26, 27

rice
    Irish experience of, 109–10
    Portuguese Clams and Rice, 150–51
    Puerto Ricans use of, 44
Richards, Ellen Swallow
    on home cooking decline, 278
    home economics education role of, 76–77
    low-income food choices advice of, 69–76,
        112–14
    New England Kitchens leadership of,
        69–75, 138
    Rumford Kitchen menu by, 74–75, 138
    WEA supporting food education by, 84
Robinson, S., 94–95
Roosevelt, Franklin Delano, 270
Roosevelt, Theodore, 270
Rorer, Sarah Tyson, 159
Rosenberg, William, 234
rum, 51, 102, 223, 224
Rumford Kitchen at Columbian Exposition
    in Chicago, 74–75, 138
Rundell, Maria Eliza, 123, 125
Russell, Malinda, 118, 146
Rutledge, S., 118
rye, 145
    in colonial bread, 12, 103, 116
    decline in consumption of, 108, 110–11
    Polish immigrants use of, 37
    Rye and Indian/Cornmeal Bread (Hale's
        and adaptation), 122–23

Safina, Carl, 165
saleratus, 106–7
salmon
    farming, 217–18
    history and industry, 167, 168, 183–84
Samp, 122
sardines, 178, 194–95
Sausage, Kale, and Potato Soup, Tillie's
    Portuguese American, 132
Scalloped Fish, 138
The Science of Nutrition (Atkinson), 70–71, 137
Scientific American, 106–7
Scott, J. M., 56
scurvy, 11–12, 67–68
servants
    Irish immigrant women as, 79–81
    middle class foods and cooking influ-
        enced by, 79–83
serving platters, 92–95
shad, 167, 183, 184, 185–87
Shaved Asparagus Salad with Goat Cheese,
    160

Shaw, Pauline Agassiz, 70
Sheldon, William, 198
shellfish. See also clams; lobster; oysters
    in Cape Cod history and culture, 42, 52–53
    threats to, 188, 190, 193–94
    Wampanoag dependence on, 52
Simmons, Amelia, 104, 123–25, 144, 148, 162,
    228
625 Choice Recipes from the Ladies of the Sec-
    ond Cong. Church, of Holyoke, Mass., 152–53
slavery
    abolition/abolitionists, 27, 224, 252
    cookbooks and, 118
    corn association with, 109
    fish use in, 176
    malnourishment and, 27
    Native American, 10
    in New England, 25–28
soup kitchens, 69–70
spirits. See alcoholic beverages
split pea soup, 127
squash, 142. See also pumpkin/pompkin
Standish of Standish (Austin), 267, 270–71
Stavely, Keith, 55, 60
Steele, Clotida "Tillie" Medeiros, 132
Stories and Folk-Lore of West Cornwall (Bot-
    trell), 95
Stuffed Peppers, 128–29
stuffing recipes
    French Canadian Turkey Stuffing, 162–63
    Plantain Stuffing, 164
sturgeon, 184–85
sugar
    in American diet, evolution of, 58–62, 59,
        223
    in baked beans, origins of, 1, 55, 58, 61–62
    in Boston baked beans, ratio increase
        from 1880 to 2017, 61–62, 62
    Caribbean production and trade of,
        223–24
    Civil War prices for, 232, 237
    consumption from 1820 to 2000, 59
    cornbread with, introduction of, 118–19
    English immigrant/settlers usage of, 58
    gingerbread with molasses compared
        with, 232
    market in 1600s and early 1700s, 50–51,
        58–59, 223–24
    molasses consumption contrasted with,
        232–33
    Pilgrims and availability of, 50–51
    prices, evolution of, 60, 224, 232
Sweeney, Joanna, 84

sweeteners. *See also* maple syrup; molasses; sugar
  honey history and usage, 50, 221, 223, 244
  in New England 1620, availability of, 50–51
  in New England 1700–1800s, availability of, 162
  Wampanoag early use of, 54–55
Sylsby, Myrle, 154

Temperance movement, 247–49
Thanksgiving
  chicken pie inclusion at, 272, 273
  Child's poem impact for, 251, 270
  cranberry consumption at, 235, 236, 271–73
  Hale's influence on, 273
  menu, 1845 example of, 271–72
  national holiday origins, 268–71
  New England food origin myths with first, 2–3, 50, 99, 267, 269–71
  oysters in stories of first, 270–71
  Pilgrim's first, myths and realities of, 2–3, 50, 99, 267, 269–71
  presidential proclamations of, 270, 271
  pumpkin at, 274–75
  recipes, 162–64
  religious culture role historically in, 267, 268–69, 271
  Standish of Standish role in creation of Pilgrim, 267, 270–71
  turkey role historically at, 163, 270, 271, 273
  Wampanoag role in first, 269
  during World War II, 272
Thomas, E. S., 57–58
Thoreau, Henry David, 165, 248
Tillie's Portuguese American Sausage, Kale, and Potato Soup, 132
tomatoes
  African American early consumption of, 29
  Herb and Cheddar Easter Tomatoes, 159
A Treatise on Bread, and Bread-Making (Graham), 115
Treaty of Paris, 204
Tried Recipes Collected by the Ladies of the Mission Circle of the First Church, 156
turkey
  French Canadian Turkey Stuffing, 162–63
  Puerto Rican Thanksgiving Turkey, 163
  in Thanksgiving tradition, 163, 270, 271, 273
turtle, 13, 28–29, 52

Underwood, William, 169, 170, 195–96
urbanization
  cooking equipment and kitchen conditions with, 82–83
  growth of, 5–6, 65, 82, 108
  immigrant food habits impacted by, 65, 83, 113
  New England foods/foodways relation to, 13, 65, 82–83, 108

vegetables
  Chinese American consumption of, 42
  for English settlers, 13
  Italian immigrant use of, 33–34
  kale, Portuguese immigrants use of, 38–39, 132
  New England Kitchen menus absence of, 66–67, 71
  Shaved Asparagus Salad with Goat Cheese, 160
  Victorian food science on, 67–68, 70, 73–74
  Victorian ideals on artful serving of, 92
Vermont
  cheese making, 159, 257–65
  cheese making, newcomers and elites role in, 259–60
  cheese making prior to 1850, 264–65
  farm villages historically in, 6
  flatlanders and tourism in, 259–62
  maple production in, 220
Victorian era. *See also* food science, Victorian
  artful serving of vegetables in, 92
  home economics, 76–79
  New England foods/foodways impacts under ideals of, 2–3, 63, 67–74, 76–77
  nutrition understanding during, 67–68, 70–74
The Virginia Housewife (Randolph), 228
vitamins, 67–68, 72

Wack, Mary F., 126
Wampanoag peoples
  about, 49
  bean cultivation and use by, 51–55
  clambakes, early evidence of, 49
  conditional sedentism for, 52
  crops grown by, 8–9, 52
  first Thanksgiving and, 269
  food storage habits of, 52–53
  King Philip's War between Pilgrims and, 4, 10, 54, 252
  New England foods origin myths and, 2, 3
  Pilgrims impacting availability of food sources for, 4, 8, 54

pottage in diet of, 54, 55, 121
pumpkin use by, 274
recipes of, 121–22
sweetener use by early, 54–55
Washington, George, 14
Washington Pie, 154
WEA. *See* Women's Education Association
Wendell, Barrett, 60
whale meat, 182–84
*What Mrs. Fisher Knows about Old South-
ern Cooking, Soups, Pickles, Preserves Etc.*
(Fisher), 146
wheat
bread making logistics and costs, 100–101,
102–3, 105
in cornbread, rise in use of, 117
English settlers preference for, 100–103,
105
expense of, 102, 105, 112–13, 119
increase in use with price decline, 107–8
pie increase relation to availability of, 228
Wheat Bread of Distillery or Brewer's
Yeast, Catharine Beecher's, 139
whole, promotion of, 115
wheat bran biscuits, 126
Whitehead, Jessup, 87
Whitney, Madame, 95, 98
whoopie pies, 154, 234–35, 277
Wilde, William, 16
Williams, John, 204
Williams, Roger, 49, 221
Wilson, Woodrow, 41
Winning Stuffed Quahogs, 151
Winouker, Harry, 234
Winslow, Edward, 53, 269–70
Winthrop, John, 49, 221

Women's Education Association (WEA),
83–84
Wonder-Working Providence (Johnson), 100
Wood, William, 53
working class. *See also* poverty/low-income
population
home economics advice conflict with
realities of, 78–79
immigrant, food choices for, 113–14
New England Kitchens on foods for, 69–
70, 112–13
World War I, 60, 61, 206
World War II
cranberry usage during, 241
fishing after, 206–8
lobsters during, 170–71
Thanksgiving during, 272

Yankee pot roast. *See* New England boiled
dinner
Yankees
defining, 5, 11
diet of earliest, 11–12
elites/elitism, 14, 60, 64, 65
pie identification with, 227–28, 230–31
Puritan background and beliefs of, 60
yeasts
bread making and, 82, 101, 104, 108, 139
chemical leavenings compared with, views
on, 106–7
distillery, 104, 108, 139
for doughnuts, 155
Wheat Bread of Distillery or Brewer's
Yeast, Catharine Beecher's, 139
Yellow Split Pea Soup, French Canadian, 127
Young, A., 270

ABOUT THE AUTHOR

MEG MUCKENHOUPT writes about food, history, and the New England environment. She is the author of *Cabbage: A Global History* and *Boston Gardens and Green Spaces*, a *Boston Globe* Local Bestseller.